An Ethic of Responsibility for Nigeria

Engaging Corruption with Human Dignity

Kefas U. Kure

© 2025 Kefas U. Kure

Published 2025 by Langham Academic
An imprint of Langham Publishing
www.langhampublishing.org

Langham Publishing and its imprints are a ministry of Langham Partnership

Langham Partnership
PO Box 296, Carlisle, Cumbria, CA3 9WZ, UK
www.langham.org

ISBNs:
978-1-78641-054-2 Print
978-1-78641-221-8 ePub
978-1-78641-222-5 PDF
DOI: https://doi.org/10.69811/9781786410542

Kefas U. Kure has asserted his right under the Copyright, Designs and Patents Act, 1988 to be identified as the Author of this work.

All rights reserved. No part of this publication may be reproduced, stored in a retrieval system or transmitted, in any form or by any means, electronic, mechanical, photocopying, recording or otherwise, without the prior written permission of the publisher or the Copyright Licensing Agency.

Requests to reuse content from Langham Publishing are processed through PLSclear. Please visit www.plsclear.com to complete your request.

Scriptures taken from the Holy Bible, New International Version®, NIV®. Copyright © 1973, 1978, 1984, 2011 by Biblica, Inc.™ Used by permission of Zondervan.

British Library Cataloguing-in-Publication Data
A catalogue record for this book is available from the British Library

ISBN: 978-1-78641-054-2

Cover & Book Design: projectluz.com

Langham Partnership actively supports theological dialogue and an author's right to publish but does not necessarily endorse the views and opinions set forth here or in works referenced within this publication, nor can we guarantee technical and grammatical correctness. Langham Partnership does not accept any responsibility or liability to persons or property as a consequence of the reading, use or interpretation of its published content.

Dr. Kefas Kure's book, *An Ethic of Responsibility for Nigeria*, comes from a rising African theologian with a fundamental point: corruption thrives all over the world as a result of people's insatiable desire for self-importance, status, and power. Examining this universality, Dr. Kure argues that corruption occurs because people refuse to protect their fellow humans, as the tale of Cain and Abel in Genesis demonstrates. As a consequence, people are struggling to understand the concept of responsibility, let alone realize the breadth and scope of God's moral duties to them. To cure this evil, Kure implores readers to accept moral responsibility in order to combat the danger of corruption: the ruin of God's image. Corruption is a terrible human trait, and this book demonstrates just how bad it is. It is for this reason Kure argues that corruption taints all aspects of our social, political, economic, and moral existence. This is a vital book for Christians to read.

Sunday Bobai Agang, PhD
Provost and Professor of Christian Theology and Public Policy,
ECWA Theological Seminary (JETS), Jos, Nigeria

In his book, Dr. Kefas Kure convincingly links three important contemporary ethical discourses: on developing an ethic of responsibility, recognizing human dignity, and combating corruption. With reference to Nigeria, he demonstrates the devastating effect corruption has on the recognition of human dignity, especially of poor people. He presents a strong case for adapting an ethic of responsibility approach in combating corruption that is both Christian and African in nature. Building on the work of proponents of a Christian ethic of responsibility, and related work of African theologians and philosophers, he presents the outlines of an African Christian ethic of responsibility on which the foundation of human dignity could be safeguarded in fighting corruption in Nigeria. This book is a wake-up call for African Christians, especially those in leadership positions, to take up their responsibility to effectively combat corruption in the African context.

Etienne de Villiers, PhD
Emeritus Professor of Dogmatic and Christian Ethics,
University of Pretoria, South Africa

Religion plays a pivotal role in shaping moral values in many African societies. This insightful book confronts the paradox that even in deeply religious contexts like Nigeria, corruption remains a persistent issue. Dr. Kure proposes that a renewed commitment to responsibility ethics can empower churches and Christians to combat corruption and its detrimental effects. I wholeheartedly recommend this thought-provoking work to theologians, church leaders, and all those concerned about the pervasiveness of corruption in African communities.

Dion A. Forster, PhD
Professor of Public Theology,
Vrije Universiteit Amsterdam, Netherlands

I dedicate this project to God Almighty for wisdom, knowledge, strength, and patience, and to my dear family for standing by me throughout these years of studying. To my late father, your parental guidance and advice are always fresh in my mind.

and

To all Nigerians who have suffered and are suffering all forms of dehumanisation due to corruption, your voices are being heard, and your dignity shall be recognized and be enhanced.

Contents

Acknowledgments xi

Abstract xiii

Abbreviations xv

Chapter 1 1
Corruption, Human Dignity, and an Ethic of Responsibility in Nigeria
    Introduction and Background to the Study 1
    1.2 Preliminary Overview of Existing Literature 4
        1.2.1 Nigeria, Religion, and Corruption 4
        1.2.2 Corruption and Its Impact on the Dignity of
            Human Persons 10
        1.2.3 Responsibility and an Ethic of Responsibility 15
    1.3 An Overview of the Research Process 17
        1.3.1 An Introduction to the Research Problem 17
    1.4 Research Question, Aim and Objectives 18
        1.4.1 Research Question 18
        1.4.2 Secondary Research Questions 18
        1.4.3 Research Aim 19
        1.4.4 Research Objectives 19
    1.5 Research Methodology 19
    1.6 Outline of the Chapters 21
    1.7 Chapter Summary 23

Chapter 2 25
Conceptualizing Corruption in Nigeria
    2.1 Introduction 25
    2.2 Some Background on Corruption 26
        2.2.1 Theological-Anthropological Background to
            Corruption 27
        2.2.2 Political Corruption in Nigeria 30
        2.2.3 Corruption and the Nigerian Church 33
    2.3 Nigeria and Governance 37
        2.3.1 Democracy in Nigeria 38
        2.3.2 Governance and Democracy in Nigeria 39
    2.4 Some Causes of Persistent Corruption in Nigeria 43
        2.4.1 Failure of Leadership 43

  2.4.2 Failure in Moral Upbringing...47
  2.4.3 Loss of A Sense of Humanity..50
  2.4.4 Holistic Poverty 52
  2.4.5 Greed..56
 2.5 Some Effects of Corruption in Nigeria..58
  2.5.1 Effects of Corruption on the Nigerian Economy...............58
  2.5.2 Effects of Corruption on the People.....................................62
  2.5.3 Effects of Corruption on Society..63
  2.5.4 Effects of Corruption as a Catalyst for Terrorism...............64
 2.6 Some Ways of Curbing Corruption in Nigeria................................72
  2.6.1 The Government Instituted Agencies of
   Anti-corruption: The EFCC and ICPC....................................72
  2.6.2 The Role of Civil Society in Fighting Corruption in
   Nigeria..78
  2.6.3 Religious Institutions as Anti-corruption Agents in
   Nigeria: The Role of the Church...82
 2.7 Chapter Summary 85

Chapter 3 89
Human Dignity and Corruption in Nigeria
 3.1 Introduction...89
 3.2 Why Talk About Human Dignity? 90
 3.3 Towards a Historical Survey of Human Dignity 93
  3.3.1 Human Dignity in Early Christian History: Era of
   the Church Fathers..95
  3.3.2 Human Dignity in the Middle Ages:
   Thomas Aquinas (1225–1274)..99
  3.3.3 Human Dignity and Moral Philosophy:
   Immanuel Kant (1724–1804)..105
  3.3.4 Human Dignity and Theological Ethics 109
 3.4 Perspectives on Human Dignity...110
  3.4.1 The Image of God (Ontological) Perspective of
   Human Dignity..112
  3.4.2 Inherent and Inviolable Perspective of Human Dignity.....115
  3.4.3 The Social and Psychological Perspective of Human
   Dignity 117
  3.4.4 Humanist Perspective of Human Dignity.........................121
  3.4.5 Christian Anthropological Perception of Human
   Dignity 124
 3.5 Human Dignity in Nigeria 133
 3.6 Human Dignity and Human Rights...137

    3.6.1 Some Views on Rights from an African Context 139
    3.6.2 Fundamental Human Rights 144
    3.6.3 Perspectives of Human Rights 146
  3.7 Chapter Summary 152

Chapter 4 155
Towards a Survey of Ethics of Responsibility
  4.1. Introduction 155
  4.2 Max Weber on an Ethics of Responsibility (1864–1920) 158
    4.2.1 Weber's Socio-political Involvement in the German
        Public Life 158
    4.2.2 A New Dimension? 163
  4.3 Other Perspectives on Ethics of Responsibility: Some
      German Perspectives 171
    4.3.1 Dietrich Bonhoeffer 171
    4.3.2 Hans Jonas 179
    4.3.3 Wolfgang Huber 188
  4.4 Ethics of Responsibility: Some American Perspectives 197
    4.4.1 Henry Richard Niebuhr and Reinhold Niebuhr 197
    4.4.2 William Schweiker 203
  4.5 Ethics of Responsibility: Some African Perspectives 214
    4.5.1 African Theology and the Notion of Responsibility 215
    4.5.2 The Notion of Responsibility in Sub-Saharan Africa 217
  4.6 Chapter Summary 219

Chapter 5 223
Etienne de Villiers and Ethics of Responsibility: The African Context
  5.1 Introduction 223
  5.2 Some Background on Etienne de Villiers 224
    5.2.1 Theological and Christian Tradition 224
    5.2.2 Etiene de Villiers's Interest in Theology and Ethics 230
  5.3 Theology and Ethics of Responsibility 232
  5.4 Interactions of de Villiers with Other Scholars 234
    5.4.1 Interactions with Max Weber 234
    5.4.2 Interactions with Hans Jonas 243
    5.4.3 Interactions with the German Christian Version of
        Ethics of Responsibility 246
    5.4.4 Interactions with the American Version of Ethics of
        Responsibility 250
  5.5 Etienne de Villiers and the Contemporary Christian Ethic
      of Responsibility 253

    5.5.1 Features of de Villiers's Contemporary Ethics of
         Responsibility..254
    5.6 De Villiers on Moral Issues 264
         5.6.1 Corruption 265
         5.6.2 Human Dignity..268
    5.7 A Critical Reflection on de Villiers's Ethics of Responsibility 270
    5.8 Chapter Summary 274

Chapter 6 277
Toward an Ethics of Responsibility for Safeguarding Human Dignity in the Context of Corruption in Nigeria
    6.1. Introduction 277
         6.1.1 First Research Question: Corruption in Nigeria...............280
         6.1.2 The Second Research Question:
             Human Dignity in Nigeria 294
    6.2 Proposing Some Features of an Ethics of Responsibility for
        the Nigerian Context..306
         6.2.1 A Matter of Urgency 309
         6.2.2 Dialogical Dimension 312
         6.2.3 Strong Ethical Value-oriented......................................314
         6.2.4 Guided by Integrity, Fairness and Equity.......................315
         6.2.5 The Need for Confession 318
         6.2.6 An Orientation towards the Future...............................320
         6.2.7 Relational Anthropology..323
    6.3 Chapter Summary 326

Chapter 7 329
Summary and Conclusions
    7.1 Introduction 329
    7.2 A Discussion of the Major Findings 330
    7.3 Contribution of This Research...338
         7.3.1 Theological Ethics...338
         7.3.2 The Nigerian Context..338
    7.4 Possibilities for Future Research..339
    7.5 Final Conclusion 340

Bibliography..343

Acknowledgments

First, I would like to express my deepest gratitude to my supervisor, Professor Dion A. Forster, for his timely encouragement, guidance, motivation, and kindness – not only during the writing process of this dissertation, but since I met him at the Stellenbosch Faculty of Theology. Professor Dion, you have been a model to me that I will live to remember and replicate. You introduced me to many theologians and thinkers whom you also learned from and still talk about in most of our conversations. I am both humbled and deeply grateful for your mentorship.

My sincere thanks also goes to all the lecturers at the Faculty of Theology; your love and care have been tremendous.

My deepest thanks also to our dear department of systematic theology and ecclesiology; being in your midst has been enriching. Your counsel, motivation, support, and guidance have been massive.

My gratitude also goes to Emeritus Professor Etienne de Villiers, the pioneering champion of theological ethics of responsibility in Africa. Your humility and insights from when you agreed to meet with me in Stellenboch and throughout this academic journey has been tremendous. Rest assured that your legacy will continue to thrive.

Many thanks, also, to the Dutch Reformed Church for your financial support toward my studies.

Special thanks to my brother, Dr. E.U. Kure and his family who have been my sponsors from the beginning of this academic journey; you occupy a special place in my heart. Your sacrifice and the trust that you have in a younger sibling cannot be forgotten. To my Mum, and other siblings, you are so dear to my heart.

Lastly, to all my friends far and near, I remain grateful for the friendship.

Abstract

Corruption is one of the greatest impediments preventing Nigeria from achieving its maximum potential. It drains significant resources from the country's economy, impedes development, weakens the social contract between the government and its people, and has created structures that undermine human dignity. Nigerians view their country as one of the world's most corrupt in the world. They struggle daily with the impact of corruption while feeling incapable of making any significant or lasting change. In an effort to halt corruption, or at the very least to minimize it, many anti-corruption agencies and campaigns have existed with the desired results yet to be achieved. This calls for more work to be undertaken to address corruption from various perspectives in the Nigerian context. This certainly includes contributions from theology and ethics.

This thesis aims to address the implications of corruption on human dignity in Nigeria by engaging Etienne de Villiers' proposal for a contemporary Christian ethic of responsibility that addresses public morality. The study begins by presenting some background on the nature of corruption in Nigeria, outlining some causes, efforts toward curbing it and their limitations. It also considers how corruption in Nigeria threatens the dignity of persons. The study argues that the safeguarding of human dignity is an important theological and ethical concern. With the effects of corruption on human dignity being a point of concern, the question of 'responsible action' arises. Who is responsible for stopping corruption and safeguarding the dignity of persons in Nigeria? As a way to suggesting an answer to this question, the study engages with the notions of an ethics of responsibility as a theological resource to contribute towards the struggle against corruption while safeguarding human dignity. In particular it considers the work of Etienne de Villiers. First, this is because he proposes a contemporary Christian ethic of responsibility that can address issues of public morality. Second, because he is an African Christian theologian whose work holds promise for contextualisation in Nigeria. The study makes a proposal for what such a contextualized ethic of responsibility for Nigeria may need to consider.

The study shows that corruption is antithetical to human dignity. Yet, it is kept alive in Nigeria through inadequate leaders and their lack of responsible leadership. It is argued that an ethics of responsibility emphasises the need for co-responsibility between various social actors in political, economic, and religious life, in order to combat corruption and safeguard human dignity.

The project makes the following contributions to scholarly knowledge and the Nigerian context: An ethics of responsibility is argued to be relevant as a contribution to engage with various public moral issues – in this study the emphasis is upon corruption. Moreover, it provides new theological and ethical frameworks, that are based on Etienne de Villiers' ethics of responsibility, that can be considered in the Nigerian context. In this regard, this study is the first to consider Etienne de Villiers' ethics of responsibility as a resource to theologically engage corruption and human dignity in Nigeria. The outcome of this task is that the study provides some theologically contextual resources to strengthen theologians, the churches, and Christians in their work for a corruption-free Nigeria in which the dignity of human persons is protected and upheld.

Abbreviations

EFCC	The Economic and Financial Crimes Commission
ICPC	The Independent Corrupt Practices Commission
IDP	Internally Displaced Persons
WTO	World Trade Organisation

CHAPTER 1

Corruption, Human Dignity, and an Ethic of Responsibility in Nigeria

Introduction and Background to the Study

One of the often-talked-about problems in majority modern democracies is the daunting increase in corruption. In some quarters, ongoing protests either demand the resignation of corrupt officials, the counteracting of ineptitude, the removal of corruption with impunity or all three. Among other issues, the protesters demand for good representation, accountability, transparent leadership, adequate and affordable infrastructure and, the provision of basic human needs. This is because the absence of these elements has effects on human beings here and now, and also future generation. This is also a peculiar situation in Nigeria where this study is situated.

Corruption endangers the dignity of human persons everywhere, particularly in Nigeria. Different models to control this menace have been in place for some time now, with the required result not yet achieved. That calls for further investigation for ways to control the continuous spread of corruption to ensure salvaging the dignity of human persons. This research presents a theological resource that could contribute to the enhancement of the existing anti-corruption agencies and/or policies in Nigeria to first, provide a theological understanding of the concept of human dignity, and second, to situate corruption as a theological-moral issue. This chapter, therefore, serves as an introduction and gives the background to the study while also giving an overview of the general structure of this study. Additionally, the chapter provides the research problem, states the primary and secondary research questions, the aims and objectives, the research methodology employed while providing justifications for the choices made before closing with an outline of the chapters.

The corruptible human nature has brought untold hardship to the world and itself. Beginning from leadership inadequacies to the quest for every material and immaterial thing, the human person is often the focus. On the one hand, material things needed for survival often classified as basic human needs, are required to enable sustainability and survival. Immaterial things, on the other hand, involve important things but those which a human person could survive without. As a result of the latter needs, corruptible action becomes inevitable when an unguided moral reason prevails, which in turn undermines human dignity.

The nature of the world we live in has attracted more research on human dignity in recent times. Ranging from brutality, human trafficking, social and economic inequality, political instability, religious fanaticism, racial discrimination and terrorism, all target humanity . Humanity has been reduced to a usable object at the expense of things, resulting in the daunting undermining of its dignity. This has sparked the interest in scholarship and other forums, all seeking to salvage the dignity of human persons from all forms of violation. However, despite these realities of human dignity violation, there comes the question of whose responsibility it is to protect human dignity from continuous violation.

One challenge humanity faces in the face of these cruelties to human dignity is the question of responsibility. Taking actions in the context of need has raised concerns within humanity and has given way to a blame-game instead of taking adequate decisions. Within such contexts, when actions are not taken, cruelty is considered a norm and the perpetrators celebrated as heroes. So it becomes important that the concept of responsibility be taken seriously within the context of human dignity violation.

This study is concerned with the effects of corruption on the human dignity of Nigerian persons. With a survey of a few anti-corruption agencies in Nigeria, a theological resource – an ethic of responsibility – is introduced to contribute to the ongoing struggle against corruption. This study argued for the recognition and enhancement of human dignity from a theological perspective, its protection, respect, and promotion for the common good.

To do this, the study provides a sort of an analysis of Nigeria's congested religious context which is yet further complicated by corruption at different forms and levels.

Corruption has become a global concern infiltrating the flourishing of nations at different magnitudes. Considering that majority of nations are governed by democracy, studies have shown this to be a major boost for corruption, especially within weak leadership systems.[1] One example is reported by Transparency International on corruption perception index. First, that "corruption is much likely to flourish where democratic foundations are weak, and second, where undemocratic and populist politicians capture democratic institutions and use them to their advantage."[2] This led to calls for concern from citizens of different nations on whom the effects of corruption rest. On such efforts, Transparency International indicates that recent anti-corruption protests, including voters' frustration with corruption, are re-shaping the politics of several countries. Such aggressions by citizens of these nations occur in demonstration of the politicians' abuse of office and attempts to limit their accountability. Hence, the agitators insist that "leaders riding waves of discontent to positions of power must pay more attention than lip-service to anti-corruption, perhaps it should enter the DNA of their policies and reforms"[3]. These concerns are similar to what is happening in the African continent in general, and sub-Saharan Africa where Nigeria is located.

The African continent, like other regions of the world, is troubled by corruption to varying degrees. The report from two surveys conducted, one by the United Nations;[4] and the other by Transparency International/AfroBarometer,[5] submit the following findings of corruption in Africa. First, the range of corruption challenges that African citizens face is complex and multifaceted, requiring fundamental and systemic changes. The reports also indicate that while most people feel corruption increases in their countries, a majority felt that they, as citizens, could make a difference in the struggle

---

1. See for example: Ebegbulem, "Corruption and Leadership Crisis"; Tella, Liberty, and Mbaya, "Poor Leadership, Indiscipline & Corruption."
2. Transparency International, "The Corruption Perception Index," 4.
3. Transparency International, 2
4. United Nations' Economic Commission for Africa, "African Governance Report IV."
5. Pring, and Vrushi, "Global Corruption Barometer Africa 2019."

against corruption.[6] Such determination to engage in the struggle against corruption by the citizens of African countries suggests the impact that corruption has had in their lives and communities. On the effects of corruption in Africa, the Global Corruption Barometer Africa acknowledges that corruption[7] is hindering Africa's economic, political and social development. As such, corruption has become a major barrier to economic growth, good governance and basic freedoms including the freedom of speech or citizens' rights to hold governments to account. Corruption affects the wellbeing of individuals, families, and communities. Although this varies extensively across countries and public institutions, corruption harms hundreds of millions of citizens by undermining their chances of a stable and prosperous future. Since corruption chips away at democracy to produce a vicious circle where it undermines democratic institutions, given that weak institutions are less able to control it, the Transparency International warns that if left unchecked, democracy is under threat around the world.[8] The index shown on a recent report on African countries, particularly sub-Sahara, is very low in terms of the effectiveness of anti-corruption crusades.[9] These are indicators that African democracies are already under threat from corruption, whose cruel effects rest on human persons with underdeveloped infrastructure.

Since this study focuses primarily on Nigeria, it calls for an in-depth survey of corruption there. As part of this exercise, a background of Nigeria's return to a democratic regime is provided concerning its contested religious beliefs yet entangled in the shackles of corruption.

1.2 Preliminary Overview of Existing Literature
1.2.1 Nigeria, Religion, and Corruption
Since the return of Nigeria to civil democracy in 1999, the nature of participatory politics assumed and continue to assume a sectional nature with much emphasis on tribal and religious identities.[10] Additionally, another research

---

6. United Nations, "African Governance Report IV," 1–73; and compare with Pring and Vrushi, "Global Corruption Barometer Africa 2019," 1–68.
7. Pring and Vrushi, "Global Corruption Barometer Africa."
8. Transparency International, "The Corruption Perception Index," 3.
9. Pring and Vrushi, "Global Corruption Barometer Africa."
10. Akindola and Ehinomen, "Military Incursion," 8.

suggests that the quest for power, land acquisition and access to available resources pitch various groups against each other, resulting in conflicts that are usually difficult to resolve.[11] In part, this results from the desperate quest for political power by political office contenders, who promise immense political and economic rewards of jobs and opportunities to their passive group members from whom they recruit political thugs and militias. In turn, the exploitation of these differences by political elites has resulted in sectarian conflicts mostly between members of Christian and Muslim faiths, and between several ethnicities agitating against their socio-political exclusion. Often, the conflict results in population displacement, abduction, disturbing civilian casualties and concomitant poor infrastructural development and healthcare delivery that complicates the problems. While the conflicts continuously assume worrying dimensions, the state is unable to deliver on the democratic dividend in terms of public goods and services to the people. This leads to a growing concern about the "failure of the government to develop basic infrastructures and effectively deliver public goods and services including security, to the citizenry."[12]

Given the numerous incidences of violent conflicts in Nigeria, one would imagine that the complex ethnic and religious nature of Nigerians does not emphasize respect for human life nor encourage its sanctity. It also indicates that the priority of elites with the mandate to protect the interest of the citizenry at various levels could be more on personal interests than their well-being.[13] Despite its rich human and natural resources, Nigeria is trapped in a cycle of political, social, economic, and religious conflicts. The reasons that have been offered to explain this state of affairs include, but are not limited to poor management of the rich resources, and the inability of the relevant authorities to address the challenges, which hampers socio-economic and political development.[14] It is also the case that despite its saturated religiosity, Nigeria has not done enough to curtail the spread of corruption. One of the reasons why this remains so is the lack of moral formation which makes

---

11. Akper, "Is God in Nigeria," 66.
12. Ukiwo, "Politics, Ethno-religious Conflicts," 115.
13. As contained in the Nigerian constitution, the governing authorities owe the citizenry an obligation to protect them and their properties from harm, see Dada, "Human Rights under the Nigerian Constitution"; Olalekan, "Human Rights, Governance."
14. Jev, "Politics, Conflicts, and Nigeria's Unending Crisis."

it possible for corruption to infiltrate all facets of life in Nigeria including the church.[15] This lack of moral formation, considered as a result of "a weak and ineffective church," is a "hindrance to the proper functioning of the state."[16] Embedded in these explanations, however, is a concern that both occur because of various forms of corrupt practices.

Even though it has become common practice in everyday life, defining corruption is still difficult. It is difficult because the concept embodies numerous forms of criminal actions and inactions that vary in degree and harm.[17] In some instances, research equally indicates that corruption is both destructive against humans and it is difficult to trace or identify its existence.[18] Some definitions of corruption have been surveyed for purposes of this study. Theobald conceptualizes corruption from three different angles,

> the first referring to the process of physical decay, disintegration and decomposition with associated unwholesomeness and putrefaction. Secondly, corruption is used to signify moral deterioration and decay; a loss of innocence or decline from a condition of purity. . . . the third . . . relates specifically to the sphere of government and administration, to the discharge of *public* duties: "Perversion or destruction of integrity in the discharge of public duties by bribery or favour; the use or existence of corrupt practices."[19]

Similarly, Caiden defines corruption as simply,

> something spoiled; something sound that has been made defective, debased and tainted; something that has been pushed off course into a worse or inferior form. When applied to human relations, corruption is a bad influence, an injection of rottenness or decay, a decline in moral conduct and personal integrity attributable to dishonesty. When applied to public office, . . . the practice has been to spell out specific acts of misconduct

---

15. Igboin, "Corruption in Nigeria."
16. Forster, "God's Kingdom," 79.
17. Ackerman, *Corruption and Governance*; Robinson, *Corruption and development*; United Nations Economic Commission for Africa. *Measuring corruption in Africa*.
18. Agang, "Globalization and Terrorism."
19. Theobald, *Corruption, Development*, 1–2. Emphasis original.

that disgrace the public office and make the offenders unfit to remain there.[20]

Also, corruption is conceived as an abuse of public power for private gain that hampers the public interest.[21] Again, corruption is seen as a vast misallocation of public and human resources that impede the functioning of government and the economy.[22] We also contend that corruption involves a public official who exploits their office to further their personal interest instead of the public interest. To substantiate these definitions, a background understanding of corruption in Nigeria is vital, thus:

> Corruption has become a household word in Nigerian society from the highest levels of the political and business elites to the ordinary person in the village. Its multifarious manifestations include the inflation of government contracts in return for kickbacks, frauds, and falsifications of accounts in the public service, examination malpractices in our educational institutions including the universities, the taking of bribes and perversion of justice among the police, the judiciary, and other organs for administering justice, various heinous crimes against the state in the business and industrial sectors in collusion with multinational companies such as over-invoicing of goods, foreign exchange swindling, hoarding, and smuggling.[23]

In terms of the applicability of these definitions to the Nigerian problem of corruption as described above, one sees that Theobald's third definition is more suitable to the Nigerian context and this study because it encompasses other elements found in other definitions. First, the definition relates corruption to government administration with the discharge of public duties through the "abuse of public roles or resources for private benefit."[24] Such benefits are used by minority corrupt players while impairing economic development that would benefit most of the population, thereby denying

---

20. Caiden, "Corruption and Governance," 19.
21. United Nations, "Global programme Against corruption: UN anti-corruption policy."
22. Fisman and Golden, *Corruption: What Everyone*.
23. Caiden, "Corruption and Governance," 26.
24. Robinson, *Corruption and Development*, 3.

them access to basic human needs. As such, it opens way to political instability, poor infrastructure, poor educational systems, poor health, and other services, thereby resulting in violent activities.[25] Robinson's definition of corruption comprises the perversion of integrity in the discharge of public duties through bribery or favour seeking. With regard to perversion of integrity, the definition cautions that "corruption breeds distrust of public institutions, undermines ethical principles by rewarding those willing and able to pay bribes and perpetuates inequality."[26] Here, perversion is used to indicate that the gains of these corrupt practices[27] are "made at the expense of others."[28]

The effects of corruption in Nigeria include the inadequate provision of basic public goods and services, harm to human lives and the denial of dignity emanating from irresponsible leadership. Secondly, the use of human beings as a means of achieving ends instead of as ends in themselves as a form of distortion to the dignity of human persons is prevalent. On the basic public goods and services, "Nigeria is one of the food-deficit countries in sub-Saharan Africa although better in terms of production than others."[29] This is because the web of political and social conflicts from poor management of resources has led to the inability to provide the basic human needs of the citizenry.[30] It is also the case that Nigeria has suffered a major setback from various insurgencies[31] resulting in the loss of numerous lives and

---

25. Agang, "Globalization and Terrorism," 3.

26. United Nations, "Global programme Against corruption: UN anti-corruption policy," 8.

27. "Abuse of public office to secure unjust advantage may include any planned, attempted, requested or unsuccessful transfer of a benefit because of unjust exploitation of an official position. For instance, an official may seek sexual familiarity, money, gifts, economic influence, hospitality, or lucrative business opportunities in exchange for official action or forbearance" United Nations, 8.

28. Caiden, "Corruption and Governance," 19.

29. Ojo and Adebayo, "Food Security in Nigeria," 201.

30. Jev, "Politics, Conflicts, and Nigeria's Unending Crisis."

31. The activities of the Boko Haram sect and the sudden rise of Fulani herdsmen have resulted in loss of countless lives. Boko Haram sect which believes that "Western education is forbidden" emerged around the year 2002 as a local Islamic movement mainly for preaching and charity to people in Maiduguri, Borno state. These activities metamorphosed from 2009 onwards, after the Nigerian government crackdown on its followers leading to their spiritual and political leader, Mohammed Yusuf being killed. Shuaibu, Salleh, & Shehu, "The Impact of Boko Haram."

displacement[32] of others, owing to the poor measures taken in protecting human lives and property.[33]

Despite the knowledge of its destructive effectson human wellbeing and national development, efforts towards curbing corruption in Nigeria appear to be an issue of concern.[34] It is of interest to note that government institutions, religious institutions as well as civil society organisations are in place to put a stop to this menace but are yet to successfully wipe out corruption in Nigeria. On the political scene, there are in existence anti-corruption agencies whose responsibility lies in prosecuting officials involved in corrupt practices.[35] Albeit with some degree of success, these agencies have not done enough to curb the prevalent spread of corruption since it continuously disguises through different forms. On the religious scene, Christian organizations[36] and theologians have been and still are involved in anti-corruption wars through prophetic declarations, crusades and teachings.[37] Similarly, civil society organisations are making giant strides in the struggle against corruption, but are also yet to achieve maximum success.[38] Although success, to some degree, has been reported, corruption persists in Nigeria and continues to cause more harm than good through a vicious violation of the dignity of human persons. Hence, it is argued that "corruption persists because human beings have lost the sense of human dignity, thereby blindly placing material value over and above human value."[39]

---

32. The news of 250 school girls that were kidnapped from Chibok in April 2014, and in February 2018, where another set of 106 school girls were kidnapped in Dapchi, a town in Yobe state all in the North-Eastern region of Nigeria are issues of great concern on deprivation of the dignity of those young students amidst several other cases of human displacement championed by the sect, Shuaibu et al, "The Impact of Boko Haram."

33. Eseoghene and Efanodor, "Boko Haram Insurgency," 308–345.

34. Mentioning some of the consequences of corruption, Kunhiyop, suggests the following; oppression of the weak, erosion of moral values, general development, ineffective development and administration, destruction of the moral fibre of society, poor productivity, incompetence, loss of public trust, disregard for the rule of law, increased social evils, and lack of transparency, *African Christian Ethics*, 167.

35. These include, the Economic and Financial Crimes Commission (EFCC), the Independent Corrupt and Practices Commission (ICPC), among many others.

36. Prominent among these organizations is the Christian Association of Nigeria (CAN). It is a body that speaks for the Nigerian church, especially when addressing the government.

37. Anthony, "New Nigeria"; Ige, "John the Baptist Approach"; Ogbuehi, "Christian Ethics."

38. Akinyemi, "Civil Society"; Tonwe and Oarhe, "Corruption Management"; Ukase and Audu, "The Role."

39. Agang, "Globalization and Terrorism," 2.

1.2.2 Corruption and Its Impact on the Dignity of Human Persons

The study of human dignity has gained more interest recently than in the past for a number of reasons. Namely, the desire to gain a clearer perspective on what the concept entails as emerges from different contexts, and the wake of enlightenment arising from the understanding of human dignity, which has given it more meaning than was the case before. It is also the case that the continuous violation to human wellbeing and flourishing, the misplacement of human values in favour of material things have led to the quest for a more contextual understanding of what it means to be a human person. Even so, different schools of thought have emerged with different explanations of what human dignity is or how it should be conceptualized (chapter 3 provides details on this). Of more interest to this study, however, is the focus on how corruption results in undermining this precious gift to humanity – human dignity.

Some argue that dignity is a key concept in both secular and theological ethics yet its meaning is often taken for granted.[40] Although it is treasured in numerous documents, it has often been called into question by several authors with their interpretative models of the concept. Human dignity remains the most debatable concept in the languages of ethics and politics, and is widely used in legal and ethical discourse today. The problematic nature of this concept, as seen in another study, has led to examining why it does not mean anything anymore to many people,[41] suggesting a serious concern toward understanding and appreciating its worth. This is because the meaning of human dignity is argued severally as a "difficult word to define,"[42] or "it cannot be easily defined,"[43] or "no common understanding has emerged for human dignity."[44] The complexity in understanding human dignity leads to its non-recognition through human perception and interactions. Two broader perspectives, however, have emerged to explain human dignity, namely a universalized perspective that acknowledges every human being as worthy

---

40. Kirchhoffer, *Human Dignity*.
41. Bedford-Strohm, "Human Dignity."
42. Moltmann, *On Human Dignity*, x.
43. Koopman, "Some Theological and Anthropological," 177; Steinmann, "The Legal Significance of Human."
44. Schuster, "Human Dignity," 3.

of dignity, irrespective of their social status, and the personalized perspective, where human dignity is accorded through performance.

Viewed from a personalized perspective, human dignity loses relevance on occasions of non-performative action. Such a view of human dignity endangers the universality of treating all human persons with respect accorded to them. It also intensifies the argument that non-recognition of human dignity depends on a person. Being in practice before the wake of the enlightenment, arguments are that such a view makes human dignity far rooted in personality, which sees it as nothing more than a privilege or prerogative or even simply decorum.[45] Another research admits that such perception reduces human dignity to a possession that is taken for granted, and is based on one's social standing.[46] Understanding human dignity as such only points to a few individuals capable of attaining it, which would pay less or no attention to the violation of the dignity of others. Such a view only identifies complex issues like the brutal killing of individuals, rape, and intense torture as a distortion of human dignity. Human dignity viewed as such would lead to a delusion and opens spaces for several human activities not considered as distorting that priceless gift of God to humanity. This view, however, is not in any way inconsiderate but would be made better if what constitutes distortion to the dignity of a person is considered from a broader perspective. Seeing the limitations of the personalized view of human dignity, a reconsideration has been made since the enlightenment so that the concept is reviewed universally to incorporate every human person.

As a universalized concept, human dignity does not depend on one's social background but on being human because "being human suffices for having human dignity."[47] This view deconstructs certain restrictions to having dignity while arguing for all-inclusiveness of all created beings as having dignity. Thus, it sees human dignity as equal to the "worth of being human."[48] In this regard, de Villiers declares "all people deserve equal respect from fellow human beings and institutions, such as the state."[49] Since human dignity is

---

45. Moltmann, *On Human Dignity*, ix.
46. de Lange, "Having Faith."
47. de Lange, "Having Faith," 215.
48. Moltmann, *On Human Dignity*, ix.
49. de Villiers, "The Recognition," 265.

universalized, its protection and enhancement become the sole responsibility of all human persons. Significantly, human dignity has a value that is beyond human comprehension, which should be treated and cherished with reverence. Koopman understands this well and attests that

> we have dignity because we are created in God's image; we have dignity because God became human in Jesus Christ and redeems us; we have dignity because the Holy Spirit, as God at work in the world, is actualizing in and through us the new humanity that is a reality in Jesus Christ.[50]

Given this universality, one could agree that "human dignity has no price, no equivalent, no quantitative dimension,"[51] but something that needs to be respected, protected and promoted.

Looking at the personalized and the universalized perceptions above, one wonders that the latter does not only see complex situations as distortions to human dignity but also, and more practically, sees beyond it. Deducing from this view draws attention to the focus of this study, where Koopman attests that dignity is violated where the basic human needs are not met.[52] Accordingly, Koopman classifies basic human needs into various categories describing them as "basic,"[53] which implies that not meeting them equals a violation of human dignity. Following from this, we could agree that human dignity undergoes violation when a person is treated as a means to achieve an end and not an end in itself. Or as Wood, echoing Kant's view observes, human dignity is not to be treated in such a way that gives it value and worth of what makes humanity an end in itself.[54] Understanding human dignity in that manner expands our horizon to seeing various human activities as contributory efforts towards depriving human dignity.

---

50. Koopman, "Some Theological," 180.
51. Wolbert, "Human Dignity, Human Rights," 167.
52. Koopman, "Some Theological," 180.
53. He classifies these vital needs of whose violation attest violating human dignity as follows; firstly, those he calls the primary needs include, water, food, clothes, shelter, protection, medical care, education. Secondly, the secondary needs including, the need to have social relations, economic, political, and cultural life. Thirdly, those described as tertiary needs including, the need to develop and actualize potentials like the artistic, aesthetic, cultural, intellectual, Koopman, 178.
54. Wood, *Kantian Ethics*.

The Kantian description of human dignity clearly portrays the worth in a person, with a distinctive explanation. He sees humanity not as a thing that can be dealt with as a means, but as that which must, at all times, be regarded as an end in itself.[55] No one is therefore at liberty to dispose of that humanity which institutes a person, either by killing, maiming, or mutilating it. From Kantian categorical clarification, it is argued that the fundamental value of humanity or rational nature rests on a concrete reality that portrays humans as an end and not merely as a means.[56] As such, depicting a human being as an end demonstrates respecting the value of what makes it an end and not merely a means. For instance, "rational beings should not be subjected to deception or coercion"[57] but instead "we should seek to harmonise our strivings with those of other rational beings toward their end,"[58] thus echoing the imperative nature of our responsibility that aims at "respecting and enhancing the integrity of life."[59] The two perspectives to human dignity (personalized and universalized) give us a description of what it should be. This study, however, goes ahead and provides a theological connection to what human dignity entails.

Given the complexity of human dignity, a working definition from a theological perspective is used in this study. The choice of which definition to use is based on the idea that a common, inviolable, inalienable human dignity can only be acknowledged theologically, if a theological concept characterises human beings[60] as simply human beings.[61] The image of God concept, with reasons supporting it, is suggested as being this theologically suited concept

---

55. Kant, *Groundwork for the Metaphysics*.

56. Wood, *Kantian Ethics*.

57. Agang, "Globalization and Terrorism," 6. This term and many others such as coercion, taken closely, informs us of the certain practices - notably corruption, which forms part of this study that have demonstrated the inefficiency and incapability of various authorities living up to their expected responsibilities while violating human dignity at all cost. It is possible to maintain that there is no denying fact that our world has been taken captive by governmental and economic systems that make it extremely difficult to promote values that create human dignity and flourishing.

58. Wood, *Kantian Ethics*, 87.

59. Schweiker, *Responsibility and Christian Ethics*, 32.

60. The use of human beings here includes full dignity to all persons who are not (or not any longer, or not yet) Christians. Oberdorfer, "Human Dignity."

61. Moltmann, *On Human Dignity*, ix; Oberdorfer, "Human Dignity"; Vorster, "A Theological Perspective."

for this challenge.⁶² To this end, the creation narrative in the biblical book of Genesis sets the background that human beings are created in the image of God. Contemporary scholarship has, however, made efforts to not only explain this image of God, but also show its relevance for an ethical assessment of human dignity. These include the agreement to it as a qualification of human dignity that cannot be underestimated,⁶³ while others see the image of God (see section 3.3.1) as the basis of human dignity.⁶⁴ Such dignity is given to human beings by their connectedness with God through a relationship that cannot be destroyed by human misbehaviour, not even by murder, as one of the most despicable forms of moral misconduct.⁶⁵ Theologically, "human dignity attests that human beings are God's property."⁶⁶

This would suggest that we see human dignity as both a gift and a right from God for every human being (see section 3.3.2) - the right to simply be human and exhibit God's-likeness. In this regard, human dignity is viewed as a gift from the perspective that man is God's representative with a dignity that is inviolable as a gift from his creator.⁶⁷ Here, being created in the image of God means that man must be good in himself because he has inherent dignity and value. This explains why human dignity becomes something that is attributed, something that cannot be lost or denied by others and as an idea with high relevance for contemporary issues, and the greatest cultural achievement of Judeo-Christian tradition.⁶⁸ Human dignity, seen as such, could be described as a possession rightly owned by human beings who are God's image dignity bearers. Human dignity as a person's most basic property is the right to dignity⁶⁹ thus, making human dignity a key concept in the worldwide struggle for fundamental human rights.⁷⁰

---

62. Oberdorfer, "Human Dignity."
63. Bedford-Strohm, "Human Dignity."
64. Schuster, "Human Dignity."
65. Bedford-Strohm, "Human Dignity," 214.
66. Voster, "A Theolgical Perspective," 2.
67. Schuster, "Human Dignity."
68. Bedford-Strohm, "Human Dignity."
69. Vorster, "A Theolgical Perspective."
70. By fundamental human rights here we mean those rights and duties which belong essentially to what it means to be truly human, because without their being fully acknowledged and exercized, human beings cannot fulfil their original destiny of having been created in the image of God. (Moltmann, *On Human Dignity*).

It is clear in contemporary scholarship that there is a link between human dignity and human rights. Human dignity, not human rights, is the focus of this study, although references and important connections between these two concepts will be made as the study progresses.[71]

Despite various efforts having been put in place to stop the continuous spread of corruption in Nigeria as indicated above, the menace still manifests. This study seeks the common good of the Nigerian persons where corruption undermines human dignity. As such, the study suggests that further efforts are needed to bring an end to the menace. As an academic discipline, this study presents a theological resource called an ethic of responsibility to contribute to the struggle against corruption in Nigeria. This theological resource is not a new anti-corruption agency seeking to replace the existing ones, but a booster to the agencies that already exist. To this end, the concept of an ethic of responsibility is briefly introduced below and discussed in detail in chapters 4 and 5.

1.2.3 Responsibility and an Ethic of Responsibility

The word responsibility covers a range of human interactions. It is a concept that is commonly characterized with leadership from where there are expectations requiring reasonable actions. Some of these actions include answering a question for one's actions or inactions. When actions are morally justified, the agent of responsibility receives praise, and when actions are not justified, the agent is blamed. Given that blame is often avoidable even in the context of inactions, such attitudes intensify the quest for responsibility. Although responsibility talk occurs in different academic fields,[72] it is looked at from a moral theological perspective in this study. Nevertheless, as an ethic, responsibility emanated from a German sociologist, Max Weber. A detailed exploration of the concept is provided in chapter 4 (see section 4.2) of this study.

---

71. For proper connection between human dignity and human rights in this study, the following scholars were consulted and their views discussed in chapter three: Moltmann, *On Human Dignity*; Wiredu, *Cultural Universals and Particulars*; Kirchhoffer, *Human Dignity*; Wolterstorff, 2013; Muis, "Human Rights and Divine."

72. The discussion of responsibility from different background and perspectives is in chapter 4.

Responsibility has had an interesting history in modern theological ethics[73] and has developed and grown over the ages.[74] This shows that responsibility is not a new topic in moral-ethical inquiry considering its appearance in many traditions foremost among them English-speaking moral philosophy and theological ethics.[75] Even so, the idea of responsibility remains exceedingly complex and relates to all questions in ethics, including those relating to "value and power."[76] As a way of clarification, responsibility refers to being answerable for action or being accountable for it.[77]

There would perhaps arise a concern as to what an ethic of responsibility has to do with the discussions involving corruption and human dignity and, with emphasis on Nigeria. First, the study deals with corruption, and the underlying effects it has on human dignity. Second, although there have been efforts to combat the continuous spread of corruption in Nigeria (see section 2.6), the scourge keeps spreading and the dignity of people continues to be in jeopardy. The introduction of an ethic of responsibility is, therefore, used as a theological contribution to enhance the activities of the existing anti-corruption agencies. More importantly, an ethic of responsibility is presented in this study as a virtue that invites every individual to imbibe in the view of promoting ethical living in society. By so doing, we become sensitive to what is detrimental to the lives of others when recognizing and enhancing the dignity of others is viewed as a societal obligation (see section 6.1.2.3). It is also the case that human dignity has a personal dimension (see section 6.1.2.1) where one does not only seek the enhancement of other people's dignity but looks inwardly to avoid living in moral exhaustion. Regarding that view, this study agrees that there is a relationship between human dignity and personal liberty (section 6.1.2.2). Understanding responsibility as such, suggests that other people's dignity would be rightly recognized and enhanced when we discover and seek to enhance our own dignity. That would mean the responsibility to live and act ethically, which requires a collective effort,

---

73. Fletcher, *Situation Ethics: The New Morality*, 232 mentioned some of these proponents as Buber, Brunner, Barth, and Bonhoeffer who wrote on this interesting theological ethical topic.

74. Lucas, *Responsibility*, 93.

75. Huber, "Toward an Ethic"; de Villiers, "Prospects of a Christian."

76. Schweiker, *Responsibility and Christian Ethics*, 1.

77. Lucas, *Responsibility*, 93.

and when considered in the struggle against corruption is a call for inward evaluation toward responsible actions.

Such is the concept of the ethic of responsibility that the German sociologist Max Weber delivered in Munich, in his 1919 essay entitled "Politics as a Vocation,"[78] which is further discussed in section 4.2. Following his return from America,[79] Weber, in the year 1904, suggested in a letter to a colleague, that Germany should borrow America's "club pattern" as a means of re-educating Germany.[80] This was said following the autocratic system of leadership in Germany that appealed to only a few persons. Realizing this, Weber sought the involvement of the younger generation, which he emphasized in the essay "Politics as a Vocation." Starr highlights Weber's contention in the 1919 essay that the vocation of politics is ultimately not about whether politics can or should be ethical, but rather what kind of ethical framework is most appropriate.[81]

1.3 An Overview of the Research Process

1.3.1 An Introduction to the Research Problem

Nigeria could best be described as being in "a state of emergency" due to the endemic spread of corruption. Perhaps one could say that corruption has reached a breaking point in Nigeria, and adequate actions are needed more than mere rhetoric and lip-service.

Previously, it was regarded solely as a political and an economic problem responsible for the poor infrastructural development, perpetuated by politicians and public office holders. As a point of departure, however, this study views corruption with its detrimental effects also from a theological-moral perspective as being responsible for lack of provision of basic human needs which, in turn, undermines the dignity of human persons. As such, engaging corruption through a different lens (theological) requires that further emerging ways towards curbing it to safeguard the dignity of human persons is not only prominent, but in the Nigerian context, urgent. While perspectives from

---

78. de Villiers, E. "In Search."
79. Weber's trip to America is detailed in chapter 4.
80. Weber, *From Max Weber*, 104.
81. Starr, "The Structure," 408.

Christian theology provide useful tools for understanding the uniqueness of human dignity that corruption endangers, they also help us to understand corruption in ways other than from the political and economic point of view. In the choice of a theological resource, this study engages Etienne de Villiers, a South African Sytematic Theologian, who is an expert in the field of ethics of responsibility from the African context. While de Villiers' proposal for a contemporary Christian ethics of responsibility holds great promise to engage with issues distorting the moral fabric of most African societies, it is considered as lacking some resources to critically and clearly speak to the African person because of its Western character. Yet, because he is the pioneering champion of theologial ethics of responsibility from an African context, engaging his work is prominent for this study. A detailed discussion on Etienne de Villiers' work on ethics of responsibility is found in chapter 5 of this study.

1.4 Research Question, Aim and Objectives

1.4.1 Research Question

Given the state of affairs in Nigeria with regard to corruption and its eminent threat to human dignity, this study sought to answer the following research question:

How could an ethic of responsibility contribute towards the safeguarding of human dignity within the context of corruption in Nigeria?

1.4.2 Secondary Research Questions

1. How could corruption be understood in the Nigerian context?
2. In what ways is the dignity of human persons challenged by corruption in Nigeria?
3. What theological resources could an ethic of responsibility offer to address corruption in the Nigerian context?
4. How might these identified ethical resources contribute to the safeguarding of human dignity in Nigeria?

1.4.3 Research Aim

The aim of this study is to explore the perception of corruption and its effects on human dignity in the Nigerian context, in order to offer a theological contribution to curbing the scourge and safeguard human dignity.

1.4.4 Research Objectives

In order to respond to the research question and achieve the aim of this study, the following research objectives were formulated:

- To gain an understanding of how corruption is perceived in Nigeria, the way in which and the extent to which it violates human dignity
- To unpack the concept of human dignity with the variation in meaning, and how the lack of a coordinated perception of it results in violation through various human actions such as corruption
- To interrogate the theological contribution that an ethic of responsibility could offer in the struggle against corruption in Nigeria
- To examine the ways in which theological-ethical resources could contribute to the recognition and enhancement of human dignity in Nigeria.

1.5 Research Methodology

This study takes the form of a literature study. The literature study comprises three major sub-topics, namely corruption, human dignity, and an ethic of responsibility. Various sources were reviewed among them books, journal articles, monographs, edited books and reports from the government and NGOs. A detailed description of sources of specific importance to the study follows here below.

As the key problem for the study is corruption, literature from different perspectives, such as theological, moral, political, and economic, was used. As to the theological perspectives, the following work leads the conversation *The Eccentric Existence: A Theological Anthropology* which was consulted to offer some background to human depravity that led to sin, hence, corruption.

Others include in *Many Faces of Evil: Theological Systems And The Problem Of Evil*.[82] These works were used to provide some theological background to corruption in chapter 2 (see section 2.2.1). Other literature on corruption provided the moral dimension of corruption. In this section, however, different works lead the conversation.[83] Since the discussion on corruption in chapter 2 focuses on Nigeria, the above sources comprise majorly of Nigerian voices for contextual reasons. Another form of corruption considered in Nigeria is the political perspective in which these works lead the conversation.[84] These resources provided the nature of corruption in Nigeria, the causes, and the effects.

Regarding the theme of human dignity, the literature considered included theological, sociological, and philosophical perspectives. From the theological perspective, the noted works lead the conversation.[85] A few works were consulted on human dignity from a humanist perspective.[86] Human dignity was considered from a philosophical perspective and similarly a few works were consulted.[87] Discussing the ideas of Kant in the section (see section 3.2.3) was prominent because he influenced moral discussions, particularly on human dignity.

Accordingly, the theme of an ethic of responsibility formed the third major segment of this research which was studied from sociological, theological, and philosophical perspectives, and in different contexts. Since the idea of an ethic of responsibility was initiated by sociologist, Max Weber, his works set the pace for the discussion in this section.[88] This was followed by the works of theologians from the German and American contexts. For the German contexts, the works of Dietrich Bonhoeffer on ethics and Wolfgang Huber were

---

82. Kelsey, *Eccentric Existence*; Feinberg, *The Many Faces*.

83. Agang, "Globalization and Terrorism"; Igboin, "Corruption in Nigeria"; Yagboyaju, "Religion, Culture, and Political"; Onongha, "Corruption, Culture and Conversion"; Ogbuehi, "Christian Ethics."

84. Yagboyaju, "Political Corruption"; Omotola, "The Intellectual Dimensions"; Mercy, "The Effects of Corruption"; Moyosore, "Corruption in Nigeria"; Fatile, "Corruption and the Challenges"; Suleiman, "Political Corruption."

85. Aquinas, *St Thomas Aquinas*; Moltmann, *On Human Dignity*; Soulen and Woodhead, *God and Human Dignity*; Bedford-Strohm, "Human Dignity"; Koopman, "Some Theological."

86. Soyinka, *The Climate of Fear*; Akper, "An Ethos of Hospitality."

87. Kant, *Groundwork for the Metaphysics*; Harbermas, "The Concept of Human."

88. Weber, "Domination and Legitimacy"; Weber, *From Max Weber*; Weber, "Max Weber: An Intellectual"; Weber, *Politics as Vocation*.

considered to provide a theological version which served as representation for others.[89] From the American context, the works of Niebuhr was phenomenal in establishing some understanding of an ethic of responsibility.[90] Similarly, the works of Schweiker were central for a continuation from the previous generation of theologians in the American context.[91] From the philosophical perspective, the works of Hans Jonas served as a roadmap.[92] Regarding the African perspective, the whole of chapter 5 was dedicated to the works of Etienne de Villiersand, particularly, his proposal for a contemporary Christian ethic of responsibility was well studied.[93]

Aware that corruption is a continental issue, this study focused on the negative implication of corruption and the threats it poses on human dignity amongst the Nigerian populace. Also, in full acknowledgment of the complexity of human dignity, this study focused on the theological understanding of human dignity, with particular reference to the image of God inherently possessed by every human being that is created by God. Finally, is the notion of the ethic of responsibility. Here, the study did not exhaustively present discourse on the subject but successfully studied the works of Etienne de Villiers alongside other proponents. As a result of the study, some guiding factors that a contemporary ethic of responsibility in Nigeria could take into consideration, if such ethic would be effective for salvaging the undermining of human dignity caused by the scourge of corruption were provided.

1.6 Outline of the Chapters

The study comprised of seven chapters, which in clear terms focused on interrelated questions

- Chapter 1 sets the stage for the entire study by explaining what is contained therein. It spells out the background, the conversation

---

89. Bonhoeffer, *Ethics: Dietrich Bonhoeffer's Works*; Bonhoeffer, *Dietrich Bonhoeffer Ethics*; Huber, "Toward An Ethic"; Huber, *Violence: The Unrelenting*.

90. Niebuhr, *The Responsible Self*.

91. Schweiker, "Radical Interpretation and Moral"; Schweiker, *Responsibility and Christian Ethics*; Schweiker, *Theological Ethics and Global*; Schweiker, "The Ethics of Responsibility."

92. Jonas, "Technology and Responsibility"; Jonas, *The Imperative of Responsibility*.

93. de Villiers, "Who Will Bear"; de Villiers, "The Vocation of Reformed"; de Villiers, *Revisiting Max Weber's Ethic of Reponsibility*.

partners, methodology, and the research questions that are answered in the chapters ahead.

- Chapter 2 specifically focuses on outlining the case of corruption in Nigeria. In doing this, it provides some background perception of corruption from political and religious perspectives. A few causes of corruption, the effects of it, and the efforts to curb it from further spreading are all contained in this chapter. It was found that corruption continues to thrive because human beings, ranging from political, religious, public and private settings, have chosen to become its marketers and distributors. To disembark this endemic problem, the chapter concludes that there is an urgent need for building societal moral fibre through moral transformation from individual to societal levels.
- Chapter 3 focuses primarily on understanding the notion of human dignity. The concept was looked at from different perspectives and backgrounds, which provided its broader perception, and a trajectory was established that human rights exist to safeguard human dignity. The chapter also argues that human dignity is violated due to variation in perception of it, but also due to cruelty of human action toward others.
- Chapter 4 sets the tone to survey the concept of an ethic of responsibility. Doing this, the chapter highlights different persons, contexts – other than African, and perceptions of the concept. The findings from this chapter transpose the study to the next chapter which is more contextual and specific. One of the things found in the chapter is the irreconcilable tension among the proponents of ethics of responsibility which, in turn, affects its applicability in different contexts and issues.
- Chapter 5 specifically focuses on an African theologian, Etienne de Villiers, the pioneer of the topic of a Christian ethic of responsibility in the African context. The emphasis was on his projection for a contemporary Christian ethic of responsibility to salvage public morality and enhance ethical living.
- Chapter 6 forms the crux of the study. With Nigeria being the context of the study, this chapter provides a proposal for an ethic of responsibility that could be useful, first to contribute to the

effectiveness of the current anti-corruption struggle in Nigeria and, second make a case that recognition and enhancement of human dignity both have a communal and personal dimension.
- Chapter 7 summarises the findings, makes suggestions for further research, and concludes the study. The chapter concludes with suggestions that corruption is endemic, which requires collective effort to engage it to salvage human dignity from continued violation.

1.7 Chapter Summary

This chapter offered an introduction and background to the study. This was followed by the statement of the problem, the research question, aim and objectives of the study. A brief overview of the literature study and some of the sources that formed the bedrock for the review in the various chapters was provided. The next chapter attempts to conceptualize corruption in the Nigerian context.

CHAPTER 2

Conceptualizing Corruption in Nigeria

2.1 Introduction

The previous chapter gave the general background of the study and introduced an outline of the chapters that make up this research report. This chapter offers a conceptual and contextual analysis of corruption concerning the Nigerian context. The reference to Nigeria does not dispute the endemic global challenge of corruption, but to limit the scope of this study. Also prominent in this chapter is the overview of corruption from different viewpoints while referring to some root causes, effects and the efforts being made towards curbing corruption in Nigeria.

Through conceptual and contextual analyses, corruption has been discussed from a theological- anthropological viewpoint as well as other perspectives that are relevant to the scope and focus of this study. This is important because it will help us focus on the scope of this research as well. Regarding the scope of this study, however, we limited the survey of corruption to three dimensions, namely the theological, the religious and the political dimensions. The reason for focusing on these perspectives is to understand the leadership landscape of Nigeria and how it encourages the continuous spread of corruption that has become detrimental to human dignity, but also to see the roles of religious institutions in spreading and curbing corruption in Nigeria.

The chapter has five main divisions: part one deals with perspectives in conceptualizing corruption; part two is an analysis of the nature of governance in Nigeria; Part three focuses on the causes of corruption in Nigeria; part four examines the effects of corruption in Nigeria; part five examines the efforts towards curbing corruption in Nigeria, before closing with a summary of the chapter.

2.2 Some Background on Corruption

A study conducted attests that corruption is recognized as an issue of serious political, economic and moral significance, representing a cost for growth and development.[1] Surprisingly, many corporations claim they do not suffer any damage by corruption. Some of these firms and organizations, he argues, could either be deceiving themselves and the public or have a weak control mechanism that benchmarks the extent of corruption. Although corruption is not a living being, the gravity of its effect is felt when left unchecked.

In a document compiled in collaboration between the United Nations Economic Commission for Africa (UNECA) and the African Union Advisory Board on Corruption (AUABC), a comprehensive background of corruption in African context is provided.[2] This document states that corruption is undoubtedly the most pressing governance and development challenge confronting Africa today, and whose corrosive effects are greatly felt on the progress, stability and development of the continent. This menace, the report shows, impedes economic growth by discharging foreign investments, creating distortion in resource allocation, and generally increasing the cost of doing business. Of utmost concern is the political realm where "corruption undermines the rule of law, respect for human rights, accountability, and transparency, and weakens government institutions. Its social costs, however, include deepening income inequality, power, and adversely affect good moral values in society."[3] In its moral realm, corruption undermines human dignity and deadens societal moral fibre while weakening people's consciences. This report summarizes the situation of corruption in the African continent at large, although the degree differs from one state to the other due to diversity in governance within the continent.

Similarly, Nigeria being the context of this study, has its specific description of corruption. Although a variety of literature on corruption in Nigeria

---

1. Kreikebaum, "Corruption As A Moral."
2. AUABC, "Combating Corruption, Improving Governance," 3.
3. AUABC, 3.

comes from diverse disciplines including but not limited to political scientists, sociologists, economists and ethicists, they all aim at portraying the extent of corruption.

By its very nature, corruption is socially transitional in that it evolves along with society, assuming new meanings across time and space.[4] This being the case, corruption has become a complex and persistent phenomenon which, in the case of Nigeria, bedevils.[5] By bedevilling, "corruption is not only complex and persistent but a common household name in most human societies with its impact leaving people in devastating conditions on a daily basis."[6] However, another study finds that corruption in Nigeria appears to be "ubiquitous, so much so that Nigerians themselves view their country as one of the world's most corrupt."[7] Another study classifies corruption as unethical behaviour that runs counter to acceptable social norms and moral values. It is a behavioural pattern, which seriously hurts public morality and leaves society worse for it.[8] Following these portrayals of corruption, we would agree with the previous description that corruption has reached a breaking point in Nigeria, to the point of warranting a state of emergency.

2.2.1 Theological-Anthropological Background to Corruption

Tracing corruption from a theological perspective would unravel its root causes from when humanity fell short of God's standard. To this inquiry, the work of David Kelsey on theological anthropology is considered primarily because of the background and the link he provides in understanding the relationship between the creator and the creation.

To begin with, Kelsey in his two volumes, *The Eccentric Existence*, emphasizes the nature and reason for the interrelationship between the creator and the created. He asks the question, "what does the specific Christian conviction that God actively relates to us imply about what and who we are and how we are to be?"[9] In essence, he complicates the answer to the above question

---

4. Igboin, "Corruption in Nigeria," 45.
5. Obuah, "Combating Corruption," 27.
6. Fatile, "Corruption and the Challenges," 47
7. Page, *A New Taxonomy*, 3.
8. Ighaekeme, Abbah, and Gaidem, "The Effect of Corruption."
9. Kelsey, *The Eccentric Existence*, 159.

with two beliefs, namely that God "is understood in a triune way, and that the triune God actively relates to us in three interrelated but distinct ways; as one who creates, grounding our reality and its flourishing; as one who promises us an eschatological consummation and draws us to it; and as one who reconciles us in our multiple estrangements."[10] In the light of these three ways in which God relates to us, a few things would require further extrapolation to help us situate Kelsey's explanation to our understanding of corruption.

The first medium of relating that God creates and grounds our reality and flourishing has an eschatological dimension. These two components, creating and flourishing, relate to God's intention in declaring good what was created as presented in the biblical narratives. This once good created, however, later rebelled against the creator, thereby resulting in the intrusion of disobedience that broke the initial relationship between the creator and the created. The quest for reconciling the broken relationship between the creator and the created, therefore, arose. This confirms Kelsey's point that God relates through reconciling us in our various estrangements, such as resulted from disobedience in Eden.

The doctrine of sin reminds us of how creation got estranged from the creator. The estrangement as observed in another study occurred when Satan brought sin into the world and disrupted that perfect fellowship that God had initiated.[11] Sin, however, tore apart our perfect fellowship of love with God, for we were expelled from the garden of Eden where Adam and Eve had lived in regular communion with God. It also damaged our relationships with each other. The doctrine which explains the concerns of natural theology and creation has been developed both by classical and contemporary theologians: notably Augustine, Barth, Brunner and several others. It is, therefore, very important to recognize their inputs to the conversation.

Similarly, another study tries to situate Barth's contemporary natural theology to the classical theologies of Calvin and Augustine on natural theology.[12] Although Barth differs from Augustine on natural theology in his understanding of human nature without a theology of original sin, he does not deny its existence. In his assertions, Barth affirms how the human condition

---

10. Kelsey, 605.
11. Aben, "The Trinity and Public Theology."
12. Allen, "Sin and Natural Theology," 14.

is marked by "certain depravity and why the whole of human nature requires Christ's redemption. "[13] This depravity consists of the resistance to God's condition to act lawfully and rightly, which was promoted by humanity. The depravity "gave humanity precedence to their own selfish desires, interests and objectives, and they became self-absorbed, displeased God and hated one another."[14] The assertion further suggests that redemption is required to renew the broken relationship, which also concurs with Kelsey's point above that God relates to us by reconciling creation back to the creator. Such declaration affirms why the original sin is seen as a "fault and corruption of the original flawlessness of humanity. "[15] This sort of understanding, as championed in traditional Christianity, seeks to understand humanity's broken relationship with God through the rebellion of Adam and Eve in the Garden of Eden. Perhaps, understanding the original sin this way, backed by the Augustinian tradition, "helps us understand the extent to which humankind has free will to determine a choice between good and evil."[16] From this backdrop, we realize that choosing evil rather than good, as humankind's initiative, helps our understanding of Kelsey's point that God relates to the created by reconciling us from our various estrangements.

Now, the original sin that came through free will suggests how and why corruption originated from Eden. Corruption, as seen from above, includes the choice of evil over good, which comes in different dimensions, namely either as natural evil to include pains, diseases, earthquakes, floods, fires, pestilences, hurricanes and famine, resulting from human activity, but could occur also without the action of the agent; or as a moral evil that arises from human activity that challenges the omnipotence of God over the existence of evil in the world which, most times, does not involve an agent.[17] When corruption involves an agent, the reality in free will and choice of either good or evil ensues. Such human activity involves choices whose consequences cannot be blamed on others since they arise from human free will. In such choices, the existence of immoral behaviour, such as corruption, that are detrimental

---

13. Allen, 14.
14. Aben, "The Trinity and Public Theolgy," 43.
15. Rondet, *Original Sin: The Patristic*, 40.
16. Linden, "The German Christians' Influence," 10.
17. Feinberg, *The Many Faces*, 16.

to both human and societal wellbeing become prominent. As a result, "we are still scarred by sin, and those scars are warping our understanding of what it means to live in the image of the Trinity."[18]

Free will, as Augustine explains, should be used as a tool for the right action and not for evil. This is because Augustine sees no sense in a human person who is good but cannot act rightly unless he/she wills, hence, the need for free will to enable right acting.[19] From this backdrop, we could relate corruption emanating from the inappropriate and deliberate misuse of free will for evil rather than good.

2.2.2 Political Corruption in Nigeria

From the root sense, this form of corruption simply emanates from the political activities involving politicians. As it were, politicians control the affairs of the state, aligning decisions that either enhance the wellbeing of the nation or distort it. As such, political corruption involves any act of a public official aimed at changing the normal or lawful course of events for personal interest or the interest of a group of persons.[20] This form of corruption includes manipulation of political institutions' procedures, which influences the political system and frequently results in institutional decay.[21] When this happens, the difficulty of actualizing a truly representative democracy that allows full participation intensifies, thereby denying the citizens accessible knowledge of the responsibility of the authorities for and towards them.

Another study observes that political corruption is in two phases, namely misuse of government power to embezzle and accumulate wealth, and the use of state allocation to preserve power for a political ally and party functionality.[22] This, he adds, frequently leads to institutional decay, which in turn, distorts the functional capacity of the relevant authority. Such is a description of unethical exploitation of the state, the effect of which hampers socioeconomic growth and brings about political instability.

---

18. Aben, "The Trinity and Public Theology," 43.
19. Feinberg, *The Many Faces*, 56.
20. Yagboyaju, "Political Corruption."
21. Suleiman, "Political Corruption"; Aleyomi, "Corruption and Democratization Process."
22. Suleiman, "Political Corruption."

Perusing the extent of political instability, gross economic meltdown, government failure, underdevelopment, and the stagnation of democracy and development in Nigeria, several studies attest to political corruption as the propeller.[23] Despite being a multi-ethnic country with a complex religious nature, Nigeria's hope for a sustainable democracy shows only limited progress. In part, the nature of participatory politics takes a sectional dimension, favouring the fortunate minority with the political wheel with little or no regard for the unfortunate majority. Such politics often declines the central democratic mechanisms leading to the economic meltdown and government failure in various ramifications.

Political corruption, like any other type of corruption, remains the most critical impediment to achieving the Sustainable Development Goals (SDGs) whose aim has been to reduce poverty and underdevelopment rates across the nations. Like a deadly virus, corruption attacks the vital structures and systems that endanger the progressive functioning of the society.[24] One of these vital segments of the state is the economy, which is the bedrock of the national treasury. The national treasury is commonly known in Nigeria as the "national cake," referring to the country's wealth that attracts the interest of anyone in a place of power, or who desires power to run for their share of the cake. This has turned the quest for leadership to grasping a share of the cake with little or no interest for representative leadership.

Political corruption either influences the growth and flourishing of a nation's economy or devalues it. The latter results when politicians, who champion the course of policies, are non-intentional in formulating sustainable economic policies or devalue them when they lack the capacity. The extent of their decisions determines the management capacity of resources and appropriately channelling them to use, with the aim of enhancing the development and sustainability of human well-being and infrastructures that enable tremendous contribution to development.

The influence of political corruption on the Nigerian economy could be the main contributor to the increasing difficulty in meeting the basic human

---

23. Suleiman, "Political Corruption"; Yagboyaju, "Political Corruption"; Awojobi, "Political Corruption and Underdevelopment."

24. Ene and Dunnamah, "Corruption Control"; Ajie, and Gbenga, "Corruption and Economic Growth."

needs of the citizenry, although the needs, the provision and equity in distributing the resources rests largely on the leadership capacity to both decision-making and proper management. Considering political corruption as having to do with the misuse of power, a study suggests that bad management and misappropriation of public funds are the reasons people's needs are not met.[25] As a nation blessed with human and natural resources, perhaps with some not yet discovered, the political leaders who are decision and policymakers, rather prefer to squander these resources for self-gratification.[26] Importantly, political leaders selfishly amass wealth on things they could live without but fail to think of the felt needs of the poor majority of Nigerians.

This makes it necessary to distinguish between the real and felt needs bedevilling the human persons. Felt needs here refer to anticipations, wants and dreams of what one thinks of actualizing someday. They are needs which an individual could live and survive without. Real needs, on the contrary, include those needed in urgency to enable the living and survival of a human person. They are not futuristic but present needs, needed here and now. These include but are not limited to the next meal, the next clothes to wear, the next bill to pay, or the next place to run in search of shelter. Having access to felt needs does not only impact human well-being and survival but societal development. The influence of political corruption characterized by decision making largely retards social development, increases the chances of poverty, limits the growth of the nation, undermines economic growth, and leads to poor implementation of public service reforms.[27] Regarding felt needs of the citizenry, availability of a workable system that guarantees the free flow of policies would bring to order a society whose needs are regarded as real, instead of as felt needs. This does not undermine the place of real needs because they would have to be real before they are felt. When the focus on basic human needs is considered and seeks to solve the felt needs beyond and above the real needs, it would mean placing importance on the human well-being, which triggers treating and valuing them as ends in themselves and not mere means to the ends.

---

25. Ighaekeme, Abbah and Gaidem, "The Effect of Corruption."
26. Ajie and Gbenga, "Corruption and Economic Growth."
27. Ajie and Gbenga, "Corruption and Economic Growth"; Odi, "Impact of Corruption."

So far, it has been presented here that political corruption largely distorts national growth and development. Saddled with the power of making decisions and implementation, politicians being policymakers, have a larger share of the blame. This is because both the resources and the power to put policies into appropriate usage are under their control. The problem, as seen in the preceding paragraphs, involves the misplacement of priority and inappropriate discharge of the vested powers which result in an increase and in corruption in Nigeria. Poor discharge of duties, valuing self-aggrandizement over human wellbeing, characterize the Nigerian political landscape, making it a breeding ground for corruption. Although more emphasis, and perhaps blame, could be laid on the political institution for perpetuating corruption, other sectors are not spared in this regard, notably the religious institutions.

Since Nigeria operates under a democratic system of governance, it is often assumed that corruption applies only to those actively involved in the state and partisan politics. It could be true, as seen above, that politicians and other public office holders stand at higher risk with corruption, yet the practice is not exclusively perpetrated by them. In that sense, this study unveils corruption in other sectors, notably the religious institutions with particular reference to the church.

2.2.3 Corruption and the Nigerian Church

If politicians were the only persons indicted with corruption, it would mean that corruption does not apply to religious institutions, particularly the church. Such assumptions could arise from the fact that the church is filled with a deep sense of morality where everyone lives, behaves and should act morally well, and wrong acts are condemned. Being part of society and consisting of individuals participating in public affairs, there would be no justification to exempt the church from cases of corruption. As it were, churches could either be harbouring corrupt individuals within itself, or be negligent in addressing corrupt-related practices and, therefore, cannot be exempted in this line of discussion. Attempting to do that would mean denying the depravity of the human mind that is susceptible to influence. Nevertheless, this section surveys the nature and extent of corruption in the Nigerian church, most importantly, the effects and their implication in distorting the societal moral fibre.

Earlier assertions in Nigerian history hold that concepts such as shame, honesty and honour, that regulated morality, were effectively a controlled group behaviour.[28] At that time, activities constituting public or private shame were strictly considered amoral and, therefore, not tolerated. This was because the societal moral values were held in high regard through the influence of religion, perhaps the Christian beliefs and practices. Today, however, the tide has changed, such that religion has been so commercialized that anything goes on, so much so that the moral and societal decay have higher momentum daily.[29]

As a moral concern infiltrating the Nigerian church, corruption is an immoral human act that perverts and converts human consciousness from sensitivity to insensitivity, depriving one of moral discernment. When that happens, it results in justifying misappropriation, misrepresentation, and mismanagement of church funds and properties. The difference here, with political corruption discussed above, is that the resources in the church, unlike the public's, are in most cases privately owned, particularly in recent times where most churches, especially in Nigeria, are operated by individuals. Such misuse of resources includes human and material resources, lack of accountability, lack of transparency, sexual scandals, payment for religious duties such as prayers, healing and miracles. Also, when the church fails to "be guided against simply being co-opted by the state," it loses the potential to exhibit the core of the gospel through social and moral transformation.[30] Going by those factors attests to why the church is accused of failing to enhance the significant reduction in the perpetration of corruption in Nigeria because, in itself, it is corrupt.[31] The failure in moral formation and discernment, therefore, significantly affects the efficacy of the Nigerian church to stand and uphold its identity.

The content of the gospel messages parading most Nigerian churches also influences corruption. As a religiously complex nation, Nigeria does not have one single religion or church denomination. This goes with the nature of the teachings at these worship centres, which makes it complicated aligning to

---

28. Onongha, "Corruption, Culture and Conversion," 75.
29. Adenuga, and Omolawal, "Religious Values and Corruption," 522.
30. Forster, "God's Kingdom," 81.
31. Yagboyaju, "Religion, Culture and Political."

what is taught. Some of these teachings include, but are not limited to, "saying what the congregants would always want to hear" such as how to either succeed, have breakthroughs, instant healing, instant miracles, or how to acquire instant wealth. On the contrary, little or no emphasis is made on things that concern public moral life such as honesty, the dignity of labour, persistence and faithfulness with regards to public engagement.

It is believed that some of these churches use "fear, and sometimes lies, to control and manipulate people for the advantage of a selected group of persons."[32] When the emphasis is placed on uncertainties rather than assurance and hope, these church groups succeed in inflicting fear, hence, holding their followers hostages to do and act as instructed. Such are the attitudes that have resulted in the commercialization of religion and the gospel by making it the quickest way to material freedom. In this regard, research has shown that the Nigerian church has drifted from the evangelism of salvation to that of prosperity even when it entails robbing or other forms of ill-gotten wealth.[33] This happens, Faleye adds, "when pastors and other religious leaders collect tithes and offerings without recourse to the source."[34] Often, this occurs through the association of religious heads with top public officials, many of whom are parading the streets with convicted corrupt cases.[35] As a result of such association, the nature and the content of their message changes. Instead of speaking against immoral practices, such as corruption, it is replaced by misinterpretation of biblical injunctions such as "not judging others" because God would do. Such forms of interpretation portray how corruption misleads through "crooked indoctrination"[36] of people's consciences.

Following the first point, it can be argued that corruption infiltrates the Nigerian church because of the nature of messages. Primarily, the principle of disciple-making has ceased from being the focal point in most Nigerian churches. At some point, total focus on eternity made the Christians aliens in the world with the assumption that the gospel is associated with rejection – as seen in the cross of Christ – and poverty to be the only hope of the

---

32. Faleye, "Religious Corruption," 175.
33. Faleye, "Religious Corruption," 176.
34. Faleye, 177.
35. Yagboyaju, "Religion, Culture and Political."
36. Faleye, "Religious Corruption," 176.

masses. In this regard, a study suggests that the church should not focus on life eternal only, but more importantly, teach about purity, holiness, diligence, the dignity of labour, and even the tendency to failure and success as these are human tendencies.[37] Such would enable Christians become earthly relevant while, at the same time, remaining eternally minded. Being relevant in terms of admonishing adherents to imbibe values and virtues that promote peace, orderliness, and shunning immoral behaviour like corruption and exhibit control to become pacesetters for society.[38] These virtues would enable the church to become beacons and regain her place as the "salt and light" to the world. This is the much-anticipated role of religion in society. Failure, in this regard, results in the prevalence of corruption that continuously distorts the societal moral fibre.

Financial misappropriation is another form of corruption prevalent in the Nigerian church. The depravity of the human mind that deadens human conscience to make it insensitive and amoral is the root cause of accepting abnormality as normal. This happens when church leaders partake in "robbing their congregants by manipulating the gospel for their gains, and sometimes making them commit crimes, theft, take and give bribes in the name of meeting up with church requirements."[39] On other occasions, it ranges from the theft of church money to ritual killing for money, which the church inhabits in her teachings.[40]

The prevalence of sexual harassment is another form of corruption in the Nigerian Church. It has, unfortunately, become prevalent where church leaders are listed as perpetrators of sexual affairs with church members for selfish gains in the form of promises.[41] On some occasions, it is either for children – in the case of women who are desperately wanting to have children – or for some spiritual cleansing by the "man of God." It is imperative to note here that these actions have selfish interests as their motivation. It could be summarized here as a suggestion, that the reason behind these scandals perpetrating the Nigerian church has been "the inclusion of strange

---

37. Adenuga and Omolawal, "Religious Values and Corruption."
38. Adenuga and Omolawal, "Religious Values and Corruption."
39. Faleye, "Religious Corruption," 177; Omonijo et al., "The Proliferation of Churches."
40. Adenuga and Omolawal, "Religious Values and Corruption."
41. Omonijo et al., "The Proliferation of Churches"; Adenuga and Omolawal, "Religious Values and Corruption."

teachings[42] and practices that have shifted the attention of the true gospel message from an emphasis on moral values to accept virtually everything."[43] Without focusing on developing positive attitudes on followers, the church dwindles from being the church.[44] In his assertion of the church as the community of character, Hauerwas insists that being that kind of community, "the church helps the world to understand what it means to be the world since the world has no way of knowing without the church pointing to the reality of God's kingdom."[45] To do what Hauerwas pointed out is to have a different ethic of living. Since human depravity has resulted in tolerating what was disrespectful, shameful and embarrassing, including corruption, and every amoral behaviour found in the church in the time past by making it the norm, therefore, it becomes timely that the church takes up a stand to provide guidance and direction for the world.

We have so far seen how corruption permeates different phases of human interaction. The assessment identifies the infiltration of corruption in different stages and perspectives, both in the political sector and in the church. Going by this assessment, it is appropriate to delve deeper into the nature of governance that allows the above happenings, despite their impending consequences on humanity.

2.3 Nigeria and Governance

So far, it is established that corruption is multifaceted and disguised in various forms and natures. The concern in this section, however, is to examine the nature of governance in Nigeria. In this section, we shall uncover the current leadership trend in Nigeria to ascertain the context where corruption is bred. By doing this, we can arrive at a connection between corruption and leadership.

---

42. Some of these strange teachings have shifted away some African moral values such as shame, communal life obedience, and any honouring act from African Christianity which Kunhiyop warns against. Kunhiyop, "The Challenge of Africa," 169.

43. Omonijo et al., 641.

44. Hauerwas, *A Community of Character*.

45. Hauerwas, *A Community of Character*, 100.

2.3.1 Democracy in Nigeria

The democratic system of governance has been described as the widely emphasized system of governance around the globe because its ideas and principles are people-centred.[46] Considered as the system of governance in most Western states, Majority World countries have equally adopted this form of governance. Unfortunately, the democratic practice seen in these Majority World countries, particularly in Africa, has taken a different tune. Here, Nigeria is not exempt.

In the year 1999, after a long military historical dispensation, Nigeria returned to a democratic system of governance.[47] At this new dawn in the country, "a large section of Nigerians saw it coming as the time to reposition the nation on the path of good governance, democratic dividends and a corrupt-free society."[48] Such wide expectation led to "an equally wide anticipation for a governing process that allows people to choose their leaders and, in turn, guarantees them a wide-range of civil rights and dividends as some of its features suggest."[49] Better still, democracy having in its tenets "'the government of the people by the people and for the people', is enough to have raised high expectations at its emergence."[50] These are true of an ideal democratic system, which "rests on good governance, and whose determinant is on how its policies bring about growth, stability, and the wellbeing of the citizens."[51] Unfortunately, after more than two decades of this system of governance, "these hopes have been dashed by the perils of the time and almost at the verge of being swept under the carpet of ethno-phobia, nepotism, religious fanaticism, self-centeredness and militarisation."[52]

Although democracy has been accepted both locally and globally as the best form of government, whose core values include serving the greatest happiness for the greatest number of people the case remains different in

---

46. Asaju, "Sustaining Democratic Rule," 1
47. Aleyomi, "Corruption and Democratization Process," 2; Asaju, "Sustaining Democratic Rule," 4.
48. Ukase and Audu, "The Role," 183.
49. Asaju, "Sustaining Democratic Rule," 3.
50. Aleyomi, "Corruption and Democratization Process," 9.
51. Asaju, "Sustaining Democratic Rule," 4.
52. Kure, "Leadership, Corruption," 3.

Nigeria.[53] Indeed, many years down the spiral, "Nigerians are yet to fully taste the benefits of democracy and the luxury of justice that comes with it."[54] The system is in practice, but realities are still distant from actualisation. This has remained the case because what constitutes a democratic system of governance remains a mirage, so much so that questions begin emerging as to whether democracy was the better option in the first place.[55]

Although the democratic system of governance has constituents that make it acceptable and most spoken about, these constituents are still a mirage in Nigeria. Though described severally as the rule of, or by the people, and as the government of the people for the people and by the people, a democratic system of governance has a completely different connotation in Nigeria.[56] In Nigeria, a democratic system of governance refers to "a system of government structured by a political cabal with the power of some people formed by influential people to intimidate other people."[57] Such is a system favouring a few fortunate minorities while disregarding the unfortunate majority, who are left at the mercies of those controlling the system. Understood from this view, it appears that Nigeria's form of democracy is a reversal of other democracies around the world, which is perhaps the reason for the various uncertainties that lead to the creation of chasms between the rich few and the masses.[58] This calls for a reversal of what constitutes democratic governance whose components include good governance, protection of human rights and dignity, fair distribution of resources and adherence to the rule. Collectively, these describe the features of good governance and democracy, whose reversals are termed undemocratic resulting in poor governance.

2.3.2 Governance and Democracy in Nigeria

The focus here is to outline what constitutes good governance and its responsibilities to the governed. This is done with the aim of ensuring strict adherence of a constituted authority to its laid down responsibility which when

---

53. Yagboyaju, "Political Corruption."
54. Ukase and Audu, "The Role," 183.
55. Kure, "Leadership, Corruption," 3.
56. Ene and Dunnamah, "Corruption Control."
57. Suleiman, "Political Corruption," 1.
58. Suleiman, "Political Corruption."

achieved, would provide us with an understanding of what the implications of irresponsible representation entails and its effects on society.

Good governance is described as "the use of political authority and exercise of control over society as well as the management of its resources for social and economic development."[59] This involves the strong political will to decision-making that is central to the needs of the led. Other elements of good governance include the functioning of the state's institutional and structural procedures, decision-making, policy formulation, enactment capability, information flows, effective leadership, and the relationship between rulers and the ruled.[60] It also involves adequate maximisation of the available resources that are geared towards the enhancement of societal and human wellbeing. As it concerns good governance, service provision and delivery to the populace is central.[61]

Good governance is characterized by the ability of those in places of power to fulfil the terms of the social contract with people, which implies adherence to transparency and accountability.[62] A transparent government ensures[63] strict adherence to the rule of law, which involves adequate formulation and implementation of policies, and the right placement of the governed. Adherence to the above-mentioned concepts calls for a conducive society where justice, equity and respect for human dignity flourishes[64] otherwise, the absence of these constituents would demonstrate a loss of human conscience that places "material value over and above human value."[65]

In a further description of the responsibility of a good democratic government, the following observations have been made. First, Asaju finds that true democracy rests on good governance and is a major determinant of whether the government is good or bad. Second, it ensures effective policy formulations with regard to how to bring about growth, stability, and more

---

59. Fatile, "Corruption and the Challenges," 49.
60. Doig, "Good Government."
61. Yagboyaju, "Political Corruption"; Mercy, "The Effects of Corruption."
62. Fatile, "Corruption and the Challenges."
63. Yagboyaju, "Political Corruption"; Fatile, "Corruption and the Challenges"; Mercy, "The Effects of Corruption."
64. Mercy, "The Effects of Corruption"; Umaru, "Corruption as a Threat."
65. Agang, "Globalization and Terrorism," 2.

importantly, the overall well-being of the citizens.[66] Such a system of governance ensures the transformation of society and its citizens through the provision and equitable distribution of basic human needs.[67] Often, the provision of basic human needs in Nigeria becomes a tool for political debates where it is reduced to acts of favour rather than as obligation to the citizenry. In Nigeria, a multi-ethnic society, the distribution of basic human needs is determined by "who gets what, when, and where by the elites."[68] Such concerns are suggested to being elements of "identity politics."[69] Fukuyama sees this becoming a prominent feature in democracies with the "failure of the system to fully solve the problem of people's inherent cravings for the recognition of their selfhood."[70] As this scenario succinctly describes the Nigerians situation, it nullifies the perception of good governance that includes adequate and equitable service delivery to the populace.[71] It is for this very reason that identity politics has been described as one of the features of the Nigerian democracy.[72]

Good governance is a product of true democracy, which involves the capacity of the state to function in providing services to the populace and adhere to the rule of law.[73] In relation to service provision, good governance ensures transparency and accountability by the policymakers and office holders. Besides, further study has shown that the will of the people is best suited to allow all the people to have access to freedom, dignity and adherence to the rule of law.[74] Such freedom allows the citizens the right to choose their leaders and the eligibility to exercise their civil rights through participatory engagement in public affairs.

The underlying features of a democratic government are measured by good governance and open representation, but these have become susceptible to political corruption.[75] Being the major obstacle to democratic stability in

---

66. Asaju, "Sustaining Democratic Rule."
67. Ene and Dunnamah, "Corruption Control," 11.
68. Umaru, "Corruption as a Threat," 226.
69. Fukuyama, *Identity: Contemporary Identity Politics*, 10.
70. Fukuyama, 10.
71. Mercy, "The Effects of Corruption."
72. Kure, "Leadership, Corruption."
73. Yagboyaju, "Political Corruption."
74. Makinde, "Global Corruption and Governance," (2013); Asaju, "Sustaining Democratic Rule."
75. Yagbyaju, "Political Corruption"; Asaju, "Sustaining Democratic Rule."

Nigeria for various reasons, political corruption deprives democracy of meaning through disallowing participatory politics thereby limiting participation to a few persons.[76] As such, it becomes politically corrupt when there is no true representation, which in turn does not open to listening and responding to concerns. Such democratic practice has become the most topical issue in the discussion of deepening crises and contradictions in recent times, particularly with Nigeria.[77] Formulating policies befitting growth and sustenance in Nigerian democracy has, therefore, remained a concern because of unethical, illegal, uncritical and unauthorized decisions often for sectional or personal gain.[78] Here, atrocities committed against humanity are explained rather than finding lasting solutions to them,[79] and sectionalism prioritizes the lives of some over others.

The above survey on good governance reveals the features of good democratic governance. The survey revealed this form of leadership as transparent and open for participation. It also revealed that good governance ensures accountability and transparency. This way, the public resources undergo checks and balances to ensure service delivery. Simply put, a government with such a description is less susceptible to corruption, which has become a bane to development in Nigeria. Unfortunately, the scenario remains so because of poor and weak leadership lacking a strong wheel but also harbours corruption that is antithetical to human and societal wellbeing. As argued, such stagnation in democratisation has been hampered by several forces, notably, corruption being multifaceted and disguised in different forms.[80] In the next section, therefore, we will be looking at the causes of corruption in Nigeria that continuously hamper the intended good governance described above.

---

76. Yagboyaju, "Political Corruption," 177.
77. Omotola, "The Intellectual Dimensions."
78. Yagboyaju, "Political Corruption."
79. This has recently become the song in some parts of Northern Nigeria where people are killed but the authorities justify and give reasons for such actions instead of arrests, prosecution, and appropriate the machinery under its power.
80. Aleyomi, "Corruption and Democratization Process."

2.4 Some Causes of Persistent Corruption in Nigeria

Having seen the permeation of corruption in both the political and religious institutions, this section will survey some of the root causes of the pandemic that is in Nigeria. Surveying the cause of corruption is important to this study because it provides good knowledge of the effects on both human and societal development, thereby intensifying the urgency in curtailing further spread.

2.4.1 Failure of Leadership

Leadership is the rudder that pulls societies or organisations from the usual to the rare. It informs the direction in which society goes and sets goals for its vibrancy. In part, a leader with such vision understands their followers so much that their wellbeing and societal development is a topmost priority. Such leaders are decisive and willing to act for the interest of the people. As such, they lead the people from where they are, to where they ought to be. The human society is, however, bereft of such leaders today. No wonder most societies, particularly in the developing world, continue to struggle. They struggle not because there are no leaders, but because their leaders lack vision and the capacity to lead. Often, the leaders think of and for themselves more than they do of those they are leading. Such leaders are bereft of the capacity of "influencing others for maximum productivity"[81] as they seek to "take people from where they are towards wholeness of life."[82] They, instead, become builders of self-images while their societies or organizations crumble without human wellbeing and infrastructure. Such leadership aids in the breeding of immoral conduct such as corruption in society.

Leadership in its various forms is responsible to guide and direct society for development and prosperity. Attesting to this, leadership is seen as both adhesive and as a catalyst that binds citizens of a given country in two ways.[83] First, it triggers their motivation towards the achievement of both individual and group objectives. Second, it holds the key to unlocking transformation questions. In some spheres, actualizing societal goals requires that it has leadership that is both motivated and enthusiastic. First, to ensure that policies are made and, second that policymakers adhere to their implementation.

---

81. Kure, 5.
82. Kretzschmar, "The Formation of Moral," 18.
83. Anazodo, Igbokwe-Ibeto, and Nkah, "Leadership, Corruption and Governance."

When this happens, it demonstrates that the leaders are visionary, purposeful, and capable of taking constructive initiatives.[84] That is when the vision for a moral society where vices such as corruption, that are detrimental to the enhancement of human wellbeing lose significance. When the leader lacks foresight and the wheel to lead, however, the survival of societal vices, which are "detested both in interpersonal relationships and group behaviour"[85] grow wings. Such leaders should be called immoral because they are capable of leading communities on self-destructive paths to misery.[86] The areas where inept leadership leads to continuous spread of corruption are outlined below.

First, the leadership in Nigeria contributes to the spread of corruption through a lack of or poor strong will. Given that the responsibility of leadership in democratic societies entails sustenance and maintenance of stability, the case in Nigeria is the opposite. It is arguably true that "the Nigerian society has never been well-governed since independence because good and strong leaders have never been in charge."[87] This is because the nation has been managed by selfish and corrupt leaders, whose goal is to accumulate wealth at the expense of national development. Often, these leaders have blighted the lives of Nigerians who now wallow in poverty, illiteracy, hunger, and unemployment. This, in turn, has made the problem of corruption in Nigeria a "political one perpetrated by the leaders."[88] These problems continue down the spiral because the leaders in charge of affairs lack a strong will and are indecisive in unequivocally piloting national affairs for the common good of society. As a result, a study finds that this promotes "weak institutions of government, a culture of affluent, and get rich syndrome has become a way of life of public officials."[89] When this happens, an average Nigerian citizen is made to think that "there is an inextricable link between corruption and democracy."[90]

Second, leadership in Nigeria enhances corruption through mismanagement of the nation's human and material resources. Africa is considered "the

---

84. Anazodo, Igbokwe-Ibeto and Nkah.
85. Fatile, "Corruption and the Challenges," 47.
86. Kretzschmar, "The Formation of Moral."
87. Ebegbulem, 223.
88. Aleyomi, "Corruption and Democratization Process," 11.
89. Moyosore, "Corruption in Nigeria," 29.
90. Ebegbulem, 225.

poorest continent in the world, and the richest in terms of natural resources."[91] Unfortunately, the image of this blessed continent is "battered by corruption and a leadership crisis."[92] Nigeria, in particular, a nation blessed with rich human and material resources, has become the "epicentre of poverty and conflicts due to mismanagement of these resources."[93] The public office holders either use these resources for themselves or channel them to inappropriate sectors where they are, in turn, made to their benefit. These resources are national wealth that should put in place modalities for human welfare by developing functional, advanced and accessible infrastructure, which would, in turn, boost economic growth. The interest of the leaders, however, is rather on the "persistent widening of the gap between the ruled and the rulers resulting in poverty, unemployment and underdevelopment."[94] Such leadership decisions "subject the workforce to poor welfare, poor reward and low numeration for public servants."[95] Left in such conditions and facing societal pressures and competition, the tendency to indulge in acts of corruption for a better living is created. As such, if an individual is not guided by strong ethical values, they join the line of corruption. When leaders cannot manage what they have toward the goodness of the governed, it is an indication of failure from their side.

Third, leadership in Nigeria breeds corruption through the abuse of the rule of law. Adherence to the rule of law in society promotes unity and harmony among the inhabitants while enabling the setting up of ethical principles to safeguard human lives and property only if the leadership is determinant. That is why Aristotle observes that "when humans lack virtue, they become the most unholy and the most savage of animals, and the most full of lust and gluttony."[96] Unfortunately, in Nigeria, adherence to the rule of law is difficult from the top, down to the bottom. The legislature is a product of political corruption as "elected officials get into power through the rigging of elections."[97] While this continues to happen, the leadership, through a lukewarm attitude,

---

91. 221.
92. Ebegbulem, 221.
93. Jev, "Politics, Conflicts, and Nigeria's Unending Crisis." 147.
94. Tella, Liberty and Mbaya, "Poor Leadership, Indiscipline & Corruption"212.
95. Moyosore, "Corruption in Nigeria," 29.
96. Aristotle, *Politics*, 6.
97. Ebegbulem, 221.

has "failed to enforce the law on perpetrators."[98] Additionally, the failure to adhere to the rule of law "extends to failure of the ruler to be accountable to the ruled, and the inability to neither make officials accountable for their actions nor the corrupt ones to justice."[99] Such actions are products of "weak institutions of government"[100] as well as the "failure and the visual collapse of governance."[101] Such leaders are described as "selfish, mediocre, tribal leaders, and opportunistic small-minded people masquerading around as leaders."[102] They are those leaders, whose concern for self-gratification, surpasses the desire to engage with social vices like corruption, which brings about debilitating effects.

It is such an attitude of leadership that promotes budget paddling and the demand for kickbacks before service delivery. Kleptocracy is the order of Nigerian politicians who would only pass national budgets when they are paid, and when allocations in the budget suit their demands. Studying this situation critically, a study reports that in kleptocracy, where corruption flows down, the top receives vast oil profits, and payments flow down in a patronage system.[103] Similarly, corrupt civil servants access public funds through widespread contract fraud. On the side of the politicians and officials, they "enrich themselves through corruption more or less at will, at times moving into the economy by converting whole state agencies into profit-seeking enterprises, and ambitious businesspeople with official protection and partners take on a quasi-official status as they build their enterprises."[104] For such systemic corruption to persist uncontrollably, the demonstration of failure of leadership becomes the motivation which, in turn, treats corruption with mild and soft hands. Failure of justice which, in a sense refers to "the bond of men, and as the principle of order in political society,"[105] is absent in the Nigerian system.

---

98. Moyosore, "Corruption in Nigeria," 29; Fatile, "Corruption and the Challenges."
99. Aleyomi, "Corruption and Democratization," 12.
100. Moyosore, "Corruption in Nigeria," 29.
101. Fatile, "Corruption and the Challenges," 47.
102. Ebegbulem, 223.
103. Chayes, *Thieves of State*.
104. Johnson, *Syndromes of Corruption*, 23.
105. Aristotle, *Politics*, 6.

2.4.2 Failure in Moral Upbringing

Leadership occurs at different levels in human society for many reasons. On the one hand, it influences the growth and development of virtues and restricts the nurturing of vices. On the other hand, leadership provides synergy for maximum productivity towards the common good. The growth of virtues or vices, however, determines the goals, priority and the perspectives of the policymakers responsible for upholding them. In this section, therefore, we shall consider leadership from the grassroots, namely family, society and schools, and how these have influenced the spread of corruption in Nigeria. This follows from what we have seen above regarding the role that Nigerian political leadership plays to enhance the spread of corruption. These institutions are considered here because they form the bedrock of moral formation and have consequences for safeguarding societal morality. This echoes what Aristotle asserted, that "since the state is made up of households, we must speak about the management of the household before speaking about the state."[106]

In this regard, a study suggests that these institutions provide practical moralities by assigning roles and rules that involve the acceptance of responsibility.[107] The value of this responsibility follows its expression when confronted with external forces such as peer influence. At some point, the influence of peers either enhances the virtues already embedded or subverts them. When the former occurs, the values are shared and learned, respectively. When the latter occurs, it signals suspicion of one's societal moral standard. In either case, there is a tendency that the influence of peer pressure could subvert one's sense of morality that has been entrusted on one as a responsibility to safeguard.[108] Such a person, therefore, becomes duty-bound to ensure the sustainability of such values and guards against trading them for vices.

In the case of rampant increase of corruption in Nigeria, these institutions have compromised the needed moral guidance and modelling. The decline is attributable to a lack of moral strength by individuals.[109] In instances of caregivers' role in imparting moral formation, the content and approach

---

106. Aristotle, *Politics*, 6.
107. Williams, "Infrastructures of Responsibility."
108. Tella, Liberty and Mbaya, "Poor Leadership, Indiscipline & Corruption."
109. Igboin, "Corruption In Nigeria."

of modelling taught at the family level, school or church, impacts how the individual internalises moral lessons.[110] As it were, the internalisation of these moral lessons builds sustainable values in terms of moral decision-making. Two of the values are honesty (words in conformity with reality), and integrity (reality in conformity with words).[111] These two virtues, Igboin adds, progressively enhance a transformative moral life that seeks to preserve the sanctity of human life from all forms of corruption. As such, they appeal to a higher form of morality rather than instinct or materialism.[112] Following Igboin, another study finds that virtues such as honesty and integrity are taught to help protect the name, honour, image and the integrity of families.[113] Since corruption becomes pervasive, "maintaining moral standards from the family level is substituted with immoral acts driven by selfish motivation, marring what is good and generally acceptable on moral grounds, hence resulting in moral failures."[114] These failures, however, expose children and make them vulnerable in a corrupt society. They grow to think that self-gratification, illicit rewards and the acceptance of unmerited rewards have moral validation.

The contemporary Nigerian society has not done enough to inculcate discipline from the grassroots. Moral values had, at a point in time, been held in high esteem in Nigeria. Those were times when dealing with vices was a collective responsibility of society, while virtuous behaviour was the goal. Those were moments that some forms of habits were approved and others were outrightly rejected as shameful, barbaric, and were regarded unacceptable in society. Affirming this, a study observes how vices were treated in some Nigerian societies in the time past with two examples. Taking honesty as the first example of virtues, anyone who did not think it wise to make honesty a personal value easily ran into trouble with others in society.[115] Second, theft was considered a societal crime with severe penalties. Anyone who was found guilty of theft did not carry the shame alone but with friends, family, relations, and was asked to go around the community, carrying the object they stole. Such an embarrassment, Idang suspects, "was enough to discourage

---

110. Oladipo, "Moral Education."
111. Igboin, "Corruption In Nigeria."
112. Igboin, "Corruption In Nigeria."
113. Salawu, "Towards Solving the Problem."
114. Igboin, "Corruption In Nigeria," 54.
115. Idang, "African Cultural Values."

even the most daring thief."[116] Research into the Nigerian societal moral fibre, however, reveals that those punishments and embarrassments that Idang imagines above have done close to nothing in curtailing amoral behaviour in the country. Another study, for example, reveals that Nigeria harbours more unethical conduct now than ever.[117] Gberevbie says this with the concerns for underdevelopment such attitude causes, while making the observation that for development to occur in Nigeria, it must position itself in terms of good policies and conduct among its citizens. The two voices point us to the need to revitalise societal values. If corruption could be considered a theft, and punishment that was associated with theft in the time past brought back and implemented on corrupt officials today, there might be some reawakening in the subconscious minds of those that are currently corrupt and to those that see corruption as a good adventure to desist from it. Unfortunately, society celebrates corrupt persons through failure to mould people of character.[118]

Corruption has also eroded the institutions of learning in Nigeria. While institutions are expected to be motivators for academic excellence through hard work, they have become avenues for fuelling corrupt practices in Nigeria. Such practices range from paying money for admissions, forging of certificates, fraudulent promotions, and leadership instability, practices which have disrupted the academia in Nigeria from being a pacesetter for intellectual and moral upbringing. It is one thing to have a good structural organization with policies, yet a different thing to allow smooth operation and exhibition of duties without interference with justice and equity. Suggested in a study, social justice arises in the context of unequal and uneven distribution of rewards and other privileges that enhance the human sense of wellbeing. In part, such occurrences result in frustration and aggression, which has ended in unresolved crises and destruction of lives and property in Nigeria.[119] Similarly, unequal treatment and distribution of resources contribute to unemployment opportunities, insecurity and the dearth of infrastructure.[120] These effects have led to increased incentives and opportunities for corruption.[121]

---

116. Idang, "African Cultural Values," 102.
117. Gberevbie, "Ethical Issues."
118. Tom, and Bamgboye, "The Role of Religion."
119. Tella, Liberty and Mbaya, "Poor Leadership, Indiscipline & Corruption."
120. Anazodo, Igbokew-Ibeto and Nkah, "Leadership, Corruption and Governance."
121. Moyosore, "Corruption in Nigeria."

The above comments attest to inadequate leadership, political thuggery and indiscipline, which are products of indecisiveness to firmness on what works for the common good that allows the pervasion of corruption.[122] This has been the problem with the Nigerian public leadership structure which is very good at making policies but poor in converting them into actionable realities, hence influencing the downturn of affairs. It is, however, suggested that morals built from the family level hold great promise toward a moral society.

The above summary calls for rediscovery to the saying "charity begins at home." The three institutions in question (family, church and school) have a greater contribution towards enhancing moral values at a foundational level. The inhabitation of these moral values, however, ensures the subjection of vices that a human person could live as a responsible citizen. By responsible citizen we mean one who responds adequately to issues related to human and societal wellbeing, and able to declare vices such as corruption as anti-human, anti-social and amoral.

2.4.3 Loss of A Sense of Humanity

We argue in this section that corruption occurs when human persons lose their sense of wellbeing, perhaps abusing their consciences. The argument identifies with few schools of thought in mind, particularly, a sociological and philosophical concept of *tabula rasa* that justifies the ancientness of the human heart that is influenced and contaminated only by society.[123] Complicating the matter, Aristotle affirmed that it is a characteristic of man that he alone has any sense of good and evil, and of just and unjust.[124] Since this study identifies moral bankruptcy as a cause of corruption, following the sociological concept of *tabula rasa* would limit the theological conceptualization of human depravity that explains the fallen-ness that gives rise to the evil perpetrated by humanity against God and itself.

The notion of human depravity is embedded and presented severally in religious books. From the Christian perspective, beginning with the fall (Gen 3) to rebellion (Gen 6) to rejection of a theocratic leadership (Judges), and the rejection of God's moral standards (Rom 1 and 2), all attest to moral

---

122. Moyosoro, "Corruption in Nigeria."
123. Duschinsky, "Tabula Rasa and Human."
124. Aristotle, *Politics*.

bankruptcy. From the Islamic point of view, corruption and all its constituents are also forbidden.[125] In its positive form, the human mind manufactures, nurtures, processes and implements thoughts from the heart. The human person is, therefore, an intellectual who has the responsibility to promote intellectualism either in the form of information or restraining others from immoral practices that damage the societal moral order.[126] Additionally, intellectuality of the human heart can contend with vices. There is evidence, however, that corruption has engulfed this central sector, the engine room responsible for processing thoughtful and responsible ideas. Although discourse on the intellectual dimension of corruption is still far from crystallizing, a study views this as the perversion of intellectual responsibilities for personal gain at the expense of others, deliberately or otherwise.[127]

In an effort to determine the root cause of this form of depravity, a study on the doctrine of human depravity offers some insight.[128] Pink contends that the Adamic nature in every human being granted that they possess no degree of moral rectitude but have desperately wicked hearts. He articulates this while relating to the loss of human moral judgment as responsible for why corruption has invaded every part of human nature, overspreading the whole of humanity's complex being. The gravity of this depravity explains that humanity is born with seeds of every form of evil, and radically inclined to sin – an objection to the theory of *tabula rasa* mentioned above.[129] This is why Igboin warns corrupt individuals from "confessing that the devil pushed them into the act"[130] but rather suggests that they accept the reality emanating from the loss of moral integrity.[131] These corrupt individuals would, thus, come to resolve that at the heart of the issue of corruption is the nature and selfishness of the human heart.[132] Gleaning from these thoughts, we see that no human being is immune from one form of moral depravity or the other. Although the reality of human depravity blinds the mind, it hardens the

---

125. Suleiman, "Political Corruption."
126. Omolola, "The Intellectual Dimension."
127. Omolola, "The Intellectual Dimension."
128. Pink, *The Doctrine*.
129. Pink, *The Doctrine*.
130. Igboin, *Corruption: A New Thinking*, 6.
131. Igboin, "Corruption In Nigeria."
132. Onongha, "Corruption, Culture and Conversion."

heart so much so that it remains under the ravages of depravity.[133] While one operates under the grace and mercies of God and strives toward moral transformation, however, moral judgments rule above depravity. That is a process of transformation at both personal and cultural levels that is characterized by a rupture with the past and a radical restructuring for the future.[134] So, from Pink, Omotola, and Igboin above, we see that intellectual corruption refers to an individual-induced form of corruption that operates within a mind lacking moral strength. Put simply, corruption freely operates within a mind whose conscience is inactive to moral transformation.

The foregoing conversation suggests that corruption occurs within an unguided moral heart. To this end, a term "auto-corruption" is coined referring to another form of corruption, which describes an individualized form of corruption. While other forms of corruption involve collective decisions of more than one person or organisation, "auto corruption" is an activity with a one-way flow of benefits to the individual involved.[135] It is self-induced, thus, conforms with the notion of human depravity that authenticates and validates unreported revenue, misappropriation of property, salary and pension and re-looting. As to the notion of re-looting, chances are there when "public convicted resources are not returned to the appropriate channel, but diverted by the individual involved. "[136] That is such a cunning way of alluding smartness when corrupt practices are improperly investigated and not prosecuted, which, in turn result in perverting justice, or what has been described as "corruption mocking justice."[137]

2.4.4 Holistic Poverty

It is paradoxical to mention poverty as a causative agent of corruption instead of the contrary. Here, it is important to note that poverty, just as corruption, is a multifaceted and complex concept whose understanding and application varies. This study considers poverty one of the factors responsible for

---

133. Pink, "The Doctrine of Human."
134. Igboin, "Corruption In Nigeria."
135. Page, *A New Taxonomy*, 19.
136. Page, 19.
137. Sebahene, "Corruption Mocking at Justice."

spreading corruption in Nigeria, which makes the connection between the two concepts possible.

On a general level, poverty refers to a situation in which individuals or society live and cannot provide for their basic needs. Others see poverty in terms of "deprivation of basic goods, or a low income that limits people's access to basic goods."[138] In some cases, poverty is described in terms of a nation's GDP from which a study affirms does not fully capture the phenomenon.[139] Instead, Chetwynd and Spector cited the World Bank's report that was given in 2001 about the broadness of the concept which reveals that poverty includes "low income, low levels of education and health. It involves vulnerability (to health, natural disaster, crime and violence, and education curtailment); voicelessness, and powerlessness (feeling discrimination, lacking income-earning possibilities, mistreatment by state institutions, and lacking status under the law)."[140]

Such a view of poverty makes it holistic, encompassing all other dimesions beyond simply financial. This broad perspective implies that poverty is a relative term whose impact differs from one context to another. To be in state of poverty is to have inadequate possessions for enabling a good quality of life, a lack of intellectual insight to discern what is harmful, and the inability to create modalities for livelihood. Poverty as holistic involves the a person or society having insufficient knowledge of how to conduct themselves, which could result in competition over fewer resources for survival. That is why another study explains that poor countries are more corrupt than rich societies because they cannot, among other reasons, devote sufficient resources to set up and enforce an effective legal framework.[141] Affirming the above claim, another study attests that causes for poverty in lower-income countries are due to factors such as poor government infrastructure and inadequate legal system.[142] Here, Igboin concludes that failure of structures in society is a reflection of human failure in institutions and processes, which enables

---

138. Banda, "Poverty," 113
139. Chetwynd, Chetwynd and Spector, *Corruption and Poverty.*
140. Chetwynd et. al., 19.
141. Mauro, "Corruption: Causes, Consequences."
142. Ene and Dunnamah, "Corruption Control"; Onongha, "Corruption, Culture, and Conversion."

corruption to boil down to problems of individual character and personality.[143] Such poor individuals are more likely to abandon their moral principles to imbibe on immoral acts.

Similarly, countries experiencing chronic poverty are seen as "natural breeding grounds for systemic corruption due to social and income inequalities, and perverse economic incentives."[144] Such scenarios occur because of what Igboin calls a "non-transformative moral life that seeks to preserve the sanctity of human life from all forms of corruption."[145] In addition, a study[146] attests that certain cultures have a greater proclivity for corruption than others. Putting the two thoughts together, non-transformative moral life and cultural differences, and bringing the view of holistic poverty mentioned above, we arrive at the argument that poverty (be it of the mind, moral, or physical), and cultural influence, make significant contributions to the spread of corruption.

In the case of Nigeria, the nature of holistic poverty cannot be overemphasized. It is seen among the "haves" and "have-nots," among the intellectuals and the non-intellectuals. The gravity of poverty in each of these groups varies significantly. In a study conducted in Abuja, Nigeria, it was gathered that poverty is the result of economic, political and social processes that interact with each other, and frequently reinforce each other in ways that exacerbate the deprivation in which people live.[147] The controlling agents of either political or economic strategies are, in the case of Nigeria, made of intellectuals and politically elected and appointed officials. Holistic poverty from the above conversation involves an abuse of conscience from which comes the justification of evil for good; powerlessness to resist any form of oppression, particularly where freedom of expression is not economical; and the inability to make decisions without interference.

Following the above discussion, we could outline some relationship between corruption and poverty further. First, that corruption is not a major cause of poverty. Second, some correlation exists between the two concepts

---

143. Igboin, "Corruption In Nigeria."
144. Chetwynd, Chetwynd, and Spector, *Corruption and Poverty*, 10.
145. Igboin, "Corruption In Nigeria," 58.
146. Onongha, "Corruption, Culture, and Conversion."
147. Action Aid Nigeria, *Corruption and Poverty*.

but that this relationship is an indirect one. The first view holds that corruption itself does not produce poverty, rather it has a direct consequence on the economic and governance factors which, in turn, promote poverty. For instance, corruption is responsible for insufficient jobs and poor infrastructure while creating the impression that there is competition in society.[148] In that sense, the impression that public office is the answer to poverty intensifies the quest to occupy one. With such intentions, an individual from a poor living condition becomes susceptible to corruption for the sake of getting out of poverty by amassing public resources at the expense of others. Such is the description of the poverty of the mind.

The poverty of the mind is the inability to think beyond oneself. Ironically, such a mind has no recognition that thinking for the good of others ignites the quest for their well-being as well. From the wealth of the mind (intellectual articulation) springs understanding, listening and a willingness to empower others. In instances where poverty of the mind takes precedence, however, chances ensue that would intensify physical poverty. When this happens, the end result is the circulation of poverty in that everyone desperately seeks to attain a position of dominance, but out of the wrong intentions, for self-aggrandizement. With such desperation, engaging in all forms of corruption becomes the norm, provided that the ends justify the means. Such situations result in poor remuneration and compensation of the labour force, which later breeds poor and incompetent workforce who, in turn, breed their kind. From poverty-stricken backgrounds, engaging in illegal acquisition of compensation marks the beginning and continuity of corruption in the system. In that case, young people, especially in Nigeria, end up taking bribes to commit crimes and work as thugs for politicians just to meet their poverty demands among other things.[149] Others end up indulging in sex trafficking for a living due to poor handling of the rich human and material resources that the country is blessed with.[150]

Concerns contributing to this kind of poverty vary from circumstantial to those imposed. In the case of the latter, poor remuneration of wages, salaries and pensions to those eligible makes them poor. As part of their responsibility

---

148. Action Aid Nigeria.
149. Mike, *Corruption in Nigeria*, 2018.
150. Jev, "Politics, Conflicts, and Nigeria's Unending Crisis."

to cater for the needs of their households, countless people choose to indulge in illicit means of getting wealth. Given this state of affairs, corruption is more likely to take place when civil servants are paid very low wages, which pushes them to resort to taking bribes in order to feed their families.[151] In another sense, diversion and siphoning from poverty alleviation programmes and agencies diminishes their impact on poverty and inequality, thus creating avenues where more poverty breeds more corruption.[152]

2.4.5 Greed

The human society is characterized by numerous needs that vary because of the cohabitation between the rich and poor. A few among human society acquire more than is needed for their survival with little or no concern for the others. In this section, we argue that "desiring more than is needed," which in this study refers to greed, contributes to the spread of corruption in Nigeria.

Greed as a concept has been described from different fields of knowledge. From the Western theological thought, St. Augustine of Hippo considered greed as injustice. He wrote, "greed is not a defect in the gold that is desired but in the man who loves it perversely by falling from justice which he ought to esteem as incomparably superior to gold."[153] Speaking from the theological point of view, greed is described as "an inordinate desire that excludes other values. As an attribute, greed is one of the seven deadly sins that deforms the soul."[154] In general humanities, greed is "a direct outcome of dissatisfaction, emptiness, and discontentment."[155] Hence, we can conclude here that a greedy individual has the capacity to act in ways that guarantee them to acquire more resources, admiration and power, often at the cost of the happiness of others. The contrary perception of greed is from economics that sees it as having a positive relevance. A study citing John Locke reiterates how Locke renamed greed as "self-interest whose advantages would expand trade and bring prosperity for everyone."[156] Looking critically at D'Souza's quote, the desire of a greedy individual would perhaps be to enjoy and make

---

151. Mauro, "Corruption: Causes, Consequences."
152. Chetwynd, Chetwynd, and Spector, *Corruption and Poverty*.
153. Augustine, *The City of God*, 259.
154. Griswold, "Formal Capacities and Relational," 88.
155. D'Souza, "Greed: Crises, Causes," 1.
156. Nikelly, "The Pathogenesis of Greed," 67.

merry over the acquired resources. Affirming this, another study shows that both Aristotle and Plato believed that "greed does not bring satisfaction, but encourages destructive ambition and corruption, and is a potential catalyst for a civic breakdown."[157] From these voices, we can argue that greed influences corruption anywhere, and Nigeria is not exempted.

The Nigerian public space has become the epicentre that houses greedy individuals. It is pertinent to know that ascending to a public office in Nigeria is considered a gateway to partake in the sharing of the "national cake."[158] Ensuring continuity in the public office, even at retirement, someone is employed to remain in the bureaucracy to help continue their lucrative way of distributing proceeds from the public service.[159] Igboin describes such greedy individuals as a few "crooks" in a society whose corruption is occasional through giving and receiving bribes.[160] Despite its description as an illusion that lacks meaning, greed, with an endless array of redundant material possessions that never brings complete satisfaction, still has subscribers.[161] Although such actions cause untold hardship, they do not matter to the greedy since their desire for public offices keeps growing.

In addition, greed is a concept that has been among several causative agents of human problems resulting in suffering, extreme poverty, social instability, economic crisis, wars and massacres.[162] As another study puts it, greed is the single underlying motivator to engaging in acts of corruption.[163] It distorts the free flow of both human and material resources which could benefit and alleviate the difficulty. This is further described as the "passion for selfish gratification in the amassing of wealth and the worship of money, through fraudulent and deceptive tactics in society."[164] As such, greed has deprived millions of citizens of their livelihood, their identity and their self-respect that causes them enormous monetary loss as well as psychic trauma. It

---

157. Balot, *Greed and Injustice*, 66.

158. "National cake" in Nigeria refers to the country's wealth that those benefiting feel it belongs to only those who have the opportunity of being in places of authority.

159. Chayes, *Thieves of State*.

160. Igboin, "Corruption In Nigeria," 53.

161. Nikelly, "The Pathogenesis of Greed," 65.

162. D'Souza, "Greed: Crises, Causes"; Akindola and Ehinomen, "Military Incursion."

163. Igboin, "Corruption In Nigeria," 53.

164. Nikelly, "The Pathogenesis of Greed."

can be deduced, therefore, from the assertions above that they all attest to the fact that human greed posits a huge impediment to a flourishing society. It has and still causes wounds to our institutions rather than seeking for the healing that would ensure equality, fairness and justice for everyone. Following that conversation on greed from different perspectives mentioned, we can conclude by describing greed as a causative agent of corruption.

In summary, this section has surveyed a few possible causes of corruption in Nigeria. It highlighted these through four divisions, namely failure of governance, failure from the grassroots, lost sense of human wellbeing, holistic poverty and greed. These factors, among others, have been shown to be the major causes of corruption debilitating the Nigerian state from growing and developing. As the status quo holds, there have been effects on different dimensions that require attention to enable a return to ways of supporting human and structural development. The next section, therefore, ushers us into describing the effects of corruption in Nigeria.

2.5 Some Effects of Corruption in Nigeria

The aim of this section is to outline some effects of corruption in Nigeria. Doing that would enable us to see the magnitude of the harm corruption has caused and is causing in terms of the denial of human dignity and national development.

2.5.1 Effects of Corruption on the Nigerian Economy

Here, we shall focus on the negative impact of corruption in Nigeria's economy. Described as the study of the law or rules of a household or country, a study insists on the significance of having a knowledge of economics.[165] The study's author avows that having a knowledge of economics helps us to distinguish between income and capital inequality, and how to measure inequality in society. This is important to this study because poor economic policies limit the extent of service delivery.

As part of the effort to fight corruption and strengthen the economy, Nigeria embarked on an "aggressive pursuit of economic reform through banking sector reform, anti-corruption campaigns, privatization and

---

165. Naudé, "Economics."

deregulation, institutional reforms, improvement of the infrastructure, and the establishment of clear and transparent fiscal standards since the year 1999."[166] Despite these government efforts aimed at stabilizing the economic growth and development, a study argues that corruption manifests in forms of "abuse of position and privileges, low level of transparency and accountability, inflation of contracts, bribery/kickbacks, misappropriation, and over-invoicing false declaration, a form of fraud known as 419."[167] Similarly, ghost workers syndrome, offering wrong advice for personal advantage, violation of ethics governing businesses, aiding and abetting examination practices, condoning indiscipline, and other unwholesome conduct are all associated with economic corruption.[168] Noting these features of economic corruption, another study observes that "unless the policymakers in Nigeria harmonise and get them under control, the trend would hamper the economy from functioning."[169]

Corruption affects Nigeria's economic growth in various ways. Firstly, corruption affects the economy by increasing inequality and the poverty rate in society. While poverty is attributed to economic reforms, the decisions that are made determine the level of inequality. In Nigeria, corruption results in "inappropriate public planning and implementation from which poverty, poor infrastructure and poor services to the citizens emanate."[170] Similarly, further study opines that "corruption cripples the state's ability to deliver for its citizen's enjoyment of even the minimum social and economic rights including health and education."[171] Still, another study finds that corruption breeds poor economic growth and increases poverty rate.[172] The three voices have an agreement that the effects of corruption on the economy result in a high risk of poverty and inequality. Within such a context, economic growth cannot happen because of poor infrastructure that allows the easy transport

---

166. Ola, Mohammed and Audi, "Effects of Corruption," 209; Odi, "Impact of Corruption," 42; Ajie and Gbenga, "Corruption and Economic Growth."
167. Ogbonnaya, "Effects of Corruption," 122.
168. Ighaekeme, Abbah and Gaidem, "The Effect of Corruption."
169. Ogbonnaya, "Effects of Corruption," 127.
170. Odi "Impact of Corruption," 45; Adenike, "An Econometric Analysis."
171. Ola, Mohammed and Audi, "Effects of Corruption," 212.
172. Udo, Samuel and Prince, "The Effects of Corruption."

of goods and people.[173] Indeed, when poverty sinks into a people, variation in class, race, gender, inequality and devaluation of human lives becomes inevitable. As a result, decisions that are taken by the policymakers significantly contribute to this way of life. For instance, little[174] to no job creation with poor remuneration has a strong impact on people and how they live their lives. Since corruption distorts the viability of the economy and promotes poor economic policies, poverty and inequality remain issues to ponder.

Second, corruption affects Nigeria's economy by way of reducing foreign and domestic investments. The World Trade Organization (WTO) is the body that deals with the global rules of trade between nations. One of its functions is to ensure a smooth and free flow of global trade. Ola et al assert that the WTO increases impediments on trade if a country maintains an "out-of-control" level of corruption or extortion, on the one hand. On the other hand, what that implies is that should a nation deal with these problems, "the WTO will decrease the impediment and provide that nation with an incentive to reduce skyrocketing corruption levels."[175] Like other developing nations, Nigeria is still grappling[176] with the dilemma of corruption that has largely retarded social development, undermined economic growth and discouraged foreign investments. It is worrying to note that Nigeria's economic turmoil is not only at the global scene but also locally in that within the country, are concerns with investments. Omenka posits that "corruption hinders the development of market structures and distorts competition, thereby deterring investment."[177] One huge impact of corruption is that it gives Nigeria a bad image and discourages genuine foreign investors from coming in to run businesses in the country.[178] From the WTO's functional guidelines, Nigeria has been shown to fall behind from receiving the incentives to help her fight corruption that is already a killer disease to the country's development. A few things stand out here worth pondering; the first is that corruption denies an opportunity to foreign investors and businesses which would boost the

---

173. Naudé, "Economics."
174. Ola, Mohammed and Audi, "Effects of Corruption," 209.
175. Ola Mohammed and Audi, 213.
176. Ajie and Gbenga, "Corruption and Economic Growth"; Adenike, "An Econometric Analysis."
177. Omenka, "The Effect of Corruption," 42.
178. Ajie and Gbenga, "Corruption and Economic Growth."

economy through job creation. Second, the self-image of Nigerians and the country is tainted with corruption, particularly at the international level. Third, the inequality and poverty gaps widen uncontrollably, thereby exposing the populace to denial of social and economic rights. These rights include food, health, shelter, education and security, which we refer to as basic human needs in this study. They are those needs whose absence has been equated to the denial of human dignity.[179]

The third effect of corruption on Nigeria's economy is that it distorts and exploits public investment and reduces public revenues. As such, an ailing economy struggles because its tax income is generally far below what is required to carry out basic functions.[180] In Nigeria where there is a poor state of power, health, education and communication, the situation results in "untold hardship for small and informal business owners."[181] Although these informal and small business enterprises generate revenue for the government and are great contributors to its GDP, the consequences of poor service delivery intensify their struggle for survival. In turn, it reduces public revenues that the government would have used for infrastructural development. Here, another study confirms that "the poor state of these basic needs (power, transportation and communication) is a major handicap for doing business in Nigeria."[182] The more these infrastructures are in a debilitated state, the more the economy dwindles, and the more poverty levels increase.

Beyond losing revenue, poor service delivery equally distorts and exploits public investment. As indicated in a study, the "effects of poor service delivery cause debilitating injuries on service efficiency and effectiveness in relation to workers' morale and productivity, the pervasion and frustration of development goals and objectives, as well as threatening the corporate existence of the Nigerian state."[183] With the poor implementation and service delivery, the condition results in poor economic performance, decaying infrastructure, and a constant rise in the cost of living and other essentials.[184] Here, we have two important points to note, namely that corruption distorts and exploits

---

179. Koopman, "Human Dignity in Africa."
180. Ola, Mohammed and Audi, "Effects of Corruption."
181. Odi, "Impact of Corruption," 45.
182. Ola, Mohammed and Audi, "Effects of Corruption," 209.
183. Odo, "The Impact and Consequences," 179.
184. Mercy, "The Effects of Corruption."

public investment and it reduces public revenues. To the first point, poor service delivery, staff welfare and poor work ethic result in the distortion and exploitation of public investments due to poor performance on public investments. On the second point, poor service delivery results in poor or no economic growth, thereby distorting the flow of revenue which, in turn, affects the government, who should provide the citizens with the basic human needs for better livelihood.

2.5.2 Effects of Corruption on the People

Corruption is not a living being that speaks but is made known by its effects. The nature of these effects speaks loud of their gravity, especially on human beings. For instance, a study describes corruption as a plague,[185] a disease and a tool of evil wielded by the wealthy individuals of developing nations who, in turn, make themselves more powerful. Similar studies warn of how corruption has become a clog in the wheel of progress in Nigeria because of poor control of its continuous spread.[186] Bringing these thoughts together, we see that the impact of corruption is felt by human beings that are deprived of privileges and opportunities by those in places of control and power. This happens when there is poor implementation of policies that should enhance respect for the dignity of others. Instead, policies are focused on self-gratification, which triggers the undermining of human dignity with different ramifications through lack of provision of basic human needs.

One of the basic human needs is health, which in this study refers to wholeness. Being a responsibility of the state, an adequate, affordable and accessible healthcare system is expected to be a right of humans. In another study conducted, adequate healthcare delivery is measured by efficiency in a transparent combination of financial and human resources, supply and timely delivery of services to the vulnerable populace.[187] The transparency required here involves the placement of appropriate medical personnel, the prompt supply of medical facilities, and routine supervision to ensure medical service delivery. This includes the services of the government or the organization responsible for the supply and placement of the medical specialists and

---

185. Ola, Mohammed and Audi, "Effects of Corruption," 4.
186. Esidene, "Effects of Corruption," 3; Ijewereme, "Anatomy of Corruption."
187. Tormusa, and Idom, "The Impediments of Corruption."

medical equipment. Whatever the beauty of this sequence might be, however, its reality is elusive in the Nigerian health sector. With corruption and self-interest as the priority of the policymakers, it is eroding the implementation of policies on effective healthcare delivery.[188]

As a region with health challenges, health care should have been prioritized above sentiments. Just like corruption, however, Nigeria is tagged with some of the worst health issues that result in wasting of lives on a routine basis.[189] From malaria to mother-child mortality, and several other forms of illness, Nigeria is ranking low. Even when international organizations, such as UNICEF and WHO, provide immunization equipment and vaccines, they become avenues for personal enrichment. The continuous exposure of lives to sicknesses that could have been prevented does not matter to the policymakers since their interests are self-satisfaction. While countless lives, with the majority being the poor, die owing to the poor health facilities, the rich minority travel with public resources to the Western world to access advanced medical attention for themselves and their families. Attesting to that sad reality is that corruption kills.[190] Its killing gravity results in undermining humanity's sense of dignity through poor health systems that lead to ineffective and inconsiderate provision of the basic health care that is available, effective and affordable by all and for all members of society.

2.5.3 Effects of Corruption on Society

Even though corruption through all its dimensions affects the human persons, yet some reflections on its effects on society is crucial. When the damages caused by corruption are only concentrated on human beings (as important that is) without considering the effects on the society which they live in, a continuous threat to their wellbeing lingers. A similar scenario relates to discussions on a holistic perception of salvation which does not concentrate on human lives and neglect the environment they live in.[191]

By society, we refer to infrastructures contributing to making it habitable, including societal behavioural values and life patterns. As it were, the

---

188. Tormusa and Idom, "The Impediments of Corruption."
189. Tormusa and Idom, "The Impediments of Corruption."
190. Hanf, et al., "Corruption Kills."
191. Moltmann, *God in Creation*.

flourishing of a society is measured by the provision, implementation and an even distribution of resources that focuses on enhancing human well-being. Such a society ensures no existence of poor service delivery since it reduces the quality of goods and services.[192] In a society where human beings and other creatures cohabitate, poor services result in counterfeit infrastructure.

In some instances, as argued, it is marginalization which results in unequal distribution and implementation of resources.[193] As such, marginalization brings about inequality, injustice, poverty, unemployment and often, in the case of Nigeria, results in religious or ethnical clashes. In the case of unemployment, a contributing factor to poverty, this remains rampant because of the insincerity and insensitivity of the authorities who are saddled with power.[194] Massive and uncontrolled unemployment has, in turn, resulted in social crimes as a means of survival. For instance, prostitution, child labour, children hawking the streets, and other social crimes have become paramount because there are no suitable conditions for survival in a country blessed with rich resources.

The sum of societal effects of corruption on the inhabitants are numerous but a few are mentioned here. The prevalence of injustice, either in the treatment of human beings or in the distribution of resources that would enhance their well-being is the sure way that corruption affects a society. In part, the availability of infrastructure such as affordable hospitals, food, shelter and education to the populace influences a reorientation of how life is viewed by those whose sense of livelihood is lost. In a reversible situation where these amenities are in short supply, young people see no reason to pursue further education and instead resort to crime. An example is the Boko Haram perpetrators, who see no value in Western education hence, decide not only to reject it but see it as profane.[195]

2.5.4 Effects of Corruption as a Catalyst for Terrorism

Corruption and its consequences are a global phenomenon that hinders and threatens human and infrastructural development. In the Majority World,

---

192. Moyosore, "Corruption in Nigeria"; Odo, "The Impact and Consequences."
193. Shuaibu, Salleh and Shehu, "The Impact of Boko Haram."
194. Obamwonyi and Aibieyi, "Boko Haram Menace."
195. Akinbi, "Examining the Boko Haram."

the challenges corruption poses to humanity and societies are detrimental to their well-being. Some of these include poverty, mortality, an alarming unemployment rate and insecurity to mention but a few. This section, however, considers corruption as a catalyst harbouring the spread of terrorism, particularly in Nigeria as it is elsewhere. In doing so, we shall be engaging some literature as follows.[196] This selection of literature is based on these authors' ideas relating the intersection between corruption and terrorism in Nigeria, and beyond.

Terrorism has taken Nigeria to a saturated point that news concerning conflict is overwhelming, which includes the loss of lives, destruction of properties and displacement. While terrorism in other places is fuelled by religious fundamentalism, in Nigeria it has corruption as one of its promoters.[197] However, while acknowledging corruption as the cause of terrorism, a study added that mismanagement of resources through corrupt practices results in poverty which, in turn, enhances terrorism.[198] Such a dilemma of unfair distribution and management of resources has resulted in competition for survival in Nigeria with the fortunate always favoured. This competition does not only lead to the destruction of physical structures but is also responsible for causing death and injury to countless others.

According to another study, "corruption of spirituality, morality and ethics is responsible for the continuing increase in terrorist activities."[199] As such, moral bankruptcy is the bedrock that breeds corruption since thoughts for bribery, coercion, sexual harassment for favour seeking and promotions, and the loss of human conscience can be credited to the depravity of the human mind. While many studies have failed to acknowledge this form of corruption as the propeller of terrorism, Agang has a contrary view. He insists that both the destruction,[200] distortion and disruption of human life and their environment, championed by terrorism, emanate from lack of respect for the sanctity

---

196. Agang, "Globalization and Terrorism"; Feldman, "The Root Causes"; Isyaku, "Terrorism: A New Challenge"; Bamidele, "Combating Terrorism"; Akinbi, "Examining the Boko Haram"; Okon, "The Root Causes"; Bappah, "Nigeria's Military Failure"; Ademowo, "Boko Haram Insurgency"; Akindola and Ehinomen, "Military Incursion."
197. Ikezue and Ezeah, "Boko Haram Insurgency."
198. Akindla and Ehinomen, "Military Incursion."
199. Agang, "Globalization and Terrorism," 2.
200. Agang, "Globalization and Terrorism," 3.

of human life. On a similar note, another study affirming Agang's position, suggests that only a transformative-*morazoicism*,[201] a concept that hinges on the moral willpower of the individual and seeks to promote greater positive change that begins at the individual level and translates to various institutions in society, is more appropriate to combat corruption on moral grounds.

Terrorism does not only arise from corruption but also helps the corrupt to get away with their secretive and calculated plans of evil against the masses. That corruption grows sparingly is not the only concern, but the alarming rate of impunity index which leaves corruption unchecked. This is another concern that occurs within a weak leadership structure where vices such as corruption receive mild adjudication.[202] Cases are caught daily, perpetrators are known, but weak actions are taken to interrogate them, which increases the rate of suspicion and anger in those on the margins. That is the very reason why corruption is described as "terrorism," "a killer disease," "serious destructive violence perpetrated against the human race by all human systems as its stakeholders."[203] The aforementioned issues relate to why "we are currently living in an Africa that we do not want because many evidences show that all is not well."[204] This invites us into considering the two terrorist groups hampering the Nigerian peaceful co-existence.

2.5.4.1 *The Boko Haram Insurgency*

The activities of Boko Haram insurgents devastatingly disrupt the peaceful co-existence in Nigeria.[205] Since their full emergence in the year 2009, they have caused unrecovered havoc ranging from loss of human lives and destruction of countless properties. Research has unanimously agreed on

---

201. Igboin, "Corruption In Nigeria."
202. Moyosore, "Corruption in Nigeria."
203. Agang, "Globalization and Terrorism," 4.
204. Agang, "The Need for Public," 3.

205. Boko Haram meaning Westernisation is forbidden, had a founder named Mohammed Yusuf, who was born in Girgir village, Yobe state, Nigeria. The name "Boko Haram" is itself derived from the combination of two words "Boko" (which means 'book' or "book-learning") and "haram" (which means those things which are ungodly or abominable in the sight of Allah). Ademowo, "Boko Haram Insurgency," 225. Further details on the origin and objectives of the Boko Haram sect, Shuaibu, Salleh & Shehu "The Impact of Boko Haram." For further reasons why the sect continues to succeed in their activities, see Obamwonyi & Aibieyi, "Boko Haram Menace."

some factors responsible for this terrorist insurgency.[206] These studies attest to poverty, illiteracy, religious extremism and political orientation, as among the root causes of terrorism across Nigeria. Yet, others indicate that there are conflicting[207] views regarding what propels the activities of the Boko Haram sect in that some call them religious fanatics, ethnic, economic, or a group that sought to make their voices heard. These views have become a hydra-headed monster threatening to cage our sense of unity and purpose as a nation-state. Nevertheless, let us outline the link between terrorism and corruption.[208]

The corrupt nature of the Nigerian educational system has left countless citizens at a disadvantage. While Nigeria still struggles to modernise her educational systems to ensure sustainability to those aspiring for a brighter future, the Boko Haran sect rather propagates the rejection of Western education. As attested in other research, illiteracy significantly contributes to the spread of Boko Haram.[209] As the number of illiterate youth increases, especially in parts of North-Eastern Nigeria where the sect has its origin, many have become willing tools of sabotage in the hands of Boko Haram. Since they teach outright rejection of Western education and consider it forbidden, they accept and become clean slates for any kind of brainwashing. They see nothing attractive in modern education which allows them to accept anything presented to them and consider it a norm.

Accordingly, their rejection of Western education arises from the "suspicion that education does bring about life transformation."[210] From the large number unemployed, looming poverty rate, and the loss of future hope perpetrated by the supposedly educated persons, the Boko Haram sect imagine such an education has no transformative power to a better society. This is so because the educated ones have become the most corrupt individuals in society, making life difficult while squandering the future of the next generation. Additionally, the poor state of the educational institutions makes pursuing or

---

206. Obamwonyi and Aibeiyi, "Boko Haram Menace"; Ikezua and Ezeah, "Boko Haram Insurgency"; Ademowo, Ademowo, "Boko Haram Insurgency"; Bamidele, "Combating Terrorism."

207. Ademowo, "Boko Haram Insurgency."

208. Ademowo, "Boko Haram Insurgency."

209. Akinbi, "Examining the Boko Haram"; Ademowo, "Boko Haram Insurgency"; Shuaibu, Salleh, and Shehu, "The Impact of Boko Haram."

210. Akinbi, "Examining the Boko Haram," 34.

supporting modern education less interesting. This perhaps could be one of the reasons the Boko Haram continuously see Western education as forbidden, something not worth pursuing. The power that comes with knowledge, in this case, is understood differently. Education as a basic human need that should teach about the transformation of humans and their society is lacking with resources meant for such development squandered by corruption. The Boko Haram sect, therefore, considers indulging in terrorist activities destroying human lives and property.

Another factor responsible for propelling Boko Haram terrorist activities in Nigeria is "poverty."[211] It is another menace roaming the country at an alarming rate which, in turn, results in further vices. The desperation in having a better life now and in the future seems illusory and has turned to a situation producing idle vibrant minds. Affirming the above claim, other studies attest to poverty as one of the reasons for the continued spread of terrorism perpetrated by the Boko Haram in Nigeria.[212] While blaming the rampant poverty on the uneven distribution of national wealth,[213] others imagine the daunting effects of misappropriation.[214] While the desperation for making a living proves abortive in the minds of these youngsters, Boko Haram takes advantage of them. Knowing the difficulty in extreme poverty, the Boko Haram "recruit these poverty-stricken youths under the disguise of exposing them to Islamic teachings."[215] Some join the terrorist sect in a wrong search for livelihood since poverty has increasingly become part of their lives. Surprisingly, being in full knowledge of such conditions, the policymakers who are saddled with the responsibility to enhance the wellbeing of these people choose to look away to other things, particularly those that are of benefit to themselves.

---

211. Akinbi, "Examining the Boko Haram," 36.

212. Adesoji, "The Boko Haram Uprising"; Shuaibu, Salleh and Shehu, "The Impact of Boko Haram"; Ikezue and Ezeah, "Boko Haram Insurgency"; Akinbi, "Examining the Boko Haram."

213. Isyaku, "Terrorism," 16.

214. Okon, "The Root Causes," 7.

215. Ademowo, "Boko Haram Insurgency," 223.

2.5.4.2 The Fulani Herdsmen[216]

As Nigeria struggles in her fight against the Boko Haram terrorists, a newly advanced sect called the Fulani Herdsmen has surfaced. With their activities similar to those of Boko Haram, the Fulani Herdsmen threaten and expose the sanctity of human life to ridicule. Fulani is a group of people found in most parts of West Africa who predominantly are nomadic and known for rearing cattle, which they do as their occupation and part of their culture.[217] Despite the contribution of these people's groups in advancing the economy of Nigeria, it is suggested that they are ill-informed about modern pastoral farming.[218] Being nomads, they move across Nigeria throughout the year in search of pasture for their animals due to variation in weather, in search of greener pasture for feeding their livestock. This results in them having to live together with stationary farmers, who have existed in mutuality for some time.

The Fulani herders have been considered great contributors to the Nigerian economy. While they do this through pastoral farming by rearing livestock, they also contribute immensely to the economy through the products of their system of farming. But since their system of farming requires frequent movement, it has become one of the reasons for their "settlements amidst stationary farmers."[219]

Their dwelling amid stationary farmers, has recently taken a new turn. Previously, the two dwelled together in a symbiotic relationship where the Fulani supply the farmers with manure to boost their farmlands and receive food in return. Such a mutual relationship has ceased to exist owing to the current clashes between the two groups with devastating effects on human persons. In some studies conducted, few reasons are considered for the

---

216. Ogbeide, "Fulani Herdsmen," 52; Ajibefun, "Social and Economic Effects," 133, take the narrative migration of the Fulani groups from the Middle East and the North Africa regions. He asserts their being involved in other forms of businesses but stresses on the continued nomadic lifestyle, which is characterized by rearing of cattle. Additionally, the migration from the zones has had these groups to spread to different parts of Africa, particularly the West African zones. Notably among these places is Nigeria, where the Fulani, though being among the minority tribes, have recently gained influence and have been made known through violent attacks on Nigerian communities. Although the cattle they rear are sources of meat consumed by a significant Nigerian population, their "recent attacks have called for some concerns" Ajibefun, 134.

217. Ogbeide, "Fulani Herdsmen"; Ajibefun, "Social and Economic Effects."
218. Ogbeide, "Fulani Herdsmen."
219. Ajibefun, "Social and Economic Effects," 134.

clashes: on the one hand, the clashes fanned by the encroachment of the farmlands by the Fulani persons, and the destruction of the farmer's crops by the Fulani herders.[220] On the other hand, the clashes are attributed to underdevelopment of Nigeria's livestock industry.[221] This intensifies the movement from place to place, which leads to competition for space between the farmers and the herders. The resultant inadequate provision and unavailability of pasture, water, and other needs of the cattle, therefore, prompts rivalry and the unpleasant relationship between the two groups.[222] After a careful observation of the senseless killings over three decades, a study sees the recent reasons beyond the ones highlighted above. It imagines it as a planned attempt where "millions of people are displaced, dislocated or have lost their ancestral place of habitation."[223] Looking at these cases, few things come to mind. First, there is a failure in the demarcation of land use and punishment of the offenders. Second, both the lack of livestock industry and failure in curtailing desert encroachment are attributed to an indecisive failure in leadership. Third, since "land is at the heart of living, belonging, citizenship and basis for indigenisation,"[224] those whose land is being forcefully taken without the intervention of the authorities sense some sort of complacency. The highlighted factors can all be attributed to corruption, which results in massive destruction of human lives and seizing of property by the Fulani Herders, "leaving countless Nigerians who once had large farms now in camps with poor sanitation with dehumanising conditions."[225]

In particular, the result of the clashes between the Fulani herders and farmers has caused effects in some ways which could be classified in two, namely social and economic effects. The classification of the social effects includes "loss of human life, sexual harassment, reduction in the quality of the social relationship and reduction in social support,"[226] while the second set are described as economic effects, which include a "reduction in output and income of farmers and the herders, loss of storage, displacement of farmers,

---

220. Ajibefun, 134.
221. Ogbeide, "Fulani Herdsmen," 51.
222. Ogbeide, 51–52.
223. Akper, "Is God in Nigeria," 62.
224. Akper, 63.
225. Akper, 63.
226. Ajibefun, "Social and Economic Effects," 134.

scarcity of agricultural products and loss of properties."[227] Both of these effects have direct consequences on the nation in some ways. For the social effects, the continuous threats to human lives suggest exposure to ridicule, which leaves them helpless in search of a sense of belonging and asking "why these things continue to happen to us?", "who is going to help us get out of them?" and "for how long would this continue?" Here, Akper highlights the need for a new morality he calls "the ethos of hospitality."[228] In a sense, the concept of hospitality, in this context of farmers/herdsmen clashes, goes beyond just accommodating the other but includes listening to and empathizing with them in those dark moments.

Worryingly, the continuous rampaging of terrorist activities of the above sects in Nigeria have some reasons where three are outlined in conjunction with security ineptitude in curtailing terrorist activities in Nigeria. First, the erosion of military professionalism and civil administration that occurred because of the subjective control of the military by the civilians after the nation's return to democracy. Second, poor handling of the war against the Boko Haram insurgency is characterized as a show of incompetence by the military. This also includes poor dissemination of information by the military either about their successes or the philosophy of their attacks. Third, "indecisive leadership as another reason for military failure to curb insurgency in Nigeria."[229] In addition to inadequate leadership, lack of neutrality in Nigerian leadership has brought about the colluding of some officers with the terrorist group, which makes defeating them a daunting task.[230] The porosity in leadership creates an avenue for ghost soldiers, dead personnel still considered alive, or those not in active service are not detected.[231] Such are leaders who have turned a blind eye to the cries and affliction of the poor citizens, living them at the mercies of their killers.[232]

This section argued by attributing the sustainability of terrorism in Nigeria to corruption. Several factors were considered including indecisive leadership, poor welfare of the security agency, the erosion of military professionalism

---

227. Ogbeide, "Fulani Herdsmen," 53.
228. Akper, "An Ethos of Hospitality," 288.
229. Bappah, "Nigeria's Military Failure," 151–52.
230. Obamwonyi and Aibeiyi, "Boko Haram Menace."
231. Feldman, "The Root Causes."
232. Kure, "Leadership, Corruption"

and civil administration, and poor strategies in handling war situations. In all, these factors continue to strive because of one central reason, namely corruption. Corruption is responsible for the poor and inadequate leadership, irregular recruitment of officers and exposure through lack of neutrality that gives ground for colluding. Until these issues are decisively addressed, the terrorists would continue to move freely, destroying and exposing human lives to ridicule as is seen happening currently in many regions of Northern-central Nigeria.

2.6 Some Ways of Curbing Corruption in Nigeria

Previously, we considered the causes and effects of corruption in Nigeria where we were able to see the havoc corruption causes on human beings, society and the Nigerian economy. While corruption continues to hamper and destroy Nigeria's socio-economic structure and growth, there are efforts to curtail further spreading of the menace. In these sections that follow, we shall, therefore, outline a few anti-corruption agencies in Nigeria that are categorized into three, namely the government instituted agencies, the civil society organizations and the religious institutions.

2.6.1 The Government Instituted Agencies of Anti-corruption: The EFCC[233] and ICPC[234]

The problem of corruption in Nigeria is an old story that has transpired through many decades of its existence as a nation during the military and civilian regimes. Since the menace inflicts national growth, different leaders in the past initiated various models[235] for curtailing corruption but with not much success. Despite these efforts of the past Nigerian leaders in waging war to ensure it reduces or stops the spread of corruption, it continues to infiltrate

---

233. This stands for "Economic and Financial Crimes Commission"

234. This stands for "Independent Corrupt Practices and other related offences Commission."

235. Some of these models aimed at tackling the problem of corruption include; the corrupt practices decree of 1975; the Public Officer (investigation of assets) decree no. 5 of 1976; the ethical revolution; the war against indiscipline; the national committee on corruption and other economic crimes. See Salawu, 392.

different sectors through different styles, which then calls for the analysis of what is going on regarding the struggle against corruption in Nigeria.

The struggle against corruption took a different tone after democracy returned to Nigeria in 1999. Following his election as the Nigerian democratic president, Chief Olusegun Obasanjo was determined to intensify the struggle against corruption that had eaten deep and hindered the growth and development of the country. Although such determination showcased the attitude of a visionary and courageous leader, it was motivated by pressures from international organizations that had ranked Nigeria among the world's most corrupt countries.[236] This external pressure with internal determination resulted in actionable steps to tackle corruption through the establishment of anti-corruption agencies which was necessary to curb the continuous spread of corruption and institutionalizing accountability and transparency.[237]

The EFCC was established in 2003 as a government tool to checkmate the activities of public servants in the country. The agency was established to tackle the lack of accountability among those occupying public offices and indulging in acts of corruption with no consequences.[238] In his public address as the elected president, Obasanjo declared war against corruption, noting that no nation grappling with vices like corruption had a future.[239] Obasanjo cemented this war by putting in place more anti-corruption agencies than any of his predecessors.[240] This suggests an intention that had plans for effective execution. In addition to this action step, an executive bill that aimed at sparing no "sacred cows" in the fight against corruption was passed by the parliament.[241] These steps suggest that there was an honest intention on the part of the authorities to ensure the drastic reduction of corruption in Nigeria.

The EFCC came into existence with the aim of prosecuting and investigating cases of corruption and financial crimes perpetrated with special

---

236. Raimi, Suara, and Fadipe, "Role of Economic"; Nwaodu, Adam and Okereke, "A Review of Anti-Corruption"; Nwoba and Monday, "Appraisal of EFCC"; Obuah, "Combating Corruption"; Salawu, "Towards Solving the Problem."
237. Nwoba and Monday, "Appraisal of EFCC."
238. Raimi, Suara, and Fatipe, "Role of Economic."
239. Nwoba and Monday, "Appraisal of EFCC."
240. Nwaodu, Adam, and Okereke, "A Review of Anti-Corruption."
241. Nwoba and Monday, "Appraisal of EFCC."

reference to the public office holders.[242] Following the pervasiveness of corruption in different forms and structures debilitating the activities of the nation from progressing, the EFCC had the task of investigation and prosecution of victims of corrupt cases. Furthermore, other goals of the agency were as follows; an agency created to protect national and foreign investments in the country, imbue the spirit of hard work in the citizenry and discourage ill-gotten wealth.[243] It was established to identify illegally acquired wealth and confiscate it, build an upright workforce in both the public and private sectors of the economy. EFCC was also to contribute to the global war against financial crimes, advance-fee fraud, money laundering, counterfeiting and illegal transfer charges.

The ICPC, on the other hand, was established as an anti-graft panel responsible for bringing corrupt public officers to book.[244] The government of Olusegun Obasanjo, in its zeal to declare war against corruption that was metamorphosing into different phases, established the ICPC to "boost the fight against corruption."[245] In terms of roles of the ICPC, they include,

> receiving and investigating complaints from members of the public on allegations of corrupt practices and prosecute them; to educate the public on and against bribery, corruption and related offenses; to instruct, advise, and assist that any officer, agency or parastatal about fraud or corruption; to mark the end of rhetorical talks to doing something and fighting corruption.[246]

It was a giant stride to convert words into action. To authenticate the activities of these two agencies, an executive bill was equally passed to enable them to serve as anti-corruption actors in Nigeria.[247]

Regarding what these agencies are doing, we shall first consider the success stories of the EFCC. The EFCC has recorded some successes in dealing with various manifestations of corruption as will be highlighted below. On

---

242. Obuah, "Combating Corruption."

243. Nwoba and Monday, "Appraisal of EFCC"; Obuah, "Combating Corruption"; Nwaodu, Adam, and Okereke, "A Review of Anti-Corruption."

244. Salawu, "Toward Solving the Problem."

245. Akinbi, "Examining the Boko Haram," 34.

246. Salawu, "Toward Solving the Problem," 395; Obuah, "Combating Corruption," 42.

247. Nwoba and Monday, "Appraisal of EFCC."

one occasion, the agency launched a crackdown on certain politicians, bank officials and private investors, who were suspected of amassing wealth illegally through corrupt dealings.[248] Additionally, Nwaodu, Adam, and Okereke affirm that the EFCC has established a sector in some government establishments, notably in the ministry of finance, to help fight corruption.[249] More recently, with the advancement in technology coming with emerging ways of theft, the agency has developed a software called "eagle claw" that enables them to identify and shut down scam email addresses and websites.[250] Equally, the agency established a whistleblowing strategy that allows Nigerians to take part in the fight against corruption by voluntarily disclosing information on the misuse of state assets and funds. In addition, several investigations and prosecution of high-profile members of the political class and security chiefs have also taken place.[251] Similarly, the arrests, prosecution, detention and the public exposure of corrupt officials have also taken place.[252] These efforts of the EFCC are worth commending. They inform us that something regarding the anti-corruption struggle is ongoing despite the speed it takes.

Regarding the achievements of the ICPC, it has been actively involved in raising public awareness about corruption and its effects, disseminating the important message that any money stolen is the public's and, therefore, the duty of each citizen to report officials and all who behave corruptly.[253] Similarly, the ICPC has provided a corridor of integrity for foreign investors who seek to do business in Nigeria.[254] These are amongst the few success stories of the ICPC as an anti-corruption agency in Nigeria. Although the impact of these stories might have been insignificant, there is no denying that something positive is happening. However, despite the aforementioned progresses, corruption remains a major concern in Nigeria. The big question, however, remains that of what could have deterred these two anti-corruption agencies from achieving maximum success as the government had intended?

---

248. Nwaodu, Adam, and Okereke, "A Review of Anti-Corruption."
249. Nwaodu, Adam, and Okereke, "A Review of Anti-Corruption."
250. Nwoba and Monday, "Appraisal of EFCC," 99.
251. Ajie and Gbenga, "Corruption and Economic Growth."
252. Obuah, "Combating Corruption"; Raimi, Suara, and Fadipe, "Role of Economic"; Ukase and Audu, "The Role."
253. Ighaekeme, Abbah and Gaidem, "The Effect of Corruption," 154.
254. Odo, "The Impact and Consequences."

To answer that question, we outline some issues undermining these agencies and the efficiency of their activities, which suggest that more work is still required in the fight against corruption.

First, these government anti-corruption agencies have been criticized for granting immunity to public officials identified with corruption cases to roam without arrest and prosecution.[255] Here, the dilemma is that although a few public officials identified with corruption cases have been arrested, others still roam around freely. Such an attitude contradicts the earlier intention of not sparing anyone found with corruption charges. Such attitude enhances the culture of impunity due to weak political will and indecisiveness, leaving some officials immune, to continue with corruption in the system.[256]

The second setback befalling these anti-corruption agencies involves the judiciary,[257] an arm of government that is bestowed with the responsibility to safeguard and provide justice in all aspects. In the fight against corruption in Nigeria, however, the judiciary has acted differently. It could be suggested that this occurs through delays, frustration, wasting of resources and time in their judgment. In another scene, the judiciary bottlenecks[258] and cripples these institutions from effectively carrying out their mandate. This happens when the anti-corruption agencies arrest offenders and send them on trial to the judiciary. Instead of prompt attention to such cases, the judiciary and the courts delay[259] trials of corruption cases brought by the commission. As such body language of the judiciary persists, it cripples the work of the anti-corruption agencies making them weak, ineffective and exposes them to ridicule by the public.

Yet, one other form of setback arises from the multi-cultural, multi-religious and multi-ethnic nature of the Nigerian state. It is a nation with different descriptions, such as "the populous black nation," "the most religious," known for "being corrupt," but also known for its "ethnic and cultural diversity."[260] Although these diversifications encourage unity and the common good, they

---

255. Obuah, "Combating Corruption"; Ukase and Audu, "The Role."
256. Nwoba and Monday, "Appraisal of EFCC."
257. Obuah, "Combating Corruption."
258. Raimi, Suara, and Fadipe, "Role of Economic."
259. Nwoba and Monday, "Appraisal of EFCC."
260. Afolabi, "The Role of Religion," 42; Agang, "Globalization and terrorism," 6; Omotola, "The Intellectual Dimensions"; Ukiwo, "Politics, Ethno-Religious Conflicts."

also could be sources of diversity resulting in clashes that end in the loss of lives on several occasions.[261] While some of these clashes take different forms and directions, they influence the effective operation of the anti-corruption agencies. For instance, the effectiveness of the anti-corruption agencies to the political party, religion, or region with the power.[262] Stated clearly, Nwoba and Monday submit that the anti-corruption agencies are tools in the hands of successive regimes to witch-hunt perceived and imagined enemies. This happens in such a way that those belonging to the favouring class are spared from arrests and detentions regardless of the corruption charges against them. This, in effect, compounds the challenges of these agencies from effectively carrying out their required duties, consequently keeping distance to the dream of actualizing a corrupt-free society since some persons are still considered "sacred cows" against the original intention of establishing the agency.[263]

On other occasions, fighting corruption is challenged by religious contention. Being religiously contested, the war among the two major religions, Christianity and Islam, influence major decisions in Nigeria. In the case when a member of one of these religions is arrested, it is interpreted as religiously biased. With such experiences, these government-established anti-corruption agencies have been deficient in controlling the continuous escalation of corruption. As it were, they have failed to continue the total war against corruption and the initial enthusiasm to "confront the monster head-on."[264]

This section outlined the activities of the EFCC and the ICPC in the struggle against corruption in Nigeria, their success stories and the hitches they encounter that reduces their efficiency. Some reasons for their inefficiency were highlighted, which include weak leadership in strengthening the anti-corruption agencies, abuse of public office that allows impunity, religious bias and political affiliation to thrive. These reasons contribute to the ineffectiveness of these agencies in curbing corruption, which suggests the need to look at other role players in the anti-corruption crusade in Nigeria.

---

261. Ukiwo, "Politics, Ethno-Religious Conflicts," 115.
262. Nwoba and Monday, "Appraisal of EFCC."
263. Nwoba and Monday, "Appraisal of EFCC," 98.
264. Nwoba and Monday, "Appraisal of EFCC," 98.

2.6.2 The Role of Civil Society in Fighting Corruption in Nigeria

The focus of this section is to unveil the activities of civil society groups in fighting corruption in Nigeria. The reason for this investigation is two-fold; first, to see if civil society groups have anything to offer in terms of waging war against corruption and, second, to see if the Nigerian system of governance provides suitable avenues that appreciate the effort of civil society groups. Civil society organizations' activities involving advocacy for others is not new both around the world[265] and in the African[266] contexts. Examples from the civil rights movement championed by Martin Luther King Jr. and the apartheid in South Africa just to mention but a few, were movements for liberation, freedom and a quest for dignity and belonging. Although every form of advocacy might differ from contexts to the focus, the idea in most cases is liberation from forms of oppression. Debates on different forms of political mobilization and self-organization in Africa refer to the established concepts of a civil society movement.[267] It is also the case that a civil society organisation analyses the features of associations in a public sphere and their role in politics and society. This description serves the focus of our investigation well as we seek to understand the role of civil society organizations in the fight against corruption in Nigeria.

Although civil society organizations do not have a clear definition, their activities have received recognition[268] at different times with significant impacts on human lives.[269] Among others, the civil society organisations

---

265. Examples include civil society in Central America playing an important part in post-conflict peacebuilding. See Nilsson, "Civil Society Actors"; the volunteers in Ukraine who turned to be more trusted institutions because of their resilience against the odds (Oleinik, "Volunteers in Ukraine") just to mention but a few.

266. The Apartheid struggle in South Africa, critical reactions and protests in the field of housing in South Africa, or protests during elections in Kenya, are representatives of a few examples from the African contexts. See Daniel and Nuebert, "Civil Society and Social."

267. Daniel, and Nuebert, "Civil Society and Social."

268. Ukase and Audu, "The Role"; Akinyemi, "Civil Society"; Nilsson, "Civil Society Actors."

269. Some examples of these would include Black consciousness in South Africa (Dolamo, "The Legacy of Black"), the fight against Apartheid in South Africa was deeply influenced by civil society (Shubane, "Civil Society"). In the Nigerian context, civil society include; Nigerian Bar Association (NBA), Parents Teachers' Association (PTA), Nigerian Labour Congress (NLC), Association of senior staff union of Nigerian Universities (ASUU), Nigeria Union

are described as "value-laden" in the American context,[270] "the most trusted institute" in Ukraine,[271] and black consciousness referred to as "salt" to the South African population.[272] Since civil society organisations exist to create space to function in mediating the society and the state, it infers that they provide a "platform for citizens to express interests, passions, preferences and ideas to exchange information and to achieve collective goals."[273]

As groups whose aim to ensure orderliness, civil society organisations seek adherence to the rule of law. As the corruption epidemic in Nigeria continues to spread through poor governance, greed, holistic poverty and failure from the grassroots (as outlined in section 2.4 above), the result has included poverty, dilapidated infrastructure which causes untold hardship on the poor in society. Being their aim to restore and build bridges between the populace and the state, civil society organizations can be trusted as "anti-corruption and anti-social agents."[274] According to Tonwe and Oarhe, the role played by civil society in decolonization, human rights campaigns and struggle against military authoritarianism, could be applied in the fight against corruption, which makes them responsible anti-corruption actors.[275] As a result of such confidence and trust in civil society organizations in the fight for human wellbeing, the organizations would play good advocacy for good governance and adherence to the rule of law.[276] Seeing their dedication to upholding the rule of law to ensure good governance, the civil society organizations can expose and condemn corrupt practices and involve in protests against public policies considered inimical to the public interest.[277] Such is a determination that civil society organisations work to ensure the restoration of equity, justice, fairness, transparency, honesty and accountability, while vices

---

of Journalists (NUJ), Nigeria Medical Association (NMA), and human rights organisations, including religious associations.

270. Nilsson, "Civil Society Actors."
271. Oleinik, "Volunteers in Ukraine."
272. Dolamo, "The Legacy of Black," 367.
273. Akinyemi, "Civil Society."
274. Tonwe and Oarhe, "Corruption Management," 16.
275. Tonwe and Oarhe, "Corruption Management."
276. Ukase and Audu, "The Role."
277. Akinyemi, "Civil Society."

such as corruption, human trafficking, and human abuse in either form are fought enthusiastically.

The second role of civil society organizations considered is their mediating role between the state and the individual.[278] This mediation is in the form of representation and mobilization for unified purposes enshrined in communal interaction. In line with ensuring the unity of purpose, the civil society organisations mobilize and sensitize the populace to effectively exercise civil responsibilities during the voting, census and other events to ensure a better society.[279] By active participation through sensitization and mobilization, awareness is created while the chasm between state-related policies gets to the grassroots. In that sense, the "civil society fills the gap where the government has failed to act responsibly, abdicate its responsibilities, or are unable to respond legitimately to people's needs."[280] By doing this, civil society organisations become mediators bridging the short-sightedness of the state regarding issues that are detrimental to human wellbeing.

Following from the above points, civil society organisations in Nigeria have performed well in providing platforms that the populace could use to query government policies and actions. Some of these policies and actions include privatization[281] and commercialization of public institutions and services, incessant fuel hikes, retrenchment of workers, implementation of prescribing conditions and unfavourable policies. As groups seeking to address issues of common concern through regulation and monitoring, they create awareness through analysis and advocacy that ensures adequate mediation between the state and the individuals.[282] This includes corruption where they frustrate the efforts of corrupt public officials and the exposure of cover-up plans of former rulers with corrupt cases. Some civil society organisation actors monitor the implementation of the budgets and demand for accountability while some have played key roles in election monitoring and evaluation.[283] Additionally, the "watch-dog role of civil society on the activities of anti-graft agencies of the government that have been sustaining anti-corruption crusades in

---

278. Akinyemi, "Civil Society"; Suntai and Targema, "Media and Civil Society."
279. Akinyemi, "Civil Society."
280. Tonwe and Oarhe, "Corruption Management," 20.
281. Ukase and Audu, "The Role."
282. Akinyemi, "Civil Society."
283. Akinyemi, 121.

Nigeria has been applauded."[284] The foregoing discussion provides us with some success stories of the civil society in Nigeria as anti-corruption agents. From the survey made, however, more is still expected from the civil society as they seek to intensify their civic engagement.

Despite the recorded efforts of civil society in ensuring a corrupt-free society, they suffer numerous challenges debilitating their effectiveness. Being the bridge between the state and the individual, the civil society is liable to face challenges from both groups. These challenges either enhance what they do or delimit the enthusiasm of their existence. One of the challenges is that civil society is robbed of opportunities to develop capacities for effectiveness, thereby reducing them to political and religious platforms.[285] As to religious biases, the ethno religious cleavages in Nigeria would not allow fair activities of the civil society else it is described as sentimental. While on the political platform, when those getting exposed are from a different political divide, their activities become unstable with some biases. In some scenes, the civil society has shown a lack of transparency and accountability in its undertakings such that they are seen as existing for selfish reasons, hence depriving it of the moral authority to challenge what it does.[286] One other possible limitation affecting the operation of civil society is the restriction to freedom of expression and the level of inaccessibility to information.[287] These limitations have reduced the effectiveness of civil society from being neutral anti-corruption actors.

Following these limitations, the effectiveness of civil society as anti-corruption agents is restricted. It is expected that one effectively fights what is antithetical to human wellbeing when one does not indulge in doing similar actions. It enables freshness in zeal and brightens the passion for seeing actions against humanity and generating enthusiasm for combating them. In the case of civil society as anti-corruption agents in Nigeria and the limitations highlighted above, their fight against corruption would certainly be ineffective. Although the desire to reduce the spread of corruption by civil society has been effective in some spheres, there are still scores of insufficiency

---

284. Suntai and Targema, "Media and Civil Society," 56.
285. Akinyemi, "Civil Society"; Ukase and Audu, "The Role."
286. Akinyemi, "Civil Society."
287. Suntai and Targem, "Media and Civil Society."

to enable a corrupt-free Nigeria, thus spelling the need for other anti-corruption agencies.

2.6.3 Religious Institutions as Anti-corruption Agents in Nigeria: The Role of the Church

A religious institution, particularly the church, is a significant segment of human society which plays vital functions both in the lives of individuals and in society for some reasons. As to some of its roles, a few are summarized, thus; the church seeks the unity of people by ensuring the exhibition of societal moral values.[288] It seeks to imbue sanity, virtue, morality, and shuns vices like corruption that deter human development. It inculcates nationalism, patriotism, respect for regulations, and laws as well as a pursuit for justice. Similarly, the church brings about national development by identifying and addressing the social, economic, and political problems.[289] It plays an important role in social change and the improvement in societal value systems, which could result in the transformation of social life and put society in holistic growth. In societies where principles of survival are placed above the reach of the masses, the people return to religion for solace. That was probably the reason why Karl Max described religion as the opium of the masses.[290] For the church to effectively exhibit its function in society, it must seriously learn how to see, how to think, how to become sensitive, how to care, and how to be present, act, and get involved.[291] These approaches would enhance the public responsibility of the church, thus:

> Calling the church to be the church is not a formula for a withdrawal ethic nor is it a self-righteous attempt to flee from the world's problems; rather it is a call for the church to be a community which tries to develop the resources to stand within the world witnessing to the peaceable kingdom and thus rightly understand the world . . . Christians are engaged in politics, but it is the politics of the kingdom that reveals the insufficiency of

---

288. Yagboyaju, "Religion, Culture, and Political," 3.
289. Akanbi and Beyers, "The Church."
290. Omonijo et al., "Religion as the Opium."
291. Smit, "Contributions of Religions," 298.

all politics based on coercion and falsehood and finds the true source of power in servanthood rather than dominion.[292]

In line with the above assertions concerning the church, we shall see what the Nigerian church is doing as anti-corruption agents.

First, there is ongoing prophetic proclamations against corruption in Nigeria, and even more is needed. The media houses, pastors and other religious leaders with consciousness about personal and societal morality, have been tirelessly preaching, teaching, and publicizing against corruption.[293] One of these media platforms is the music industry in general, but specific reference to a gospel singer as a representative. In the song entitled "The New Nigeria"[294] Anthony infers that it specifically captures and brings to light the despair and anticipation of Nigerians. It speaks against corruption and violence as the major social crises in the country but also envisions a peaceful atmosphere of rejoicing and celebration. It is when the church takes such a stand that it reveals where its integrity depends.[295] These are messaging types the church should be parading in the context of corruption in Nigeria and not the contrary. Additionally, the church must imbibe John the Baptist's approach and speak against corruption today.[296] Some of Ige's thoughts include the courage to speak against immoral behaviour such as corruption, the unjust killing of innocent lives, unjustifiable imprisonment, the courage to speak against various forms of inequality, and messages that draw people from sin to righteousness.[297] This way, the church would regain the prestige it has lost to corruption as revealed (see section 2.2.3).

Second, in workshops, seminars, and conferences, a lot of work to increase awareness regarding corruption goes on. Messages of transformation, the dignity of labour, perseverance, and contentment are a way to help remove selfishness, greed, and dishonest gain. These emphases are made to ensure the survival of dignity, prestige, and a nation whose people have become victims

---

292. Hauerwas, *The Peaceable Kingdom*, 3.
293. The Christian Association of Nigeria (CAN), a body that oversees the affairs of Christians in Nigeria has been vocal on the struggle against corruption through different press statements.
294. Anthony, "New Nigeria," 2–4.
295. Boesak, "A Hope Unprepared."
296. Ige, "John the Baptist Approach," 584.
297. Ige, "John the Baptist Approach," 584.

of an unfortunate dilemma.[298] For this to happen, the church would need a good dose of courage to speak to the authorities and persons who are involved in corrupt practices. Also, the courage to confront those in authority is a sure way to engage corruption just like the case of John the Baptist to King Herod.[299] To this end, Ige proposes that the church implements a similar strategy.[300]

The few instances highlighted above form the microcosm of the role the Nigerian church plays in the fight against corruption. Despite the challenge of moral transformation, lack of sound biblical teaching, and the unfortunate state of some church leaders and members indulging in acts of corruption, the above emphasis indicates that the church is not quiet. There are also chances that the church could intensify and harness forces in the fight against what is considered a blight hindering human and societal flourishing in Nigeria. To begin with, the church must understand its place in society and the role expected of it. Second, the church must check the content of its messages on whether they seek public morality or contribute to promoting immorality. This informs why there must be a theology that thinks about how the knowledge of God as revealed in the Scriptures impacts on matters of public concern at a specific time and in a specific context.[301] Third, the lifestyle of a church leader and members must align with the tenets of what they teach (words matching with actions where no difference is made between the public and private lives of an individual). Fourth, the church must learn how to speak while addressing issues of ethical concern such as corruption to ensure sanity in the church. The church must do this by displaying its "public role in addressing real challenges that destitute face in times of dislocation and alienation."[302] These realities are possible only when there is a "transformative moral life,"[303] genuine conversion to move in a different direction to march to a different drumbeat, imbibed Christian ethics, and its application to their daily lives.[304] Until these tenets are achieved, the church cannot give purposeful and exemplary moral guidance to society. Additionally, "the church must

---

298. Umaru, "Corruption as a Threat."
299. Ige, "John the Baptist Approach," 581.
300. Ige, "John the Baptist Approach."
301. Naudé, "Economics."
302. Akper, "Is God in Nigeria," 66.
303. Igboin, "Corruption In Nigeria," 58.
304. Ogbuehi, "Christian Ethics."

uncompromisingly adhere to and proclaim to their members the message that they owe their highest allegiance to Christ and should at all times maintain the inclusiveness and impartiality of Christian morality."[305]

2.7 Chapter Summary

This chapter surveyed corruption in Nigeria through different dimensions to provide a wider understanding of the concept. This was followed by outlining some ways responsible for fuelling the spread of corruption. Among those mentioned in the chapter include failure of leadership, failure in moral upbringing, loss of sense of human wellbeing, holistic poverty, and greed. The chapter also presented the effects of corruption on the Nigerian citizenry in four ways; that corruption affects the people, their society, the economy, and is a catalyst in terrorism activities. The roles of anti-corruption agencies including the EFCC and ICPC, the civil society organisations and the church in the fight against corruption were examined. What follows are the findings of the literature reviewed in this chapter.

Corruption was surveyed from a theological anthropological perspective where we located the origin of corruption from the origin of mankind. It was concluded that corruption began when human beings became depraved, hence abused their free will for doing wrong rather than good. We also saw corruption from a moral perspective, where we found that corruption occurs when there is an abuse of moral conscience, forcing the conscience to do and accept things that ought to be avoided.

Political corruption was considered as misuse of a public office, position, or power for personal gain at the expense of the public which results in poor policies, poor decisions, and inadequate will to drive the populace and society toward excellence. These were credited to poor governance and inappropriate administering of democratic values whose product is the increase in the spread of corruption.

The chapter equally highlighted some causative agents of corruption in Nigeria. Failure in leadership was considered the major contributor because of how the Nigerian leaders have become overwhelmed with power but use it only for personal gain at the expense of the populace. Second, poor moral

---

305. de Villiers, "Does the Christian Church," 8.

upbringing from the grassroots to inculcate moral values from the family has contributed to the rise in corruption in Nigeria. Third, the lost sense of moral wellbeing where immoral acts like corruption are not considered wrong even when they cause detrimental effects to the wellbeing of countless members of society. Fourth, we considered holistic poverty, which refers to a lack of material resources, lack of power or freedom to protest, and lack of intellectual power to think, as responsible for the rise in corruption in Nigeria. Fifth, we considered greed, which involves human desires for things they could survive without yet insisting on acquiring them. These causes of corruption have significantly affected the Nigerian society so much so that the effects are detrimental.

The chapter then highlighted some effects of corruption in Nigeria. First, the effects on people. In this case, human persons are denied access to basic needs that would enable them to live fully and truly as humans. Second, the effects on the economy with the conclusion being arrived at that corruption increases inequality and poverty rate in society, it reduces foreign and domestic investments, exploits public investment, and reduces public revenues. Third, the effect of corruption was seen in the increasing rate of insecurity emanating from poor handling and management of the security sector. Although this results in the daily loss of innocent lives and the destruction of countless property, weak decisions emerge from those in power.

The last part of the chapter outlined three anti-corruption agencies and the efforts they are making to combat the scourge in Nigeria. First, the government instituted agencies – the EFCC and the ICPC. It was concluded that these two have, since inception, made some giant strides in the fight against corruption. They have encountered some hitches contributing to their efforts. As a result, they are criticized for being government tools to hunt those who do not subscribe to the governing principles and ideologies. The second group we considered was the civil society organization. They have been involved in campaigns against corruption, election monitoring and observations, mobilization and sensitization of those in the grassroots for active participation and exercise of civil responsibility. Although these giant strides have been commendable in some spheres, they have suffered setbacks. Two of the setbacks mentioned include their lack of opportunities to develop capacities, and second is the restriction to freedom of expression and inaccessibility to information. The third group is the role of religious institutions, the church.

As outlined in the chapter, the church is doing well in prophetic preaching, teaching and admonishments at conferences and seminars. Although these are efforts worthy of commendation, the church has suffered some setbacks also. First, it must understand its place and role in society; second, check the content of its teachings/messages on how they address public morality; third, align its teaching with action; and fourth, learn how to speak appropriately while addressing public issues.

The summary of this chapter shows that corruption is still an issue of concern in Nigeria. Although several stakeholders are putting efforts to fight the menace, the desired results have not been achieved. This calls for further investigation of ways to support the ongoing campaigns. It is paradoxical to see how the efforts of the anti-corruption agencies have not yielded to either a corrupt-free Nigeria or one with fewer cases of corruption. When one considers the level of religiosity and compares that to the level of corruption, there is a great sigh as to what is taught by these religions. If all Nigeria's public office holders subscribe to either Christianity, Islam, or traditional religions, research indicates that all these religions see societal vices such as corruption as immoral acts. This means that religiosity does have transforming power to change people's moral behaviour or judge their conscience in an ideal situation. In the case of Nigeria, this is not true. Instead, religion is used to cover up corruption and ensure the further escalation of it, despite the efforts of a few religious groups who are seekers and promoters of the common good of society. This suggests that more ways and efforts to fight corruption in Nigeria are still underway which is the reason for this study. Considering the extent of corruption as highlighted in this chapter, the adverse effect which concerns this study is how it undermines human dignity. So, this study intends to provide, from a theological perspective, an understanding of human dignity and how it can be safeguarded in the context of corruption in Nigeria. To that end, the next chapter explores human dignity from different perspectives.

CHAPTER 3

Human Dignity and Corruption in Nigeria

3.1 Introduction

The previous chapter gave a general overview of corruption in Nigeria including factors that are responsible for the continuous spread of corruption, the effects, and the efforts towards controlling it from further escalation. It was concluded, therefore, that the effect of corruption on human and societal development results in undermining the dignity of the Nigerian human persons. To understand the dehumanizing tendencies of corruption on human persons, however, there is a need to establish an understanding of the concept of human dignity. The reason for this inquiry is to present a deeper, richer, more textured, and a theologically rich insight into the nature and identity of human beings, and what it means to be truly and fully human from a Christian perspective. Here, the Christian perspective refers to a view holding on the fact that "human beings are created in the image and likeness of God, and by which identity, humanity depends on God for existence and its activities."[1]

Considering the various ways in which the dignity of human beings is violated, this study will focus on two perspectives. The first follows Maslow's view

---

1. Aguas, "The Notions," 41.

that lack of basic human needs is tantamount to the denial of their dignity,[2] while the second is Immanuel Kant's forbidden use of human persons as a means to an end.[3] These two views are chosen because they will best help in addressing the primary research question as well as the methodology of this study. More importantly, they help to engage the research problem in general, namely the scourge of corruption on human dignity. Although these two perspectives have been critiqued over time, they are studied through a different lens by agreeing and disagreeing with some of the critiques simultaneously.

The chapter is divided into five parts, namely – an introduction to dignity talk, human dignity in history, perspectives on human dignity, human dignity in Nigeria, and human dignity and human rights.

3.2 Why Talk About Human Dignity?

The concept of human dignity is not new.[4] While human person and human dignity have become the "favourite concepts and bywords in contemporary discussions in different academic fields, there is still no sufficient understanding of what these concepts and realities are."[5] These concepts, including those responsible in demeaning the integrity of human beings, probably have

---

2. Maslow, "A Theory of Human," 372. Maslow outlined the basic human need from psychological perspective. He categorises these needs into four groups namely; physiological needs (the most potent of all needs); the safety needs (safety from all forms of emergencies); the love needs (sense of belongingness); the esteem needs (the desire for strength, achievement, adequacy, recognition, attention, importance, prestige, and independence); the need for self-actualisation (where one is allowed to do, and be what they can be). He, however, gives some preconditions for these basic needs as follows – freedom to speak, freedom to do what one wishes so long as no harm is done to other, freedom to express one's self, freedom to investigate and seek information, freedom to defend one's self, justice, fairness, orderliness. These conditions, he concludes, are defended because without them the basic satisfactions are quite impossible, or at least, very severely endangered. However, the non-actualisation of these basic needs is considered a pre-requisite for undermining human dignity.

3. For Kant, a human person is an unquantifiable variable with no price, hence cannot be exchanged for anything, whatsoever. As such, a human person has an entitlement for being an end and not to be taken or used to an end. Any of such attempts, he declares, denies humanity its dignity. Also, as the study progresses, we will elaborate on this reality that Kant argues. Further, Novak insists that Kantian interpretation of a human being is true for some reasons. Firstly, his understanding that the ancient philosophers of Greece and Rome, before the contact of those regions with Christianity, did not reach this principle. Secondly, that we must note the quiet but strong culture of German pietism in which Kant grew to maturity. Novak, "The Judeo-Christian Foundation," 111.

4. Enslin, "Kant on Human Dignity."

5. Aguas, "The Notions," 40.

taken the lead that quests for regaining the lost respect becoming prominent. This being the case, the reader is introduced to why the need for dignity talk has become an important topic in academic discussion before venturing to perspectives towards understanding the concept.

The search for human dignity informs what propels human desires on why and for what they exist. Helpfully so, one such explanation is the fact that human beings are "meaning-seeking and meaning-giving entities."[6] The reason for this, is that "humanity stands at the centre of the various transformations and advancements in modern society that are made by and for "human satisfaction."[7] They seek meaning to ensure their sense[8] of uniqueness among other species, and sometimes among fellow human beings; a meaning-giving group of beings to life, environment, and to others. Human beings seek to know their sense of self-worth expressed as a desire for dignity.

The desire to fulfilment, such as meaningful life, a life well-lived, a life of dignity, depends significantly on the influences brought by relationships with others.[9] In this regard, relationships suggest mutual coexistence, which triggers a sense of belonging within the community of other human species that brings their true sense of belonging. It is for this reason that "true humanity is nested in the complexity of being a person concerning other persons such that an individual would know that being fully human necessitates showing care and concern for the full humanity of others."[10] This assertion implies that belonging in a community with others authenticates our being fully human, on the one hand, while, on the other hand, necessitating our treatment of others and how we see and value their humanness. This suggests that knowing our human worth results in recognizing the worth of others.

Talking of dignity in this sense requires an understanding of the worth of human persons as the subject which is like the concept of personhood. To understand that better, a few suggestions that could be helpful. The value placed on human persons triggers their search for why human beings attract such attention. Research asks, what is it about our personhood that gives

---

6. Kirchhoffer, "Human Dignity," 10.
7. Aguas, "The Notions," 41.
8. Kichhoffer, "Human Dignity," 11.
9. Kirchhoffer, 11; Volf, *Flourishing: Why We Need*.
10. Forster, "Affect, Empathy," 3.

attention through which we have the moral status we enjoy, grounding the existence of our moral rights?[11] In response, Eberl cites Aquinas, who ascribes the term a person as "a term of dignity."[12] On another scene, human beings are described as those who share first-order desires,[13] but also capable of second-order desires. These second-order desires formulate who human beings want to be and what they want to have.[14] With these needs, human beings draw their sense of self-worth and the longing for dignity, which drives the way they engage in and within various relationships around them. The dignity that persons possess, therefore, results in their having dominion over their acts, and are not made to act as others, but act through themselves.[15] Additionally, they share, through their material bodies, "certain essential qualities with other members of their species."[16] This echoes another view of human persons as those with the freedom to formulate desires about what they want.[17]

In sum, we can say dignity talk is significant because it describes the subject, a human person, whose dignity is discussed and the freedom they have by being human that makes possible discovering, developing, nurturing their sense of belonging, and sharing inter-relationality. In other words, it both involves a symbiotic relationship where we not only contribute to the good of others but also are contributed to and enhanced by others.

The essence of dignity talk, therefore, while opening an understanding of the worth of a human person with their dignity, also informs us of our shared responsibility toward the dignity of others.[18] Having this understand-

---

11. Eberl, "The Ontological and Moral."
12. Eberl, 222.
13. First-order desires here refer to "those that human beings share with other animals which include; sex, food, sleep to mention but few" (See Kirchhoffer, "Human Dignity," 11). On the contrary, "the desire for self-worth and the desire for dignity are second-order desires which primarily are pursued by the human species" (See Kirchhoffer, 11). Such specific desires give human beings a sense of uniqueness over other animals in ways that this study will unfold as we progress.
14. Kirchhoffer "Human Dignity," 11.
15. Eberl, "The Ontological and Moral."
16. Eberl, "Aquinas in the Nature," 335.
17. Kirchhoffer, *Human Dignity*.
18. On the view of human dignity held by the society, whether consciously or unconsciously, it depends largely on many matters of basic importance. Some of these include not only how a human person interacts with and toward others, but also "his/her relationship

ing would make a significant contribution to our journey towards the discovery of the missing links in dignity discussions. This is perhaps the reason why a human person, although bestowed with dignity and good nature, is yet capable of doing "evil and inflicting harm against others."[19]

3.3 Towards a Historical Survey of Human Dignity

In this section, we shall survey the trajectories of human dignity through historical traditions. Understanding the complexity of history, this choice does not aim at covering every period in detail but is limited to a few. The reason for this is to understand how human dignity was perceived at certain periods to see if changes have occurred that would help our contemporary view, particularly in the Nigerian context. To do this well, the survey takes the periods covering the early Christian era, the Middle Ages, and the era of modernity. Again, the choice of these periods does not aim at disqualifying other periods and their proponents, but for the sake of this study, the said periods are chosen to give an overview and limit the scope of the study.

At a time in history, human dignity was described in personalized terms to be the honour of rank, and the status of a dignitary attributed to few individuals.[20] It was individualized such that only a few persons were termed to have dignity. That has, however, changed in recent times, such that human dignity now refers to "the worth of being human,"[21] and has wide acceptance within moral discourses.[22] This is attested in a declaration that "to be human is to have dignity," whereby "*Humanitas* and *Dignitas* are synonymous."[23]

---

to the material environment and the value placed on various forms of human activity." See Dales, "A Medieval View," 557.

19. Aguas, "The Notions," 40.

20. Waldron, "Dignity, Rank, and Rights," 218; Moltmann, *On Human Dignity*, ix.

21. Malvestiti, "Human Dignity," 190; Moltmann, *On Human Dignity*.

22. Although the concept of human dignity has received acceptance as a moral notion, other scholars on the subject, such as Waldron, have chosen to slightly differ. Although he agrees that human dignity has changed meaning from being a juridical idea to an all-inclusive notion described as an intrinsic worth, he sees that to be wrong. Instead, he promotes that human dignity has a legal recognition, and no need of underlying moral dignity is required. Waldron, "Dignity, Rank and Rights," 210.

23. Koopman, "Some Theological and Anthropological," 177; Bonhoeffer, *Ethics*, 374. The explanation equating humanity with dignity implies the interconnectedness of the two where one confidently says without dignity one ceases to be human, in a sense one loses their self-worth.

Humanitas and *Dignitas* synonymously describe the fundamental meaning of being human seen as a fundamental human right. This has, however, made the search for dignity key[24] in the worldwide struggle for human rights, and why several discourses have recently focused their attention to the abuse of human dignity in different contexts. It then follows that the abuse of human dignity is no longer news across regions and perhaps in Africa, but limited actions are taken towards identifying and proffering solutions to it by relevant authorities. This, however, remains a key reason why less attention is given to discussion on dignity resulting in its being undermined persistently.[25]

Besides, human beings are liable to identify certain resistive powers within them that speak a significant difference with other creatures. Part of this is seen in Macintyre's description of human beings as "vulnerable to many kinds of afflictions where most of us are afflicted by serious ills."[26] Part of the ills faced today are those caused by human beings against each other, where living becomes almost unbearable for the other. Oftentimes, we hear about "killings, kidnapping, rape, abortion, terrorist attacks, hunger, wars, and many other forms of violence. Ironically, while the human person is the victim of these menaces, human persons are equally the perpetrators"[27] which simultaneously makes them both culprits and victims. Here, our resistive powers are expressed through the feeling that our suffering is redeemable; our ability to strive upward against the downward pull of necessity. The unified answer to these assertions enabling the uniqueness of humans over other species is "the excellence component called human dignity which is highly valued."[28] The applicability of this component to the entire human family, is, however, understood differently. First, religious[29] people would locate its origin in our

---

24. Moltmann, *On Human Dignity*, ix.
25. de Villiers, "The Recognition of Human"; Moltmann, *On Human Dignity*, ix.
26. Macintyre, *Dependent Rational Animals*, 1.
27. Aguas, "The Notions," 40.
28. Kass, *Being Human: Core Readings*, 567.
29. Pope John Paul II has two links to this; first, "in his defence of the dignity of a human being, he posits universality of the human nature that transcends the limits of history and culture. Secondly, he admits with the classical metaphysical view which understands the human person as characterized by the intellect and free will" (See Coughlin, "Pope John Paul II," 66, 67). (Aben, "The Trinity and Public Theology," 40) adds that agreeing that God is a plurality of persons working together to accomplish creation, and that "mankind" is a plurality of persons made in God's image, then it follows that human beings were created to work together

God-given origin and God-being[30] whereas the secular may locate the source of dignity within ourselves as a power[31] that sets us apart from everything else that lives.

3.3.1 Human Dignity in Early Christian History: Era of the Church Fathers

During the early church tradition, specifically the Church Fathers, prominent references to human dignity were undoubtedly present. Confirming that claim, studies indicate that the term dignity was used concerning human beings in many ways during that era.[32] Interestingly, the Church Fathers neither coined the concept of human dignity nor took it over directly from the language of Scripture that grounds the dignity of human beings. Instead, they borrowed the term from Greco-Roman usage[33] "even though the Greeks did not use the term dignity for all human beings but only for a few."[34] As suggested in another study, the earliest users of the concept of human dignity were neither Jewish nor Christian,[35] but a pagan philosopher, Cicero (106–43 BCE).[36] However, another study insists that Cicero and ancient philosophers viewed human dignity from a moral perspective while arguing that "the worthiness of a being is grounded on their capacity to embed the highest features of human nature within a moral framework, defined through specified kinds of virtues."[37] Two concepts emanated from this that were used for understanding human dignity. First, *Dignitas* either referring to a designation of an individual's distinctive task in society and second by

---

to accomplish the task that God has given them, which is to care for God's creation. And given that God's creation includes their fellow human beings, their task is also to care for each other.

30. This basic dignity comes directly from God's creative act and not from any action on the part of man. See Aguas, "The Notions," 40.
31. Kass, "Being Human," 567.
32. Soulen and Woodhead, *God and Human Dignity*.
33. Soulen and Woodhead.
34. Novak, "The Judeo-Christian Foundation," 109.
35. Although propounded by pagan philosopher, Christianity, on acknowledging it insisted that every single human is loved by the creator, made in the image, and destined for eternal friendship and communion. On this ground, Christianity made human dignity a concept of universal application that became a matter of self-condemnation to use another human as a means to an end (See Novak, 109) – echoing Kantian categorical imperative.
36. Volck and Shuman, "Dignity of the Body," 126.
37. Andorno and Pele, "Human Dignity," 2.

designating humankind's distinctive place within the natural order.[38] These two ways of using the word dignity continued with considerable modification when taken further by the early Church Fathers who emphasized the latter more frequently than the former.[39]

The Church Fathers did not only borrow and use the idea of human dignity but also classified the concept based on individual performance. In fact, some writers from Clement of Alexandria to Augustine argued that human dignity could be increased[40] over time through faithfulness and the cultivation of virtue. The apologists of the second century, however, maintained that dignity was given freely[41] and irrevocably to all humankind; first, by their creatureliness in the image of God and, second as extended by God, the universal offer of redemption. Putting the views together, some conclusions could be made. In the words of Clement, the root of all dignity is of "high value and is made sacred by that which is worth all, or rather, which has no equivalent in the virtue of exceeding sanctity of the latter."[42] In other words, the measure of dignity is discovered not in the social convention, as Cicero's first designation above suggests. Instead, in God and the pattern of God's action toward humankind in creation and redemption, as Cicero's second designation connotes. Concluding from the above views, human dignity originates and is embedded in humanity by virtue of their creatureliness and not by what they do or can do – as some contemporary perspectives would put it today. It is not about social achievement earned by self, but a gift received at creation.

The early Church Fathers used three divisions to unravel the notion of dignity regarding the natural order. The first dimension is in connection with the creation theory of human beings. Cited in the study by Soulen and Woodhead, the Christian apologist Lactantius (AD 240–320) addressed the dignity that comes to human beings from God's work of creation by declaring created humankind as a sacred animal (*sanctum animal*).[43] The sacredness here includes the sanctity of human life which calls for its apt protection from endangerment. Further, the Church Fathers connected the ancient idea

---

38. Soulen and Woodhead, *God and Human Dignity*, 3.
39. Volck and Shuman, "Dignity of the Body," 126.
40. Volck and Shuman, 126.
41. Volck and Shuman, 126.
42. Soulen and Woodhead, *God and Humanity Dignity*, 6.
43. Soulen and Woodhead, 4.

that human beings have a special place in the world because of their rational capacities and their ability for self-formation. This idea of self-formation invites these rational human beings into relating with their creator, God, in whose image they are created and are redeemed.[44] For this reason, the apologist insists that God "prohibited the killing of human beings, even if in instances recognized and approved by any public law."[45] With such affirmations, it would mean that such dignity is given to human beings by their close link to God and, thereby upholding a relationship between God and human beings.[46] By such a relationship, human life is considered sacred which cannot and should not be destroyed by human misbehaviour, not even murder. It implies that even at the fall of humanity, the dignity component remained. This gives human beings a sense of honour and respect that is imbued, which should be respected and protected. This sense of honour and respect emanates from participation in God, in being God's image, at the same time, human beings participate in God's reason. For this purpose, humans can reflect on themselves and exercise free will.[47]

Similarly, St. Augustine, in line with the above conversation holds that humankind is made after the image of God. Concerning the rational or intellectual soul, the image certainly remains even after the fall despite the disfigurement of its dignity.[48] This explains the conclusion that "for the honour of man is to be the image and likeness of God which is preserved only about him by whom it is impressed."[49] From these arguments, it is established that human dignity was neither lost at the fall nor should it lose value due to any human actions or inactions.

The second dimension employed by the early Fathers to unravel the notion of human dignity involves God's "redemption in Christ and its appropriation through life and the practice of Christian virtue."[50] Unlike the previous view, this one makes distinctions on the gravity of dignity a person could have. Argued concretely, the dignity that comes through redemption is "acquired

---

44. Meith, "Human Dignity."
45. Soulen and Woodhead, *God and Human Dignity*, 3.
46. Bedford-Strohm, "Human Dignity."
47. Meith, "Human Dignity."
48. McKenna, *The Fathers*, 418.
49. McKenna, 358.
50. Soulen and Woodhead, *God and Human Dignity*, 4.

gradually over time by way of practicing virtue and discipleship."[51] Some contemporary scholarships, however, agree that human dignity should be understood in terms of the "doctrine of justification."[52] Unlike the early Church Fathers, Clement of Alexandria (ca. AD 150–215) acknowledged that such dignity can be augmented and increased, thus suggesting it could be obtained through "one's effort."[53] de Villiers, however, differs from this view and contends that dignity is "only found in human persons as something that is bestowed by God."[54] Here, if human dignity is taken as a merited value based on justification, it becomes problematic with unresolved problems. Considering such a view and its dangers, a study observes that "for dignity to be accorded to only the justified, then the sinners, unjustified and non-baptized persons, would be unequal about their dignity."[55] Considering that we are talking of the dignity of a human person in its entirety, viewing it in this sense would have many limitations that could be very problematic. In a sense, those with different beliefs or who do not subscribe to the doctrine of justification would utterly be dismissed from having dignity.

The third dimension used by the early Church Fathers to unravel the concept of human dignity is the "ultimate goal of human life."[56] It can be argued that human beings, in a broader sense, are meaning-seeking species. The campaigns to live together in "justice and freedom,"[57] the quest for a "new ethos of hospitality,"[58] and seeking "compassion,"[59] all have an underlying yearning for meaningful human life as one of the reasons. For the early Church Fathers, one tradition processed this notion of human dignity by differentiating between humankind as image and likeness of God. Prominently in this tradition is Origen, who attests that "man received the dignity of God's image to his first creation" which conferred on him "the possibility of attaining

---

51. Soulen and Woodhead, 4.
52. de Villiers, "The Recognition of Human," 268.
53. Soulen and Woodhead, *God and Human Dignity*, 4.
54. de Villiers, "The Recognition of Human," 268.
55. Wolbert, "Human Dignity, Human Rights," 173.
56. Soulen and Woodhead, *God and Human Dignity*, 6.
57. Ackerman, "Becoming Fully Human," 14.
58. Akper, "An Ethos of Hospitality," 284.
59. Forster, "Affect, Empathy," 3.

to perfection."⁶⁰ Meanwhile, St. Augustine's emphasis focused on eternal blessings such as "perishability, eternal life itself, and the immortality of the flesh and soul," which he calls unfailing *Dignitas*.⁶¹ Unfailing dignity could be placed with Helmut Thielicke's idea of alien dignity, and Karl Barth's idea of human life as a loan that ought to be guided and protected.⁶²

This third dimension and its reference to the goal of human life is essential in different ways. First, the idea of the goal of life, particularly for the redeemed, is the eternal life from where their ultimate meaning of life would be realized. Secondly, for the unredeemed whom we have established as also carriers of dignity, their goal for meaningful life could be in the area of acceptability, belonging, justice, and freedom. In either case, the idea for the goal of human life rests on the hope for the security of that life both here and now, and in the hereafter.

3.3.2 Human Dignity in the Middle Ages: Thomas Aquinas (1225–1274)

In this section, we dialogue with one of the prominent figures of the Middle Ages, Thomas Aquinas' theological and philosophical disposition on the dignity of human persons. It is the assumption of this study that the perception of human dignity in the Middle Ages would make contributions towards broadening the assumptions of the concept.

The Middle Ages comprised an era that shared a rich tradition of thought on human dignity which has received attention in recent scholarship. This forms the basis for an agreement that the medieval era all agreed to the view that "human dignity had to do with the creation of man in the image and likeness of God and his dominion over other creatures."⁶³ Importantly, another study insists that human dignity was, at this time, described as "spiritual dignity" for various reasons.⁶⁴ The first reason had to do with the fact that the term was created to

---

60. Soulen and Woodhead, *God and Human Dignity*, 6.
61. Soulen and Woodhead, 6.
62. Barth, "Respect for Life."
63. Dales, "A Medieval View," 557.
64. Andorno and Pele, "Human Dignity."

"defend and celebrate the excellence and greatness of human beings . . . the second reason was that the term appeared as a complementary perspective and a counterpart of a more pessimistic view. The worth of human beings is, therefore, ultimately based on their ability to develop and harmonise their intellectual, moral and bodily abilities while moving towards their spiritual self-realisation."[65]

Taking this further would show that there was a ferment of debate in intellectual circles about the relationship between God and man, and the idea of *dignitas* came to be used as the way of distinguishing between man and other creatures.[66] This debate involved the humanists who attempted to reconcile classical thought and dogmatic theology by emphasizing the idea that mankind has dignity because man is made in the image of God, distinguishing man from other species. Later, these views were, however, discovered to have flaws in the thoughts of medieval authors.[67] Amid this uncertainty of clarity comes Aquinas, who devises a clear concept of human unity that this defect was outstripped. In order to discuss Aquinas' conception in more detail, therefore, it will be wise to evaluate his perception of a human person from which he discusses human dignity.

3.3.2.1 *Thomas Aquinas and the Human Person*

To understand human dignity better, Aquinas chooses to first, present his view of a human person whose dignity is discussed. Other scholars who followed the scholarly tradition of Aquinas, such as Wojtyla, have written on the notion of a human person too. Although these scholars had encounters with torture, experienced by human beings from which they wrote about a human person, Aquinas differs.[68] His reason for writing on the human person

---

65. Andono and Pele, 7.

66. McCrudden, "Human Dignity."

67. Specifically, Robert Bultot, an author who specialises in the topic than anyone else. He notes that, dominated by the Augustinian concept of the dualism of the body and soul, they lacked a firm conception of human unity and considered the image and likeness of God to exist in the soul only. See Dales, "A Medieval View," 557.

68. It is general knowledge that Wojtyla "endured tragic experiences during his early life experiences that moulded his personality, his thinking, and his thoughts. He lost his mother at an early age, and his brother when he was ten years old, and he endured the different upheavals that crushed Eastern Europe during the twentieth century. During the middle years of the

is "less personal – simply because he did not experience horrors, and violence inflicted against the human person – thus making his reason for writing an objective one."[69] Adopting his definition of a human person from Boethius, a philosopher who was before him, Aquinas states clearly that "a human being is a person."[70] The name, person, signifies "an individual substance as having a property which is a sign of dignity."[71] Seen in the *Summa Theologiae*, Aquinas writes "because of the substance in a rational nature is of high dignity, therefore, every individual of the rational nature is called a person."[72]

This idea of rational nature could be problematic in a sense in reducing the foundation of being a person to rationality.[73] Being a rational nature constitutes an intellective mind, a view which Aquinas uses to distinguish human beings from other material substances.[74] For Aquinas, the rational idea of human beings is entitled to the named person because of the dignity grounded not as a human property but existing in a particularly perfect way specific for intelligent beings. And when he characterizes a person, he does not talk directly about an individual of a certain kind, but about substance in a certain nature. Aquinas, therefore, clarifies that rationality is primarily a "feature that makes it possible to decide who is entitled to the name 'person', but not the real reason for calling someone a person."[75]

Aquinas again makes a distinction between human beings from other types of beings. He, at this point, describes human beings as "rational animals."[76] He explains that this involves seeing a human person with higher gifts and

---

twentieth century, his native country, Poland, like other Eastern European countries was crushed by two brutal tyrannies, one after another: Nazism and Communism. As a young man living with his father, Wojtyla not only observed but experienced the horrors of these regimes. He too, was a victim and had his shares of pains and sufferings, first during the Nazi occupation and later during the Communist regime in Poland. Many of his friends and associates particularly the Jews, perished during the onslaught of Nazism. In these brutal and horrible events, Wojtyla saw how man can be both the agent of goodness and evil." Aguas, "The Notions," 46. With these experiences, writing about a human person for him springs freely than for others like Aquinas.

69. Aguas, "The Notions," 42.
70. Eberl, "Aquinas in the Nature," 333.
71. Piechowiak, "Thomas Aquinas: Human Dignity," 71.
72. Aquinas, *St Thomas Aquinas*, 77.
73. Such idea of a personhood is grounded in some weighty philosophical writings of the medieval era, although Aquinas chooses to differ from those (Piechowiak, 2016).
74. Eberl, 334.
75. Piechowiak, "Thomas Aquinas," 72.
76. Eberl, 334.

abilities to discern between what is good and bad, something that no other animal could do. That a human being has an extra and better knowledge about things than other animals, perhaps, informs part of their uniqueness. This assertion for a human person becomes Aquinas's claim, through which he discovered "existence (*esse*) and essence (*essential*) as the constitutive component of every real being."[77] By placing a human being as a rational animal, Aquinas sees through their material bodies that "human beings share certain essential qualities with other members of the rational animal family."[78] This indicates that, by being rational animals, human beings have a share of responsible actions of enhancing the quality of other human lives, which include but are not limited to promoting, protecting and respecting the dignity of others. Let us now evaluate Aquinas' view of human dignity.

3.3.2.2 Aquinas and Human Dignity

From Aquinas's view of personhood presented in the preceding sub-section, we shall now discuss how this fits into his dignity discourse. As discussed, a human person has dignity because he/she is a person. Additionally, Aquinas insists that this person is "most perfect in the whole of nature that subsists in rational nature."[79] Here, the perfection referred to has to do with that which a human person has, as embedded by God. This dignity is, therefore, based on a "human's spiritual sense, which is founded in the spirituality of the human essence as the principle of actuality. In a sense, we could ascribe this dignity to an expression of the high degree of beingness, actuality, and perfection that a human person possesses."[80] This expression agrees with Aquinas' understanding of grace in *Summa Theologiae*, where he affirms why a human person could only receive anything through God's gracious givenness. He observes thus, "it seems that man cannot love God above all things by his natural endowments alone without grace. For the love of God above all things is the proper and principal act of charity."[81]

---

77. Jalocho-Palicka, "Thomas Aquinas' Philosophy," 131.
78. Eberl, 335.
79. Aguas, "The Notions," 55.
80. Aguas, 55–56.
81. Aquinas, *St Thomas Aquinas*, 77.

In the prologue to the second part of the *Summa Theologiae*, Aquinas cites the *imago Dei* – the image of God – as the fundamental principle for considering the morality of human actions. This image implies that every person is endowed with the powers of intellect, choice and self-movement. In such a movement, all that matters is the goal that the only human's ultimate fulfilment is to union with God. It is interesting to note that for Aquinas, the dignity of a human person is embedded in their union with God, which is a union of love. This love indicates that God loves[82] all things that exist because all things that exist are good in their state of making. It is this union that fulfils the dignity of a human being, and not the bestowal of rights or services that may seem to cause or relieve one from pain. Since all created goods are infinite, therefore, they simply are not able to satisfy humans' yearning for fulfilment as these yearnings deepen the human longing for belonging and acceptance. Rather, only God who is the source of all goodness can satisfy the yearning that is at the heart of every human person. This being the case, we could also argue that only God the creator bestows dignity, which calls for respect through the exhibition of justice.

In *Summa Theologie,* Aquinas writes on issues involving humanity and other creation, namely the principle of justice and respect. In a sense, his view of respect is of importance in that it gives no evidence to differentiate one human person from others. He takes this notion further by differentiating between respect and piety as they relate to virtues. Citing Cicero, Aquinas attests to the virtue of respect[83] by which persons eminent in any position of dignity receive the deference of a certain service and honour. This suggests that positions or levels at which dignity is obtainable are varied. In this manner, respect, which becomes the object of dignity turns to a place of piety[84] to offer service and honour to those superior in dignity, such as parents. Gathered from these, Aquinas holds that respect and honour are variables that are given and received by human beings not because of their creatureliness, but by the position one occupies. As variables that are received, they are liable to be lost, reduced, or weakened. This view portrays Aquinas's idea that dignity is dynamic since he holds that dignity can "develop and become

---

82. Aquinas, *Nature and Grace*, 80.
83. Aquinas, *Virtues of Justice*, 54.
84. Aquinas, *Virtues of Justice*, 54.

stronger when the exercise of gifts of faith, hope and love, or it can become weaker when we sin and turn away from God."[85] This suggests that Aquinas holds to an idea of dignity that can be lost, regained, reduced and increased, which differs from views attesting that dignity is inherent, a variable that can neither be lost nor reduced. This, therefore, keeps us wondering if Aquinas agrees with the view of equality of dignity for all human beings.

Aquinas, like other scholars before and after him, is a good guide[86] through many thickets of confusion and misunderstanding when it comes to dignity. Some of these confusions, as mentioned here involved his view on the increase and reduction of dignity. On another occasion, he sees every creature as designed to enjoy[87] fellowship with God, which already has an inherent and fundamental dignity. One may want to agree and disagree with his assertion for various reasons. First, if by creatureliness a human person has inherent dignity, it applies, therefore, that by relating to God, as he puts it, dignity remains even with sin. Unlike others, however, Aquinas chooses to hold a kind of a dual view of human dignity.[88] When this view of dignity is placed with others, confusion on dignity matters increases, thereby questioning why a variable, such as dignity, has significant variation.

As noted elsewhere above on the confusion, misappropriation, and misplacement of the dignity concept, Aquinas makes useful contributions towards a better understanding of dignity in his moral philosophical writings. Unlike other views that assume human dignity as incoherent rhetoric that gets uncritically smuggled into public discourse by religious people, Aquinas sees dignity deeper and broader than his critics. For those holding views towards replacing dignity with autonomy, Aquinas chooses to differ. Instead, he focuses on the "crucial role in building respect for human life that

---

85. Guyette, "Thomas Aquinas and Recent," 119

86. Guyette, 113.

87. Guyette, 118.

88. On the one hand, within the frame of relationship with God, human dignity is to be found. While on the contrary, human dignity is dynamic that can be lost, reduced, increased, stronger, or weaker unless faith, love, and hope is applied. It suggests a kind of dignity that can be worked to earn (Guyette, "Thomas Aquinas and Recent"). It would also suggest that Aquinas' Catholic theology that remains suspicious of the reformation, informs his view of merit for salvation which by extension is mentioned in dignity. Root asserts that the reformation accusation that Catholic theology teaches some form of salvation by one's own works, and the teaching that our works can be meritorious is central to Aquinas' submission on dignity as a variable that can be reduced and be increased. (see Root, "Aquinas, Merit, and Reformation," 10)

dignity plays."[89] Such an idea encapsulates the relationality of dignity that as human beings, we depend on others who enhance our dignity in the same order which we do to them.

In summary of Aquinas' view of human dignity, a few things stood out. First, and perhaps most importantly, he attests to God as the bestower of human dignity. Second, he agrees with other scholars on the possession of dignity by every human person. Third, he slightly differs from others in that he believes in the increase, reduction or even loss of human dignity. Although this view sees dignity as something that depends on one's status, it seems contradictory when we consider his comments on grace through which humanity receives anything good.

3.3.3 Human Dignity and Moral Philosophy: Immanuel Kant (1724–1804)

Immanuel Kant, known for his academic contribution in moral philosophy, contributed enormously to the discourses on human dignity in the era of enlightenment. Kant is probably "the one who spoke to the concept of human dignity during the enlightenment era."[90] One of his crucial points in asserting dignity to all human beings is the idea of autonomy which has had several critiques over time. He did so in the light of a categorical imperative that he discerned in the rational being, and made famous this formulation of the principle of human dignity of doing to humanity either in your person or in the person of others, always as an "end and never as a means only."[91] Despite these critiques, which we shall outline below, Kant, is often considered a key figure, when it comes to the modern transition from social and political systems based on honour to those based on dignity, where honour is understood as an hierarchical measure of social value, and dignity is understood as the "inherent and equal worth of every individual."[92] He is also considered "the most influential moral theorist of modern times,"[93] "the father of the modern concept of human dignity and a crucial progenitor of the form of

---

89. Guyette, "Thomas Aquinas and Recent," 114.
90. Novak, "The Judeo-Christian Foundation," 110.
91. Novak, 110.
92. Bayefsky, "Dignity, Honour, and Human," 809.
93. Wood, "What is Kantian Ethics," 157.

human dignity that grounds human rights,"[94] and "human dignity is widely regarded as one of the most significant of his insights."[95] Thoughtfully so, human dignity was described during that era as "rational dignity,"[96] which helps to describe the process that shaped the recognition of human beings' worth between the seventeenth and the eighteenth centuries.

Being an influential figure in moral discourses, Kant identifies what lies at the heart of moral values and principles by providing a philosophical argument of our core moral conviction, while constructing a moral theory based on them.[97] In the *Groundwork for the Metaphysics of Morals,* two important imperatives are mentioned; first, the quality by which every person should be treated as an end and never merely as a means.[98] Second, act in such a way that you always treat humanity, whether in your person or the person of any other, never simply as a means, but always at the same as an end.

Although Kantian thoughts have had critics amongst scholars over the years, some have assessed his ideas differently. One of these insists that "dignity in Kant forms an integral part of Kant's moral thought, what is a sustained examination of the principle within the context of Kant's whole ethical theory."[99] That makes the Kantian view of dignity to mandate certain forms of respect from "all other individuals, society and the state."[100] Such respect, Donnelly finds, should come from the perspective that a human person is exalted above any price by being human, not to be valued merely as a means. This value he calls dignity (absolute inner worth), "is one by which a human person exacts respect for self from all other rational beings in the world."[101] One more important point in Kantian discourse of dignity involves the idea of autonomy. Described from the Enlightenment Era, a study insists that the dignity[102] of man in this sense came to be developed philosophically to portray man's capacity to be lord of his fate and the shaper of his future. That

---

94. Bayefsky, "Dignity, Honour, and Human," 811.
95. Jones, *Kant's Principle of Personality*, 3.
96. Andorno and Pele, "Human Dignity," 6.
97. Wood, "What is Kantian Ethics," 158.
98. Kant,"Groundwork for the Metaphysics."
99. Jones, *Kant's Principle*, 3.
100. Donnelly, "Human Rights and Human," 21.
101. Donnelly, "Human Rights and Human," 21, 22.
102. McCrudden, "Human Dignity," 657.

was, perhaps the basis of describing rational beings as persons whose nature already marks them out as ends in themselves, as something that may not be used merely as means. In all the above, the Kantian assertions, particularly on human dignity and autonomy, have created some controversies among scholars. A few Kantian scholars, as discussed below, have, however, tried to make clarifications to these issues.

One of Kantian's moral theories under scrutiny has been the "dignity of human persons that is said to be commonly misunderstood."[103] Such misunderstanding, Sensen observes, is due to the misconception of what Kant meant when he refers to dignity. He asserts that Kant conceives dignity as sublimity or the highest elevation of something over something else which expresses that something is "raised above" all else. What is raised here, however, depends on the context in which Kant uses dignity. While referring to human dignity specifically when Sensen posits that Kant envisions that "human beings are elevated over the rest of nature by virtue of being free."[104] This freedom does not refer to independent existence without others but suggests the reason people should be "united by ends that they freely and rationally pursue in common."[105] Pursuance of a common good here includes seeking the good of others as for ourselves. This suggests an idea of relationality that subverts the critiques of autonomy of human-independent from other social realities.

The relationality of human beings with each other is central in Kantian dignity discourses. He regards dignity as "what refers to a relational property of being elevated, and not to a non-relational value property."[106] Cited in a study, Giovanni Bognetti's explanation of human beings as autonomous does not refer to social or political ranking, as dignity was considered at some point. Instead, it is a view that has every[107] human being without exception, affirming the relational element. Moreover, "Kant's contribution to the development of dignity consists in attributing the equality ßof the human family with unconditional worth grounded in moral autonomy."[108] What this

---

103. Sensen, "Kant's Conception," 309.
104. Sensen, "Kant's Conception," 310.
105. Wood, "What is Kantian Ethics?" 162.
106. Sensen, "Kant's Conception," 310.
107. Bayefsky, "Dignity, Honor," 811.
108. Bayefsky, 811.

means is that Kant's idea of relational anthropology regarding human dignity subverts the critics who assume that the idea suggested self-autonomy.

For those claiming that Kant's notion of autonomy excludes relationality, Sensen uses three paradigms to explain their confusion. First, the contemporary paradigm of human dignity. He holds that it is a "non-relational value property human beings possess that generates normative arguments to respect them."[109] Second, the archaic paradigm of dignity which is based on the ancient Roman usage of *Dignitas*. At that time, dignity was a "political concept that referred to the elevated position on the higher rank of the politically powerful in society."[110] Such dignity, as already mentioned elsewhere, was exclusively applied to a few persons who had the tendency to be lost and be regained. Third, the traditional[111] paradigm, which applies *Dignitas* to all human beings with the thought that human beings have an elevated position in nature by reason. Additionally, to what places human beings above other creatures is what Fischer mentions, as cited by de Villiers, that human beings are created in the image of God.[112] It is from these two qualities that human beings are said to be elevated above other creatures and nature, with the responsibility to take care and not to destroy nature and other creatures. It does not, however, guarantee that human beings' exalted position calls for social ranking over other human beings – as autonomy might be understood. Rather, the reason to enhance the wellbeing of others. Simply put, this is the reason for not only identifying, but protecting, and promoting the reality therein the worth of every human being.

Autonomy exemplifies the power to act independently without the consent or help of others. Human beings, as Kant describes, are autonomous in themselves because of the freedom and their ability to reason. Such views have been under scrutiny by the proponents of disability theology in recent times.[113] de Villiers problematizes this notion through a critical consideration of Kant's placement of human beings above any price or equivalent but is recognized and treated as an end in itself which is the core of morality.[114] This

---

109. Sensen, "Kant's Conception," 312.
110. Sensen, 312.
111. Sensen, 313.
112. de Villiers, "The Recognition," 265.
113. Reinders, "Understanding Humanity and Disability."
114. de Villiers, "The Recognition of Human Dignity," 264.

does not mean a separatist idea with human beings to place others, say the abled persons, above others, say the disabled. Instead, as Kant puts it, "it is an all-inclusive notion involving both the disabled and the abled bodies in the economy of wellbeing and its enhancement."[115] Since the dignity being talked about is specifically human dignity and not of objects, it clears any boundaries to what such a human being could be. Whether an embryo, or a new-born, as de Villiers puts it, or mentally handicapped, as Koopman puts it, their meeting ground is simply, "being created in the image of God," hence guaranteeing them dignity.[116] It is not dignity that one loses because of social or political attainment or reality, but an inherent one, to which both Kant and contemporary Christian theology, attest.

3.3.4 Human Dignity and Theological Ethics

Although human dignity is a key concept in both secular and theological ethics, its meaning has, for some reason, been taken for granted.[117] It is one of the few philosophical notions that has gained currency beyond specialist academic discourses, hence, it has found its way into our colloquial vocabulary.[118] Despite its prominence in philosophical discourses, human dignity is still regarded as a source of trouble with several features not fit into one coherent ethical concept, which explains "why philosophers tend to ignore or circumvent the concept."[119] In theological ethics, however, arguments abound asking questions concerning the notion of human dignity. Some of these inquiries relate to, "when does an individual acquire dignity," and whether or not such dignity could be lost and be regained.[120] These understandings from both philosophy and theology offer some ideas to deeply seek what human dignity entails. A variety of concepts, including human dignity, historically metamorphoses in meaning and application. This assures that both the concept of human dignity, human rights, and responsibility are concepts that gained their distinctiveness under the influence of new developments

---

115. de Villiers, 265.
116. de Villiers, 265; Koopman, "Some Theological," 178.
117. Kirchhoffer, *Human Dignity*, xiii.
118. Stoecker, "Three Crucial Turns."
119. Stoecker, 7.
120. Kirchhoffer, *Human Dignity*, 3.

and philosophical ideas at the advent of modernity.[121] The very reason why research warns that it is unacceptable for Christians to uncritically embrace these concepts or claim them as part of their Christian heritage.[122] This is because human dignity was only acknowledged in European mainline churches after the end of World War II.[123] This might be surprising because of how the churches have "taken themselves for being advocates, insisting on its Christian roots."[124] There is also no reason for Christians to reject them out of hand because they are formidable to Christian ethics and belief. Their reason for the warning is that those concepts have existed in other discourses as well, where they were perceived differently from what Judeo-Christianity understands them to be.

Before this period, human dignity was denoted as the rank of honour such that it referred merely to the "status of a dignitary."[125] Such an understanding of human dignity had much concentration on the social statuses of individuals. Moreover, such understanding places "prime emphasis on one's duties."[126] That conception submits that human beings were distinguished from nature by reason and freedom, thus placed above others. If such is what human dignity entails, it is nothing more than a privilege or prerogative, or even simply a sense of decorum.

3.4 Perspectives on Human Dignity

This section discusses some perspectives that could be useful in ascertaining human dignity. There is a variety of categorisation of human dignity of which not all could provide the needed help to this study.[127] However, Nordenfelt's

---

121. de Villiers, "The Recognition of Human Dignity."
122. Oberdorfer, "Human Dignity."
123. Körtner, "Dem Risiko Trotzen."
124. Oberdorfer, "Human Dignity," 231.
125. Moltmann, *On Human Dignity*, ix.
126. Sensen, "Human Dignity," 83.
127. For instance, (Andorno and Pele, "Human Dignity.") outline categorise human dignity into five (5) stages thus; moral dignity, spiritual dignity, rational dignity, social dignity, and human dignity *stricto sensu*. Although these categories could fit into the ongoing study, only particular reference is made. Another form of categorisation is by (Galvin and Todres, "Dignity as Honour-Wound"). They see human dignity from seven (7) dimensions namely, spatial dignity, temporal dignity, embodies dignity, interpersonal dignity, mood dignity, identity dignity, and finitude dignity. Also, (Sensen, "Human Dignity") presents two dimensions of

categorization of dignity in what he called "varieties of dignity" is, however, applied here. In his assessment, four models of identifying dignity are presented. The first, he calls the dignity of merit, which involves a person who has a rank or holds an office that entails a set of rights. Such a person has a special dignity called merit.[128] This sort of dignity is called "the aristocratic, wherein dignity is perceived as outstanding honour or high standing."[129] In addition, Nordenfelt sees dignity as a moral statute, a form of dignity that is dimensional in that it varies from an extremely high position to an extremely low one. It is dependent on the thoughts and deeds of the subject. Third, is the "dignity of identity."[130] This kind of dignity, Nordenfelt suggests, does not depend upon the subject's merit – as the first one above, and has nothing to do with the person's moral status. Instead, "it is a dignity that can be taken from us by external events, by the acts of other people as well as by injury, illness, and old age."[131] Ober classifies such dignity as "civic dignity comprising of democratic practices informed by law and sustained by political culture."[132] The fourth aspect of dignity is the dignity of *menchenwürde*, a kind of dignity that differs from the previous three above. It is a dignity that we all as humans have, or are assumed to have, by being humans. It is "especially human value with which all humans have to the same degree."[133] This form of dignity is connected to the Kantian conception of intrinsic worth referred to as the "universal human dignity."[134] Perhaps, this universal dignity, in the words of Ober, and *menchenwürde*, in the words of Nordenfelt, becomes the ground from which theological notions of dignity holds. Speaking from the image of God, every creature has an intrinsic dignity that is inherent without boundaries.

---

human dignity namely, traditional and contemporary. He links the traditional model back to Cicero, Kant, and other thinkers, while the contemporary model took effect from the wake of twentieth century which later found its ground in the United Nation Charter.

128. Nordenfelt, "Varieties of Dignity," 71.
129. Ober, "Three Kinds of Dignity," 1.
130. Nordenfelt, "Varieties of Dignity," 72.
131. Nordenfelt, 74.
132. Ober, "Three Kinds of Dignity," 1.
133. Nordenfelt, "Varieties of Dignity," 77.
134. Ober, "Three Kinds of Dignity," 1.

3.4.1 The Image of God (Ontological) Perspective of Human Dignity

According to the structure of this study, this is the first model of human dignity taken from Nordenfelt's *menchenwürde* of dignity. It is a form of dignity embedded in human persons and based on human creatureliness. Earlier proponents of this view of dignity include Cicero, who used the Aristocratic Roman term *Dignitas* to universalise it to all human beings.[135] This alludes to the perception that human dignity, seen as common to everyone by being humans, has had a "long history before it was acknowledged after the end of World War II in European mainline churches."[136] On its reception by the church, the emphasis has rested on the image and likeness of God as foundational to human dignity.[137] This, then, gives human beings a sense of relationship and connectivity with God than other animals and keeps them closer to the creator. Human beings become God's companion in furthering God's completed act of creation with the responsibility to take care of what was already in existence. In this sense, the responsibility to respect, protect, and promote the existence and wellbeing of humanity began right then. From this backdrop, we would deduce the notion of human worth and its embeddedness in the image of God.

Human dignity, embedded in the image of God is a right that human beings, as God's image-bearers, have. From the theological stance, a study affirms the claim by describing humankind as "God's property."[138] This property, which was obtained from creation, becomes the first concept that defines humanity in a Christian theological context. This explains why humans belong to their creator (God) and why they are "God's workmanship with obligations

---

135. Sensen, "Human Dignity"; McCrudden, "Human Dignity."
136. Oberdorfer, "Human Dignity," 231.
137. It is also interesting to note that creation in the image and likeness of God as the basis for human dignity calls for some clarity with words often used. One of these ideas suggests three words, namely quality, duty, and relation. Although these three concepts have a great deal of history from the creation narrative, none can independently represent dignity in isolation (Oberdorfer, "Human Dignity"). For instance, if relation regards human beings as images of God because they relate to God, because of their existence in the face of God, and because of their turning to God, it would side-line people void of such relationality. In fact, such arguments could hold in terms of justification. This could go on with other variables, duty, and quality. But the idea here is to see and accept them as ways dignity could be promoted and not as ways to increase or reduce dignity, whatsoever.
138. Vorster, "A Theological Perspective," 2

to doing God's will."[139] In turn, this gives an expression that human beings have a God-given property in their person by this connection as mentioned above. This also means that their being is not the product of their work but what they owe to their creator, which limits their control either at the beginning or the end of their existence.[140] From this backdrop, we see how the uniqueness of human relational value with their creator is expressed, which gives human beings the capacity to actively relate to God, on the one hand. On the other hand, they relate to the whole creation in structures of "interdependence such that it creates room for co-creativeness."[141] This implies that God's image-bearers become part of the economy of creation whose role relates largely to the enhancement of what has already been made. From the above connection of human worth from creation, it can be used as a theological framework to explain human dignity.

The use of human dignity as a theological parameter for assessing the worth of human beings was, at a point in time, a concern which broke out as a result of an assessment of the conflict that broke out from churches about human rights. Human rights were considered to carry the spirit of secularization, representing anthropology, which focused on the individual without reference to God and was void of the commandment of brotherly love. This, therefore, granted human rights a certain kind of distrust because of its secular origins. With the idea of human rights as both separatist and dichotomizing between individuals, it made an outright acceptance of human dignity a difficult venture. The challenge of accepting human dignity as a common concept that would see every human being with equity was, however, made possible on the basis that there would be a theological concept to portray it. Such a concept is believed to "accept, accommodate, describe and present human beings as simply humans, hence, the theory of the image of God."[142]

Following that argument, the image of God perfectly suited the challenge because of some reasons. First, by being created in the image of God, it means human beings are "addressed by God and are given the ability to respond

---

139. Vorster, 2.
140. Soulen and Woodhead, *God and Human Dignity*, 6.
141. Soulen and Woodhead, 49.
142. Oberdorfer, "Human Dignity," 231.

to the word of the Creator."¹⁴³ In part, being addressed by God here has no exclusion, but portrays an all-inclusive perception for all humanity. Often, arguments abound, counteracting the reality that all human family is a carrier of dignity. One such argument is commonly found in contemporary Christian ethical discourses, giving rise to the crisis in dignity talk between proponents of "biological and technological modifications in enhancing human dignity."[144] The two concepts, biological and technological modifications, concerning human dignity, are geared towards enabling enhancement, a concept which seeks to make something, in this case, human dignity, better than it is already known. Arising from evaluating human dignity as such, the problem of dignity talk[145] is created.

Being created in the image of God applies to relationality[146] between God and humanity and between human beings with each other. This form of relating signifies caring and compassion. By caring, it involves living to fulfil the mandate of stewardship with eagerness to ensure the wellbeing of other humans. Here, caring for others manifests and is modified by how one cares for oneself. As such, caring for what makes life meaningful and worth living would mean seeing that those other human beings, by being human, have similar expectations and ambitions. Similarly, compassion signifies a sense of mutual existence. In this sense, the construction of the individual entity is reconstructed and replaced by mutuality. By this, the sustenance of others and what makes them have their self-worth, or simply put, their dignity, is prioritized above other things. When applied to human dignity, both caring and compassion would signify the eagerness to ensure mutual coexistence regarding respecting and promoting the worth of a human person. Such mutuality is an invitation that human beings are called to "communion in speech with God."[147]

The second reason authenticating the image in human dignity discourse is the "commission to multiply, implying that humanity is meant to have a future."[148] By having a future, humanity is called to planning and the suste-

---

143. Soulen and Woodhead, *God and Human Dignity*, 50.
144. Kirchhoffer, "Human Dignity," 375.
145. Kirchhoffer, "Human Dignity," 376.
146. Soulen and Woodhead, 50.
147. Soulen and Woodhead, 50.
148. Soulen and Woodhead, 50.

nance of this future. The sustainability of this future entails providing and cultivating the mechanisms with the enhancement of human worth and respect for human dignity as pointers. By this, humanity becomes the custodians to ensure that the world becomes habitable for humans – and other animals.[149] Within such a view of making the world habitable, we make it home even though we are not home yet.[150]

Third, the image of God theory holds that humans have the "dominion to cultivate the earth."[151] By cultivating the earth, human beings have the liberty to treat the earth in response to God's intended mission and vision, and not in autonomous sovereignty. God's mission for humanity and the earth includes that all creatures, particularly human beings, live to exhibit their potential and glorify God. That is what Calvin meant by the expression that the flourishing of humanity is the glory of God. The deprivation of such freedom has resulted in unjust and unequal treatment of others for self-gratification.

The reasons highlighted here place the significant distinction that human beings have for being created in the image of God. In connection with human dignity discourse, this spelt the origin of human dignity from creation, suggesting that every human being has dignity.

3.4.2 Inherent and Inviolable Perspective of Human Dignity

Holding that human beings are God's image-bearers authenticates that they have a dignity embedded in them that can neither be lost nor be violated. It is an element received from creation that distinguishes humanity from other creation.[152] It is such dignity that is equated to the worth of being human, without which, one loses their sense of humanness. Alluding to such a view

---

149. Soulen and Woodhead, 51.

150. The growth of the idea that we are home but not home yet is taken as an excerpt from the ecological ethics with the idea of taking care of the earth. Perhaps, here we could include with specification, taking care and enhancing the wellbeing of fellow human beings. Conradie develops this idea that we have to recognize that "we are at home on earth" – even though in the eschatological sense, we are not home yet- since this would help to overcome human alienation from the rest of earth community ("Human Distinctiveness," 5). Stating this, he sees being at home on this planet and knowing our place as humans implies the need to recognize and accept human limitations which we have to learn to live with so as to give limits to growth of both fellow humans and other forms of creation ("Human Distinctiveness," 5). In respect to human dignity discourse here, it gives a reminder that the work of enhancing human lives that ensures their wellbeing and flourishing be done as that modifies our true existence at home on earth.

151. Soulen and Woodhead, 50.

152. Moltmann, *On Human Dignity*.

among the apartheid campaigners in South Africa, it helped South Africans to once more believe that "all human beings possess dignity – hence an affirmation that *humanitas* and *Dignitas* are synonymous."[153] Such a form of dignity is what Andorno and Pele call human dignity *stricto sensu* to mean that all human beings have intrinsic worthiness and inalienable rights by the mere fact of being human.[154]

The term inherent dignity is further explained to mean "involved in the essential character of something 'intrinsic,' 'permanent or characteristic attribute of something.'"[155] When applied with human dignity, it connotes an inseparable worth from the human condition that is embedded and cannot be lost. Andorno, therefore, insists that dignity is not an accidental quality of some human beings, or a value derived from some specific personal features, but rather, an unconditional worth that every human person possesses simply by being human. Such dignity is further described as that which human beings already have, which implies that every person has a "worth equal to the worth of every other human person."[156] The inviolable dimension of human dignity follows from the previous. It sees human dignity as that which cannot be lost or denied by others because of its embeddedness in the image of God. While it is undebatable that human dignity is open to abuse and misappropriation, yet its relatedness guarantees that it cannot be denied whatsoever.

The inherent and inviolable idea of human dignity is also argued from the perspective of interrelatedness between human beings and the difference with other species. This dimension makes a distinction between human dignity and personal dignity as all related to humanity. This means that "being members of a species that is different from other species through the possession of certain characteristics gives human beings dignity."[157] By this description, he agrees that human beings could live on, though some members die, yet they offer an image of the flourishing of our full humanity, which he calls "human

---

153. Koopman, "Some Theological and Anthropological," 177.
154. Andorno and Pele, "Human Dignity," 4.
155. Andorno, "Human Dignity," 228.
156. Kirchhoffer, "Human Dignity in Contemporary," 19.
157. Meilaender, "Neither Beast Nor God," 3.

dignity."[158] This way of understanding human dignity has to be inclusive.[159] This is not only aggregable on the linking relationship between human dignity as embedded in the image of God but emphasizes that such dignity is only taken seriously when it applies to all human beings equally.[160] Here, Huber is right to emphasise not only the talk about human dignity for every human being but also its equality as well. In this case, when dignity is recognized, and perhaps enhanced without an equalizing dimension, would mean a form of denial of such dignity.

These two perspectives of understanding human dignity suggest that it is given and cannot be taken from the bearer because it is embedded. For any reason, undermining one's dignity signifies denying them their sense of being human in its truest form.

3.4.3 The Social and Psychological Perspective of Human Dignity

Following from the previous perspective, several critics have chosen to subscribe to none of the above. Instead, they believe human dignity is an entity that could be given, increased, reduced, or taken away from a human being for some reason. Accordingly, that idea of human dignity appeared in the nineteenth century and was explicitly or implicitly used to discuss social and political issues and to fight for a fully realized citizenship for everybody.[161] It is a view that sees humanity as a quantifiable variable, differing from what Kant had said that human beings are unquantifiable entities (see section 3.2.3). The proponents of this view neither agree in the equality of humanity nor equality of human dignity – as suggested above. Put simply, there are views that see dignity as something human beings would have to make an effort to acquire and maintain to avoid losing it. Such form of dignity is described as social dignity.[162]

The psychological view of human dignity is one that "associates a person with ideas of pride, self-respect, and integrity."[163] Here, dignity has more to do

---

158. Meilaender, "Neither Beast Nor God," 4.
159. Huber, "The Dignity," 438.
160. Huber, "The Dignity," 438.
161. Ardorno and Pele, "Human Dignity."
162. Andorno and Pele, "Human Dignity."
163. Kirchhoffer, *Human Dignity*, 88.

with how a person thinks of themselves than what others think of them. On the contrary, the social view of human dignity has to do with social norms and morals that are acceptable in the society in which a human person lives. One's dignity, in this sense, increases when he/she lives and behaves within the societal norms, or else stands the chance of a reduced dignity when their actions contradict the norms of society.

The social theory of human dignity holds that dignity is given to persons by their social realities acceptable by a given society. Two concepts have been adopted, namely self-worth and behaviour to describe these social realities. The interactive dimension of human dignity speaks "both of human behaviour in the world, and the observation that human beings act and justify their actions according to societal mores and moral norms."[164] Such conduct, he later described as "dignified."[165] They either give an individual a sense of acceptance or rejection, respect, or disrespect, so much so that one's judgment of self is determined by such descriptions. In the case of the negative attestation of one's behaviour as a pointer to their dignity, it would mean a disregard for the human quest to being treated well. When such occurs, we suffer.[166] Such description of suffering has a negative connotation on both the individual who is not treated well and their relationship with others. They find that this comes with a failure to not only being in a relationship with others but not being able to see, feel, understand, and be included, as these could generate a sense of self-worth, which could enhance our selfhood in the way we get treated by others. When that happens, we are able to "see our own dignity reflected in the eyes of others."[167]

It can be contested in today's world that gaining acceptance by setting and meeting certain standards is becoming the norm. From the economic worldview, it is the capitalist idea requiring an individual's worth such that the behavioural pattern is the determinant factor. Perhaps, from the religious perspective, one's moral standing in the faith stands out, which in some instances, is the measuring standard in which an individual is valued, respected and promoted. Such quests rest on the social reality that people

---

164. Kirchhoffer, *Human Dignity*, 21–22.
165. Kirchhoffer, "Human Dignity," 378.
166. Hicks, *Dignity: The Essential Role*, xv.
167. Hicks, xv.

generally praise what they believe to be morally good behaviour.[168] In part, the desire for acquiring praises is associated with the potential to acquire dignity through any of such behavioural pattern. Often, the desire to fulfil such potential is seen in making tireless attempts to attain some dignity in the form of self-worth[169] through striving for moral behaviour that society applauds. In a sense, this signifies that we acquire and realize dignity through our moral[170] behaviour. This view could see the treatment of an individual, who lacks morally acceptable behaviour, as having less or no dignity. In that case, it contrasts the ontological and inalienable views that see human dignity as a possession acquired by being human. Contrary to this view, Hicks makes some clarification. She agrees to the fact that everyone deserves to be treated with dignity and sees dignity as something we all deserve regardless of what we do. Equally, she frowns at the social reality that treats people based on moral behaviour because of any wrong they might have committed. Such treatment, in her view, only perpetuates the cycle of indignity.[171]

Following the social dimension of human dignity is the psychological view, which sees dignity, not in terms of behaviour but from the lens of self-worth of an individual. We should be reminded that these two views object the ontological view of dignity while proposing dignity as something one could acquire, which could either increase, decrease or be lost. In the first instance, the psychological view of human dignity signifies a sense of pride[172] and self-worth[173] on oneself. While the quest for pride and self-worth might refer to a form of the egoistic notion in some spheres, here it is a quest for one's worth as a human being living a meaningful life and worthy of respect by others.[174] Kirchhoffer, citing Bagaric and Allan, sees human dignity, in this sense, as an empowering concept that confers rights and entitlements and protects interests.[175] The idea of empowering and entitlement calls for

---

168. Kirchhoffer, *Human Dignity*, 22.
169. Kirchhoffer, 24.
170. Kirchhoffer, "Human Dignity," 379.
171. Hicks, *Dignity: The Essential Role*, 5.
172. Kirchhoffer, *Human Dignity*, 88.
173. Kirchhoffer, "Human Dignity," 378.
174. Kirchhoffer, 378.
175. Bagaric and Allan, "The Vacuous Concept," cited in Kirchhoffer, "Becoming What You Are," 45.

an agreement with another view that supports technological advancement in the promotion of human dignity.

The enhancement perception of human dignity collectively subscribes to the notion of dignity as something we acquire. In some spheres, it seeks to portray dignity as something that can be improved either technologically or biologically. Thus, Kirchhoffer explains enhancement with human dignity as it applies to making "something better than it was before, but distinct from therapy, which involves making some abnormality more normal."[176] Enhancement, in this sense, is about betterment, similar to the description of reconstruction when Mugambi discusses the need for a shift in African theological perception of salvation from liberation.[177] Mugambi's emphasis is on bettering the knowledge of salvation by African theology that would serve the African people by presenting salvific understanding in practical terms.

In the context of such debates, the proponents of the ontological view of dignity see enhancement as a violation of human dignity. On the contrary, those supporting the enhancement debate claim that human dignity obliges enhancement, thus not improving it is a violation.[178] In either case, going by the ontological view, the enhancement theory of human dignity would be a violation of human dignity. In part, it neglects the inherent value of worth a human person has by being human. This could develop an idea that either sees God's good creation as not good enough, thus needing some improvement, or not subscribe to the equality of all human beings as others do not live to the expected reality that gets applauded. When these premises are true, it violates the human rights to dignity as contained in the Universal Declaration of 1948, which is to be discussed later (see section 3.5).

The totality of the social and psychological dimensions of human dignity, however, has some conclusive views. While the proponents of these views perceive human dignity as something that can be acquired, reduced and enhanced, it is also problematic. In part, they pay no or less attention to recognizing the humanness in a human being. Such neglects fail to acknowledge that each human being has something someone else lacks, and we each

---

176. Kirchhoffer, "Human Dignity," 375.
177. Mugambi, "From Liberation to Reconstruction," 36.
178. Kirchhoffer, "Human Dignity," 376.

lack something someone else has, which we could gain by interaction.[179] Otherwise, the sense of mutual interrelatedness of human beings fails.

The social and psychological perspectives portray human dignity from a more personalized dimension than the universalized point of view (see section 3.2 above). While the psychological perspective equates dignity to pride, self-respect and integrity, the social dimension gives a description involving self-worth and behaviour. These views present human dignity as something that can be reduced, enhanced or even be lost depending on one's social realities and contributions to society. Such an understanding of human dignity contravenes the universal perception that sees every human person as having dignity without boundaries.

3.4.4 Humanist Perspective of Human Dignity

The humanist dimension of human dignity involves emotional factors that deprive an individual of having self-esteem and worth. From a theological perspective, a humanist is one who finds resources of their tradition the most relatively adequate means to articulate and answer vexing human dilemmas about how rightly to orient life in the world.[180] This insight directs our inquiry in the following section regarding the humanist perspective on human dignity.

In categorizing why the pursuit of dignity has become prominent in human society, it is suggested that "protection from fear" is one of the reasons.[181] That is, a fear of some demeaning punishment that reduces the subject to merely "something" and not a human being. It is not fear of some dreaded events that consume but of "some degrading punishment."[182] Such is the fear that creates tension in human beings, whose condition projects hopelessness to humanness for what might turn out. As to the quest for dignity, in this sense, it is for "self-preservation."[183] Such dignity grants that one lives with agreements that do not reduce them to slaves of imposition, but that are seen and acknowledged as partners of consent.[184] It involves allowing people the

---

179. Sacks, "The Dignity of," 14–15.
180. Schweiker, "The Ethics of Responsibility," 255.
181. Soyinka, *The Climate of Fear*, 85.
182. Soyinka, 85.
183. Soyinka, 87.
184. Soyinka, 88.

chance to be and feel they are human beings, to protect them from feeling like objects.

In another sense, Soyinka attests to dignity as being about recognizing, identifying, and respecting the worth of others and not about having influential power.[185] Power is important when it is applied appropriately to enhance human wellbeing and an orderly society, but when used as a tool for intimidation, it becomes oppressive to others. Important as dignity and its quest are, even in instances of powerlessness, there is resistance. It is the influence of power, on the one hand, and its abuse, on the other hand, that has given space that public morality, especially in the Nigerian context, is in a lack.

For some time now, the experience of North-Eastern Nigeria is that which has, and still experiences vicissitudes of life.[186] This situation, which has spread to other parts of Nigeria, leaves countless people, especially women and children, in a situation where they feel "life is no longer worth living as they call on God daily for help."[187] Similar to the situation in Nigeria, a South African newspaper describing such a society indicated that "we have for a long time been part of such a sick society – one that kills children, murders old people and where right is wrong and wrong is right."[188] Additionally, Akper describes the current situation in North-Eastern Nigeria as a society where the killers are protected, kidnappers operate at will with the death toll not causing remorseful attention.[189] At the heart of this mischief, the inhabitants are rendered helpless, disorientated, and are baffled. Where such happenings continue, they must be condemned as morally reprehensible.[190]

What comes to mind during these recurrent experiences is the ways to safeguard human lives and property. At some point, reprisal attacks seem to loom as the solution. On other occasions, peaceful speeches and conversations ensue. Seeing that these steps have not done enough to ensure a society void of such public immorality, new suggestions are emerging. The emergence of these new ways of thinking spring not only from concerns on the continuous loss of human lives but the socioeconomic effects leading to "hatred, hostility,

---

185. Soyinka, 88.
186. Akper, "An Ethos of Hospitality," 284.
187. Akper, "Is God in Nigeria," 67.
188. Vosloo, "Public Morality," 69.
189. Akper, 284.
190. Bagu, "Human Rights," 210.

lawlessness, the indignity of life and disorder."[191] Indeed, "the challenge posed by the moral crisis does not merely ask for peaceful co-existence or some abstract plea for the community, but an ethos of hospitality."[192]

In agreement with Vosloo's sentiments, Akper attests to there being no form of public morality needed in Nigeria today than the ethos of hospitality.[193] Akper sees this from the difficulty emanating from radical religious and ethnic intolerance looming across Nigerian societies. Attesting to this, Akper insists that the Nigerian situation is not only void of peace, but the absence of total hospitality. He sees the absence of hospitality as the root cause of cruelty, and hostility in relationships within any given society.[194] Without hospitality, challenging economic justice, racism, xenophobia, lack of communication, the recognition of the rights *and dignity* of another, would be elusive.[195] He, thus, ascribes to hospitality as a prerequisite for a moral public life.

In most cases, there is confusion in differentiating between attesting to morality as a concept or a different perception of it. In either case, Akper responds not to a lack of moral teachers or communities where morals could be taught, but understanding[196] what the right morality is, and the lack of appropriate human beings to teach and practice such morality. In the case where diverse views of morality are irreconcilable, the resultant effect is a society with disorderliness that is void of morality. The responsibility to safeguard society, both the present and the future, however, becomes a challenge of the present generation and how they perceive threats to public moral lives. To this end, it is argued that acting responsibly to avert the destruction of the future life of humankind would involve acting and relating so that the other, too, could have life, dignity, and strive for a better life of future generations by acting quite responsibly today.[197]

Putting together conditions necessary for enhancing human life and, perhaps recognizing their dignity, is a matter of interdependence. Similarly, as established elsewhere above, human beings are interdependent such that

---

191. Akper, "An Ethos of Hospitality," 285.
192. Vosloo, 66.
193. Akper, 289.
194. Akper, 289.
195. Vosloo, 66.
196. Akper, 290.
197. Akper, 293.

each is a receiver and a giver. Here, appreciating the worth of one's life and its value, calls for recognition that the life of the other has a worth, hence, deserves respect and protection. This idea calls for reasons not to destroy a human person but gives reasons to both protect and desire to see them go and live well.[198] Perhaps, the protection here includes the sense of giving which is an essential part of human dignity.

In another sense, human dignity calls for recognizing the worth of others as an obligation to them. This obligation entails that we appreciate the value of human life not to destroy but protect it the best way we can.[199] This could also be seen by appreciating the value of human life as something of unquantifiable value and the realisation that every human being wants to live and see their lives go better.[200] In this sense, recognizing the value of human life becomes an act of bestowing honour to each member of society, which ensures equal dignity.[201]

From the humanist perspective, a few emphases on what human dignity entails are outlined. First, that dignity is denied in the presence of intimidation that causes fear. Second, dignity is enhanced by recognition and identification of the worth of others. Third, dignity is enhanced with the consideration of the wellbeing of others through an ethos of hospitality. These put together, suggest that a humanist perspective of human dignity focuses on the emotional elements of a human person.

3.4.5 Christian Anthropological Perception of Human Dignity

In this section, we shall consider what constitutes the Christian anthropological perception of human dignity. In doing so, the works of Nico Koopman, particularly his assertion on the lack of provision of basic human needs as a violation of human dignity, is discussed. Similarly, Bedford-Strohm's work on human dignity is explored.

Koopman grounds his discussions on human dignity with emphasis on the African continent, a context he is very familiar with. In so doing, he

---

198. Scanlon, "What We Owe," 104.
199. Scanton, 104.
200. Scanlon, 104.
201. Sacks, *The Dignity of*, 120.

categorizes some factors which serve as violators of human dignity in Africa in some ways, namely inequality, violence, illness, and the various forms of prejudices.[202] While these factors directly have effects on the human person, he deems it fit to define the concept of human dignity from a trinitarian perspective. He asserts, thus, "we have dignity because God became human in Jesus Christ and redeemed us; we have dignity because the Holy Spirit, as God at work in the world, is actualizing in and through us the new humanity that is a reality in Jesus Christ."[203] Such a description, he finds, gives us the idea that the faith we profess has a strong human element which includes, but is not limited to "the flourishing and wellbeing, worth and value, honour and dignity of all human beings."[204] The flourishing and wellbeing of human persons is key to their human dignity. Africa is, however, enmeshed with issues that are dehumanizing both in nature and praxis as we shall see below.

3.4.5.1 Engrossed Social Inequality

Social inequality refers to the inadequate distribution of resources which this study calls basic human needs. Talking of the lack of, or poor distribution of these basic needs, Koopman worries that the African continent is more overwhelmed than other regions of the world, such that he sees a violation of human dignity in several dimensions as discussed below.[205]

Koopman envisages human dignity violation in the existing forms of social separation, which he considers as dehumanizing.[206] In a flashback on the apartheid experience in South Africa, he describes the disorientation it caused both the Black and the White people. According to him, the apartheid, disrupted the notion of human equality by dehumanizing both the parties while causing disillusionment about the value and worth of a human being.[207] Since this gab was created, the need for re-humanizing these two groups towards freeing the Whites from superiority and the Blacks from

---

202. Koopman, "Human Dignity in Africa," 240.
203. Koopman, "Some Theological," 180
204. Koopman, "Human Dignity in Africa," 240.
205. Koopman, "Human Dignity in Africa." See some of these dimensions from (Soyinka, *The Climate of Fear*) to "anti-humanism," "reduction in self-esteem," "nullification of human status" and "humiliation"
206. Koopman, "Some Theological."
207. Koopman, 178.

inferiority[208] complexes surfaced. Moreover, the dehumanizing description of others as "unhygienic, delinquent, criminal, cheaters and immoral"[209] were also of great concern to their humanity. This sprang the need to redeem the abused image of God to give South Africans "a more human face."[210] It also gave and still gives room for social disorientation in many parts of Africa today, which Koopman says "is still high."[211] In environments where such practices continue to prevail in today's African societies, issues of xenophobia, homophobia, and others of that sort are experienced.[212] In fact, Koopman could not reconcile this with the alerting and criticizing tradition of Belhar confessions that it seems to suggest that "we have forgotten the past."[213]

Citing from the Belhar confessions, Koopman reminds us that the confessions have a tradition that recognizes the forgetfulness that makes us seekers of amnesia.[214] While referring to the South African and the African experience at large, it shows that values proposed for a new society have been replaced.[215] This form of replacement has given way to other social crimes perpetrating human dignity. In South Africa, for example, the systemic crime of apartheid gave rise to a culture of violence that emanates from the victims of marginalization and poverty, involved in the organized criminality of various scores.[216] While these activities continue to define the society, the extent of dehumanisation that ensues becomes alarming. Such activities have blinded us so much that we have failed to recognize that the faith we profess has at its heart and core the flourishing and wellbeing, worth the value, esteem and dignity of all humans, and the rest of creation.

Following the human sense of forgetfulness and non-recognition of the faith we profess, there has been a failure to celebrate unity in diversity. Unity begets avenues for acceptance and compassion while creating a feeling of belonging and togetherness. Compassion also enables the recognition of

---

208. Koopman, 178.
209. Koopman, "Human Dignity in Africa," 244.
210. Koopman, "Some Theological," 178.
211. Koopman, "Human Dignity in Africa," 244.
212. Koopman, 244.
213. Koopman, "Belhar," 38.
214. Koopman, "Belhar," 38.
215. Koopman, 38.
216. Koopman, "Human Dignity in Africa," 245.

diversity, and through it, sees that humans share more in common than they differ. Referring to human dignity in this sense, Koopman uses the three articles of the Belhar confessions, namely unity, reconciliation, and justice.[217] According to him, where these three prevail, there the dignity of all life is acknowledged, affirmed, and actualized. However, such realisation would only occur when there is unity in diversity of ideas and beliefs, with the goal of humanizing people from brokenness and depressed situations. Koopman therefore concludes that "where people from diverse and even antagonistic backgrounds live in close proximity, where they are exposed more to each other, where they share in each other's daily joys and sorrows, they start to develop sympathy, empathy, and interpathy."[218] This is when the realisation that as humans we each live for one another, and that our involvement in another person's life, contributes to them realizing their essence of being human. This is perhaps the notion of compassion which states that "my humanity is tied to the humanity of other persons and theirs is intricately linked to mine."[219] As such, social inequality arises when there is a failure to see in others, our shared sense of humanity. When we feel others do not matter such that we could live and exist without them, we simply are saying that the humanity of others does not matter to my humanity.

3.4.5.2 Cultural Abuses

Following social inequality are cultural practices that are detrimental to the dignity of human persons. Understood as people's way of life, some of these cultures, especially on the African soil, are perils to the sustenance of life or demeaning to human worth. In the case of demeaning human worth, practices of female circumcision, a form of violating the dignity of women, is still a challenge.[220] Without careful consideration of the detrimental effects on the health and wellbeing of these young women, the placement of culture above their worth ensues. Despite the justifiable claims that it is "a form of teaching the youngsters about the suffering dimension of life," such claims are

---

217. Koopman, "Belhar."
218. Koopman, 34.
219. Forster, "Affect, Empathy," 3.
220. Koopman, "Human Dignity," 245.

suspicious.²²¹ In part, they suggest a kind of compromise of the inherent and unquantifiable dignity with mere lessons for suffering. Perhaps, progressive implementation of such cultural practices would constantly call for liberation to enhance the flourishing of human beings. On this note, it is suggested that the vision of liberation and dignity for all might become alive again, and might inspire and inform our public discourses, policies and practices.²²²

It is indeed the case that incest, sorcery, polygamy, and forceful delivery of many children constitute other cultural practices undermining human dignity in Africa.²²³ These are perceived as daily happenings in a continent that is religiously saturated. Wondering if the faith community could speak in this regard, Bedford-Strohm suggests that the Christian faith leads to a radical commitment to realizing human dignity in the very concrete circumstances of daily life.²²⁴ Carefully considered, these human dignity demeaning/violating factors have a human element. Sorcery, for instance, is seen to be motivated by greed, jealousy, and hatred which demeans persons for various reasons.²²⁵ It results in denial of care and attention, the two elements that Hicks describes as "being at the heart of treating people with dignity."²²⁶ In the case of forceful delivery of many children where the woman's health might be at risk, provided that the end justifies the means, it is regarded as normal. It is possible, Hicks argues, that these things continue to happen because of "our inability to speak or name these acts of indignity."²²⁷ If such practices are considered as wrongs, then the submission that "we cannot remain silent about the wrongs in church and society" becomes indisputable.²²⁸ This then becomes a reminder that "our dignity lies in the wonderful purpose, the life of quality for which God has created humanity."²²⁹ Gathered from these experiences, the argument that this could result in some psychological disorder is a possibility, which would require an adequate address. Suggestively,

---

221. Koopman, 245.
222. Koopman, "Belhar," 40.
223. Koopman, "Human Dignity," 245.
224. Bedford-Strohm, "Human Dignity," 218.
225. Koopman, "Human Dignity," 245.
226. Hicks, *Dignity: The Essential Role*, xii.
227. Hicks, xiii.
228. Koopman, "Belhar," 41.
229. Koopman, "Some Theological," 180.

"the language of dignity is an acceptable way to discuss psychological pain, humiliating and demeaning experiences."[230] By speaking against the wrongs, we liberate lives from forms of indignity and provide them with a new ethical pride and the joys of being human.

3.4.5.3 Environmental, Economic and Political Factors Affecting Human Dignity

One of the significant features of our environments is that it enables both human and non-human beings to co-exist and thrive, which suggests a hospitable rather than a hostile co-existence. If the latter ensues, the tendency to demean human dignity cannot be overemphasized. In analysing the African environmental factors that are detrimental to human dignity, the high rate of deforestation with a low rate of afforestation as a sure way to desertification is a big challenge to humanity.[231] In the case of desert encroachment, which is looming in many parts of Africa as a result of human factors causing exposure to life and extinction of various life forms to danger, calls for concern.[232] In part, such experiences could result in various forms of fear and anxiety, thereby intensifying human vulnerability about nature. Hence, as suggested, the greatest antidote lies in "speaking our fears, listening to the fears of others, and in that sharing of vulnerability, discovering a genesis of hope."[233]

Arguably, the economics and politics of globalization must aim to enhance, not compromise, human dignity.[234] As such, the influence of globalization has not only affected the politics and economics but makes the environment unconducive for human survival. Moltmann responds to this by alluding to the role of "modern industrial society in throwing out of balance the equilibrium of the earth's organism and gearing towards universal ecological death."[235] The signs of this ecological crisis have become an ecological catastrophe for those he describes as "the weaker living things which are first to perish in the process of struggling."[236] These weaker ones, although not responsible for

---

230. Sacks, *The Dignity of*, 18.
231. Koopman, "Human Dignity," 246.
232. Koopman, 245.
233. Sacks, 2.
234. Sacks, 3–4.
235. Moltmann, *God for a Secular*, 92.
236. Moltmann, 93.

the majority of ecological crises, lack the power to resist it. Moltmann sees this poverty for power as not only the worst environmental pollution but also a "form of corruption that causes poverty."[237] Indeed, a form of poverty that disorients individuals from "the hope of seeing into the sphere of future possibilities."[238]

Such disorientation about future anticipations for better human life and its flourishing is a concern for the African continent as it is for elsewhere. A place where forms of pollution, overpopulation, deforestation and desertification are on an increase, posing danger not only to human persons but also to nature. Following this concern is the fact that these ecological challenges receive little or inadequate attention in crucial visionary documents. Ever since the establishment of some of these documents, they had the protection of human dignity and the safety of the environment as one of their focal points.[239] It is, however, argued that even on the rare occasions when some of these documents mention these ecological challenges, "it is not for the sake of the environment itself, but humans."[240] These same humans do not flourish with the scanty resources due to overpopulation, which does not only lead to consumption of foodstuffs, but of the "very foundations from which people live."[241] The genesis of intense crime, and violence against the other, thus, threatening their dignity, also increases.

Worst still, the impending threats from the global market for intensifying this ecological crisis by imposing on the poor countries to cut down the rain forests and overgraze the pastureland as a strong factor to an ecological crisis. Without the power of resistance, these poor countries, including African countries, suffer from what Gandhi described as "the worst corruption,"[242] which is poverty. In either case of the environmental crisis, the tendency to humiliate and subject humanity to worst forms of dignity denial is imminent.

---

237. Moltmann, 94.

238. Moltmann, *Ethics of Hope*, 3.

239. There are numerous agencies across the African continent with the vision of safeguarding human dignity and are very critical of the wellbeing of the ecology. Some of which include; African Charter on human and People's Rights; South African Bill of Rights; and the New Partnership for Africa's Development (which houses the heart of the agenda of the African Union), see: Koopman, "Human Dignity," 245.

240. Koopman, 245.

241. Moltmann, *God for a Secular*, 94.

242. Moltmann, 93.

Koopman is therefore right to describe environmental problems as influencers and detrimental to human dignity in Africa.

3.4.5.4 Crime, Terrorism and Corruption

One other set of issues faced by the African continent relates to the high levels of criminality, terrorism, and corruption. Though the latter has been discussed in the previous chapter (see section 2.3), some comments could yet be referred to here. It is common to experience cases of crime in societies with either high unequal distribution or insufficient resources. If the former, corruption cannot be excused from being one of the propellers. In case of the latter, competition for survival ensues. In either case, the risk of breeding terrorism is high. These ills characterise Africa, so much so that human dignity is becoming "uncontroversial to the point that it does not mean anything anymore."[243] Similarly, Novak wonders why, in this century, the concept of dignity is "often sounding empty," an indication that the world has moved into a new age, with new problems, and in need of new solutions to secure the dignity of man.[244] Such controversies emanate from an inappropriate understanding of what the concept is, which calls for clarity in terms of meaning.

Although the inappropriate unified meaning of human dignity supports its denial, the attitudinal response does more. In his analysis of violence, Huber sees "human violence against other humans as the most disturbing and most challenging problem facing the world today."[245] From the struggle for food, shelter, security of lives and property, even in the contexts of abundance, it demonstrates that violence permeates our society and our whole life. Here, the attitudinal challenge revolves around using dehumanizing instances for public entertainment which Huber finds, contributes extensively[246] to preparedness to use violence in real life.

In the South African context, apartheid is described as a form of inhuman treatment, and a systemic crime.[247] This singular form of crime did not only deprive several South Africans of their sense of humanity, but also a loss of

---

243. Bedford-Strohm, "Human Dignity," 211.
244. Novak, "Human Dignity, Persnal Liberty," 67.
245. Huber, *Violence: The Unrelenting Assault*, xv.
246. Huber, xv.
247. Koopman, "Human Dignity," 245.

human conscience from seeing humanness in other people's humanity. This gave rise to the culture of violence when life is lived out of fear of the "other," with distrusts.[248] A similar example from the Nigerian context is that such violence has resulted in the displacement and alienation of a large number of people from their ancestral lands and homes, turning them to refugees and others into internally displaced persons (IDPs).[249] With these different expressions, we could agree on the need for a global ethical perspective in addressing the challenges relating to human dignity violation, which we see happening daily.[250] Given that the increase in mortality rate, malnutrition, and lack of medical attention have become global challenges, they could properly be addressed from this perspective. Until these problems are addressed, there must be a realisation that human practices infringe upon human dignity, and crimes against humanity are almost considered a norm.

The above dehumanizing elements exist because the basic human needs are not provided. These basic human needs, which we mentioned (see section 3.1) consist of food, shelter, education, health, and security, which an individual needs to enable them live fully and truly as a human.[251] With the reality in African societies, these needs have not been met, hence, giving rise to the high level of crimes against humanity.

In summary, three perspectives were considered to ascertain Koopman's portrayal of human dignity in Africa. First, he talks of engrossed social inequality, second, cultural practices, and third, the environmental factors. According to Koopman, these factors are detrimental to human dignity,

---

248. Koopman, 245.
249. Akper, "An Ethos of Hospitality," 283.
250. Bedford-Strohm, "Human Dignity."
251. Here is an explanation to these basic human needs based on this this study. First, health would mean that which is quality, functional, affordable, and assessable to all human persons. Second, by food we refer to that which is affordable, quality, available to all, especially the most vulnerable, so much that an average human person does not live thinking of where their next meal would come from. Third, shelter, refers to decent, affordable, and assessable housing where human persons could live with dignity that befits them. Fourth, security which includes instance where human persons could live and move without fear of uncertainties – as is the deplorable insecurity in Nigeria- but with confidence doing about their affairs. Last, education refers in this study as knowledge that is transformational which is quality, affordable, assessable, and encouraging. Education encouraged beyond certification but includes vocational education where human persons have access to become self-reliant in various ramifications. The provision of basic human needs is paramount to the recognition and enhancement of human dignity. The lack of them thereof, however, is what this study argues that threatens human dignity.

particularly on the African continent, where he worries that human beings propel them, hence, a call for a change of attitude. Here, the attitudinal change would require a reconsideration that we all are humans with a dependent element, which becomes a reminder that the right attitude towards the "other" for being human, connotes recognition of their dignity.

3.5 Human Dignity in Nigeria

The ongoing incidences in Nigeria could usher us into a brief survey of human dignity. These incidences that range from corruption, human trafficking, challenges of insecurity, various forms of violence, all have the human person as soft targets, with human dignity violation as a result. This leaves us wondering if the concept of human dignity matters – as already mentioned earlier. Indeed, the idea of human dignity matters to a Nigerian person, although such understanding comes with variation too.

Human dignity in Nigeria could be perceived from a cultural dimension. In this case, this study chooses to reflect on the Igbo[252] of South-Eastern Nigeria and the Ham[253] of North-Central Nigeria. Igbo people link their understanding of human dignity through cultural and traditional perspectives. In one instance, the human person is acknowledged as the apex of God's creation so much that according to a human person's right and respect, God is equally recognized.[254] That brings together the notion of recognition, which relates to justice in the community. As Emeghara observes, human dignity amongst the Igbo cannot be detached from a person's relation with others in society. Rather, "it upholds the communal relation between human persons

---

252. Igbo refers to a language and the people who speak it who inhabit the South-Eastern part of Nigeria (Ejidike, "Human Rights," 71).

253. The Ham sociocultural group is situated in the North-Central part of Nigeria, majorly found in the present-day Kaduna and parts of Nasarawa states. The people are called Ham, while the language they speak is called Hyam (John, "Narratives of Identity," 2). Regarding dignity, nothing much has been written from the perspective of Ham people. Nevertheless, the people understand what dignity entails. (The writer of this project is Ham and speaks Hyam as first language). To this end, the word dignity in the Hyam language is 'Kham', literally meaning respect or honour given to someone considered to have a higher rank; either a parent, a senior adult, or any person who deserves respect from an inferior person. Nevertheless, the Ham people accord this honour or respect on all human persons who they see deserve to be treated with respect and honour for simply being human persons.

254. Osunwokeh, "Human Dignity Stance," 1.

that no one individual lives and exists as an entity, but as one that belongs to the fold of the community."[255] Such a unique interrelation suggests how the dignity of a human person is conceptualized. The perception, however, does not shy away from various forms of dehumanization that the community exhibits on human persons, particularly on women. As Baloyi states, the subjugation of women has many facets ranging from sexuality, economics, politics, culture to religion.[256]

As for the Ham people, their perception of human dignity is linked to respect and honour. The idea that people matter more than things is a basic assumption in many African societies. While the said assumption could be dismissed in some African societies at present due to various forms of human dignity violation, a few elements are still in display. One of these few is the Ham people that Kato wrote about. He affirms that there is a strong belief in God as the maker of heaven and earth amongst the Ham people.[257] By such an indication, a Ham person is urged to see a human person as made by God. Kato goes further to point out that children are taught not to make fun of the fool, the lame, the blind, and any person considered to be with any form of disability because they all are made in the image of God.[258] These indicators show the connection there is in understanding the value placed on humanity to enable respect and honour.

From the above scenarios, we could see that human dignity is not an alien concept in the Nigerian culture as shown by the two people groups. As it was indicated, human dignity is linked to the image of God embedded in humans, which calls for respect, belonging and honour. By these cultural understandings, the human person is considered as deserving protection, provision of livelihood, security and communal interaction. Any attempt to devalue a human person through subjection, as we currently see in Nigeria, is done out of ignorance that human beings do not have equal dignity nor should they be treated equally with basic human needs equally provided and

---

255. Emeghara, "The Dignity," 130.
256. Baloyi, "When Culture Clashes."
257. Kato, "Theological Pitfalls in Africa."
258. Kato, 30.

evenly distributed. Aben aptly captures this by saying that "we all share the essential attribute of having been created in the image of God."[259]

The contested nature of Nigeria could further suggest the perception of human dignity from other dimensions fuelled by ethnicity, religiosity, and perhaps, political affiliation. Nevertheless, the emphasis on "respect for human life,"[260] and on "inalienability"[261] is relevant to usher us into the perception of the concept of dignity in Nigeria. This is due to the emphasis on how human life is of "incommensurable, incalculable worth."[262] For Lebacqz, this worth is not derived from specific human characteristics, such as rationalisation or freedom, which are limited and sometimes fleeting. Rather, each human life is of inalienable worth because each has that standing before God. Similarly, Barth sees and describes human life as "a loan that deserves respect."[263] For Barth, this respect is "man's astonishment, humility, and awe, when he meets something superior such as majesty, dignity, holiness, and a mystery, which compels him to withdraw and keep his distance to handle it modestly, circumspective, and carefully."[264] These two views remind us of the expected value a human life deserves, and which, in turn, portrays the enhancement of their dignity. With the contested religious nature of Nigeria and seeing that the above views suggest a Christian theological voice, a proper representation would require a Muslim perspective.

The Quranic view of human dignity presents God bestowing honour and favour on humanity, which confers on its privileged position.[265] Outlining three components by which the Muslims understand the place of human worth, firstl, it rests on humans' free will, second, it rests on humans' superior ability to obtain life in security and freedom from want, and third, human beings have privilege because they can exert their free will to live righteously.[266]

Despite such a background, human dignity still receives various conceptions in Nigeria. In some quarters, such as politics, what is considered

---

259. Aben, "The Trinity and Public Theology," 40.
260. Barth, "Respect for Life," 724.
261. Lebacqz, "Alien Dignity," 721.
262. Lebacqz, 721.
263. Barth, 725.
264. Barth, 725.
265. Muftugil, "Human Dignity," 159.
266. Muftugil, 159.

dignity depends on one's affiliation. This is an understanding that conforms to the social and psychological perception discussed previously (see section 3.3.3). In these situations, human dignity becomes something that could be increased, reduced or bestowed on one when there is conformity to certain principles or standards. This form of perception is informed by power. Here, from an economic viewpoint, a Nigerian is considered to have dignity by the status they occupy, a form of understanding we have previously mentioned as personalized, which has since been modified and universalized since the wake of modernity. Human dignity in Nigeria is, however, still placed on status, and as a sense of decorum.[267] It is probably because of this understanding that human dignity violation occurs at different phases in Nigeria. Within such confusion, "we should never forget that everyone, even our enemies, even the most impoverished among us, has the dignity of bearing the divine image, and so sharing something of the divine essence."[268]

These indices show that human dignity is neither a novel concept to the Nigerian person nor is its meaning alien. Rather, the analysis shows that largely, it is the variation in understanding human dignity, which makes it open to the violation. Judging from the previous theories on human dignity discussed above (see sections 3.3 and 3.4), we could place Nigeria's perception within some of those theories. First, there is a sense in Nigeria's perception that human dignity is linked to the ontological views. Second, there is a sense of a personalized view of human dignity, and third, there is a sense of physical and psychological view of human dignity. These variations suggest the complications that lie in understanding human dignity, which results in its incessant violation. As already stated, therefore, this study has as a point of departure to unravel human dignity from the ontological view with roots in the image of God that is an entitlement of all humanity without restriction. It is such an understanding of human dignity that brings together and reminds human beings of our shared sense of humanity, which is not built on self-dependency but through mutual co-existence. Within this shared sense of co-existence, there has been a violation of not only human dignity but also human rights in Nigeria, which calls for finding a link between the two concepts.

---

267. Moltmann, *On Human Dignity*.
268. Aben, "The Trinity and Public Theology," 40.

3.6 Human Dignity and Human Rights

The concepts of human dignity and human rights have occupied academic conversations in recent times, so much so that one hardly exists without the other. Also, there are often tensions in trying to unify these concepts in terms of their meaning and applicability in different contexts. This may explain why Charles Taylor suggests that various stakeholders would have to agree on the meaning and applicability of the two terms.[269] As part of this study, this relationship will be discussed, particularly the fact that human rights exist to safeguard human dignity. As a limitation, the section does not aim at giving every detail about human rights – as this does not form a major part of the study – rather it emphasizes the relationship between the two concepts to provide a grounding for understanding human dignity. To journey through establishing the said relationship, Jürgen Habermas, Jürgen Moltmann, Jeremy Waldron, and Pawel Luków among other voices have been selected. Although aware of more voices, these few are chosen because they give a much clearer view that suits the current study. In so doing, we shall have a brief analysis of why talks on human rights in general, a view of rights in the African context, and fundamental human rights.

As a pointer, discussions about human rights are heard everywhere in modern society. It can be contended, therefore, that wherever the need for rights arose, there were issues human beings tried to get rid of.[270] As such, Habermas would say, "human rights developed in response to specific violations of human dignity and can thus be conceived as specifications of human dignity as their moral source."[271] In some of these instances, the quest for rights had aimed at bringing freedom so that there could be flourishing of lives and the reclaiming of humanness in areas where that was denied. In view of this need, wherever there came to be a concept of human beings, their rights simply as human beings, were formulated.[272] Indeed, there are no contentions that the concepts of human rights and human dignity are relational. It is not a relationship in terms of similarity or difference but one of interdependence.

---

269. Taylor, *Dilemmas and Connection*, 105.
270. Muis, "Human Rights and Divine," 1.
271. Habermas, "The Concept," 464.
272. Moltmann, *Faith and the Future*, 178.

To begin with, speculations abound over the placement of human rights over and against safeguarding human dignity. While Waldron problematises this as a lack of clarity when we talk of rights that every human person has such freedom, he sees such assertions to be the very reason why some humans are in "chains and need to have freedom."[273] Similarly, Luków agrees to this claim, stressing that human rights were never backed by a substantive account of human nature and the worth, value or status of human beings. Although human dignity featured in the founding human rights documents, it was left undefined and its relation to human rights was not specified.[274] As such, there were no specifications as to whether or not human rights backed the account of human worth or if they lacked clarity. There is, instead, an internal relationship, which explains that human rights exist for effective implementation of the core moral values.[275]

While Waldron agrees to the linking relationship between human rights and human dignity, he sees a more interesting duality of uses in terms of the distinction between dignity as the ground of rights and dignity as the context of rights. In this, he stresses further that dignity is what some of our rights are rights to, but dignity is also what grounds all of our rights.[276] While Luków agrees with Waldron in a sense, his concern falls back to the meaning of human dignity. He concludes that human dignity arrives in the human rights discourse because of ideological debates. Since human dignity was not necessarily conceived as a foundation of legal norms,[277] it often expressed national corporations or the moral-ideological orientation of constitutional arrangements.[278] Habermas, however, did not only venture into establishing a link between the two concepts, but also contemplates whether an intimate conceptual connection existed from the beginning. He contends that we only agree with our intuition that tells us human rights have always been the

---

273. Waldron, "Dignity, Rank, and Rights," 211.

274. Luków, "A Difficult Legacy," 313.

275. Habermas, "The Concept," 464.

276. Waldron, "Dignity, Rank, and Rights," 212.

277. Referring to the twentieth century, perhaps a time where human dignity was conceived as a rank that only a few people were entitled to, human dignity as a concept, struggled with identity in terms of meaning. This resulted in why it found its place in political and legal discourse, retaining much of its vagueness, as can be observed in post-war international human rights. See Luków, "A Difficult Legacy," 314–16.

278. Luków, 315.

product of resistance to despotism, oppression, and humiliation.[279] Although these views cover a range of dimensions involving human dignity and human rights, a sort of agreement exists. All think that human rights were embedded in the most international laws with safeguarding human dignity as one of the pointers. Waldron puts it clearly that human dignity both forms the ground and context of human rights.[280] Agreeing to this, Habermas adds that human dignity has played a role in the construction of human rights.[281] We could, therefore, submit here that agitations for rights follow the violation of human dignity, such that these rights to operate protect human dignity, both from what has happened and against future occurrence.

An example of this is in the categorization of human concerns for sustenance and survival.[282] These exist because of the fragmented world we live in, where racism, colonization, dictatorship, and class rule are confronted as infringements of human rights. These infringements, seen in increasing measure, could have political injustice and economic inequality as propellers, thus, neglecting the awareness that those rights when granted, put people in a position to implement freedom[283] for themselves. Given the context of this study, let us further our understanding of rights from an African perspective.

3.6.1 Some Views on Rights from an African Context

It would be interesting to survey an understanding of rights from the African context. This is done to give the reader some views from an African context regarding what Africans mean when they talk of rights. More importantly, because the fact that Africa is a complex concept to define, this section does not claim to present every African view on the subject matter. Rather, it is

---

279. Habermas, "The Concept," 466.
280. Waldron, "Dignity, Rank, and Rights," 212.
281. Habermas, "The Concept," 466.
282. Human rights have been categorized into individual rights – as those over against the powers of state and society; economic and social rights – as those against capitalism and class rule; right of existence – as those coming from the impoverished and wretched people of the third world demanding the right to live and survive. See Moltmann, *Ethics of Hope*, 218; Moltmann, 180; Moltmann, *God for A Secular*, 119). In summary, these rights are distinguished between protective rights to life, freedom and security; rights to liberty, these covering freedom of opinion, freedom of association and freedom of religion; social rights to work, to the means of subsistence, and to housing; the rights to play a part in public life, and to participation in politics, industry, and culture. Moltmann, *Ethics of Hope*, 218).
283. Moltmann, *Faith and the Future*, 181.

narrowed to the western region of Africa where a few scholars are studied. Discourses on human rights are not alien to the African contexts largely because of historical experiences. From slavery to the horrors of colonialism and racism, the persecution of foreigners in xenophobic attacks, the abuse of vulnerable women and children, and the killing of people of different faiths or ethnic identities, Africa has suffered and still bleeds from the abuse of human dignity and human rights.[284] These elements have continued to hamper the socio-political and socio-economic fabrics of Africans, with close to no difference now as it was during the era of colonisation and slavery. This is, partly, because "we are still falling into the historical trap of teaching human rights in a way that is riddled with inconsistencies and exclusions . . . instead of frowning on anything that is segregated, discriminatory, and dehumanising."[285] Speaking from a trinitarian theological perspective, Aben avows that regaining the true sense of human rights and dignity in Africa would start when we remember that "everyone, even our enemies, even the most impoverished among us, has the dignity of bearing the divine image, and so, sharing something of the divine essence."[286] To this end, human rights in Africa must be seen as "belonging to Africans as human beings created by God rather than as a Western construct that is gradually being imported into Africa."[287]

Wiredu asserts that a right is "a claim that people are entitled, to make on others or society at large by their status."[288] These rights, he adds, "are claims that people are entitled to make simply by their status as human beings."[289] The issue of why human beings could come up with such rights claims requires further investigations. One way to do this is to establish the ground on which human beings claim some rights. Second, we could look at the view of the world we live in, and the effect of human activities on each other and the environment they live in.

---

284. Bagu, "Human Rights," 205; de Villiers, "A Christian Ethics"; Kure, "Leadership, Corruption."
285. Bagu, "Human Rights," 206.
286. Aben, "The Trinity and Public Theology," 40.
287. Bagu, 206.
288. Wiredu, *Cultural Universals and Particulars*, 157.
289. Wiredu, 157.

Studying the Akan people of Ghana in West Africa, Wiredu describes three elements of understanding the concept of a person which are *okra, mogya, and sunsum*.[290] Of these three elements, we shall discuss okra for two reasons. First, because okra is "held to come directly from God which is supposed to be an actual speck of God,"[291] and second because it is the concept that fits well into the ongoing discussion than the other two. By possessing *okra*, the divine element, he adds, all persons have an intrinsic value which they do not owe to any earthly circumstance but God. Prominent to this is a concept of human dignity, implying "that every human being is entitled in an equal measure to certain basic respect."[292] Applied in the Akan's tradition, okra is the right of each person, which guarantees them to pursue that unique destiny assigned to them by God. Accordingly, the presence of okra calls for an understanding as to why an Akan person has a right to its protection. This assertion brings close the conception of a right to inalienable human dignity. The idea reveals human rights more from an African perspective than a Western perception. Bagu succinctly points out that

> whereas the Western perspective of human rights tends to be individualist and increasingly secular, African approaches tend to be communal and religious . . . hence the reason why the concept of *ubuntu*, which expresses a communitarian affirmation that human rights of each member of the community to exist and thrive is used.[293]

Bagu avows further that "what the African God wants is an Africa where every person is recognized, respected and conferred with all the rights that accompany the fact that they are human."[294] The above expression forms some basis to human rights in an African context, specifically portraying some views from Western Africa.

---

290. Akan is a word referring both to a group of intimately related languages found in West Africa and to the people who speak it living mostly in Ghana. Wiredu, *Cultural Universals and Particulars*, 157.
291. Wiredu, 157.
292. Wiredu, 158.
293. Bagu, "Human Rights," 207.
294. Bagu, 201.

Moltmann elaborates rights from a more general perspective by insisting that "if rights are based on God's claim upon human beings, then there is a need to formulate the fundamental human duties that these rights and freedoms exist to safeguard,"[295] referring to the ground at which they stand to the claim of human rights. Evaluating the "why" of human rights also calls for identifying the context in which human beings live, and perhaps their environment. The world we live in is characterized by human activities threatening the flourishing of lives and the continual human existence in ages to come, simply referred to as "a morally bankrupt age."[296] This is where the effect of human activities either positively promotes their existence or negatively threatens it. Moltmann sees such a world as that which the people of the earth are entering a shared global history because they are all morally endangered.[297] Such endangerment comes as a result of nuclear threat and by the ecological crisis which the inhabitants of the earth share, that are posing harm on themselves.[298] The more the inhabitants of the earth share this global history, the more important a consensus about human rights and the rights of nature becomes.[299]

The essence of rights discourse in this context makes it possible to discern the contours[300] of a global democracy in which humanity could somehow become its determining subject. Else, Hauerwas warns, such a world would be "extremely hard to maintain our moral identity because we feel pulled in different directions by our various roles and convictions, unsure of any coherence to our lives, and become divided selves, more easily tempted to violence."[301] If understood well, Hauerwas's description of the violent world is multifaceted. It includes the effects of technological advancement on the lives of future generations, ecological degradation, and ecological justice.[302] The above views attest to the dangers befalling the human person within the

---

295. Moltmann, *On Human Dignity*, 24.
296. Hauerwas, *The Peaceable Kingdom*, 3.
297. Moltmann, *God for a Secular*, 117.
298. Moltmann, 117.
299. Moltmann, *Ethics of Hope*, 217.
300. Moltmann, *Ethics of Hope*, 217.
301. Hauerwas, *The Peaceable Kingdom*, 6.
302. Jonas, *The Imperative of Responsibility*, 51; Veldsman, "Science," 176. See also Conradie, *The Earth*.

global current realities. This explains why "we must track down the danger before it is too late, else the potential disappearance of the human species will become real irreversible destruction."[303]

Whilst the above description of the endangerment of human rights signals warning for prompt action towards protecting them, rights talk is opposed from other ends. Instead of discussing rights in this regard, others have opted to oppose the conversation and advocate to change the terms of the debate for other discussions.[304] Wolterstorff, however, outlines reasons why rights talk is under opposition.[305] The first reason for opposing rights talk is because it is seldom used to make inflated claims. This category of opposers, he opines, makes the pursuit of some ideas (such as rights) an obligation and not optional, thereby leaving some realists feeling guilty on certain claims that are seen as unrealistic. Second, rights talk is under opposition because they are often followed by rights absolutism.[306] Such critics assume, as a point of departure, that certain rights considered infallible are possibly not. Since there is no allowance for discussing these rights further to establish some absolutes, these rights might not be valid. Further, the opposition to rights talk holds that rights are made for expressing and encouraging the mentality of possessive individualism. That is to say that these rights are made to ensure the survival, and entitlement befitting a suitable society, but for only a few, hence they are opposed. Such extremism blindfolds one's obligations to cultivating virtues that would enable the enhancement of the flourishing of our lives alongside others.[307] Rights-talk, as the objection goes, "is for me claiming my possessions, you claiming your possessions, him claiming his possessions, her claiming her possessions."[308] If rights are to be understood as such, then the discussions on human rights would be deprived of its significance.

---

303. Bazin, "A Reading," 14.

304. Wolterstorff, *Journey Toward Justice*, 38 sees such opposition to rights talk amongst the Afrikaners in South Africa who spoke in defence of apartheid. Instead of agreeing to discuss rights and their implication, they suggest, rather, to discuss responsibilities, about social bonds of friendship and loyalty, about what's necessary for a well-ordered society.

305. Wolterstorff, *Journey Toward Justice*, 38.

306. Wolterstorff, 38.

307. Wolterstorff, 38–39.

308. Wolterstorff, 39.

3.6.2 Fundamental Human Rights

The concept of fundamental human rights has been discussed within several contexts and by different persons. Notably, the concept as referring to "those rights and duties which essentially inform what it means to be truly human without which human beings cannot fulfil their original destiny of having been created in the image of God."[309] As indicated by many researches, the declaration at the general assembly of 1948 of the United Nations on the fundamental human rights was adopted.[310] It states that "whereas recognition of the inherent dignity and the equal and inalienable rights of all members of the human family is the foundation of freedom, justice, and peace in the world."[311] This declaration cannot be viewed as an abstract idea, but must be looked at against the background of the suffering and the present struggles of individuals, nations and states.[312]

It can be argued, however, that the declaration was made owing to the human condition regarding the concept of human dignity. In the wake of "crimes of the fascist dictators, rights were formulated over against the powers of state and society,"[313] "based on class rule and capitalism, economic and social human rights were introduced."[314] The demands of the third world persons for the right to exist and the right to survive have been introduced into rights discourses.[315] These demands for rights, considered properly, have become concerns for the different contexts in a bid to redeem the struggling humanity from the chaotic world.

Nonetheless, the complication of these demands does not rely only upon the redemption of mankind but for other of God's creation too. In this case, an existing relationship between humanity and ecology (creation) as "exploitative" can only stop when exploitation between human beings stops, such that ecological justice can only be attained when there is economic justice.[316] Understanding Moltmann's sentiments here presents us with an ideological

---

309. Moltmann, *On Human Dignity*, 23.
310. Cliteur, Wissen, and Haag, "Human Dignity," 157.
311. Cliteur, Wissen, and Haag, 157.
312. Moltmann, *On Human Dignity*, 20.
313. Moltmann, *God for a Secular*, 119.
314. Moltmann, *Ethics of Hope*, 218.
315. Moltmann, *God for a Secular*, 119
316. Moltmann, *Ethics of Hope*, 221.

perception of the parallel relationship between human beings and other creatures, and between human rights and the rights of other non-human creatures. Such a description suggests that upholding rights demands the flourishing of creation in its entirety.

On the contrary, the ideological perception of the superiority of the human family over other creatures intensifies and widens the gap between the economic, social and ecological justice. Moltmann, again, make some clarification on this notion. He explains and validate dominion over other creatures as contained in the creation narrative only when it corresponds to the creator's lordship over the world. This is a lordship that is loving, kind, and caring, void of exploitation, plundering, and destruction, and that does not contradict their rights and dignity.[317] This points to a disengagement from modern civilisation with the idea that only human beings exist independently, as everything else exists for the sake of, and for the use of human beings.[318] They, however, conclude that "human dominion or rule over nature is made legitimate when it is exercized in cooperation and community with the environment and leads to the life-giving symbiosis between human society and the natural environment."[319] The above notion suggests two things: first, it provides an elaborative discovery to rights-talk in a way indicating the rights of creation and, second, it is a call for a re-evaluation of the dominion saga, which human beings claim to have over other creatures.

Speaking on the place of humanity and nature, and the roots of different human rights, Moltmann suggests that they have a common binding force, namely human dignity.[320] Here, Moltmann establishes the difference between human rights and human dignity. According to him, that human rights are in plural and not human dignity is a characteristic feature indicating the precedence of human dignity over many rights. The dignity of a human person is an indivisible, inalienable, and shared quality of a human being.[321] To this end, there is "never a greater or lesser dignity; it either exists entirely or not at all."[322] Human beings should, therefore, not be "exposed to any treatment that

---

317. Moltmann, *On Human Dignity*, 27.
318. Moltmann, *Ethics of Hope*, 222.
319. Moltmann, *On Human Dignity*, 27.
320. Moltmann, *God for a Secular*, 118.
321. Moltmann, *On Human Dignity*, 9; Moltmann, *God for a Secular*, 119.
322. Moltmann, 119.

calls to questioning their quality as subjects" – in Kant's words, as ends – but considered as ends in themselves.[323] Although human rights exist to safeguard human dignity, the above idea suggests the superiority of human dignity over human rights.

The placement of human dignity above human rights does not elevate human beings above all other living creatures, but is merely a "special instance of natural life."[324] This notion of human dignity is closely linked to the Christian theology view of every human creature as the carrier and bearer of dignity (see section 3.3.1). While Moltmann does not equalise human dignity and human rights, he cautions that human dignity should not be elevated through human rights at the expense of nature, but should be in harmony and have a way to benefit nature. Else, left independent of nature, human rights would experience difficulty in claiming universality.[325]

3.6.3 Perspectives of Human Rights

Given the various debates on human rights, factions exist that speak about them differently. One view considers human rights irrespective of the divine relationship, as having nothing to do with morality. Here, we will refer those views as the anthropological conception of human rights. Others see human rights from the divine point of view, concerning God, the creator of the human family. We will refer those views here as the theistic[326] conception of human rights.

3.6.3.1 Towards a Theistic Conception of Human Rights

Understanding human rights from the theistic point of view establishes a relationship between human beings and God. Such a relationship is not by virtue of choice, but by acceptance and affirmation. Muis gives a summary of this relationship thus, "we would not need to choose between God and human rights; we would not need to deny human rights if we believe in God; we would not need to reject God if we struggle for human rights."[327] With the

---

323. Moltmann, 119.
324. Moltmann, 120.
325. Moltmann, 119.
326. Muis, "Human Rights and Divine," 1.
327. Muis, 4.

above claim, we come to realize that the belief in God and human rights are two constituents that could go together perfectly well, and could perhaps, reinforce each other.[328]

Theistically, Muis analyses Wolterstorff's conception of human rights about God. In his book, *Justice, Rights, and Wrongs* Wolterstorff assumes that human rights are only possible if human beings have the same non-instrumental worth sufficient to account for human rights and greater than any non-human creature.[329] He shies away from identifying human worth in relation to human capacities; instead, he says that worth can be imparted to human beings. If this remains valid, it means human beings could impart worth to themselves and others rather than what only God will impart to them.[330] While human attachments to fellow human beings could be based on actions or inactions, God can bestow worth by loving them, and by attaching to them equality, affirming that human beings have equal worth.[331] Whereas Wolterstorff might be right in his assertions, his arguments have raised some theological concerns.

3.6.3.2 Towards a Theological Conception of Human Rights

Following the theistic dimension of human rights is the theological dimension. Here, Muis suggests two theological themes to link the discourse on human rights, namely creation and redemption.

The first divine act, Muis calls the act of creation. By the creation of human beings, specifically and other creatures in general, there is a demonstration that God has given[332] creatures the right to live. Not only are human beings created by God, but the image and likeness of God, *imago Dei*, presents then with a privileged position above other creatures. Van Husysteen explains this special privilege by ascribing human beings as the forerunner[333] of humanity, which defines the relationship between humanity and deity. This existing relationship does not only place the human person above other creatures but guarantees the safety and security of existence. Here, van Husyssteen uses the

---

328. Muis, 4.
329. Wolterstorff, *Justice, Rights and Wrongs*, 352.
330. Muis, "Human Rights and Divine," 5.
331. Muis, 5.
332. Muis, 6.
333. van Huyssteen, *Alone in the World*, 120–21.

Genesis account to explain and give a rationale for the divine prohibition[334] against the shedding of human blood because of their virtue of being created in the image of God. This assertion would include instances of capital punishment, also where a human being has a right. It also nullifies speculations that even sin could dismiss one of their rights to live.

The protection from shedding of human blood, by their relationship with God, comprises of other segments. A human person, being in the image of God, connotes a representative function that highlights their extraordinary importance. Towner describes humanity as walking representations[335] of God and not simply pieces of tissues or masses of electrons, which gives humans an exquisite value and importance. This value places and grants the human family dominion over other creatures, which calls for responsibility in two ways, namely love and justice. Love for oneself, other human beings, and other creatures seeks to enhance the wellbeing or flourishing, and seeks to secure that the person's rights are honoured, respected and promoted.[336] Justice, considered as a virtue, connotes a steady and enduring will to render to each person the rights belonging to them in order to enable them to enjoy life.[337] In sum, love and justice, as two variables placing the human person above other creatures are expressed in stewardship, nurture and responsibility toward what God loves and cherishes.[338] Love and justice about human rights suggest a legal connotation of human rights, which might not be applicable in certain situations, thus making them non-universal.

Legal human rights are not only part of human justice, but also are moral human rights that are universal. One of these moral rights is the right to live a human life.[339] The universality of the right to live as a human person emanates from the reality that every human being is a person, and as a person, is endowed with inalienable human rights.[340] Here, Moltmann agrees with our previous assertions of relating human beings to God by creation as that which gives human beings' existence its inalienable and transcendent

---

334. van Huyssteen, 120.
335. Towner, W.S. *Genesis*, 26.
336. Wolterstorff, *Justice in Love*, 101.
337. Wolterstorff, 85.
338. van Huyssteen, *Alone in the World*, 121.
339. Muis, "Human Rights and Divine," 6.
340. Moltmann, *God for a Secular*, 121–22.

dimension. In relating to the transcendent God, human beings become persons whose dignity ought to be protected by various institutions of law. They would destroy themselves if human beings are treated as objects, commodities, or as members of the work-force.[341] When this is the reality with the human family where the sacredness and sanctity of their lives are underexposed, the case of love and justice is denied, which in the truest sense, infringes on their rights. Equally, any brutal treatment of a human being denies them their universal moral rights.

In his second theological theme explaining human rights, Muis converses with Karl Barth's doctrine of justification. Important as the doctrine of justification to Christian theology is in general, and to Christianity in particular, the complex discourse on rights could be integrated. The assertion that believing, and faith in God guarantees the right to be called God's children provides an identity marker that should not be erased whatsoever. This occurs when God, through Jesus Christ, justifies a sinner, thereby establishing a relationship.[342] It turns to a union where a sinner is adopted into God's larger family, recognized, loved and treated first for being a human person, then as a justified sinner. This form of adoption is a legal act by which God gives to all human beings the right to be his children.[343] The implication of this view is in its non-inclusion of all human persons. It suggests that rights, which supposedly exist to protect and safeguard the dignity of all persons, are limited to only those in the Christian faith tradition. Considered as such, the view could be dehumanizing and would infringe the rights of others from outside the Christian faith. If human rights would only be understood from this perspective, they would cease from being universal and fundamental. Rather, they would become limited to cover only a portion of those who align with the dictums of God's divine selection and justification.

3.6.3.3 Towards an Anthropological Conception of Human Rights

By the anthropological conception of human rights here, we refer to those rights with little or no regard for moral justification. Those rights, when obeyed, in most cases downplay the sanctity of human life and its worth. Some

---

341. Moltmann, 122.
342. Muis, "Human Rights and Divine," 7.
343. Muis, 7.

of these rights have arisen in recent times with the influence of advanced technology, on the one hand. On the other hand, they are self-motivated. These would include the rights to life, including concepts such as abortion, infanticide, euthanasia, and others, which are propounded by bioethics. To understand these rights would, however, require a connection to the entitlements due to a human person, that his/her rights deserve protection.

In assessing human rights from an anthropological sense, we refer to Kant's two phrases referring to human dignity. Kant's first distinction, as cited in Muis, is between end and means. By this, Kant asserts, a human being should not be used as a means for something else but be an end in itself.[344] Second, Kant makes the distinction between price and worth, insisting they are two different variables. In this case, Kant clarifies price as something quantifiable, which is liable to be substituted with another variable of its worth. While on the contrary, worth, which refers to dignity, is a priceless variable that is unquantifiable.[345] Here, the pricelessness of human beings does not portray an order of superiority that places some human beings above others, but that which considers all the human species as priceless. Being a priceless variable, Kant, referring to human dignity, concludes that human beings have dignity because they have no price and because they are an end in themselves.[346] How then does this apply to the anthropological conception of human rights?

In this regard, Wolterstorff agrees with Kant that human beings can only have human rights if they have the same "unique human worth."[347] We could develop two scenarios that refer to "having a right and being rendered that right."[348] Kant and Wolterstorff agree on the ground for human beings having rights by similar worth. As Wolterstorff argues, it does not mean that one is deprived of worth as a person, but that one is "not enjoying what having such worth entails."[349] When this happens, the person, who is not granted what he/she has a right to, is wronged.[350] Avoiding such extremes is to apply Jesus's two love commands, namely justice and love. Wolterstorff describes

---

344. Muis, 3.
345. Muis, 3; de Villiers, "The Recognition," 266.
346. Muis, "Human Rights and Divine," 3.
347. Muis, 4.
348. Wolterstorff, *Journey Towards Justice*, 42.
349. Wolterstorff, 42.
350. Wolterstorff, 42.

it thus, "to possess the virtue of justice is to have a steady and enduring will to render each person the rights they possess."[351] Adding this to the societal role, he acknowledges a just society as that whose members are granted the rights that they possess. Such rights, in this context, refer to the recognition of the worth of human persons above any price.

If this fundamental principle is established, it can be argued further that human worth, as the right of a human person, is underestimated. One such example is the intriguing issues with infants and women who, in most African societies, are considered lesser human beings on the ground that they cannot make certain choices for themselves.[352] They are often considered as having no or little value. For instance, a child who is not up to the required age limit to vote is forced to accept any leader others impose to lead them without their consent. In other spheres, these infants are either described as disabled or minors who do not have rights of their own, hence, they are dictated to how to live their lives. This explains why theologians of disability[353] cautions that they do not only need rights, but "involvement, commitment, faithfulness and love."[354]

The actualization of these attributes on a human being, by being a person, signifies a connection with the one who demonstrates love and is committed to expressing it. Forster makes similar assumptions in his discourse on human dignity and compassion. Discussing from a social reality point of view, Forster agrees that true humanity is nested in the complexity of being a person about other persons.[355] On the rights, we can agree with Forster that our physical reality (sex, religion, class, race, fitness) does not describe our humanness, but our social reality in simply being human beings does. Human rights, from the anthropological sense that sometimes overlooks human realities from a relational perspective, therefore, nullifies the embedded sacredness of a human person. Here, treating a person with a right in a certain way other

---

351. Wolterstorff, 85.

352. See some works by a few African theologians, for example Oduyoye, "Alive to What," 195; Oduyoye "Reducing Welfare," 75; and Brand, *Speaking of a Fabulous Ghost*, 35, with emphasis on the wholeness of all creation.

353. Reinders, "Understanding Humanity and Disability," 37.

354. Koopman, "Some Theological and Anthropological" 182.

355. Forster, "Affect, Empathy," 3.

than the way they should be treated is tantamount to wronging that person.[356] In the language of rights, denial involves an act of being wronged or deprived of what one deserves owing to their humanness. This connects us with the notions of human dignity debates with various dimensions.

In summarizing the theological and anthropological conceptions of human rights, a few things call for pondering. First, for human dignity to be considered universal, it should not be confined to a certain religious belief or tradition – as a Christian theological view of selection and justification suggests. Also, for anthropological perception, human rights should not be considered from social or physical construction. Rather, they should be considered from the shared sense of humanity that sees every human being as deserving of the rights to be human. This, therefore, becomes a call to widen the understanding of what it means to have human rights. For purposes of this study, human rights are simply the right to be human without boundaries to every human species.

3.7 Chapter Summary

This chapter surveyed the concept of human dignity and the relationship therein with human rights from different perspectives. The survey helped us identify various conceptions and misconceptions of these concepts through different periods and perspectives, which influence the abuse of these two important variables in some quarters. One of the reasons for the abuse of human rights and dignity is that the meaning, from the secular perspective, is inconsistent with the theological perception that sees human dignity as God's embedded gift to mankind, which continues to rationalise the value of these variables. Nevertheless, below is the summary of the findings in the chapter and how it situates to the ongoing study.

Given that human beings are meaning-seekers, they engage in the search for the meaning of human dignity and why it is necessary. It was found that by understanding what human dignity entails, human beings become self-actualized towards themselves and their relationships with others.

Human dignity was considered from history, ranging from the early Christian era, the Middle Ages (Aquinas) and the enlightenment era (Kant).

---

356. Wolterstorff, *Justice in Love*, 86.

Although human dignity did not start from the Christian context, the idea has gained acceptance through the link made with the image of God possessed by every human being. For Aquinas, we summarized three views; first, and perhaps most importantly, he attests to God as the bestower of human dignity. Second, he agrees with other scholars on the possession of dignity by every human person by being human. Third, he slightly differs from others in that he believes in the increase, reduction, or even loss of human dignity. Kant, on the contrary, submits that human dignity cannot be lost nor be substituted for anything. Rather, human dignity is inherent and has no quantifiable value.

We considered different perspectives in understanding human dignity as follows; first, the image of God's view holds that every human being has dignity equal with everyone else. Second, the inherent view, holds that human dignity is a gift by God to human beings that cannot or should not be taken away or violated, else one loses the sense of being human. Third, the social and psychological view holds that human dignity can be given, taken away, reduced and/or increased depending on the status and the contribution made by the bearer – human being. Fourth, a humanist view sees dignity through emotional expression, which either reduces or increases self-fulfilment, courage and confidence. Fifth, a Christian anthropological view sees human dignity in terms of denial of self-fulfilment propelled through incessant endangering human activities against the other.

The final part of the chapter demonstrated a link between human dignity and human rights. Here, the findings indicate that human rights are simply rights to be human in its truest form – as this study holds – which are meant to protect human dignity from violation.

In the conclusion of this chapter, the study submits the following: First, human dignity is violated, generally, and particularly in Nigeria because there is no agreed meaning to the concept. As a result, it has become difficult to categorise an activity that violates human dignity. This study, therefore, admits that recognition and enhancement of human dignity occur when human beings are treated equally as humans and can flourish. When viewed as such, human activities, such as corruption, that are responsible for the denial of access to basic human needs, and any form of denial of livelihood is considered in this study to be a violation to human dignity. This is because such activities neither promote individual good nor societal good. Rather, they contribute to untold hardships where life, in some parts of Nigeria, is considered almost without meaning anymore because of various dehumanizing structures. Understanding human dignity as such suggests the need to involve all stakeholders in the struggle against corruption, which has become a blight to human dignity. For this to be achieved, we introduce a theological resource in the next chapter, the ethics of responsibility, to argue a case for how appropriately this task of protecting human dignity from violation could be done.

CHAPTER 4

Towards a Survey of Ethics of Responsibility

4.1. Introduction

The previous chapter focused on human dignity from different perspectives. We established, on theological grounds, that human dignity is embedded in everyone created by God and so remains a right for all human beings. The difficulty in ascertaining human dignity, however, calls for different stakeholders to take active roles in the recognition and enhancement of human dignity. This chapter, therefore, sets the background on an ethic of responsibility. It aims at analysing the perspectives of individual scholars from different contexts and backgrounds on the ethics of responsibility. The relevance of this chapter to the ongoing study is to understand how ethics of responsibility can be applied in enhancing the recognition and protection of human dignity in the context of corruption in Nigeria.

To actualise this, the chapter is divided into six parts. Part one gives a general introduction to the concept of responsibility while part two focuses on perspectives from Max Weber. Part three presents the German theological perspectives of ethics of responsibility including the philosophical perspectives of Hans Jonas's ethics of responsibility. Part four surveys the theological dimension of ethics of responsibility from the American perspective while part five presents perspectives from the African context, and part seven summarises and concludes the chapter.

An understanding of the concept of responsibility and its application to today's reality could be traced back to some earliest surviving Greek texts of the Homeric heroes who had little use for the concept of responsibility, with their central focus being on merit and kudos.[1] In these texts, both human and superhuman agents are often regarded as fair targets of praise and blame based on their behaviour.[2] It is, however, worth noting that an agent's conduct is excused because of the presence of some factors that have undermined their action. A reflection on these factors, however, gave rise to fatalism.[3] Further,

> the view that one's future or some aspect of it is predetermined in such a way as to make one's particular deliberations, choices and actions irrelevant to whether that particular future is comprehended. He insists that if some particular outcome is fated, then it seems that the agent concerned could not be morally responsible for that outcome. Likewise, if fatalism were true concerning all human futures, then it would seem that no human agent could be morally responsible for anything.[4]

Similarly, Aristotle extrapolates the theory of moral responsibility using two conditions, namely voluntariness and involuntariness by which one is held responsible.[5] Speaking on virtue and excellence with regard to actions and emotions, Aristotle, referring to responsibility, makes a similar observation that when actions are voluntary, we receive praise and blame, but when they are involuntary, we are pardoned and sometimes pitied.[6] Aristotle bases his submission on the integrity of the agent under whose power there is to perform any action.[7] In view of this, a certain kind of agent qualifies as a moral agent and is thus properly subject to ascriptions of responsibility by

---

1. Adkins, "Honour and Punishment."
2. Irwin, *Classical Philosophy*.
3. Eshleman, "Moral Responsibility."
4. Eshleman, "Moral Responsibility," 2.
5. Aristotle, *Nicomachean Ethics*.
6. Aristotle, *Nicomachean Ethics*, 52; Campos, "Responsibility and Justice," 100.
7. He adds that where it is in our power to act, it is also in our power not to act. For if we have power to act where it is noble to act, we also have power not to act where not to act is base (Aristotle, 65).

possessing the capacity for decision.[8] Such decisions are those of longing resulting from deliberation that expresses the agent's conception of what is good. Aristotle's further discussion on moral responsibility is devoted to spelling out the conditions under which it is appropriate to hold a moral agent blameworthy or praiseworthy for some particular actions or traits.[9] From these two traditions, the Homeric heroes' idea of merit and kudos, and Aristotle's blaming and praising, have strong links to retrospective or classical models of responsibility where the agent is treated based on past actions. Portraying responsibility as such pays close to no attention to the implications of what a moral agent does and its future relevance. Viewing responsibility only in retrospection is, however, beyond the scope of this study. Rather, this study explores responsibility in prospection, where the focus is on the here and now, but also with the future of human lives and societal wellbeing.

Prospective responsibility is forward-looking; something a moral agent simply must do regardless of the consequences. This prospective form of responsibility has gained the attention of recent scholarship after the first proposal by Weber, whose vision for responsibility is prospective with futurist aspirations for human and societal wellbeing.[10] Retrospective responsibility, on the contrary, is backward-looking, often associated with the legal notion of accountability in looking at the events and outcomes to determine who or what was responsible for them.[11] This has either blame or reward (as Aristotle says) or kudos (as the Homeric heroes state), even when the agent had no control over their action which is considered "unfair."[12] Of the two forms of responsibility, the prospective dimension as forward-looking captures the interest of the current study. This is because prospective responsibility is concerned[13] with the agent's responsiveness for something that might happen in the future, or for the interest or wellbeing of someone in general. The interest of this study, however, rests on the recognition and enhancement of the

---

8. Eshleman, "Moral Responsibility," 2

9. Eshleman; Aristotle. *Nicomachean Ethics*, 52.

10. Huber, "Toward an Ethics," ; Schweiker, *Responsibility and Christian Ethics*; de Villiers, *Revisiting Max Weber's Ethic*; Jonas, "Technology and Responsibility"; Jonas, *The Imperative of Responsibility*.

11. Karp, "The Responsibility to Protect."

12. Carlsson, "Blameworthiness as Deserved Guilt," 89.

13. Karp, 8.

wellbeing of human persons in the context of corruption and technological advancement threatening the dignity of human persons. The sections that follow will, therefore, guide us through different perspectives in order to gain an in-depth understanding of responsibility.

4.2 Max Weber on an Ethics of Responsibility (1864–1920)

This section presents the thoughts of Max Weber[14] on the ethics of responsibility which was first developed in an essay "Politics as a Vocation" delivered in Munich in 1919 and published later in the same year.[15] Given this understanding, it is argued that Max Weber was first to coin the concept "ethics of responsibility."[16] Although the idea of ethics of responsibility has ramified into different disciplines including theology, the emphasis here is restricted to Weber's sociological and political thoughts regarding the development of ethics of responsibility. This section, therefore, looks at Weber's involvement in the German public life of his day, including his perception and description of the German polity and the concerns he had.

4.2.1 Weber's Socio-political Involvement in the German Public Life

Socrates and Max Weber have been described as two great examples of moral and intellectual integrity in the history of Western political thought.[17] Taught

---

14. Max Weber (Eliaeson, "Max Weber and Plebiscitary") has remained a controversial political figure in Germany. He served many purposes: as the cultural hero who might have saved Germany from the disasters of the Weimar Republic, had he lived longer; as a typical representative of the unawareness among German intellectuals, of the dangers of authoritarian rule in accordance with the peculiarities of German societal development; and as a founding father of the new Federal republic after the war, inspiring a new generation of liberal political leaders; as a scholar, whose work is so rich that it can be interpreted in so many directions is not easy to grasp. In methodological matters, Weber emerges both as a positivist, supporting the side of modern science in the controversy over method and as an anti-positivist, launching the method of interpretative understanding. (Weber, *From Max Weber*), Weber rebelled against the authority of his elders in his quest for change in the democratic system operating during his time. Attesting to this was the indication in his early letters and the experiences at Strassburg that clearly showed in his later distinction between an ethic of responsibility and an ethic of absolute ends.

15. Starr, "The Structure," 407.

16. de Villiers, *Revisiting Max Weber's*, 407.

17. Villa, "Max Weber," 540.

and influenced by great minds such as Karl Marx and Immanuel Kant, Weber grew in an intellectual world that was made up of agents taking various intellectual positions.[18] This was probably Weber's starting point of interest in German public life through various dimensions, including but not limited to politics, economics, and religion.

Weber's thoughts and works had tremendously been the embodiment of moral consistency and intellectual honesty at its end for some reason. One such reason is that he stands a great disabuse in our tradition, challenging the beliefs and longings that create complacency about our virtues and self-righteousness regarding politics.[19] Within this sphere of integrity, Weber developed an interest in sanitizing the German political scene from its abusers who mismanaged, misappropriated, and mishandled political affairs. To situate Weber's political ideas in Germany would mean bringing together his experiences after visiting America.

It can be argued that Weber's passion for appropriate democracy began after his tour of America in 1904. Although Weber's tour to America was pivotally important to the development of his social and political thought, it also led to the development of his theory of plebiscitary democracy.[20] During his tour of America, Weber developed more interest in labour problems, the immigration questions and problems of political management.[21] America was, perhaps for Weber, the model of a new society for some reasons: first, because the protestant sects had had their greatest scope and in their wake, the secular, civic, and voluntary associations had flowered. Second, a political federation of states had led to a voluntary union of immense contrasts. Third, Weber saw a new type of party organization that was essentially devoid of ideology and lacked a formal programme, especially at the lower level of the political system.[22] Here, local and regional party bosses represented a new brand of politics that belonged to the future. These were in preparation to shape Weber's political values as a pioneer of parliamentary democracy in Germany.[23]

---

18. Ringer, *Max Weber: An Intellectual*; Eliaeson, "Max Weber and Plebiscitary."
19. Villa, "Max Weber," 540.
20. Mommsen, "Max Weber in America."
21. Weber, *From Max Weber*.
22. Mommsen, "Max Weber in America."
23. Eliaeson, "Max Weber and Plebiscitary."

Following the model of democracy in America, Weber saw things from a broader perspective on his return to Germany. Being convinced that politics is not to be judged solely as a moral business, his attitude was rather destined to see Germany "take its place among the mightiest nations upon the earth using a certain model."[24] From his observation in America, Weber discovered a system of politics called "machine politics," which was indispensable in a modern mass democracy, particularly with the German political system in mind. Machine politics refers to the "management of politics by professionals, by the disciplined party organization, and its streamlined propaganda, where the whole process tends toward increasing rational efficiency."[25] Those were among the reasons that Weber repeatedly cautioned his countrymen not to underrate America politically or economically.[26] Rather, he insisted that democracy must oppose "bureaucracy as a tendency towards a caste of mandarins, removed from the common people by expert training, examination certificates and tenure of office, . . . democracy has to promote what reason demands and democratic sentiment hates."[27] With such a concern, Weber suggested that Germany should borrow the American club pattern as a means of re-educating themselves.[28]

Following these observations, Weber noticed the need for reforms, partly on the social and political life of the German world of his day. Here, reforming an existing system did not imply outright rejection of the existing policies in some spheres, but to either strengthen or beautify them. In the case of the German situation, Weber's quest for reformation centred on the transformation of the political institutions which guaranteed participation that shapes the future.[29] That, in his view, would ensure that no form of dualism existed between different generations.[30] Although such efforts arose because of his interest in national issues, they were also for freedom of the autonomous

---

24. Weber, *From Max Weber*.
25. Weber, 107.
26. Mommsen, "Max Weber in America."
27. Weber, *From Max Weber*, 18.
28. Weber, *From Max Weber*; Farris, *Max Weber's Theory*.
29. Ringer, *Max Weber: An Intellectual*, 64.
30. Weber, *From Max Weber*.

personality that characterized the politics of his day, which increased Weber's interest and concern to venture deeper into the German political scene.[31]

In his effort for further distinction, Weber evaluated the relationship between politics and science as one of the key hubs of his thought.[32] Considering these two elements, it is discovered that science provides humanity with objective knowledge but has nothing to say about the fundamental questions of politics, which concerns values.[33] One of these fundamental questions relates to the welfare and security of the populace which, for certain reasons, is buried in modernity's consumerist ideology. This could be called scientific rationalization, which Weber attests has limitations in promoting values. In part, the limitation of scientific rationalization is not only incapable of guaranteeing happiness, freedom or justice, but may prevent[34] the realization of these ideals. These three are the beginning point toward building societal moral fibre. An attempt to cripple them through rationalization of science, as Weber observes, would result in opening other channels, such as injustice, to prevail. On the contrary, although rationalizing science has costly limitations, its contribution to modernity cannot be underestimated.

Modernity cannot also be discarded for its contribution. In a sense, modernity has subjected its function of welfare through the establishment of the rule of law and rational-legal administration and creation[35] of liberal democratic order. On this, Ferrera insists that modernity has, on the contrary, allowed for the emergence of a distinctive value sphere that is nested within the wider political community such that professional political elites now compete for the common good by providing the political community a sense of direction through the infusion of values. This situation has made the state more and more inaccessible to forms of morality[36] and welfare. This inaccessibility happens where the ideals of politics and democracy are misplaced and misappropriated. Such are the situations parading majority democratic governance today, including in Nigeria, where the political misappropriation overshadows societal welfare. As a result, vital elements, among them human

---

31. Ringer, *Max Weber: An Intellectual*, 60.
32. Ferrera, "Objectivity, Political Order," 256.
33. Ferrera, 257.
34. Gane, "Max Weber," 549.
35. Ferrera, *Max Weber: An Intellectual*, 272.
36. Ferrera, "Objectivity, Political Order," 272.

dignity, are under severe abuse because the provision of basic human needs is distanced from actualization.

Furthermore, the tragic disjunction of scientific progress and political freedom were issues of Weber's greatest vision of disenchantment from political power which contrasts with his view of political[37] leadership. For Weber, "political leadership entails more active than passive mediation of fate that the political leader faces the ethical irrationality of the world, and takes responsibility for its bearing on political action."[38] Certainly, even in his day, the political leadership was of such great concern that Weber came close to taking up the calling of politics but was stopped,[39] for some reasons, by regional party officials, and his health – or his innermost instincts. For him, such efforts were to ensure the appropriation of what political leadership entails and to explain the expected role of the political leader. Weber suggests why a political leader must take cognizance of the fact that political means, ends and consequences do not either correspond as intended or ethically justify one another, on the one hand. On the other hand, "a leader strives both for political success and for an ethical correspondence of political means, ends, purposes and consequences."[40] Even so, Weber concludes on the condition to which this is achievable, thus, proposing the reconciliation of two opposing ethics; the ethics of responsibility and an ethic of conviction, which he sees would amalgamate the political leader and their leadership responsibilities to the political community. Or more appropriately, that the two concepts could bring close the existing distance between the political class and the masses whose mandates they seek to represent.

In his efforts to bridge the said gap between politicians and those they represent, Weber thought of an alternative way of engaging with the public issues of his day. His new view was aimed at making a distinction between what could be called traditional politics – the nature of political leadership and participation he saw that informs the motivation people had toward political participation – and what could bring motivation toward political involvement. In what characterizes the political scene, Weber attests to

---

37. Gane, "Max Weber," 549.
38. Gane, 549–50.
39. Ringer, *Max Weber: An Intellectual*, 41.
40. Gane, "Max Weber," 550.

violence as a means, that is, the exercise of the threat of coercion which only produces restrictions[41] on the physical freedom and even destruction of life. That is in existence only to the extent that coercive resources are centralized in a given structure that can impose on the members of the territorial community obligations which are fulfilled only because of the awareness[42] of the probability of physical coercion backing up such obligations. Weber describes such a political community as "a group whose members share the subjective feeling of 'belonging together' primarily based on effectual and/or traditional orientation."[43] Here, he describes the fundamental role of politics "as to build people together in stable territorial groups, sharing fundamental socio-cultural traits to safeguard their ordered interactions."[44] Seeing the havoc that such practice has caused to communities and persons, however, Weber resolved to introduce a different perspective to politics which, for him, could revive the lost interest the younger generation was developing.

4.2.2 A New Dimension?

Should there be a new way of ascertaining political participation that presents decent intentions and practice of it? Or, why is there misappropriation of political responsibility by political leaders? This section seeks to provide answers to these questions by using Weber's thoughts as a roadmap.

With concerns emanating from the nature of power play, Weber seeks a further investigation to ascertain the missing link to that effect. In his findings, Weber explored a notion that ought to be embedded in political participation that any intended political actor needed to know. He, therefore, suggests that politics be taken as a vocation.

4.2.2.1 A New Ethic of Political Engagement

Any attempt to place political vocation with other disciplines comes with considerations from current events demanding such a claim. The need to answer questions like "what is going wrong?", "how should we go from where we are?"

---

41. Ferrera, "Objectivity, Political Order," 268.
42. Ferrera, 268.
43. Ferrera, 269.
44. Ferrera, 271.

and "what is the implication of the current situation?" arise. In attempting to answer these and related questions, Weber's thoughts are helpful tools.

In his famous lecture delivered in the winter of 1919 in Munich, Weber outlined reasons for a change in political irrationality practiced in his day. In the aftermath of World War I, in a dramatic moment for Germany and Europe, Weber aimed to warn the young university students against the dangers of political extremism, whether marked by an excess of idealism or an excess of realism.[45] Shockingly to his audience, Weber made clear some disappointments they found in the lecture, in what Villa calls the "disillusioning realization that no conviction or cause, no matter its purity or success, can transform the stuff, the material of politics into something edifying."[46] By such disappointments, Weber dislodged his audience from concentrating on his speech about building their passion for politics, to encouraging them to learn to develop the right attitude towards it. In so doing, he infused into his students a new attitude to politics than what was seen, perceived and practiced. To put this differently, Weber deconstructed the minds of his audience from two ideals, namely material and immaterial. On the one hand, those whose foremost care is for the salvation or purity of their souls should stay out of politics. On the other hand, "those who can state that they love their city (nation or cause) more than their souls are ready to pursue politics as a vocation."[47]

One thing to note here is that the above assertions differentiate between "casual involvement in politics" and "the intentional taking of politics as a vocation. As for Weber, the debate about the vocation of politics is ultimately one not about whether politics can or should be ethical, rather "about what kind of ethical framework is most appropriate to political life."[48] Such intriguing thoughts fall back to his imperative "to do what must be done to meet the demands of the day in whatever sphere one finds oneself."[49] This gives us an idea of what choosing politics as a vocation would necessitate.

---

45. Pellizzoni, "Responsibility and Ultimate Ends."
46. Villa, "Max Weber," 542.
47. Villa, 541.
48. Starr, "The Structure," 408.
49. Villa, "Max Weber," 540.

Weber suggests the characteristics of an intending politician who desires taking politics as a vocation. These characteristics portray an extended exercise in "forcing idealistic youth to view politics in its least aspect, entirely stripped of the euphemisms political theory normally deploys to disguise the exercise of power."[50] Power, as understood in politics, relates to coercion influenced by political leaders, signalling that this is all politics involves. Such assumptions had deluded the minds of the youth so much that, in Weber's view, they saw venturing into political affairs an unedifying task. This is true in many domains when the interest of political leaders is swapped from nation-building to selfish gains and ambitions – an indication that leaders, as such, have no regard for politics as a vocation but as a mere profession to serve themselves. To deconstruct such ideologies, specific features of a political leader who takes politics as a vocation are outlined. First, anyone taking politics as a vocation must see that national life, in its entirety, "remains viable, durable, sustainable, even at the expense of their causes."[51] In essence, the normativity of the vocation of a political leader has not only a private aspect (calling) but also a public one which relates to the terms of the pursuit of the causes, the chosen virtues, hence making a political figure a public servant eager to champion the cause of public life, its sanctity and integrity. Further, Davis elaborates more features of politics as a vocation as follows:[52]

1. He must be a person of passion and devoted to a cause
2. He must have faith in the cause – in a "matter-of-fact" way
3. He must have a "sense of proportion."

Weber describes a political leader with the above qualities as a responsible person who is thoughtful, flexible and able to protect his choices, yet is not essentially indifferent to a firm or settled persuasion in the following manner: first, an eagerness to critically and repeatedly assess the predictable consequences of one's actions; second, a willingness to abandon or change the course if one has reason to believe such action will result in consequences harmful to other, more valuable or important ends and obligations; and third, an ability to justify one's final course of actions to others.[53]

---

50. Villa, 542.
51. Ferrera, "Objectivity, Political Order," 273.
52. Davis, "Max Weber on Religion," 40.
53. Davis, 40.

To illustrate the place of vocation in politics, Weber enumerates the structure and context from which such vocation could emerge. In an age of bureaucratized, massified politics, a vocation in politics would famously affirm the possibility of political leadership.[54] This was observable by Weber from the political realities in which those taking politics beside vocation operated. In that process, the marginalization and infringement of political decisions became the order. To demystify such assumptions, Weber affirms that politics, when taken as a vocation, could address such wrongs. One of the wrongs was a sort of advent of plebiscitary democracy, leading to the revival of the demagogue in Western politics, that could cripple an ideal political responsibility of politicians.[55] Understood properly, such leadership style had little or no recognition of inward conviction to leadership as a vocation. As such, Weber suggests that "without inwardly called" leadership, politics devolves into the nihilism of administrative despotism, the rule of the "clique" through the "machine."[56] Such an attitude to political leadership probably informed Weber's quest for an ethic of responsibility, that will be discussed later.

Having a calling for politics implies that one has a specific[57] and rare form of moral integrity. Moral integrity comprises one's ability to adhere to both morality and ethics in principles and practice, having sound moral character, hence, demonstrating sincerity to a cause. Applying to leadership, this calls for the apt demonstration that one could convincingly answer for their actions and inactions to be called a responsible person. Indeed when politics is taken as a vocation and the politician a moral actor, a commitment[58] to a cause that does not "allow the diversion through the influence of external temptations arises."[59] The enthusiasm to withstand pressures, however, is what most political office seekers, even in our African context, lack. Instead, one finds "sterile excited"[60] intellectuals who are intoxicated by politics, or mere "power politicians," who pursue power for its own sake, and are intoxicated with themselves. When such attitudes fully develop, they produce two deadly

---

54. Villa, "Max Weber," 542.
55. Villa, 542.
56. Villa, "Max Weber," 543.
57. Villa, 543.
58. Davis, "Max Weber on Religion."
59. Enderle, "The Ethics of Conviction," 85.
60. Villa, "Max Weber," 543; de Villiers, "The Recognition of Human Dignity."

political sins, namely "lack of objectivity and irresponsibility,"[61] or moral sins in the political world such as "lack of realism and lack of responsibility."[62] These two political and/or moral sins suggest weak moral integrity that cannot withstand the seduction of vanity, thus nullifying the interest of individuals with such weakness in taking politics as a vocation. In such a case, the political leader would require to combine a passion for their call or what they want to get into, with passion and responsibility to pursue politics as a vocation.[63]

Besides moral integrity as a prerequisite for a vocation in politics, a politician must also have some sense of economic freedom and control to help them keep off the proceeds springing from politics. Understandably so, political involvement could take a new tone, particularly in areas where political involvement has financial enrichment as the sole goal. It keeps politics off the shores of vocation such that professionalism is substituted for an occupation where "only what is got out of it is the motivation." In addressing this, Weber has a different view while suggesting taking politics as a vocation. Here, Weber indicates two[64] inclusive scenarios that one desiring politics as a vocation should consider, namely one either lives "for" politics or lives "off" politics in thought and practice. In the sense of practice, the politician lives by benefitting from the naked possession of the exerted power or by nourishing inner balance and self-feeling by the consciousness that life has meaning in the service of a cause, as in the sense of thought.[65] The concern Weber tries to clarify here relates to control and discipline in the economic operation of the polity. He refers to the politician, who takes politics as a vocation, to be one who is wealthy or must have a personal position in life which yields a sufficient income.[66] Similar to this is what Ferrera cited that "politics in this sense lies where the subjectivity of purposes begins and the exercise of political power encounters axiological polytheism."[67]

These guiding thoughts from Weber connect us to what he meant by a proposal that politics be taken as a vocation. Yet, Weber did not stop here;

---

61. Villa, "Max Weber," 543.
62. Enderle, "The Ethics of Conviction," 83.
63. Gane, "Max Weber," 555.
64. Weber, *Politics as Vocation*, 9.
65. Weber, 9.
66. Weber, 9.
67. Ferrera, "Objectivity, Political Order," 272.

he balanced these views with what participating in politics as a vocation demands. This would include expectations from the politician who has agreed to venture into a political vocation, and the roles awaiting his/her performance. To demonstrate this better, Weber presents the concept of ethics of responsibility as a guide to political vocation.

4.2.2.2 Ethics of Responsibility

In his discussion of two ethics, Weber identifies the most important reason[68] for the relationship between politics and science and their relation to conviction and responsibility as the two ethics. In Weber's discourse on politics as a vocation, both ethics of conviction and responsibility form a distinction. Thus, the two concepts are best understood as a distinction between mutually exclusive ethical worldviews.[69] The distinction between these two mutually exclusive ethics is that although portrayed differently but subsumed together, they are "not irreconcilably opposed but as supplements."[70] The midpoint of these two worldviews makes them so exclusively connected that both have a share of Weber's value-rational social action and instrumental-rational social action. To bring the two together, "an ethic of conviction recognizes a given hierarchy of values as the context for moral endeavour; while the ethic of responsibility acknowledges value obligations, but assumes the absence of any given hierarchy of values and the inevitability of value conflict as the context for moral endeavour."[71] Comparing these two against Weber's multi-layered perception of value conflict, his ethic of responsibility emerges as a more coherent and contextual ethical perspective for moral discourse.[72]

Consequently, there are reasons to adapt Weber's ethic of responsibility other than an ethic of conviction as mentioned above. Before venturing into that, let us highlight some weaknesses of an ethic of conviction that makes it incapacitated as outlined.[73] First, an ethic of conviction cannot generate purposeful goals from first principles. Second, the indifference of this ethic to hard realities and its neglect of the need to match means to ends is inadequate.

---

68. Ferrera, 274.
69. Starr, "The Structure," 407.
70. Enderle, 83; Starr, "The Structure," 409.
71. Starr, 409
72. Starr, 407.
73. Ferrera, "Objectivity, Political Order," 274–75.

Third, it is entirely unfit for politics. Finally, choosing an ethic of conviction seems to entail complete disregard for consequences.[74] So, to salvage the inadequacy of the ethic of conviction, Weber brought an alternative ethic to strengthen the weaknesses.

The question one might ask here relates to why Weber would choose to dwell on an ethic of responsibility as a theoretical framework for moral and political discourse other than an ethic of conviction. Perhaps the pre-eminence of the ethic of responsibility seems consistent with Weber's epochal diagnosis, namely rationalisation as a relentless process. Considering what vocation in politics comprises, conviction forms a large part of it, yet not for this course of action. In the light of this, Weber's description of an "ethic of responsibility represents a coherent ethical perspective, one that he recommends as the most adequate moral framework for taking up the vocation of politics."[75] Further, Ferrera points out that Weber admitted an ethic of responsibility as the most politically adequate type of ethics.[76] Considering these reasons keenly, one notices that the coherency of this ethic relies on it seeing politics as a vocation in which responsibility is required, which suggests a kind of superiority over other ethics.

Indeed, the sounds of superiority become clearer in this course as Ferrera suggests. In the first place, responsibility is programmatically geared towards directly affecting this (imperfect) world and achieving success in the pursuit of causes that are ethically justified.[77] This ethical stance, Ferrera adds, is one that is fully adequate to the logic and rationale of the political sphere, which includes community building and community steering through purposive practical strategies. In the second instance, the superiority of an ethic of responsibility over an ethic of conviction is that it is the only one suited to the means that are specific to that sphere where the coercive resources monopolized by every political community are made available to its leaders.[78] Following these assertions, one could argue that an ethic of responsibility is spelled out and the vocational politician understands their role for, and

---

74. Pellizzoni, "Responsibility and Ultimate Ends."

75. Starr, "The Structure," 408.

76. Ferrera, "Objectivity, Political Order," 274, see also: Pellizzoni, "Responsibility and Ultimate Ends."

77. Ferrera, "Objectivity, Political Order," 275.

78. Ferrera, 275.

in, the political community. This is because the political leader is left to face the ethical irrationality of the world where they require decisiveness to act responsibly, to use a human-machine to curb all forms of harm, killing, and undermining of human dignity in a given political community.[79]

The emergence of an ethic of responsibility as the preferable form of ethics by Weber relates also to his understanding of the ethically chaotic nature of the world.[80] In a world where so many problems are created by the clash between communities – especially religious communities – something more, as responsibility, is required. From the moment he considered interests in politics, Weber's discoveries of the nature of manipulation and the onward movement of political leadership were sometimes unbearable. Thus, his careful choice of an ethic of responsibility was "Weber's formulation of a political stance adequate to address morally serious endeavour in a world characterized by inevitable and irresolvable value conflict."[81] An ethic of responsibility, in such a case, identifies with an anthropological reality of personhood. This includes a realisation that while we are born as persons or individuals, we must become personalities by systematic devotion to a cause, a value, which we share in a calling.[82] In this case, adopting an ethic of responsibility is rather an objective imperative that follows from the fundamental and specific nature of the political activity, thus, making responsibility the defining feature of the political vocation.[83]

From the above discussions, Weber's choice of an ethics of responsibility over an ethic of conviction in moral political discourse deserves mention. As to the "what" of responsibility to Weber, he considers it as one's ability to acknowledge value obligations with an absence of any given hierarchy of values. Here, he sees responsibility as having to do with the power of the mind in discerning ethical decisions on the one hand. The "why" of an ethic of responsibility for Weber, on the other hand, is in what he describes as the coherent ethical framework for those taking up the vocation of politics.

---

79. Gane, "Max Weber," 549; Ferrera, "Objectivity, Political Order," 276.
80. Davis, "Max Weber on Religion."
81. Starr, "The Structure," 409.
82. Starr, 414.
83. Ferrera, "Objectivity, Political Order," 276.

4.3 Other Perspectives on Ethics of Responsibility: Some German Perspectives

The concept of ethics of responsibility has grown through different fields of study, including Christian theology. Albeit having its development from non-theological perspectives, theologians over the years have developed the Christian versions from different contexts. Thus, contained in this section is a developmental survey of the ethics of responsibility from the German and American Christian versions. For such a survey, this section looks at German theologians such as Dietrich Bonhoeffer and Wolfgang Huber only as a representation. The reason for this choice is that these theologians have developed ideas and perspectives that suit this study better than others. The second subsection focuses on the English-speaking world, particularly, America, where the works of the Niebuhrian brothers and William Schweiker are discussed. Having looked at the German and American perspectives, the next chapter will explore the works of Etienne de Villiers, a South African theologian, who has made some great and insightful contributions on ethics of responsibility from an African perspective.

4.3.1 Dietrich Bonhoeffer

Peculiar to Bonhoeffer's interest in ethics in general, and responsibility in particular, is the realized eminent fall of Hitler's Nazism that brought about Germany's moral and political failure. At this time, Bonhoeffer saw that these realities had already conspired against Hitler's Nazi government with the willingness to participate in rebuilding a new Germany. Perhaps, it was for this reason that Bonhoeffer returned to his homeland while ministering abroad, which also informed his interest in writing *Ethics*.[84] This is the context within which Bonhoeffer's ethics could be understood.

Dietrich Bonhoeffer was the first theologian to speak programmatically about ethics of responsibility in the period of his involvement in the political conspiracy against the National Socialist dictatorship.[85] He understood responsibility as an answer given through living one's own life, to God's address to the human. Bonhoeffer saw the structure of the responsible life "as

---

84. Kim, "Dietrich Bonhoeffer's Ethics," 44.
85. Huber, *Ethics*, 90.

marked by the harmony of freedom and the attachment of self-transcendence and the living of one's life."[86]

Although his view of responsibility sprang from the above context, Bonhoeffer had consultations with other scholars regarding this field of academic inquiry, notably Karl Barth and Reinhold Niebuhr, who equally delved into the inquiry. In his interaction with Barth, Bonhoeffer presented what he considers urgent themes that theologians of the confessing church could work on. Of these themes, responsibility became one which Bonhoeffer thought Barth would write on, but eventually explored the topic himself at length in his ethics.[87] His motivation in exploring responsibility came from the reflection on the German church struggle where he observed a crucial phenomenon called civil courage was missing. This concept could only grow out of the free responsibility of men which resulted in him developing the topic under the title "the structure of a responsible life."[88]

Unlike other voices in the field of responsibility ethics whose concern emanated from either flaw of former ethics (Jonas), the nature of former ethics and the challenges of our time while seeking to provide a different kind of ethics of responsibility (Huber), Bonhoeffer differs. Bonhoeffer bases his survey of responsibility from a biblical[89] point of view rather than philosophical (Jonas), sociological (Weber), theological (the Niebuhrian brothers, Huber and Schweiker). From this backdrop, we will look at how Bonhoeffer theologically portrays the concept of ethics of responsibility; using his major work on ethics as our primary source.

Foremost in his ethical discussions are concerns on the human quest for a good life and wellbeing. Efforts to realize these have faced challenges of rationality, objectivity and the influx of modernity, so much so that arriving at absolutes is problematized. Bonhoeffer, however, engages this notion by, first giving a description of both the uniqueness of a human person and how they live. His comments show that any description of the good reflects the

---

86. Huber, *Ethics*, 90.
87. Wannenwesch, "Responsible Living," 129.
88. Bonhoeffer, *Ethics*, 129.
89. Bonhoeffer, 255.

fact that human beings have a life that is situated in a unique person, Jesus Christ.[90] He refers to our act of living as

> our encounter with other human beings and with God that is bound together in a unity of contradiction, in selfless self-assertion, and in self-assertion that is a surrender of myself to God and other human beings. As such, we live by responding to the word of God addressed to our whoe life in Jesus Christ.[91]

By living in response to the word of God suggests that we do not live as isolated human persons but in connection with God and others. By such living, we become stewards to both our lives, the lives of others and to God.

Bonhoeffer defines a responsibility as that life in answer to the life of Jesus Christ which denotes the complete wholeness and unity of the answer to the reality in Jesus Christ as opposed to the partial answers that we might give.[92] From a different note, he stresses the concreteness of responsibility according to which every individual is to respond in their life at the very place in which they find themselves.[93] In this case, Bonhoeffer takes responsibility to mean "risking one's life in its wholeness, aware that one's activity is a matter of life and death."[94] Recalling his point of departure, the biblical perspective, from which he situates responsibility, Bonhoeffer differs from other views. He regards responsibility from the biblical sense as primarily a response given at the risk of one's life to the questions people ask about the Christ event. He puts it thus,

> at the risk of my life, I give an account and thus take responsibility for myself, for my actions; I do not justify myself. Rather, I take responsibility and answer for Christ Jesus, and with that, I naturally also take responsibility for the commission I have been charged with by him.[95]

---

90. Bonhoeffer, 254.
91. Bonhoeffer, 254.
92. Bonhoeffer, 255.
93. Wannenwesch, "Responsible Living," 131.
94. Bonhoeffer, *Ethics*, 255.
95. Bonhoeffer, 255.

Taking it further, this involves being responsible to Christ, who is life, before human beings and before God. We concurrently represent Christ before human beings and embody human beings before Christ. When this happens, Bonhoeffer states,

> I can take responsibility for myself before God and before human beings . . . taking responsibility occurs before God and for God; before human beings and for human beings; as always answering and being responsible for the sake of Jesus Christ through which way I become responsible for my own life."[96]

In all these, Bonhoeffer puts together these concepts, responsibility, answering and accountability as those that exist only in confessing[97] Jesus Christ in word and life. This makes responsibility only as the life lived in answer[98] to the life of Jesus Christ.

4.3.1.1 *The Structure of a Responsible Life*

Following the preceding discussion, it is worthwhile to look at what Bonhoeffer considers as constituting the structure of a responsible life. In his imaginations, Bonhoeffer presents two[99] concepts as parameters for this inquiry, namely life's bond to human beings and God, and the freedom of human's own life. Such bonding force reminds us of the human interconnections, first with God and with other humans through which we live in response to God. By this bond of relationality, we make choices, which also constitute freedom. While making these choices, however, we face the complexity of selflessness, a significant constituent in Bonhoefferian analysis of responsibility.

In his commitment to elucidating selflessness, Bonhoeffer uses the concept of vicarious representative action, acting or doing an action for or on behalf of someone, who has no power to do for themselves. Vicarious representation involves freedom to act on behalf of others which, in the context of Bonhoefferian assertion on responsibility, emanates from the existing bond between God and human beings. This freedom "exhibits itself in one's accountability for their living and acting and the scheme of concrete

---

96. Bonhoeffer, 256.
97. Bonhoeffer, 256.
98. Wannenwesch, "Responsible Living," 131.
99. Bonhoeffer, *Ethics*, 257.

decisions."[100] It is, therefore, within this framework, that we consider the structure of responsible life.

Responsibility based on vicarious representative action is most evident but not exclusively in relationships where one is required to act for the sake of others.[101] In the case of relationships, which Bonhoeffer calls deputyship elsewhere, they constitute one who acts in the place of others,[102] say a father for his children, a statesman for the society, or an instructor for a learner. In this case, a father bears in him the responsibility of working, providing, intervening, struggling, and even to the point of suffering for his children, which makes him stand and act in their place. In so doing, he bears in him the selves of those looking up to him that he must act responsibly, else he denies it when he attempts thinking of being isolated.[103] At an occurrence of such attempts, Bonhoeffer describes it an act of irresponsibility. This informs us of vicarious representative action found in relationships.

Responsibility based on vicarious representative action also involves individuals in isolated circumstances who might not directly have others they have to stand on their behalf but occurs through choice and freedom. Here, choice and freedom could be seen in an interconnection where freedom of will comes with choices which, though having consequences, one freely chooses anyway. The prominent example of this is Jesus Christ[104] who, having no attached responsibility like a father above, does not exclude him from the domain of responsibility. Jesus Christ, Bonhoeffer asserts, was an individual who sought to achieve some personal perfection but only lived as the one who in himself has taken on and bears the selves of all human beings with all

---

100. Bonhoeffer, 257.

101. Bonhoeffer, 257.

102. A similar example of such vicarious representative actions could be seen in society: how a statesman relates and treats others. In the case of a nation, we could agree with Bonhoeffer's assertion of irresponsibility when there is denial to take and assume responsibility to protect, promote, enhance, and sustain the existence and flourishing of human life. A prominent example could be derived from Bonhoeffer's personal life. We would recall that in the plot to assassinate Hitler, Bonhoeffer's participation was not a blind embracing or a refutation of his pacifist claims. Rather, it was a decision to act vicariously on behalf of those who could not act and to shoulder the sin of that action.

103. Bonhoeffer, 258.

104. This symbol reminds us of Jesus's vicarious act through the incarnation, crucifixion, and resurrection on behalf of humanity that cannot be enacted independently from the power of God in Christ.

their guilt. This real vicarious representative action, therefore, makes Jesus the responsible human being par excellence.[105] It is interesting to note that Jesus's attitude went beyond and above desiring self-glorification or dwelling in self-perfection, but a portrayal of selflessness. No wonder Bonhoeffer insists that "vicarious representative action and responsibility is possible only in completely devoting one's life to another person. Hence, only those who are selfless live responsibly which means that only selfless people truly live."[106]

Taking the idea further one can reflect on some thoughts of a fourth-century influential figure, Ambrose of Milan, regarding acting for the betterment of others.[107] Bonhoeffer echoes Ambrose saying that "the person who fails to deflect an injury from his neighbour when he is in a position to do so, is as much as at fault as the one who inflicts it."[108] While such realities may be hard to find in today's society, a few exceptions of selfless persons could demonstrate a sense of responsibility for others without a boundary limit. Reacting to those who insist that doing good should only be restricted to the benefit of oneself, Ambrose defers. He declares that "the motive for carrying out one's duties should not be to benefit and bring glory to oneself or one's state but to honour God and bring him glory."[109]

Jesus's vicarious action includes voluntariness to accepting the guilt of humanity upon himself. Although being guilty involves one's wrong action, but in Jesus Christ, the tone differs. He chose to willingly accept the guilt without sin, hence, Bonhoeffer sees such action as the origin of every action of responsible deputyship.[110] For fear of guilt, selflessness loses its grip and substance. This keeps us from acting for the common good of others either by standing[111] isolated when we need to get involved or otherwise. Through Jesus Christ, Bonhoeffer affirms, it becomes an essential part of responsible action that the man who is without sin loves selflessly[112] and for that reason incurs

---

105. Bonhoeffer, 259.
106. Bonhoeffer, 259.
107. Granville, "Christianity and the Responsibility."
108. Granville, 317.
109. Granville, 317.
110. Bonhoeffer, *Dietrich Bonhoeffer Ethics*, 241.
111. Bonhoeffer, *Ethics*, 269.
112. Bonhoeffer, *Dietrich Bonhoeffer Ethics*, 241.

guilt. It then suggests that responsible persons called to act responsibly place their actions into the hands of God and live by God's grace and judgement.

4.3.1.2 *The Place of the Ethic of Responsibility*

With the structure of a responsible life characterizing and suggesting a responsible life, action, and living, it is significant to understand the place of ethics of responsibility. It would mean the context at which this structure strives and why it is necessarily so.

In discussing the place of ethics of responsibility, Bonhoeffer uses the concept in ethics, namely a vocation to link an interplay with responsibility. It is that concept that has appeared in different contexts including, but not limited to, secular and biblical ethics respectively, but in other spheres as well. While Weber digests its constituents from a social perspective, Martin Luther makes similar engagement with the concept but sees vocation merely as the justification and sanctification of the worldly orders, particularly in the New Testament. Bonhoeffer, however, chooses to differ from them to focus on biblical evidence.[113]

Bonhoeffer begins this search by first, clarifying a sort of correspondence between responsibility and vocation. Taking from biblical evidence, he aligns vocation as God's gracious call of human beings into salvation, and a life that calls for action. While responsibility, on the contrary, is the involvement and intentional response of this call for all its essence, namely forming and living in a community with other like-minded people. Bonhoeffer stresses this scenario to substantiate the claim that through an encounter with Jesus Christ, an individual experiences God's call which extends to a life in community with Jesus Christ.[114] By this, Bonhoeffer refers to the reality of the divine call of humanity through grace, and thus made these human beings God's possession. As God's belonging, the essence of this call extends to unity with the one who calls, but also with others that are called and have been justified. With this, Bonhoeffer opines from Christ's perspective that this life is now my vocation, and from my perspective, it is my responsibility.[115] By this unity, the boundary of vocation is broken not only vertically through

---

113. Bonhoeffer, *Ethics*, 289.
114. Bonhoeffer, 290.
115. Bonhoeffer, 293.

Jesus, but also horizontally, about the extent of responsibility. It indicates, however, the extent of what we owe others with whom we are stewards, how we take care of God's good creation.

Further, we could also equate this boundless responsibility with the responsibility of the church to the world, as Hauerwas suggests while referring to the social task of the church. In his discussions on the social responsibility of the church to the world, Hauerwas makes a strong emphasis on the church as being a community. With the realities of our times, some of which are leading to enmity between the world and the church, Hauerwas reminds us that these are two relational concepts and none can exist without the other. They are companions on a journey that one would not survive without the other. The often perceived ground for enmity goes to misplacement of priority that the church tries to deny its role in the world, which suggests some sort of dismissing the world as irredeemable but transforming itself into a triumphalist subordination of the world.[116] The church, Hauerwas insists, ought to identify God's boundless redemption work such that the world should not be left in a helpless and hopeless situation but be a people with a hope sufficient to sustain both the world and us. Hauerwas's conclusion on the social responsibility of the church, therefore, goes beyond the vocation of God's gracious call of the human persons to be the church and help the world understand itself as the world. So, for the church to be the church, it is not to be anti-world, but rather attempt to "show what the world is meant to be as God's good creation."[117] For this to be actualized, Hauerwas adds that God requires that a church be a community of discourse and interpretation that endeavours to tell the stories about the character of God revealed in the stories of Israel, and Jesus, and form its life in accordance to them.[118] Bonhoeffer would have agreed with Hauerwas on this view of the saintly community called the church with a vocation as the "called out ones," but with a boundless responsibility. This sort of responsibility informs how we deal with those outside the shores of the church in responding to God's call in us for them, namely, to be stewards to God's good creation. Bringing this view to the context of this study would mean that we are called to, either as

---

116. Hauerwas, *A Community of Character*, 2.
117. Hauerwas, *The Peaceable Kingdom*, 100.
118. Hauerwas, *A Community of Character*, 92.

individuals or community of believers and general society, remember that we are responsible to God in the way that we treat others, especially those we have an edge over to protect.

4.3.2 Hans Jonas

This section presents another German version of the ethics of responsibility, the philosophical perspective of Hans Jonas.[119] His central argument is on reimagining ethics for the technological age that focuses on safeguarding and enhancing the wellbeing of the future generation. The section delves into his view of an ethic of responsibility and why he thinks it is necessary than the previous forms of ethics. Studying the thoughts of Jonas is necessary because many proponents of ethics of responsibility, both from Germany and America, began inquiries in ethics of responsibility after the publication of his book, *The Imperative of Responsibility: in Search of An Ethics of Responsibility for the Technological Age*, which serves as our major literature resource for this review.

4.3.2.1 What Informs Jonas's Ethics of Responsibility

Jonas, like other philosophers of his time, "drew upon his wartime experiences and the enormous technological advances of the post-war years to offer a controlling critique of the age."[120] As a passionate scholar, he wrote with equal perspicacity on various subjects, raising issues which were brought together in a fluid and concise work.[121] Two of the issues he raised include the flawlessness of former or traditional ethics, and the negligence and revitalisation of environmental ethics. These two concerns originated from Jonas's view that a new ethics is required, which he along with other scholars, refers to as the ethics of responsibility.

---

119. Jonas (1903–1993) was one of the greatest German-Jewish philosophers of the twentieth century. He, like other philosophers of his time, drew upon his wartime experiences and the immense technological developments of the post-war years to offer a powerful critique of the age. More so, he devised an ontologically grounded ethics which he hoped might be able to rise to contemporary challenges, foremost of which was the environmental ethics. And yet, in the English-speaking world, Jonas has never achieved anything like the status of his peers, despite being highly regarded in Germany and Italy (Morris, *Hans Jonas' Ethics*).

120. Morris, *Hans Jonas' Ethics*, 105.

121. Morris, *Hans Jonas' Ethics*.

As such, nature, in the form of environment, has been and still is a significant aspect of human existence and interaction. In it, human beings exist and interact with other non-human creatures, thus calling for an ethics of care, nurturing and enhancement, for progressive and continual existence. Jonas's philosophy also informs the analysis of the environment such that environmental science relies heavily on his analysis for the essential elements of its work concerning nature and responsibility.[122]

Accordingly the theme of responsibility has, for some time, not received meaningful attention from environmental theories. The reason for this is two-fold: first, because of the moral character of responsibility, and second, because of the influence of welfare policies.[123] The moral character of responsibility focuses beyond what is immaterial as taken by human beings, to strictly what is significant (having to do with nothing but human beings). In this case, Jonas suggests that "individual responsibility be widened to collective responsibility and further extended out to future generations."[124] Here, both the moral and the welfare policies, as these concern responsibility, apply in Jonas's above submission of extending it to the future. His idea and concern for the future generation agrees with Schweiker's imperative of responsibility for "the enhancement of the integrity of life," hereafter, the reality in calling to order or revising old traditional ethics which could bring about the integration of ecological preoccupations of social and political ethics.[125]

The second theme in Jonas's ethics of responsibility is "the flawlessness of former ethics." By former ethics, he refers to traditional ethical discourse with limitations to combat the devastating influence of technological advancement created by and for humans' satisfaction. These former ideas of ethics,

> whether in the form of issuing direct enjoinders to do and not to do certain things, or in the form of defining principles for such enjoinders, or in the form of establishing the ground of obligation for obeying such principles has in common, that the human condition, determined by the nature of man and the nature of things, was given once for all; that the human good on

---

122. Bazin, "A Reading," 2.
123. Bazin, 2.
124. Bazin, 2.
125. Schweiker, *Responsibility and Christian Ethics*, 35.

that basis was readily determinable; and that the range of human action and therefore responsibility was narrowly circumscribed.[126]

It, indeed, follows that former ethics in Jonas's view, does not apply to the realities of contemporary challenges influenced by technological advancement. He discloses why this remains so in three ways: first, through his perception of the changing nature of human action and, since ethics is concerned with action, it should follow that the changing nature of human action calls for a change in ethics as well.[127] Second, Jonas discloses that "former ethics presented man as the maker of his life qua human, bending circumstances to his will and needs, and except against death, he is never helpless."[128] Third, in former ethics, nature was not an object of human responsibility. The changing nature of human action is, however, greatly influenced by the influx of modern technology that enhances human power beyond anything known or even dreamed of before. So, the power from modern technology is a power over matter, over life on Earth, and over human self which is growing at a fast-tracking pace.[129] Such power, as Jonas understands in the former ethics is anthropocentric, concentrated on magnifying and increasing the human capacity to control, subdue and subvert other non-humans.[130] Sadly, the influence of such human power goes beyond non-human beings, but has become detrimental to human beings in what he calls the worst kind of violence.[131] The focus of such power, however, is on "the here and now of occasions as they arise between men, of the recurrent, typical situations of private and public life."[132]

In part, Jonas's identification of the above challenges, as championed by the influence of technological advancement, has both benefits and threats to humanity and nature. The beneficial aspects of technology could be seen throughout history to have been enthusiastically welcomed because of their potential to liberate us from hunger, disease and poverty. Perhaps, it has been

---

126. Jonas, "Technology and Responsibility," 31; Jonas, *The Imperative of Responsibility*, :xiv.
127. Jonas, "Technology and Responsibility," 31.
128. Jonas, 31
129. Jonas, *The Imperative of Responsibility*, xiv.
130. Jonas, "Technology and Responsibility," 35.
131. Huber, *Violence: The Unrelenting Assault*.
132. Jonas, *The Imperative of Responsibility*, 5.

celebrated as the source of material progress and human fulfilment.[133] On the contrary, critics[134] of modern technology see it as a threat to authentic human life because it leads to uniformity in a mass society, a narrow criteria of efficiency, impersonality and manipulation, uncontrollability and the alienation of the worker.[135] Of the benefits of modern technology building an ideological base that humans could both have control over their lives and nature, Jonas calls these "novel powers of modern technology and asks how this technology affects the nature of our actions, and in what ways it makes acting under its dominion different from what it has been through the ages."[136] Such quest calls for a dramatic analysis of the features of former ethics and why Jonas calls for a new ethic of responsibility for the human future and non-human nature.[137]

4.3.3.2 Features of Former/Traditional Ethics

From the start of this section, we saw that Jonas had indicated flaws in former or traditional ethics. In his analysis and observation, Jonas neither seeks to condemn former ethics nor reject it, but is concerned about the irrelevance of these former ethics in the era of technological advancement for salvaging future generations from today's human cruelty. With his concern about the consequences of human action in the present and their effects for the future generation, Jonas reminds us about former ethics in a number of ways.

First, Jonas describes all traditional ethics as anthropocentric in that it does have humans as its centre of attraction, such that ethical significance belongs to the direct dealing of man to man, including dealing with himself.[138] This argument stems from de Villiers's question on why human beings peculiarly differ from other creatures, with answers from history it is because of humanity's possession of reason,[139] and their creation in the image of God. Jonas's second feature of former ethics states that it focuses on the here and now, with little or no emphasis on the future or yet unborn. He argues this

---

133. Barbour, *Ethics in An Age*, 4.
134. Read further on critics of technology (Barbour, *Ethics in An Age*, 10–14).
135. Barbour, *Ethics in an Age*, 10.
136. Jonas, "Technology and Responsibility," 32.
137. Barbour, 10.
138. Jonas, "Technology and Responsibility," 35; Jonas, *The Imperative of Responsibility*, 4.
139. de Villiers, "The Recognition of Human," 265.

in agreement with certain maxims showing confinement to immediate setting of actions, including the golden rule and certain maxims.[140] In all these maxims, however, the agent and the "other" of his action are solely sharers of a common present with no reference to the future. On the third feature, Jonas describes former ethics as one which the entity, man, and his basic condition was considered constant, and not itself an object of reshaping *techne*.[141] It follows from the fact that humans, in themselves, could not tame their use of technology. Rather, they embraced technology in its totality without caution on its usage on the future generation.

From these features of former or traditional ethics, Jonas expresses their relevance in today's world context with challenges of technological advancement. He does not nullify the existence of technology in time before now, but his concern is on "why modern technology has introduced actions of some novel scale objects and consequences that the framework of former ethics can no longer contain them."[142] Further, as a way of a critique of former ethics, Jonas insists that "no previous ethics had to consider the global condition of human life and the far-off-future, even existence of race. After all, no previous ethics prepared for us a role of stewardship and the dominant scientific view of nature, even less."[143] Some former ethics, in his view, portray "denial of all conceptual means to think of nature as something to be honoured after it has been reduced to the indifference of necessity and accident, and divested it of any dignity."[144] Consequently, it

---

140. Jonas sees some of these actions as those centered in the here and now with limited significance for the future generations or those not at the present. These include, "love thy neighbour as thyself"; Do unto others as you would wish them to do unto you"; "instruct your child in the way of truth"; "strive for excellence by developing and actualising the best potentialities of your *qua* man"; "subordinate your individual good to the common good"; "never treat your fellow man as a means only but always also as an end in himself" (Jonas, "Technology and Responsibility," 4); Looking into these maxims carefully, one could notice their reference to the present here and now. How could we do what to who when we do not have the knowledge of these "others?" This ethics focusing on the here and now, however, was of occasions as they arise between men, of the recurrent, typical situations of private and public life and it was only the good man could meet these with virtue and wisdom (Jonas, *The Imperative of Responsibility*, 5).

141. Jonas, "Technology and Responsibility," 35; Jonas, *The Imperative of Responsibility*, 4.

142. Jonas, "Technology and Responsibility," 38.

143. Jonas, 40.

144. Jonas, *The Imperative of Responsibility*, 8.

becomes not a new thing anymore to ask whether the condition of extra-human nature, the biosphere as a whole and parts now subject to human power, have become a human trust as has something of a moral claim on us not for our ulterior sake but its own and in its own right.[145]

What we could draw from this is the realisation of human loss of stewardship in three-fold, namely for themselves, for others and for the rest of creation. In this case, the human focus exclusively gears towards attaining human good, which implies humans live for self-recognition and attainment.[146]

Observing these flaws from former ethics, Jonas delves into proposing a more appropriate ethic, one that is applicable in addressing the concerns of modern technology than did former ethics, whose concern focused only on the here and now with limited attention on the hereafter. He, however, insists on formulating the ethics that go beyond using non-humans to satisfying human ends, rather as that which seeks for the recognition and enhancement of both. Hence, we turn to Jonas's proposal for ethics of responsibility in the era of modern technological advancement.

4.3.3.3 Jonas's Ethics of Responsibility for the Technological Age

Here, we will briefly outline what Jonas sees as adequate ethics for the technological age. Perhaps observing the flaws of the former ethics, he considers appropriate and sufficient ways that ethics could combat human consumerist ideology over nature, which subdues both human and non-human beings for human satisfaction.

Technology has turned humans into creators[147] of self-images that entertain them such that they become the makers and the doers for their future that calls for salvaging human life from continuous human manipulation. Being the reality with both human and non-human beings, such ideological behaviour calls for retrospection. In that case, the human mind would require to be reminded of its place of stewardship, which goes beyond coercive power for dominance. To ensure compliance to that cause, we must rethink how to redress and readjust our commitments that bring reduction to the human

---

145. Jonas, "Technology and Responsibility," 40.
146. Jonas, 40.
147. Jonas, 41.

extremist ideology of using non-humans as means to ends with no or little concern against technological effects. Here, Jonas suggests an integrative and intentional stewardship that reminds human beings of their sole responsibility to God, other human beings and nature.

A new ethic of responsibility suitable for the modern technological age demands a reconsideration of the human relation and perception of nature.[148] As a gift to humanity, nature assumes central placement in human affairs as the source of life and living. Such arguments could face objection when nature is perceived to exist solely for human satisfaction and benefit. That is an "earthly point of viewing nature which makes it reductionistic and guarantees human's mismanagement of it thereof."[149] Since by human definition, nature has limited resources, Jonas cautions that "irresponsible economic and technological growth threatens to destroy the resources of this earthly nature."[150] Arguing further, "nature has a right to life just as much as does man."[151] In this regard, Jonas could not take any dichotomies between man and nature, which gives man hierarchy and autonomy at the expense of nature. Instead, he "establishes a continuum of which the common point is the organism–as it continues its existence."[152] Should we not here detect Jonas's perception of the vulnerability of nature as a result of human control of it using technology? Jonas, in this regard, presumes danger in the lifespan of both humanity and nature when he considers how human beings seek independence and detachment from the roots (nature) by living and doing what they so wish. As such, he "appeals to a collective consciousness" sparking an ethical jumpstart of responsibility, whose goal is to awaken human's responsibility towards saving existence itself."[153]

An ethic of the future seeks to instil in us the fear whose guidance we need, where that which is to be feared has not yet happened and has perhaps no analogies in past or present experience.[154] Such fear also includes the acts of justice and fairness in the actions of the present and their implications for

---

148. Jonas, 51.
149. Bazin, "A Reading," 3.
150. Bazin, 4.
151. Schelling, *First Outline*, 23.
152. Bazin, "A Reading," 4.
153. Bazin, 5.
154. Jonas, *The Imperative of Responsibility*, 27.

future generations.[155] Such affirmations indicate that if there are no future generations, there can be no more doing justice and no more exercise of responsibility. In presuming any fear for the future generation of humans, we must understand what is presently at stake and why the fear. It means we would need to know the significance of courage to understand the extent of the fear for the future. In our search for future ethics of responsibility for the technological age, Jonas puts it that it is an "anticipated distortion of man that helps us to detect in the normative conception of man which is to be preserved from it."[156] It is from knowing what the danger is that we would value the strategy to safeguarde against it. Otherwise, we would not know what to preserve and why, but only to know what is at stake when we know it is really at stake[157] It, thus, becomes our duty to seek to know what we need to preserve and why it needs to be preserved. In this case, we talk about the preservation of human life and nature at present, but more importantly, for their continued existence in the future. Such a search, Jonas suggests, requires an effort of reason and imagination that can instil in us the fear whose guidance we need. That, however, becomes in itself the first duty of the ethics we are speaking about.[158]

Arguably, imagination and reasoning do not completely portray the quest for future ethics but require a consistent and intentional commitment to engaging what is imagined or reasoned. In this case, Jonas suggests education as a parameter. He puts it that we "must educate our soul to a willingness to let itself be affected by the mere thought of possible fortunes and calamities of future generations so that the projections of futurology will not remain mere food for idle curiosity or equally idle pessimism."[159] Instead, they would turn to realistic goals where our educated mind converts knowledge into engaging actionable steps fostering societal and human wellbeing. Therefore, "bringing ourselves to this emotional readiness, developing an open attitude to the stirrings of fear in the face of merely conjectural and distant forecasts concerning man's destiny, is the second preliminary duty of the ethic we are seeking."[160]

---

155. Muers, "Pushing the Limit," 39.
156. Jonas, *The Impertive of Responsibility*, 26.
157. Jonas, 27.
158. Jonas, 27.
159. Jonas, *The Imperative of Responsibility*, 28.
160. Jonas, 28.

In Jonas's search for the ethics of responsibility for the technological age, it is needful here to refer to some of his claims and references to concepts. One of these concepts relates to the golden rule, which signifies either the effects or significance of our current actions on the future generation. He puts it thus, "in your present choices, include the future wholeness of man among the objects of your will."[161]

Another concept Jonas uses to describe the future ethics of responsibility for the technological age relates to some decisions taken by leadership structures. Considering the nature of modern societies, leadership has taken a representation that decisions are taken on behalf of others. In a situation where such structures make decisions, particularly when those decisions have effects, it raises concerns. Jonas engages this scenario having the future generation in mind that he cautions the decisions taken here and now that have effects beyond here and now. Here, he expresses dismay over the "insufficiency of representative governments to meet the new demands on its normal principles and its normal mechanics."[162] Jonas's concern about the representative government is in its one-sided representation whereas the same decisions are set to affect the future generation while they are not here now. In this case,

> it serves the present decision-makers well if they realize that the non-existent has no lobby, and the unborn are powerless and so accountability to them has no political reality behind it . . . in the present decision-making and when they can make complaints then, we, the culprits, will no longer be there to either accept or reject blames for our actions and inactions.[163]

In Jonas's view, because decisions have a lasting impact (either positive or negative), they should be informed by the context and nature of people who would live with those decisions.

In summary, Jonas presented us with three ideals to help us unravel his proposal for the future ethics of responsibility in the technological age. First, he identifies his problem with former ethics, which is no longer fit to contain the challenges of the technological age, signalling the need to change to a

---

161. Jonas, "Technology and Responsiibility," 44.
162. Jonas, 51.
163. Jonas 51.

new ethic that is profitable to address current realities and shows potential for salvaging future generation. Second, he outlines the ineptness of former ethics and its focus in three areas, namely that it was solely anthropocentric; it focused only on the here and now without consideration for future generation; and that it was one which puts man, and his basic condition above being an object of reshaping. Third, he offers a proposal for ethics for the technological age, which has the potential to salvage the destruction of humans and nature in the future.

4.3.3 Wolfgang Huber

In this section, the ideas of Wolfgang Huber[164] (1942–2023), another German theologian who has written widely, not only on the ethics of responsibility, but theological ethics at large, are explored. We will journey with Huber on his interest, development and concern for ethics of responsibility and what it means for us today. In this section, we will, as we have done with others earlier, come up with his suggestive conclusions on what and how ethics of responsibility that is suitable for our time should be constructed.

4.3.3.1 Huber's Interest in Ethics of Responsibility

In his reflections and imaginations of events, Huber sees as a challenge to the twenty-first century's witness of a paradigm shift in the field of ethics, which he characterized into three broad classes. First, the era that sees and evaluates life, perhaps human life as a project. This involves planned births under certain circumstances, pregnancies being rejected, and in short, people becoming authors of their life histories.[165] These challenges are easily associated with the advancement of science and technology, where human beings are trying to replicate themselves. Such a scenario often possesses questions

---

164. Huber is a former Bishop of Berlin-Brandenburg in the German Evangelical Church and served as Chairperson of the National Council of the Evangelical Church in Germany (EKD), until his retirement in 2009. He is currently an Extraordinary Professor of Theology at Heidelberg University as well as at Humboldt University, Berlin, and a Fellow of STIAS at Stellenbosch University, South Africa (Huber, *The Dignity*, 427). In his academic career, among many other things, Huber taught systematic theology, especially Christian ethics, at two German Universities. Also, he was at some time both a staff member and a deputy director of a church-affiliated research institute, the Protestant Institute for Interdisciplinary Research, in Heidelberg (Huber, *The Dignity*, 428).

165. Huber, *Ethics*, vii.

on how particularly, Christians ought to live in such a world. Huber was once asked similar questions too. During one of his ministry moments, the question of how a Christian church can face the great challenges of our times that are shaped by science and technology, by the presence of military means of mass destruction, and the growing global disparity.[166] From this moment, Huber concentrated on how Christian churches, as communities of faith, take public responsibility, the topic which became his interest from then onward.[167] He did this while affirming why ethics does not just involve the questions of what we can do and what we ought to do, but also the question of who we are.[168]

Equally, Huber observed the uncontrollable violence of humans against humans as the most disturbing and most challenging problem facing the world today, that immediately invites attention to the signs of the times.[169] Similar to American theologian William Schweiker, who attests that we are in the "time of many worlds," and insists that every work in ethics must provide[170] some account of what is going on. Both descriptions have human wellbeing and integrity as the focus. This is because as an interconnected set of creation who do not live in isolation as separate entities, we equally share our humanness through identifying with the concerns of others. This is why ethics, as a reflection on the conduct of human life, becomes our primary shape and differentiates our understanding of humanity.[171] Much more, Huber realized that such situations would need a new and broad public debate on such issues on a clear ethical basis.[172]

The third motivation for an ethics of responsibility, or rather for a new intentional ethic is in his agreement with Hans Jonas on the consequences of our present actions on the future generation. This again has the influence of science and technology as a factor but also our attitude toward the present realities. In a sense, modern technology increasingly equips humans with power that is ambivalent in its effects for the future.[173] This sense of

---

166. Huber, "The Dignity of," 428.
167. Huber, 428.
168. Huber, *Ethics:The Fundamental*, vii.
169. Huber, *Violence: The Unrelenting*, xv, xi.
170. Schweiker, *Theological Ethics and Global*, xi.
171. Huber, *Ethics: The Fundamental*, 2.
172. Huber, *Violence: The Unrelenting*, xvi.
173. Huber, "Toward an Ethics," 576.

reasoning, which is anthropocentric, has tendencies to deviate our attention from considering the effects of these ambivalent power we acquire. In this case, Huber suggests the need for human beings to not only worry about the present experiences but also the future. This because that can only happen when we develop an ability for collective anticipatory reactions, which is what he sees responsibility to be all about.[174] Here, the present generation must also be willing to make a deliberate change of attitude towards the path of technological and economic development that continuously widens the gap between the rich and the poor. Else, it will increasingly experience a discrepancy between the living conditions it produces for the future and the notion that humans are free and, therefore, capable of responsibly shaping their destiny.[175] The three issues highlighted here form Huber's key concerns in which he calls for intentional ethics of responsibility in such times we live in, that would adequately address these issues, and place priority once more on human beings.

4.3.3.2 Huber's Conception of Ethics of Responsibility

Discourses on ethics have been central to Huber's academic work and life for some time. In some of these, he has devoted so much interest in the concerns of contemporary challenges and their effects on humanity, both in the present and future. With this consideration, his view on the ethics of responsibility also fits into the conversation. As a result, he attests that "responsibility is not a new topic in the moral inquiry since it has a firm placement in the traditions foremost of English-speaking moral philosophy and theological ethics."[176] This view differs from foremost views on the newness of the concept of responsibility by others, such as Niebuhr, that it is of relatively recent origin.[177]

To avoid rushing into proposing a different view on what is already under attention, it is pertinent to evaluate what others have said and still say concerning responsibility and ethics. In this case, Huber identifies a few theories visible in the sphere of responsibility ethical debates as a result of which he

---

174. Huber, "Toward an Ethics," 576.
175. Huber, 577.
176. Huber, 573.
177. Niebuhr, *The Responsible Self*, 47.

offers his critique, thereby proffering the model he assumes is befitting to our time.[178] First, the theory of free will applicable to responsibility "is one in which an agent is held morally responsible for either what they do intentionally, or choose to do, or doing certain actions resulting in either praiseworthiness or blameworthiness."[179] Others hold on the correlation of responsibility and freedom, arguing for the presence of responsibility in the case of inevitability. Still, other theories differentiate responsibility from virtue, arguing in favour of the differences between responsible action and virtuous character. Other proponents undertake to discern "moral responsibility from causal responsibility and liability for punishment."[180] Finally, there are those who "distinguish between the normal situation of role responsibility and the exceptional situation of vicarious responsibility."[181] These debates, Huber argues, "are characterized by their continuity with earlier moral theories that do not reflect the specific problems and challenges that confront ethical reflection today."[182] Deviating from these limitations and what he sees as "old theories unfit for us today," he makes the following suggestion. Regarding ethics of responsibility suitable for our time, "it seems that the first contribution of theological ethics to the ongoing debate consists in the explicit acknowledgment of, and reflection on some specific characteristics of the present socio-political situation that demands a specific kind of ethical evaluation."[183] While referring to these theories as old, Huber does not in any way nullify their relevance. At some time past, these theories had been relevant to address ethical problems. Currently though, the challenges confronting our demand, in Huber's view, is a new dimension and a new language is needed to speak about these issues. In that case, he suggests three challenges that invite a new way of speaking about responsibility in our time.

The first, of these challenges he calls collective crimes of disobedience.[184] It is often easy to deny responsibility for wrongdoing, particularly when one was not actively involved during the action. On the other side of the coin,

---

178. Swinburne, *Responsibility and Atonement*, 34.
179. Huber, "Toward an Ethics," 573.
180. Talbert, "Moral Responsibility."
181. Bonhoeffer, 252.
182. Huber, "Toward an Ethics," 574.
183. Huber, 574.
184. Huber, 574.

however, when the action does yield praiseworthiness, anyone desires to be identified with it, whether the action was done with their knowledge, consent, approval, or even rejection, they associate themselves with the action. This suggests how much the human heart yearns for anything good. We all want to be associated with a good testimony, a good name, a good record against one's profile, even when it means being rejected or connected with people of high calibre, that we sometimes refer to as "dignitaries"– those whom we consider to be more human in our common usage. The same cannot be said of accepting responsibility for crimes committed even if they were done by people we value, love and cherish.[185] These circumstances are in connection with the old fashioned theories of responsibility that are unfit to address the moral challenges of our time.[186] In his response to the humanity we share for simply being humans, Huber points out why that should invite us to accept responsibility for any form of violence, either committed in the past or present against humanity.[187] Doing so would remind us that we live in mutual dependence within this one world and that the human self is relationalby nature, and that we depend on others from the very beginning of our lives until the very end.[188] Hannah Arendt writes that humanity, "when purged of all sentimentalities, has the very serious consequences that in one form or another, men must learn to accept/assume responsibility for all crimes committed by men and that all nations share the onus of evil committed by

---

185. Dietrich Bonhoeffer in his discourse on ethics refers to this model of responsibility which he calls "vicarious representation." By this, he refers to giving and accepting responsibility for others, even when these "others" have done nothing deserving it. He uses the sacrificial representation of Jesus for mankind to portray this.

186. Huber, *Violence: The Unrelenting*, 7

187. His reference here goes to his German context and the experience of the past. The "intense provocation for an ethics of responsibility in the twentieth century must be found in the brutally planned and executed genocides and mass murders of our time. In memory of these events, he continuous, we realize that there are historical events that are not part of the past but are always a part of our present" (Huber, "Toward an Ethics," 574). By this, he refers to those who see themselves as free born, in the sense they were born after these events, as not having a share of responsibility. Rather, the concern here is the attitude of these free born toward what history presents to them regarding brutality of human beings done and how they respond to the past and react to the present. Similarly, is the scenario of Apartheid in South Africa, where those born after the period claiming innocence for what was done during the time of Apartheid. With these two contexts in mind, Huber submits that "past crimes result not only in a general and common co-responsibility of all humans but likewise in specific co-responsibilities of human as members of smaller communities within humankind." Huber, "Toward an Ethics," 575.

188. Huber, *Violence: The Unrelenting*, 7; Huber, "The Dignity of," 434.

others."[189] It seems that the idea of humanity which Arendt points to above does not fit into the understanding of others that celebrating inhumanity is considered an act of obedience.[190] Here, Huber cautions that "obedience conformity, and fear are the normal mechanisms by which people accept, tolerate passively, or even contribute actively to the harm done to others."[191] One could, therefore, argue that collective crimes of disobedience do not justify humanity from accepting responsibility for self and others. Also, for fear of rejection and condemnation, the commitment towards enhancing the integrity of human life by virtue of being humans created in the image of God, calls for the rejection of all forms of crimes against humanity.

The second challenge Huber foresees that should call for a new ethic of responsibility is what he describes as the globalisation of modern technology.[192] The present age has had different descriptions and characterisations.[193] As such, globalisation, which informs various parameters such as religion, economy, politics, terrorism, and corruption, has the goal of unifying the world into what has been described as the proverbial "global village" with both present and future implications.[194] In one sense, Huber sees new scientific and technical possibilities to have been accompanied by far-reaching and, sometimes, utterly unforeseeable consequences for the future. In this sense, we must take into account not only the positive opportunities that open up here and now, but also the risks that are linked to them for future generations.[195] In his concern for responsibility in such a world, Huber follows Hans

---

189. Arendt, "Organized Guilt and Responsibility," 133.

190. Celebration of inhumanity refered to here does not necessarily mean applauding inhuman activities done to human beings, rather the inactiveness in responding to these activities ensures irresponsibility to act when there are calls for acting. Perhaps the integrity of human lives in such cases ceases to be the priority, but blind obedience to what should be unthinkable and unacceptable against humanity.

191. Huber, "Toward an Ethics," 575.

192. Huber, 576.

193. The present age is called "the time of many worlds" signalling the fact that human beings always inhabit some space of meaning and value structured by cultural and social dynamics (see Schweiker, "The Ethics of Responsibility," xi). Our world as "a public spectacle of British economics, military muscle, and governments in servitude to mammon and its godlings" (Huber, *Violence: The Unrelenting*, xi).

194. The concept of the world as a global village was coined by Marshall Mcluhan in the 1960s. It is a phenomenon that describes the world becoming more interconnected as the result of the propagation of technologies, particularly the media.

195. Huber, "Why Ethics," 28.

Jonas whose focus of responsibility centres on the challenge of technological advancement on the future existence of humanity. In Jonas's view, the progress of modern technology made it necessary to expand the concept of responsibility.[196] This advancement of technology, despite its usefulness to mankind, is disruptive in another sense, both for the survival and flourishing of humanity at present and in the future. In the case of the present, technology provides us with the possibility of collective nuclear self-annihilation, nuclear fission and the decoding of the genetic code, which have given humanity unknown possibilities for determining its future. Additionally, technology offers humanity an increase in power to both preserve and develop human lives but also new possibilities of destroying it. In the case of the future, these technological advancements enforce self-manipulation of the human species.[197] Huber warns that these developments, regarding equipping[198] human beings with an increase in power, are deeply ambivalent in their possible effects. This is similar to Jonas's declaration on why responsibility for the future of human life on earth is a fundamental moral imperative for every person.[199]

It thus becomes a challenge calling for collective awareness and effort from different stakeholders to combat and save humanity's future and present of the ambivalence of technological advancement. This is because the challenges emanating from technology have both human and societal significance. From the human perspective, these advancements promise the elongation and the possible extinction of human life through choice, on the one hand.[200] On the other hand, the challenge of natural resource usage, promoted by a consumerist ideology, has a possible extinction of human life now and in the future. In this regard Huber suggests,

> if measures to limit the rise in global temperatures are to be effective, it is not enough for individuals, groups, or nation-states to take them; the international community must agree on a speedy reduction in worldwide carbon dioxide emissions. Nor is it enough to pin one's hopes on politicians; rather, groups

---

196. Huber, *Ethics: The Fundamental*, 89.
197. Huber, 89.
198. Huber, "Toward an Ethics," 576.
199. Jonas, *The Imperative of Responsibility*, 28.
200. An example is the theory of pro-euthanasia.

in civil society must become advocates of sustainable development, and they must set a good example. Global responsibility demands genuine cooperation among states, as well as strong networks in civil society that transcend the borders of nations and continents.[201]

Yet, Huber identifies another reason why the ethics of responsibility is appropriate for confronting the challenges of our time. This third reason he calls the ambivalence of modernity project.[202] This feature and the previous one have similar ideas on ambivalence (uncertainty) about what they each portray. The above considerations suggest that the project of modernity is undefined in its emphasis on the refusal of all forms of heteronomy and the declaration of human self-sufficiency. It also presents ideas and concerns around issues of human dignity, autonomy and freedom of the human subject. There is also the emphasis on the anthropocentrism that challenges the notion and possibility that only human beings are gifted with specific dignity.[203] Additionally, it involves the display of human power, both over other human beings and on other creatures. In this case, violence is inevitable when the power of humanity is involved, hence the very reason Huber insists that the search for basic core of ethical orientation is inevitable since the responsibility to care for the earth – with all that dwell in it – is bestowed on humanity.[204]

This ambivalence of modernity is in continuity with the era when bishops and princes decided about human destiny.[205] In this case, Huber labels ethics as the thinking about human responsibility.[206] This responsibility has the influence of the nature of power that human beings exhibit. If this power confines itself to the after-effects of coexistence with the nearest neighbour, as long as its consequences are applied to those who are in this world with us, the responsibility is limited.[207] This limitation holds if the neighbour Huber refers to is strictly a human personality without the inclusion of other creatures. It

---

201. Huber, *Ethics: the Fundamental*, 89.
202. Huber, "Toward an Ethics," 577.
203. Huber, 577.
204. Huber, *Violence: the Unrelenting*, 125.
205. Huber, "Toward an Ethics," 577.
206. Huber, *Violence: the Unrelenting*, 125.
207. Huber, 126.

goes as far as explaining what happens to the future inhabitants of the earth entrusted to the care of humans. When these two scenarios are excluded from the human power that Huber talks about, the power becomes limited. Only when power is understood as the ability to influence and shape our environment, does the reality surrounding us, and the cautious reflection of the effects of our decisions, and actions on the future life of the earth and those who would inhabit her become the power of responsibility.[208] In this case, Huber suggests that you act so that "the consequences of your actions remain compatible with the future existence and dignity of human as well as non-human life in the biosphere, or avoid actions that are incompatible with the future existence and the dignity of human as well as non-human life biosphere."[209]

Consequently, an ethics of responsibility for Huber could be interpreted as a golden rule stating as follows: respect others' principles as much as you would want others to respect your own.[210] Perhaps this is why Huber concludes that the dominant trait in contemporary ethics lies in it becoming an ethics of responsibility.[211] With these references, Huber makes a summary of what he describes as a substantial criterion for responsible action as follows:

1. Prospective care for a shared natural, social, and cultural space of living together
2. Fairness toward the weaker as the test for the legitimacy of actions
3. Critical evaluation of the contextual conditions of action
4. Self-limitation concerning the rights of future generations and to the dignity of nature
5. Respect for the freedom of conscience for others as for oneself.[212]

---

208. Huber, 126.
209. Huber, "Toward an Ethics," 587.
210. Huber, 589.
211. Huber, "Why Ethics?"
212. Huber, "Toward an Ethics," 589.

4.4 Ethics of Responsibility: Some American Perspectives

The English-speaking world has not been left out of the discourse on ethics of responsibility. Although the trend seems to have gone cold for some decades, the recent academic endeavour has returned to its quest with vibrancy. Notably, among recent scholarship on this topic is the Chicago-based theologian, William Schweiker, who has written on the Christian theological perspective of ethics of responsibility from the American perspective. To understand recent scholarship on the subject matter, however, it is needful that we return to earlier voices who preceded and informed Schweiker's views. We will, therefore, start the survey with the Niebuhrian brothers before returning to Schweiker.

4.4.1 Henry Richard Niebuhr and Reinhold Niebuhr

To understand the emergence and development of responsibility discourse in the English-speaking world, we cannot but start with Henry Richard Niebuhr and his brother, Reinhold Niebuhr. Although the two brothers differ significantly in their theological dispositions, yet in terms of responsibility, they shared fundamental insights about the situated character of the human agency.[213] Were it not for the two brothers, the theory of responsibility would have perhaps become a neglected theme in the English-speaking world, but their legacies provide an appropriate place for the English-speaking theologians to resume this conversation and connect to the ongoing discussions.[214] The Niebuhrian brothers in their rich theological assertions, besides their disparity, provided the English-speaking world with their views on the concept.

Although being the younger of the two, Henry Richard Niebuhr, had responsibility in his work in the mid-1930s, especially concerning the church and its tasks, but also with a theory of agency.[215] This theory concerns moral choice, in which he argues that it is embedded in networks of social processes that trigger the right action, and is not determined by an isolated, autonomous agent or an objective calculus. Instead, he sees the right action growing out

---

213. Lovin, "Becoming Responsible," 309.
214. Lovin, 390.
215. Ottati, "The Niebuhrian Legacy," 400.

of responsiveness to the whole of reality.[216] For Reinhold Niebuhr, however, the language of responsibility enters his work in the early 1940s, where it chiefly concerned an interpretation of sin as well as a view of the responsibility of the United States – particularly in the post-World War II circumstance.[217] Reinhold's views concerned the political realities of the day in that his political realism paid attention to everything that is happening, both within the state and individuals. This explains why his view of a responsible self relates to a decision-maker,[218] who resists the temptation to think about all reality and its infinite possibilities, but focuses on the available choices at a given moment. These sharp contrasts give the two brothers explicit identities they earned from their distinct theological dispositions.

The Niebuhrian brothers are either identified as "Christian realists"[219] or neo-orthodox theologians. Their engagement in ethical issues and resolutions gave rise to these identities that distinctively made them different from other theologians of their day. Two such reasons include: first, when the two participated in a turn away from certain forms and/or assumptions of global theology during the 1930s. Second, they both made use of theological ideas articulated by classical figures, such as Augustine and Jonathan Edwards, to frame their theologies and to critique what they saw as sentimental faith and ethics in the modern West.[220] This could, however, not deal with their contrasting views, even as they were both described as realists.

For H. R. Niebuhr, realism meant a turn towards the reality of God or the religious object, and a turn away from an anthropocentric attitude that values human beings as the central aspect of reality who try to subject all things to human control and are overly optimistic about human progress.[221] This sort of argument suggests that human beings, if detached from the central aspects of realities and left only to focus on God alone, could lose sight of the reality that human responsibility is to God, to fellow humans and nature. Reinhold, however, cautions against such a perception of reality, and insists on the impossibility of humans, given the variety of uncertainties they face,

---

216. Lovin, "Becoming Responsible," 390.
217. Ottati, "The Niebuhrian Legacy," 400.
218. Lovin, "Becoming Responsible," 391.
219. Ottati, "The Niebuhrian Legacy," 401.
220. Ottati, 401.
221. Ottati, 401.

to attain perfection.²²² On the contrary, realism for Reinhold Niebuhr, was bound up with a forthright recognition of human limitations and corruption together with the frank admission of an irreducible tension between the ethical ideal of love and our historical possibilities.²²³ This, Reinhold affirms, unlike his brother, that "responsibility is knowing that we are men, not God; we are responsible for making choices between good and bad, between greater and lesser evils."²²⁴ Deduced from his view, we could say that responsibility involves intentional involvement, but also our objective recognition of responsibility as a calling on us. This provides us with a space to venture into their language of responsibility.

4.4.1.1 H. Richard Niebuhr and Reinhold Niebuhr's Language of Responsibility

Here, we look at the final thought resolutions of the Niebuhrian brothers about their views on responsibility. The two brothers made remarkable contributions to the theological perspective of responsibility in America. In the view of H. R. Niebuhr, the idea of responsibility was a perennial and major element of his thinking that later matured and extended into expression in the responsible self where he gave an introduction to Christian ethics.²²⁵ This view characterized his claims regarding responsibility in various ways. Here, he identified responsibility as the core idea in a deep pragmatist understanding of human agency, which he came into conversation with other scholars. In his classification, H. R. Niebuhr came up with three images to describe the agency: man-the-maker (teleological), man-the-citizen (deontological), and man-the-answerer (responsibility). These three images²²⁶ support different approaches to ethics, which can be distinguished because they construe the moral question differently.

In his famous collected essays, which were later published as *The Responsible Self*, H. R. Niebuhr made the concrete and justifiable distinction between these images, with close attention to the human quest for living and

---

222. Niebuhr, "Must we do Nothing," 425.
223. Ottati, "The Niebuhrian Legacy," 401.
224. Lovin, "Becoming Responsible," 391.
225. Ottati, "The Niebuhrian Legacy," 403.
226. Ottati, 404.

the search for truth.²²⁷ He identifies the human quest in general as that which lies in seeking for the truth about ourselves and in our quest for existence. This is similar to what Ijatuyi-Morphè, a Nigerian scholar, says regarding Africans as seekers of "social life and religion."²²⁸ H. R. Niebuhr first describes the two images by analysing their weaknesses to fulfil the human quest for existence and search for the truth about human selves. By that, he observes their limitation to satisfy the human quest, which then resulted in the third image and later became his preferred image in ethical discourse above the others.

In their search for truth and knowledge of themselves, humanity imagines their autonomous position over other creation as agents in charge of their conduct and capable of making good out of existence. Such imaginations inform of the realistic symbol of the maker, or rather the fashioner – one who creates, makes, constructs, and reconstructs things according to an idea for the sake of an end.²²⁹ This human anticipated end, we could see, echoes Aristotle's ethics in which he explains that such an end aims at some good for the one inquiring, in this sense, the agent. For Aristotle, beyond all the arts of bridle-making and horse-riding and military strategy, there must be an art of arts, a master art, whose end is the actualisation of the good man and the good society, whose material is human life itself.²³⁰ Teleologically, this image illustrates the direction of the human quest that H. R. Niebuhr writes about, and which concerns this end for their existence. This end, as seen involving the desire for truth, and knowledge of themselves and the other, sums up the duty of the image, man-the-maker, whose concern is in creating to make meaning out of their endeavour. This image, however, is not enough to adequately explain the human condition in search of this truth and knowledge, thus, Henry Richard Niebuhr suggests the second image.

The quest for knowledge and truth does not satisfy and guarantee the solution of the human problem of who they are, who they should be, who they want to be, or how they ought to live. In the case of "who humanity should be or who they are," it could be suggested that this notion portrays the general character and behaviour of our lives as agents under the law (deontological).

---

227. Niebuhr, *The Responsible Self*, 56.
228. I-Morphé, *Africa's Social and Religious*, 11.
229. Niebuhr, 48.
230. Niebuhr, *The Responsible Self*, 49.

This symbol, H. R. Niebuhr calls the image of a man-the-citizen who lives under the law.[231] The law, which sets to guide and ensure strict adherence for better individuals and society, as mentioned by the man-the-maker image above, also applies to the enhancement of the agents' character and conduct, ensuring both their wellbeing and the society's.

One peculiar aspect of this symbol, H. R. Niebuhr observes, is that it has applicability to all our existence in society. He suggests the reality of this applicability in that we have been influenced under the various laws of the family, neighbourhood, nation, and are often subject to the regulation of our actions by others. Despite the existence of, and our familiarity with these rules, we still find it ethically right to consent to some laws, to give ourselves rules, or administer our lives according to some discipline. From this can be seen some complexities within this image of the law abider, who is surrounded by various domains. When it sets loyalty to the internal concerns (self), the external concerns (of others) arise. That is why H. R. Niebuhr attests to the difficulty in achieving the unity of the self, the organization of manifoldness called personality, as these become challenging to the administrative self.[232] These two symbols, man-the-maker and man-the-citizen (law abider), may only be primordial or only a cultural symbol despite enabling us to understand large areas of our existence and to find guidance in making complex decisions. Yet they remain images[233] and hypotheses, not truthful copies of reality and that something more and something different needs to be thought and done in our quest for the truth about ourselves and our quest for true existence. Hence, the emergence of the third image which he calls man-the-answerer.

The emergence of the third image is a result of the limitation observed from the previous images, and their inability to successfully provide humans with adequate truth and knowledge about themselves, others and their environment. This image, Niebuhr calls man-the-answerer, is considered the new symbolism of responsibility that could bridge the gap between the former two images. The interesting thing about this image is that man engaged in dialogue,[234] – man acting in response to action upon him – thus becomes a

---

231. Niebuhr, 53.
232. Niebuhr, 54.
233. Niebuhr, 56.
234. Niebuhr, 56.

synecdoche. This becomes a way of understanding ourselves as a whole when we use the image that forms part of our activity that enables us to think of our actions as having the pattern of what we do when we answer another who addresses us. In other words, how we respond to questions others expect us to answer, whether those we are directly involved in or not, provided that we are agents, perhaps responsible ones, we ought to respond. Such responses we give to others have this character of being reactions, and answers to action upon us.[235] Such anticipated questions, Niebuhr observes, have unique characters that make them different from any other sort of question. Perhaps they are questions of responsibility. Hence, he declares that responsibility in every moment of decision and choice inquires to know what is going on.[236] Knowing what is going on does not answer the question of good or bad (teleology), nor to right and wrong (deontology), but rather the fitting action – one which interacts as a response and as anticipation for further response – is alone conducive to the good and what is right.[237]

To put this properly into the right usage and understanding, Niebuhr outlines what he calls elements in the theory of responsibility.[238] He makes this suggestion having in mind how to present the idea of responsibility without reference to the images already highlighted. The first of these elements in the theory of responsibility is the idea of response. At this level, he states how all actions, including those we indeterminately call moral action, are a response to action upon us. At the second element, it is not only responsive action but responsive by our interpretation of the question to which is being given. The third element, he mentions accountability which though has meaning linking it with legal action, but has a more definite meaning when we understand it as referring to the part of the response pattern of our self-conduct. Putting these elements together, H. R. Niebuhr sees responsibility as depending on the agent who stays with his action, who accepts the consequences in the form of reactions and looks forward in a present deed to the continued interaction.[239] This idea of responsibility may be abstractly defined as the idea of an agent's

---

235. Niebuhr, 56.
236. Niebuhr, 60.
237. Niebuhr, 61.
238. Niebuhr, 63–64.
239. Niebuhr, 64.

actions in response to action upon him by his interpretation of the latter action and with his expectation of response to his response.[240]

In all these assertions, however, Niebuhr still battles with a question of responsibility he is unclear about. When we consider the images and the elements he mentioned, it is still unclear to whom ought we be responsible to, or for. This is because Niebuhr asks a similar question himself when he mentions what we should consider our life of responses to action upon us. We should have this question in mind, he suggests: to whom or what am I responsible, and in what community of interaction am I?[241] This question expands the horizon of our discussions on responsibility by providing possibilities to whom Niebuhr had in mind, and what we face that we need the theory of responsibility in our time here and now.

This theory of responsibility interests this study, particularly, because it involves our co-responsibility for ourselves, others, and the environment we live in. It involves speaking toward safeguarding the pervasiveness of public morality which, in the case of this study, includes corruption. Although the devastating effects of public morality abound, this study streamlines one of the many, namely non-recognition of human dignity. In agreement with Niebuhr, to ensure what or to whom one is responsible for and stand responsible therefore, becomes adequate when dealing with theories as important as responsibility. On a similar note, this concern for what and to whom one seeks to be responsible for or to, continues in the American context of this discourse. To further analyse it, William Schweiker, who is informed by the thoughts of the Niebuhrian brothers, takes the discussion further in the American context.

4.4.2 William Schweiker

William Schweiker (1953–present) was born in Des Moines, Iowa, and ordained a Methodist minister. In terms of his academic life, he studied widely and is currently a Professor of Theological Ethics at the University of Chicago, USA.[242]

---

240. Niebuhr, 65.
241. Niebuhr, 68.
242. Schweiker is Edward L. Ryerson Distinguish Service Professor of Theological ethics at the University of Chicago. He is the director of the Enhancing Life Project, composed of 35

4.4.2.1 Responsibility and Agency

Questions about responsibility are as old as human civilisation itself, and are at the heart of most contemporary moral and political debates.[243] As a result, the idea of responsibility is exceedingly complex and relates to all questions in ethics.[244] Hence, Schweiker insists on why it becomes a duty upon the theologian or philosopher to not only distinguish, but also relate the elements of responsibility within ethical reflections.[245] He makes such declarations while holding that responsibility provides the means to articulate the moral demands on the exercise of power by moral agents. By moral agents, he refers specifically to human beings whom he sees at the centre of technological advancement with the dividends thereof.

The question of technological advancement forms only part of contemporary challenges that ethics of responsibility seeks to address. As an age of religious violence and ecological crisis, what is needed in ethics is a renewed vision of the moral vocation of human beings, not against but within the wider compass of life on earth.[246] Others include the various societal moral decays such as corruption, rape, abortion, diseases, war, conflict, and other forms of terrorism that, succinctly, continue a rampage through technological advancement as a result of globalization. Within such a context, a renewed vision of the moral vocation of human beings within the wider compass of life on earth becomes an urgent call. This form of coordination fits into Agang's description, whereby humans are increasingly interconnected, which also increases worldwide interconnectedness.[247] In such interconnectedness, the dilemma of human self-satisfaction over other creatures prevails.

In his other research focus, Schweiker carefully studies the catastrophic eruption of events in the twentieth century with their devastating effects on humanity. In this case, Schweiker's stance is for the survival and flourishing of human beings within the context of what he calls the "time of many

---

international scholars in various fields. He refers to himself as a "theological humanist" ("The Ethics of Responsibility," 254).

243. Schweiker, *Responsiiblity and Christian Ethics*, 9; Schweiker, "Radical Interpretation and Moral," 613.

244. Schweiker, *Responsibility and Christian Ethics*, 1.

245. Schweiker, 1.

246. Schweiker, "The Ethics of Responsibility," 251.

247. Agang, "Globalization," 7.

worlds."[248] This assessment is similar to Hauerwas's assertion that people do what was at some point seen unthinkable, which has resulted in a morally chaotic world where we feel the only alternative is for each person to choose or create the standards they live.[249] In such a world, Hauerwas maintains, it is extremely hard to maintain our moral identity because we feel pulled in different directions by our various roles and convictions, unsure of any coherence to our lives, and become divided selves, more easily tempted to violence.[250] This is similar to what Schweiker describes as the time of many worlds that include "horrors of mass death and terrors of tyranny, and in which meaning and orientation are difficult to attain."[251] Considering such an age, it is not surprizing that the idea of responsibility should be so central to moral reflection and debate.[252] Such reflections and debates would, in Schweiker's view, involve identifying why he calls for the radical interpretation of moral responsibility.

By radical interpretation of moral responsibility, Schweiker refers to a "means whereby critical reflection on moral values and norms transform moral sensibility that gives rise to the sense of responsibility."[253] He articulates this radical interpretation as basic to moral self-understanding which ought to be taken concerning claims about God, if we are to make sense of the idea of responsibility in our contemporary situation. Moral responsibility means that someone or some community can and must give an account, and provide an answer for what they have done, or intend to do. In that case, moral responsibility requires a form of answering for either what is done or would be done, thus explaining why Schweiker argues that "every work in ethics must provide some account of what is going on."[254] A sort of understanding of what is going on, which in this case, Schweiker describes as "the time of many worlds," and an answer to the question of what is going on triggers the nature of moral action required. In those instances of many worlds characterized by either deliberate human actions such as infliction of pain, hardship, and

---

248. Schweiker, *Theological Ethics*, xi.
249. Hauerwas, "The Peaceable Kingdom," 2.
250. Hauerwas, 6.
251. Schweiker, *Theological Ethics*, x.
252. Schweiker, "Radical Interpretation," 613.
253. Schweiker, 615.
254. Schweiker, *Theological Ethics*, xi.

other human activities undermining the integrity of their lives, then moral action is required. There are instances in "the time of many worlds" where human activities, such as the technological advancement, indirectly affect and distort the sanctity of human life not only now but also for the future as Jonas proposes. In these times, Schweiker suggests that being a moral agent "involves being responsible for oneself in and through responding to others and being accountable for bringing something into being through the exercise of power that is not coercive but persuasive."[255]

Drawing from Schweiker's view, we could see that being responsible and taking responsibility demands the freedom to act and to express oneself, and a realization of the indivisibility of our humanness in terms of relatedness. Also, it suggests "development and the expression of truly and fully humans by not forsaking the conditions necessary to be genuine selves and to have relations with others."[256]

4.4.2.2 *The Essence of Responsibility*

By presenting the essence of responsibility, we will be looking at what Schweiker's views contained in responsibility. It means what is required in being responsible by the agent we have described above, seeing that Schweiker's concept of responsibility comes from a Christian theological perspective.

In his search for the meaning of responsibility, Schweiker attests to the late arrival of the word in Western ethics, with the first appearance in German, English and French in the seventeenth century.[257] He attests to the early usage of the word not only among philosophers, such as David Hume and Aristotle, but also theologians, such as Dietrich Bonhoeffer and the Niebuhrian brothers. As a result of its late arrival in the moral lexicon of the West, the idea of responsibility manifests the complex and social progress of modern history, which has yielded three ideas. First, that it entails a naturalistic view of reality where events are explained in causal terms with human beings appearing as unique creatures because of our capacity. Second, the language of

---

255. Schweiker, "Radical Interpretation," 618.
256. Schweiker, *Responsibility and Christian Ethics*, 15.
257. Schweiker, 58.

responsibility has contributed to the growth of individualisation in Western societies. Third, it has brought about an interiorization[258] of the moral life.

From the etymological sense, Schweiker shows that the word responsibility "derives from Latin, *Respondeo,* which means to promise a thing in return for something else, and also, in legal discourse, to give an opinion, advice, decision, or, generally, an answer when one is summoned to appear in court."[259] In the legal meaning, he sees it coinciding with the German *Verantwortung,* which means answering. From here, Schweiker describes a responsible agent as one who can "answer for his/her actions and intentions before someone and in the process of which the bond between a person and his/her deeds is acknowledged."[260]

Schweiker's ethics of responsibility has a human agent as its central focus and their responsible life with both selves and to God. With this emphasis, he formulates the core of his responsibility towards the enhancement of the integrity of life before God. He puts it clearly that responsible actions and relations are ones that "respect and enhance the interaction of complex goods and also manifest and contribute to moral goodness and integrity."[261] In sum, he states "in all actions and relations, respect enhances the integrity of life," which makes up the distinctiveness of Christian ethics.[262] With this description, he concludes by giving his best definition of an ethics of Christian ethics of responsibility as that form of moral reflection which, in distinction to other forms of ethics, uses responsibility as the means for relating systematically the dimensions of moral inquiry.[263]

4.4.2.3 Theories of Responsibility

Schweiker's theological inquiry into ethics of responsibility draws him to identifying theories of responsibility. Although these theories make significant contributions in helping us understand work within Christian ethics on the theme of moral responsibility, they unsatisfactorily explain what he wishes to

---

258. Schweiker, 58–59.
259. Schweiker, 55.
260. Schweiker, 55.
261. Schweiker, *Theological Ethics*, xiv.
262. Schweiker, *Responsibility and Christian Ethics*, 34.
263. Schweiker, 38.

propose.²⁶⁴ Nevertheless, in his quest for theological ethics of responsibility, Schweiker resonates with three theories that are outlined below.

The first is the agential theory where Schweiker has conversations with other voices, such as Immanuel Kant and Paul Tillich, that have reasoned on this theory. From his personal view, Schweiker groups the agential theory as that which grounds responsibility in the acting agent. This, he says, "focuses on the connection between an agent as both a causal force in the world and the evaluation of his/her acts."²⁶⁵ This theory determines the rightness of acts of praise and blames concerning the connection between the agent and his/her deeds such that an agent becomes morally responsible when they caused an action to happen or has no excuse to justify his/her innocence. On the contrary, if it can be shown that an agent did not cause an action to happen, or while causing the act had excusing reasons, then the agent is not morally responsible.²⁶⁶

Schweiker's interaction with Kant on the agential theory of responsibility illustrates the categorical imperative as being the principle of non-contradiction applicable to will. For Kant, acting such that one's action could be used as a universal law is seen as the sole condition under which a will can never contradict itself.²⁶⁷ Such is considered a foundation to the morality of an agent acting autonomously from will and freedom. The burden of Kantian ethics, in this regard, shows that while human beings are moved by desire, inclination, and remain subject to the causal laws and universe, there is more to be said about the agent. If so, it can be argued that the central problem of how to govern our lives would become less an issue of concern. Schweiker here understands Kant trying to show that a person can legislate maxims for their actions, thus suggesting freedom as moral agents.²⁶⁸

Schweiker also engages Tillich's idea of *theonomy* in his agential theory of responsibility in the context of freedom.²⁶⁹ In this, Tillich argues, the moral law, the law of our essential nature, is not simply something imposed on ourselves (autonomy), nor is it simply imposed on us by another foreign will

---

264. Schweiker, 43.
265. Schweiker, 41.
266. Schweiker, 78.
267. Schweiker, 80.
268. Schweiker, 80.
269. Schweiker, 82.

or power. Instead, our true freedom is *theonomous*,[270] the moral law of God, which is nothing else than our true being. The true moral being, however, can only be asked by man because he alone can look beyond the limits[271] of his being and every other being. Similarly, this true being, Schweiker asserts, is paralleled to our actual being which indicates that our lives are marked by a fragmentation of problems. Such fragmentation includes Schweiker's assertion that the voice of man's essential being is silenced, step by step; and his disintegrating self, his depersonalization, all show the nature of the antimoral act and, by contrast, the nature of the moral act.[272] Such fragmentation, we see in Tillich, that is the answer to the question "how shall this self be integrated?" is found in love, and is the ultimate principle of morality.

In our examination of agential theories, we have found that these theories focused on the relation of the agent to him/herself. Moreover, they attempted to specify the grounds that validly relate "causal and evaluative judgements that the agent could act morally."[273] Schweiker's conclusion on Kant's and Tillich's views of the agential theory of responsibility includes what he describes as being necessary for integrated ethics of responsibility which he proposes.[274]

The second theory of responsibility, which Schweiker calls the social theory, focuses on social roles, vocations, conversations and communal unity, one that pays attention to practices that constitute the identity and roles of persons and communities.[275] Here, Schweiker converses with philosophical (Marion Smiley), social (Peter French A), and Christian (Stanley Hauerwas) theories of responsibility. Human societies, it can be contended, are characterized by identity markers for human conduct, either as good persons, with a sense of attractive morals to societal praiseworthiness, or those capable of attracting blameworthiness. In either case, the contribution expected by an

---

270. Theonomy is expressed by Paul Tillich in different ways. In one of these ways, he sees theonomy as a condition in which the spiritual and the social forms are filled with the import of the unconditional as the foundation, meaning, and reality of all forms. It fills the autonomous forms with sacramental substance by creating a sacred and a just reality at the same time (Taylor, *Paul Tillich*, 58).

271. Tillich, *Systematic Theology*, 207.

272. Schweiker, 83.

273. Schweiker, 85.

274. Schweiker, 86.

275. Schweiker, 86, 93.

individual relates to social roles that bring about building up communal unity which, in turn, enhances the integrity of human lives.

Being philosophical theorists, they reject the modern metaphysical view of moral responsibility as depending on the agent. Stressing this, Smiley argues that "our causal responsibility is not purely objective or independent of our normative expectation of those being blamed."[276] Rather, her pragmatic reconstruction of the notion regards moral responsibility as a social matter.[277] In her view, this happens because of our attitude of holding persons responsible for actions they are not directly involved. Thus, she "insists that practices of blaming and praising be keyed to social roles."[278] Her argument further discloses why the source of responsibility is the practice of blaming and not an individual's free will that causes the event.[279] Here, she "contests the assumption that responsibility is something we discover about individuals rather than what we assign to them."[280]

French argues from a social dimension that a social theory of responsibility is the maintenance of identity within a community.[281] This form of identity involves social actions we impose on individuals and "what they make them become or feel while citing shame, as an example in this regard."[282] From these two theorists, Schweiker concludes that for a social theory of responsibility, "praise and blame function in terms of shame and esteem concerning the social identity of agents and their conduct and, calls them strong theories of responsibility."[283]

---

276. Smiley, *Moral Responsibility*, 179.

277. Smiley, 179.

278. Smiley, 4.

279. Smiley, 4.

280. Her argument is summarized as follows: If we want to argue openly with one another about our responsibility for the suffering of others and explain the differences that arise among us, we will have to stop thinking about responsibility as a purely factual discovery and begin thinking about it on the basis of our own social and political points of view. One of these judgments is that harm was the consequence of an individual's action. The other harm was that the individual was herself worthy of blame (see Smiley, 4).

281. Schweiker, *Responsibility and Christian Ethics*, 90.

282. French, *Responsibility Matters*, 207. In another place, French postulates a foundational theory that allows treatment of corporations as members of the moral community. He argues, corporation can be full-fledged moral persons, hence could be held to account for what they do. French, "The Corporation," 207.

283. Schweiker, 90.

Schweiker also identifies Christian ethicists with similar theories, such as Stanley Hauerwas, besides the social theorists of responsibility. Schweiker describes Christian theories of responsibility as weak theories because their primary concern is on the formation of Christian identity and not responsibility assignment.[284] Here, Hauerwas argued that it is important to base theory as the responsibility of what informs the identity of Christians and what they believe. This presents a form of moral guidance that is designed to help believers conform more completely to their beliefs.[285] As a characteristic of Christian ethics, however, it should be concerned with the formation of a society shaped and informed by the truthful character of the God revealed in the stories of Israel and Jesus.[286] These and other similar stories inform the Christian identity, hence forming the basis on which Hauerwas propounds the theory of responsibility that Schweiker calls "weak."[287] This Christian identity informs the character and conduct of individuals and their public life, that should reflect their actions and capability of accepting the consequences of those actions. Hauerwas states not that what we do is unimportant or secondary, but rather, what one does or does not do is dependent on being "self sufficient to take personal responsibility for their action."[288] Getting this to a Christian theory of responsibility, his account expresses a social dynamic in the question of the formation of moral identity through social practices.[289]

In view of social theories of responsibility, it is shown that they are concerned about the social role of an individual in making the society a better place but do not spare the agent of either blame or praise, as these form part of human instinct. The social theory is, however, seen to rightly specify the integrity of human and social life as a function of the practice and discourse which form the identity of life. Responsibility is "assigned not simply based on discrete acts, but the character and social role or vocation of an agent."[290]

---

284. Schweiker, 90.

285. Hauerwas, *A Community of Character*, 90.

286. Hauerwas further attests to this Christian identity of Christian ethics because of the fact that it does not begin on principles, but by calling our attention to a narrative that tells of God's dealing with creation (Hauerwas, *The Peaceable Kingdom*, 25).

287. Schweiker, 91.

288. Hauerwas, *A Community of Character*, 113.

289. Schweiker, *Responsibility and Christian Ethics*, 92.

290. Schweiker, 93.

To its limitation, the difficulty this theory has is that of the authority of social practices, a similar problem with the agential theory.[291] Those limitations suggest why Schweiker presents the third theory.

The third theory of responsibility, which Schweiker notes as popular in modern theological ethics, is presented in two basic forms and formulated by two figures. First, is Karl Barth's divine command ethics alongside the Niebuhrian brothers, Bernard Häring and Charles Curran, which has some continuity with agential theories mentioned earlier but recasts the agency in terms of an encounter with the other. Here, we concentrate on Karl Barth and his divine command ethics since we have discussed the Niebuhr's above. These figures have a strong link with the social theory, and also in relation to the demand to respond to others.

Barth and the divine command ethics contained in his *Church Dogmatics* combine normative and metaethical dimensions of divine command ethics.[292] In these descriptions contain the placement of humanity from creation, redemption and what ought to constitute a human way of living, and their interaction with other non-human creatures. In one sense, this living invites responsiveness to others (fellow human beings), obedience to the other (God), and taking care of others (non-human creatures). These, in sum, suggest our moral responsiveness, stewardship and obedience.

For Barth, a human person understands God both as "one who made them God's partner in history but that this knowledge is futile when we know nothing of Jesus Christ in whom all history begins and proceeds."[293] This sets the basis of human obedience to God that Barth presents. He, however, insists that this "came right before man was, and before the world was, that God drew him to Godself when He destined him to obedience to His command."[294] A human being, were it not for this historical connection with God, could not know the history of Jesus because, as the true God is the God who is and acts and reveals in Jesus Christ, so true humanity is one who is bound to this

---

291. Smiley, *Moral Responsibility*, 4.
292. Schweiker, *Responsibility and Christian Ethics*, 95.
293. Barth, *The Christian Life*, 20.
294. Barth, *Church Dogamtics*, 517.

connection. He is such a person about whom we are asking, the man who is responsible to the commanding God.[295]

4.4.2.4 Schweiker's Quest for an Ethics of Responsibility

Having considered these theories concerning responsibility, Schweiker seems unsatisfied with them. His dissatisfaction arises from the contemporary challenges of our time, of which he describes as "the time of many worlds." Looking into the theories, however, he notices limitations and calls for "an integrated theory of responsibility."[296] This theory, in his view, although it reflects the existing ones, differs significantly in how it encompasses previous theories. One limitation of the existing theories of responsibility is that although they both draw on diverse moral phenomena in speaking about responsibility, it is not clear that they are speaking about the same thing despite the use of common discourse. Moreover, what scholars have presented on responsibility from different dimensions and the conclusions and criticisms from those formulations add to the conundrum. These, therefore, become the reasons why the existing theories are inadequate.[297]

Postulating this integrated theory, Schweiker wants to avoid the errors already encountered by the earlier theories so much, that he suggests the characteristics of this new theory of responsibility. The first of these characteristics is that an "adequate theory of responsibility must account for the insights of these other positions about the nature of the moral life."[298] In his thoughts on the moral life, he affirms why contemporary ethics has taken it to be of utmost importance to determine whether persons and communities invent morality or discover it.[299] Such articulations inform us how diverse other theories identify and consider the morality of life. It can, therefore, be deduced that the extent to which moral life is perceived would inform how it is treated, even amid public morality calling for responsible actions. In this case, Schweiker insists that we must conceive of the moral life as the dialectical relation between actualization of self and encounter with others mediated by

---

295. Barth, *The Christian Life*, 20.
296. Schweiker, *Responsibility and Christian Ethics*, 103.
297. Schweiker, 103.
298. Schweiker, 103–4.
299. Schweiker, 106.

social roles and vocations. This leads us to his description of what it means to act morally, which he sees "requires an agent's understanding of the actualization of their own life in response to others concerning the rules and vocations they have in social existence."[300] He calls this the agentic-relational account of persons from the perspective of integrated ethics of responsibility.

The second characteristic of integrated ethics of responsibility, Schweiker writes, is that it must account for the relation[301] between the good which persons are to respect and enhance, and the principle for right action. The idea of good and wrong reminds us of the man-the-maker image (teleology), and the idea of respect here connotes the presence of man-the-citizen (deontology), while the idea of enhancing right action brings in man-the-answerer (responsibility). The relation of these concepts denotes Schweiker's idea of integration. In his assertions, he notes that this character of integrated ethics of responsibility involves different levels of value rooted in basic human needs, and articulates an imperative of responsibility.[302] For him, through this integration, we can make sense of the demand to be responsible for self – which is the central insight of agential theories – while respecting the insights of the dialogical and social theories of responsibility.

4.5 Ethics of Responsibility: Some African Perspectives

The ongoing discussion has demonstrated views of ethics of responsibility from contexts other than the African context. The reason they preceded the African perspective is basically because the idea of ethics of responsibility is developed among Western philosophers and theologians, rather than in Africa. It could also be argued that Africa is leaning on already established documents from which to build and develop its model. The view of an African perspective of ethics of responsibility, however, basically comprises theology, philosophy and economics/business among others. The aim here is to evaluate the previous Western views presented, and how they could be relevant to address public morality confronting the African continent. This section

---

300. Schweiker, 104.
301. Schweiker, 104.
302. Schweiker, 104.

is, therefore, divided into four sub-sections. First, we shall look at African theology and the notion of responsibility; second, we shall consider African philosophy and the concept of responsibility; third, we will present the notion of responsibility in economics/business; fourth, we shall consider African notion of responsibility and public morality.

Although Africa is a generic name for the continent, Africa is not a single entity, but rather one rich in diversity of cultures, traditions, beliefs, and comprises of various independent nations. Mugambi is correct when he says "when studying and making general remarks about Africa, keep in mind that the continent has many distinguishing differences between ethnic groups."[303] Similarly, Maluleke points out that Africa is "vast, complex and differentiated, which we should never pretend to speak representatively and comprehensively about."[304] These suggestions caution our usage of, and reference of Africa. For the sake of this study and section, therefore, Africa will be considered as a continent, except where we make specific references to certain regions.

4.5.1 African Theology and the Notion of Responsibility

The African continent has had a history of theological engagement over time. It is estimated that for over fifty years, Christian thinkers, both theologians and non-theologians alike, have articulated their brands of Christian theologies consciously and deliberately, which has today given rise to various forms of emerging theologies in the continent, as elsewhere.[305] These theologies, ranging from African Christian theology,[306] black theology of liberation,[307] reconstruction theology,[308] feminist theology,[309] ecological theology,[310] and

---

303. Mugambi, *African Christian Theology*, 3.
304. Maluleke, "African Theology," 486.
305. Maluleke, 485.
306. John S Mbiti of Kenya, Kwame Bediako of Ghana, Byang Henry Kato of Nigeria and several others.
307. Allan Boesak of South Africa has been at the front line of this movement.
308. Jesse N. K. Mugambi of Kenya is said to be the "father of reconstruction theology," the movement he began in the early 1990s at the advent of twenty-first century.
309. Mercy Amba Oduyoye has been influential in her writings from this perspective.
310. Ernst Conradie of South Africa has been prominent in advocating for the salvation of creation.

now theology of an ethic of responsibility[311] have emerged and are thriving. Of these forms of theology, correlations are gearing towards the wellbeing and flourishing of an African person.

Despite its rich theological history and theologians, the notion of ethics of responsibility in African theology is not prominent. Recent research on the subject of responsibility affirms that nothing much has been done on ethics of responsibility from the African context.[312] This notion of "nothing much," only suggests that nothing substantial regarding the ethics of responsibility but does not dismiss some elements of it. For instance, the awareness of technological advancement and its effects on humanity is mentioned by a few African theologians. In his assessment, Bujo affirms,

> it has become a trivial observation that people indulge in self-destruction by pursuing solely the total domination of the world and the reckless exploitation of nature . . . therefore, people be prepared to account for the technical achievement attained so far and ask themselves the question of whether nature is regarded as a co-creature in this process.[313]

Although Bujo in the preceding quote did not refer to Jonas, his thoughts were attuned with Jonas's concern above (see section 4.3.3.1) and Kant's categorical imperative on the consequences of our actions and inactions. Similarly, the call to build up communities whose cultural, social, political, and economic structures reflect values of responsibility, respect, care, and love is what Mugambi and Wasike ascribe as a duty for Christians.[314] This is a call to reflect on the notion of responsibility in terms of the collective effort for societal wellbeing. It invites African theologians to incorporate in their thinking the notions of responsibility, particularly for human and societal wellbeing. It reflects notions of responsibility for salvaging others and nature

---

311. Etienne de Villiers of South Africa leads the discussions on this emerging field of discourse.

312. Neequaye, "Towards an African Christian," 176.

313. Bujo, *The Ethical Dimension*, 215. Similarly, "the impressive, dramatic advances of science and technology are opening up new horizons of human thought and action and are challenging Christians to seriously address themselves to social ethical issues . . . these and many new social, cultural, and political elements have created a host of new issues and serious problems which undermine the very sacredness of human life today" (Mugambi and Wasike, *Moral and Ethical Issues*, 1).

314. Mugambi and Wasike, *Moral and Ethical Issues*, 1.

from threats that technology poses. The notion of responsibility, however, infuses the works of a few notable African theologians, which this study considers prominent, in order to narrow the focus to sub-Saharan Africa, where Nigeria, its immediate context, is located.

4.5.2 The Notion of Responsibility in Sub-Saharan Africa

The sub-Saharan region of Africa is not left out in discourses regarding the ethics of responsibility. Interestingly, both theologians, and particularly philosophers, have helpful contributions to guide our search. For that reason, a few theologians and philosophers, both from Ghana and Nigeria are our conversation partners in this section.

In what he calls discourses on the external and internal influences on human life, Kwame Gyekye reflects on the Akan of Ghana's perspective of responsibility. Alluding to his Western philosophical counterparts with the assumption that if "every event is caused,"[315] then human action and conduct are caused too, hence we cannot be held morally responsible for those actions.[316] In response, he brings close to his African belief and tradition, regarding his nativity, the Akan of Ghana. In the Akan's view, the cause of every event does not eliminate or subvert the role of the individual in human actions. In that case, "to do the right thing either in a moral situation or otherwise, an individual should be held responsible for it was within human capacity to do it correctly."[317] Even though the action had no intention to cause harm or pain, the agent was involved in the action. In that situation, "the agent must accept the responsibility for the action because it was performed, even though the consequences turned out contrary to the original intention."[318] Although Gyekye could not specify either retrospective or prospective responsibility, his submission seems to involve both. Since for him, the character of one determines the state of their action, a person is responsible because their character has the capacity to reform and improve. He concludes that

---

315. This view is called determinism (Gyekye, *An Essay on African*, 120).
316. Gyekye, *An Essay on African*, 120.
317. Gyekye, 121.
318. Gyekye, 122.

the Akan philosophy holds that "human beings are free and must, therefore, be held morally responsible for their actions and behaviour."[319]

Another dimension of responsibility from sub-Saharan Africa relates to corporate social responsibility. This has to do with business and economic regulations that help private or public companies or enterprises be socially accountable to themselves, clients and the general public. In a few sub-Saharan countries such as Nigeria, Ghana and Cameroon, the role of corporate social responsibility raises similar concerns on the ethics of responsibility. In a study conducted, for instance, concerns were raised to indicate how technological advancement and social organizations continue to impose risk and limitation on the efficient performance of the biosphere. The conclusion to that study indicated that an effort of corporate social responsibility required an "in-depth analysis in terms of theoretical underpinnings and a new complex, increasing-charging business environment."[320] Also in the report was changing values, principles and norms of society in order to integrate its broad dimensions into the sustainable development agenda. Although the above reference focuses on companies and organizations, the focal point remains societal and human wellbeing which technology poses. Suffice to say that the idea of responsibility for salvaging ethical living in our globalized society is not strange to sub-Saharan Africa, although it might not be prominent as we have seen.

From the above summary, we could say that the discussion on responsibility is ongoing through different dimensions with almost a unified goal. Theology, philosophy and economics/business are all involved with societal and human wellbeing as leading concerns. We, therefore, attest to de Villiers's description that "transformation of society should have one of its goals as the desire to humanising the society."[321] Here, humanizing society includes creating a conducive ground that humanity may flourish. That would ensure a more humane society that houses individuals responsible for their actions, be they intentional or unintentional. Such a society would hold firm the goal for recognition and enhancement of dignity of human persons. These indications of responsibility are, however, insufficient in that they lack depth

---

319. Gyekye, 123.
320. Ogini and Omojow, "Sustainable Development," 15.
321. de Villiers, "The Vocation of Reformed," 526.

for intensive academic investigation. If all there is to responsibility is to be explored, either a new dimension or context becomes a requirement. Else, detailed information about ethics of responsibility would remain unknown to, particularly African contemporary society. The next chapter will, therefore, explore the works of a South African theologian, Etienne de Villiers, who has not only devoted most of his life to writing but has produced substantial academic resources. His deep interaction with famous and earlier proponents of ethics of responsibility in other parts of the world cannot be overemphasized. As such, his writings easily connect the reader to the broader picture of responsibility.

4.6 Chapter Summary

This chapter has surveyed the development of responsibility and ethics of responsibility. It considered the concept of ethics of responsibility from different academic disciplines (sociology, theology, and philosophy) and contexts (German, American, and African).

The first part considered Max Weber, a sociologist, who is considered the pioneering champion of the ethics of responsibility. In his case, the German political landscape was problematic in that young people found no interest in politics until his lecture in 1919 titled "Politics as A Vocation." He argued that politics, when taken as a vocation, gives room for improvement and by extension, provided reasons for responsible practice and politicking. Weber's view on politics is that the younger generation should not discard it by standing aloof, but that they can get involved with a different perspective. Such perspective includes the "what" and "why" ethics of responsibility interests him over the ethics of conviction. In his conclusion, however, Weber considered that responsibility has to do with the power of the mind in discerning ethical decisions and in acknowledging value obligations in the absence of any given hierarchy of values. Moreover, he ascribed ethics of responsibility as the coherent ethical framework for those taking or who would develop the intention of taking politics as a vocation.

Following Weber is the theological notion of responsibility in Germany with Dietrich Bonhoeffer. Taking his search into this concept from a biblical perspective, he considered two facts, namely the structure of a responsible life and the place of responsibility. In the structure of responsible living,

Bonhoeffer used the imagery of vicarious responsibility, using Jesus's story as an example. More so, the father, a statesman as well who has others looking up to them for the fulfilment of needs. In the case of the father who has a family, Bonhoeffer insists that such a person has no justification, whatsoever, to think of living alone without thinking of those under his care, namely his family. Any attempt of such, he affirms, becomes an act of irresponsibility. Such action requires accepting the guilt of others and the willingness to become guilty in their stead, such as Jesus did. As a vicariously responsible representative, Bonhoeffer sees Jesus as one who, without guilt, willingly accepted to become human and share the guilt of humanity. Jesus is therefore described by Bonhoeffer as a responsible representative per excellence. On the second component, Bonhoeffer discussed the place of ethics of responsibility, where he uses the imageries of vocation and responsibility to explain God's gracious choice and call to humanity and what role there is for these human beings to fulfil as a result.

Next is Wolfgang Huber, another theological voice from the German perspective whose focus, unlike Bonhoeffer, centred more on theological ethics. He argued about the concerns of our time and how a new ethical approach is needed to address them. This is because, in his view, previous ethical theories fitted well to address previous ethical issues, but have become almost uncertain to our time here and now. Huber's concerns are on the characteristics of the modern time that are saturated with diversities. Having observed the insufficiency of former ethical approaches in our time, he suggests that our time which is characterized by socio-political situations of many kinds, demands a specific kind of ethical evaluation that would adequately and relevantly address ethical concerns of our time.

The last perspective from the German world came from a philosopher, Hans Jonas, whose concerns are for the future generation. Jonas has issues with the former or traditional ethics, which he described as being concerned with the ethical significance of the here and now. Significant as those, Jonas worries, who have little or no concern for the future generation and who would live when the present generation, whose choices could be detrimental to their lives, might have ceased to exist. Particularly, Jonas's concern centred on the technological advancement that has taken over the control of human affairs to the point of presenting illusions to what humans can do. While these technological advancements are important, Jonas cautioned about the effects of our actions for the future generation.

The American perspective took the tone from two traditions, namely the Niebuhrian brothers and William Schweiker. The Niebuhrian brothers, Henry Richard, and his brother Reinhold Niebuhr, were concerned with analysing the human quest in search of truth and knowledge about themselves. From this search, they propounded the three images of man, namely man-the-maker, man-the-citizen, and man-the-answerer. Of all these images, they disclosed the third image, man-the-answerer as more appropriate than the other two images. The reason being that it is the image that seeks to first, ask the question "what is going on?" before venturing into finding solutions to it, unlike the other two images. For Schweiker, on the contrary, his quest for responsibility ethics rests on three theories, namely the agential, the dialogical, and the social theories. Here, he discovered the three as insufficient to present a theological-ethical model of responsibility and instead proposes an integrated theory that encompasses the three. For him, none of the theories is enough to stand isolated, but when put together with others, they would form an integrated model whose concern gears towards the enhancement of the integrity of human life.

These views have presented the development of ethics of responsibility from contexts other than of this study (Africa, and particularly Nigeria), which calls for concern. It is not negligence that the African perspective of the concept was not discussed in detail, but the fact that a specific chapter is dedicated to discussing ethics of responsibility from an African perspective. The next chapter, therefore, deals with Etienne de Villiers, a South African theologian, from whose ideas, we discuss the ethics of responsibility from an African point of view. Although de Villiers is a South African, he has developed ethics of responsibility whose concepts could sufficiently serve as a springboard for the Nigerian context. Learning from his methodology, de Villiers's view of responsibility ethics will propel this study towards developing ethics of responsibility for the Nigerian context, the immediate context of this study.

CHAPTER 5

Etienne de Villiers and Ethics of Responsibility: The African Context

5.1 Introduction

In the previous chapter, we primaily studied the development of ethics of responsibility from contexts and personalities other than the African. In the survey, German and American perspectives of ethics of responsibility developed by theologians and other academics were studied as well as their perspectives. This chapter, however, takes the reader to an African version of ethics of responsibility perspectives from Etienne de Villiers, a South African theologian. de Villiers has written constructively by engaging the earlier proponents from other contexts and he now proposes contemporary Christian ethics of responsibility from an African context.

This chapter seeks to do two things: first, to engage de Villiers's scholarship with specific reference to his proposal of contemporary Christian ethics of responsibility. Second, to present de Villiers's reception of the foremost German and American versions of ethics of responsibility and how he applies ethics of responsibility in addressing the scourge of corruption and human dignity. To this end, the chapter is divided into sections that will help the reader navigate through the views of ethics of responsibility from an African point of view. The first section provides de Villiers's background, which comprises his interest in theology and ethics; section two ventures into his views on ethics of responsibility, how he agrees and disagrees with other proponents; the third section provides de Villiers's proposal of contemporary Christian ethics of responsibility; section four portrays de Villiers's engagement with the notion of corruption and human dignity in the African context while demonstrating how ethics of responsibility could help to address the two concepts. Section five is a critical engagement of de Villiers's contemporary ethics of responsibility, its viability in addressing moral issues, such as corruption, and how human dignity could be recognized and enhanced.

5.2 Some Background on Etienne de Villiers
5.2.1 Theological and Christian Tradition

Etienne de Villiers (1945 – present) is a South African Systematic Theologian who is multidimensional in his writings.[1] In terms of his faith tradition, de Villiers identifies himself as coming from a conservative Reformed Theological background.[2] Thus, de Villiers's strongest characteristic, in a typical Reformed fashion, has been to emphasize and champion involvement in the world.[3] This would include his active involvement in addressing public morality, particularly in the South African context. While this is true as we shall see through his later writings, it is proper to situate his background further.

It can be contended that the environment one grows in has great influence in their life. While it is true in some instances that one takes along the values and norms of the environment as they grow, the case may differ with others. In a nutshell, de Villiers grew within a world characterized by three major experiences in his life. First, he grew up in the upsurge of Afrikaner nationalism. Second, he grew up at the start of the political reign of the National Party in South Africa. Third, he grew up during the introduction of

---

1. He is Emeritus Professor of the Department of Dogmatic and Christian Ethics in the faculty of Theology, University of Pretoria. He studied Theology and Philosophy at the University of Stellenbosch and was awarded a doctorate in Christian Ethics at the Free University of Amsterdam (de Villiers, *Revisiting Max Weber's Ethic*, IV). He is a reformed Theologian (de Villiers, "Religion, Theology," 16). In his assessment (Naudé, "Virtue and Responsibility," 2) describes de Villiers as "a church theologian in the possible sense of the word; an ordained pastor and professor in the service of the church and, through the church, he is in the service of the gospel in the wider society."

2. de Villiers, "The Distinctiveness," 1; de Villiers, "Christian Ethics and Secularisation," 1–9.

3. van Niekerk, "Personal-Ethical Perspectives," 3.

the apartheid policy in South Africa.⁴ More importantly, he grew up with typical Afrikaner parents, in a house whose loyalty to the National Party was taken for granted, and the policy of apartheid never questioned.⁵ Growing up with such experiences would have been enough reason for de Villiers to venture into living and acting in conformity with what he later would refer to as evil, namely the apartheid policy and its theological justification. He, rather, chose to be different. It was probably then that he began nurturing the idea of responsibility – which would later become his research focus.

His Christian conviction is also of prominence to his formation and choice of being different, and as an advocate for justice and peace.⁶ de Villiers particularly declares how his interest in being a Christian, even his becoming a theologian, happened. His father being a theologian and a preacher, was involved in presenting sermons and other theological discussions. It was during one of the sermons by his father, particularly, a Pentecost sermon, that de Villiers got convinced of the calling to become a minister.⁷ This, for him, was incredible, yet he had a focus as to what to do with the call. His purpose was "to help evangelize the world, especially with the political turmoil in the country at that time and he was concerned by the challenge that modernization and secularism posed to the church and the Christian faith."⁸ Since he had chosen to look and think differently from the country's then political situation, his zeal to address injustices in the South African society grew so much that the challenge posed by the Enlightenment to the Christian faith should be faced.⁹

His concern for what goes on within the society where human beings live, challenged him to reflect intensively on rediscovering the vocation of a Reformed ethicist in the present South African society. He perceived it as a concern that adversely affects God's good creation. Here, he imagined that "a world marked with sin should be where a Christian calling to serve God's purpose ensues, which unavoidably for him, implies the calling to work for the

---

4. de Villiers, "How my Mind," 17.
5. de Villiers, "How my Mind," 17.
6. Veldsman and Wethmar, "For and About."
7. de Villiers, "How my Mind," 17.
8. de Villiers, 17.
9. de Villiers, 17.

transformation of the world and, more specifically, society."[10] In this regard, the Reformed ethicist is left with an obligation to "help fellow Christians to contribute to the transformation of society" and explain what the practical implication for the gospel of Christ for the transformation of society entails.[11]

In terms of his theological formation, three phases which were central have been suggested. Veldsman and Wethmar explain how: "Originally coming from a background of evangelical pietism, his exposure to the Enlightenment influences, which he encountered at Stellenbosch and Amsterdam, led to a first attempt to cope with the challenges by rationalist and empiricist critics of the Christian faith." This began the first phase of theological development.[12] de Villiers later admitted that he was "transformed from a pietistic and church-centred Christian" to one who sees differently and seeks to address issues that concern society.[13] This first attempt developed in him a concern which would later lead to his doctoral thesis in 1978, in which he defended a view contrary to his Professor. Before then, on arrival in Amsterdam, discussions on apartheid by both South African and Dutch theologians and intellectuals "further awakened in him the desire to reflect more intently on relevant political and economic issues."[14] Perhaps this added to his interest so that the shift to Christian ethics became almost natural and inevitable. That was possibly the boiling point of conviction on Christian morality that later brought about their sharp contrast with his promoter. He held to the fact that "Christian morality has a distinctive content in opposition to his promoter, Professor H.M. Kuitert's idea of a natural clarity of moral notions."[15] One thing he admits which stood out for him during the first phase of his theological development was that both the theology and philosophy classes he attended, as well as his involvement in student politics resulted in the transformation that "broke his intellectual naiveté."[16] Henceforth, he became actively and more openly involved in engaging public issues that concern societal morality, and particularly, the church within a liberal democratic South Africa.

---

10. de Villiers, "The Vocation of Reformed," 521.
11. de Villiers, 521.
12. Veldsman and Wethmar, "For and About," 1.
13. de Villiers, "How my Mind," 17.
14. de Villiers, 18.
15. Veldsman and Wethmar, "For and About," 1.
16. de Villiers, "How my Mind," 17.

de Villiers's second theological formative stage began when he was at the Huguenot College in Wellington (South Africa) as a lecturer.[17] One prominent challenge he was confronted with at Wellington was the "turbulent events in the South Africa of the 1970s and 1980s."[18] In his own words, "he again became active in the church matters."[19] Faced with the reality of the time, de Villiers in his second phase of theological development devoted himself to work on issues related to justice and peace. He, particularly, kept on defending the position that "Christians are called not to conquer a particular enemy but enmity as such."[20] Amidst the turbulence of apartheid South Africa, he was further involved in expressing diverging views, focusing on analysing and evaluating apartheid, its theological justification in the official documents of the Dutch Reformed Church, and "the criticism of the ecumenical world, and the rejection of apartheid by the Dutch Reformed Mission Church and the World Alliance of Reformed churches in the early 1980s."[21] This firm standing later got backing from other proponents of Reformed churches that stood against the justification of apartheid and other social evils that permeated the South African society.[22] In essence, as apartheid struggle intensified in the second half of the 1980s, de Villiers "turned his attention on discussing moral issues, particularly the security situation in South Africa."[23]

This commitment reflects his later submission regarding the vocation of a Reformed ethicist in South Africa and its concerns on the transformation of society. The concept of societal transformation largely focuses on humanizing society. In his words, the "transformation of society should have as one of its goals, the desire to humanization"[24] of both humanity and nature."[25] This echoes Moltmann's view regarding the health of human beings and their surroundings. In his view of health, Moltmann sees it to be between the

---

17. de Villiers, *Revisiting Max Weber's Ethic*, iv.
18. Veldsman and Wethmar, "For and About," 1.
19. de Villiers, "How my Mind," 18.
20. Veldsman and Wethmar, "For and About," 1.
21. de Villiers, "How my Mind," 18.
22. See the works of Allan Boesak, Steve Biko and several other South African theologians, particularly black theologians, who stood against the justification of apartheid and its insistence to having a theological background.
23. de Villiers, "How my Mind," 18.
24. de Villiers, "The Vocation," 526.
25. See further discussion on care for nature by Bujo, *The Ethical Dimension*, 19.

"'individual and society,' 'society and nature,' and 'past and future,' which he calls the holistic concept of health."[26] Like Moltmann, de Villiers sees that transformation of society necessitates humanizing it entirely so that humanity might live truly and fully, while they flourish. To borrow from ethics, it would mean "a good life or 'life worth living,' which evokes an image of a living thing thriving in its proper environment."[27] Concluding his thoughts on these, de Villiers submits that "the optimal protection and enhancement of all life on earth or the flourishing of all God's creatures are formulations of a more inclusive goal that may be worthwhile to explore."[28]

The third phase of de Villiers's theological development began within a unique period in South Africa. First, he was appointed[29] in 1994 – the year South Africa became a democratic state – to the faculty of theology at the University of Pretoria, the same year that the African National Congress (ANC) took over power. As can be argued, this third phase of de Villiers's theological development became the landmark of his extended engagement with issues of public morality, particularly with the emergence of liberal democracy. He again was faced with the challenge of making relevant his views on public morality within the sphere that was almost strange to the former Nationalist constitution. First, the new liberal democracy that held on the greater separation between church and state made it difficult for all churches to effectively contribute to the solution of society.[30] Earlier, his criticism of apartheid and its theological justification had been "fiercely resisted in the Dutch Reformed church, including by the liberal theologians, who saw active support of the armed struggle of the liberation movements as the only legitimate moral stance for Christians."[31] This made futile de Villiers's effort in helping to draft a report for the Western Cape Synod of the Dutch Reformed church, and his exploring the implications of the biblical message for the enhancement of peace in South Africa on the "peace task of

---

26. Moltmann, *God in Creation*, 271.
27. Volf, *Flourishing: Why We Need*, ix.
28. de Villiers, "The Vocation," 526.
29. de Villiers, "How My Mind," 18.
30. de Villiers, 18; de Villiers, "The Vocation," 524.
31. de Villiers, "How my Mind," 18.

the church."[32] This, however, did not make de Villiers relent in his effort to preach and teach peace for South Africa, particularly within the church.

His second challenge within that era involved balancing church life with the political reality that had sterned the separation from the previous Nationalist government. This, indeed, posed threats to his views and efforts, some of which had been unacceptable by theologians themselves as seen above. The process of modernization and secularization held back by previous political dispensation now proceeded swiftly and almost unabatedly. Worst of all, de Villiers saw the negative implications of these processes on church life, which became noticeable over more than a decade after he said this.

One last but most significant aspect of de Villiers's third theological development phase has to do with a question that he still tries to answer. The significance of this question is manifold. In the first phase, it seeks to revitalise the lost interest in public issues. Second, it seeks to help the church understand its political role and responsibility to society. Third, what should be the responsibility of liberal democracy to humanity and society in general. This question has to do with "what the task of the church and Christian ethics should be in the public sphere of liberal democracy."[33] Perhaps this concern, as we shall see further, might have contributed to his interest in developing a contemporary Christian ethic of responsibility, of which he has become a leading voice within the African theological context.

Clint Le Bruyns's writing concerning post-apartheid South Africa and the need for public morality laments the need for renewal of human solidarity. In his conclusion, he suggests that the "renewal of human solidarity is an ethic to be sought and lived out and experienced in the manifold spheres of society" he finds that "revisiting the value of transcendence for the self and the community is one step in the right direction."[34] Le Bryuns's idea of renewal of human solidarity portrays similar challenges with living as responsible agents, a view de Villiers has elaborated and made his current research interest. We could, at this point, return to de Villiers's engagement with theology and ethics.

---

32. de Villiers, 18.
33. Veldsman and Wethmar, "For and About," 1.
34. Le Bruyns, "Human Dignity and Moral," 210.

The three phases of de Villiers' theological development mentioned above became prominent in what had defined his theological focus. Due to the exposure of different theological traditions, and the stance of the church and some theologians' position, de Villiers chooses to focus on promoting a campaign that would "help the world to understand what it means to the world."[35] Henceforth, public issues understood differently by liberal democracy, and during the turmoil of apartheid could be re-imagined and re-strategized. That, again, echoes the first social task of the church, when it houses "people capable of remembering and telling the story of God we find in Jesus."[36] Additionally, the church should also be a community that is not only telling and remembering the story of God but also living it out. Put simply, the church becoming a living testament.

5.2.2 Etiene de Villiers's Interest in Theology and Ethics

de Villiers's concern over the negative impact of previous political regimes on the church intensifies his quest to addressing public morality in South Africa. Perhaps, the reason why he chose theological ethics.

In his description of the times, Schweiker laments the significance that every work in ethics must provide some account of what is going on. In his assessment, human beings live in a world and are surrounded[37] by uncertainties at the same time inhabiting some space of meaning and value structured by cultural and social dynamics. Similarly, Hauerwas imagines Christian ethics as a self-conscious activity as rather a recent development, yet being a Christian has always involved moral claims.[38] The above two voices challenge our thinking concerning what Schweiker has called "the time of many worlds"[39] where human beings contend with the limits that time places on life that it is swept in and out of existence. The quest for speaking against the tyranny of the time and how it affects human existence and flourishing, however, invites us to study Etienne de Villiers's views with the South African experiences of the past and the present.

---

35. Hauerwas, *The Peaceable Kingdom*, 100.
36. Hauerwas, 100.
37. Schweiker, *Theological Ethics*, xi.
38. Hauerwas, *A Community of Character*, 89.
39. Schweiker, *Theological Ethics and Global*, xi, xii.

Going by two views above, de Villiers would agree with them in his theological-ethical engagement with issues in society. In his imaginations, de Villiers posits that "the features of an appropriate ethical approach to public issues in the contemporary context of late-modernity are one of the crucial questions that Christian social ethics faces today."[40] His submission does not deny the prevalent existence of public issues calling for redress, it rather emphasises it with more intensity. He points out that "we are faced with the challenges of the increasing number of new ethical issues brought by technology which are hard to combat."[41] And so, a call for the "formulation of new moral values and norms" which is suggestive of the intense need to diversify our search for ways to deal with diminishing public morality.[42]

The growing concern for decline in public morality has become an area of interest for de Villiers in his ethical deliberations. During his time of study in Amsterdam, de Villiers was introduced to Christian ethical thoughts, but also to the "challenges posed to Christian ethics by analytical moral philosophers, evolutionary ethicists, anthropologists and sociologists."[43] In his quest for understanding the idea of Christian morality, de Villiers countered the view that there is nothing distinctive about the content of Christian morality – the view held by his professor – "and that only the motivation Christians have for doing what is morally right could be described as distinctive."[44] The result of this argument drew him into "the academic field of Christian ethics."[45] Understood from his idea of a distinctive Christian morality "it would support us in grasping, at an individual level, the radical and universal character of the commandment to love our neighbour, whilst any content that corresponds to the morality of others renders collaboration with others desirable."[46] Similar views are shared among scholars, like Jean Porter, who, in her *Moral Action and Christian Ethics,* argues that Christian ethics can make a distinctive

---

40. de Villiers, "The Vocation," 1.
41. de Villiers, "The Vocation," 7; *Revisiting Max Weber's.*
42. de Villiers, "The Vocation," 7; *Revisiting Max Weber's,* 217.
43. de Villiers, "The Distinctiveness," 1.
44. de Villiers, 1.
45. de Villiers, 1.
46. van Niekerk, "Personal-Ethical Perspectives," 5.

contribution to the debates on Christian morality – either in moral substance or in terms of underlying moral justification.[47]

Porter's point highlights the constituents of a distinctive Christian morality as caring and respect for others as we would want for ourselves (the golden rule). It is this distinctive nature that brings to bear the wellbeing of those outside our circle of influence, which echoes Vosloo's view of morality as being "not merely about common values but about (uncommon) people who embody these values ... People who are formed in communities through certain truthful narratives and role models."[48] This description of morality suggests some sense of hospitality. For Vosloo, hospitality is having the potential to enable a more creative and responsible rethinking of the relationship between identity and otherness, or sameness and difference. In that sense, an ethos of hospitality as openness to others and otherness challenges the mindset of enclosed and stuffy identity.[49] The point of interest here is that the human person, unlike lower animals, directs their action by "a reasoned understanding of the good."[50] The ongoing conversation invites different stakeholders if issues of public morality and a distinctive Christian morality is to be understood. In his submission on this, de Villiers emphasizes "the need to work together with other people with the same intent to promote the protection and flourishing of all life in God's creation, which he calls our responsibility."[51]

5.3 Theology and Ethics of Responsibility

In this section, the reader is introduced to de Villiers's interaction with other proponents of ethics of responsibility, his views on theological ethics, and how he agrees and disagrees with other voices. Following that, his proposal for a contemporary Christian ethic of responsibility will be reviewed.

In their introduction to the book *Modern Theologians: An Introduction to Christian Theology since 1918*, Ford and Muers explain why theology has

---

47. Porter, *Morality and Christian Ethics*, 1.
48. Vosloo, "Public Morality," 65.
49. Vosloo, 67.
50. Porter, *Morality and Christian Ethics*, 102.
51. de Villiers, "The Distinctiveness," 7.

become, and should be seen and engaged as modern.[52] In their inquiry, the explanation goes that through the influence of certain major events in the European world, the impact has reached different areas of human engagement. As theologians have been involved in the conversation with scholars of other disciplines, it has influenced the way that we think and do theology, hence making theology modern. As such, the modernisation of theology has given room to its engagement with different issues of public morality confronting the life existence, particularly in late modernity. With the expansion of human knowledge and wisdom, the result has been global public morality which leads Stanley Hauerwas to say that "the fragmentation of our world is not 'out there' but in our souls, such that it is extremely hard to maintain our moral identity."[53] The concerns baffling the world we live in invite us to rethink appropriate ways to address them for which de Villiers, just as Weber, suggests an ethic of responsibility.

de Villiers's view of ethics of responsibility is rooted in the concerns that the modern times pose on humanity and nature. One of these, he attests, in agreement with Hans Jonas, is technological advancement. But unlike Jonas, de Villiers sees technological advancement to have created what he calls the "responsibility gap,"[54] that requires "comprehensive responsibility."[55] Collectively, he sees an "acute expansion of this gap in moral responsibility as proportional to a growing inability to bear such responsibility as one of the most disturbing paradoxes of modern times."[56] What this means is that despite being a blessing, technological advancement creates an adverse effect in expanding the responsibility gap, which then creates more problems than those it solves. Since it is already taking over what humans in other centuries could do, de Villiers's question on "who will bear moral responsibility"[57] becomes relevant and requiring urgent attention and response. To deal with the responsibility gap caused by technological advancement with negative consequences for both present and future generation, de Villiers suggests the need to supplement the classical notion of responsibility (retrospective) with

---

52. Ford and Muers, *The Modern Theologians*, 1.
53. Hauerwas, *The Peaceable Kingdom*, 6.
54. de Villiers, "Who Will Bear Moral," 16.
55. de Villiers, "An Ethics of Responsibility," 5.
56. de Villiers, "Who Will Bear Moral," 16.
57. de Villiers, 1.

the new notion (prospective).[58] This suggests that de Villiers's contemporary Christian ethic of responsibility is built more around the new notion than the classical.

Taking a look at prospective moral responsibility, one would agree with de Villiers that threats of global public morality invite us towards rightful thinking on their effects for the future. In agreement with Jonas, de Villiers advocates for the responsibility to "actively prevent future harm to humans and nature."[59] With technological advancement, however, de Villiers reveals that responsibility talk is becoming more problematic resulting in blame games on either the human beings who manufacture the machinery, or those operating them, or the technological gadgets themselves. In all these, the call for who will bear moral responsibility gets louder as the gap widens. To this note, de Villiers calls on "both philosophers and lawmakers to radically rethink the notion of moral accountability or retrospective moral responsibility in order to make adaptations to the classical model."[60] If understood properly, de Villiers's advocacy here suggests a concern for the survival, sustenance, and flourishing of human life and nature both here and now, but also for the future generation.

5.4 Interactions of de Villiers with Other Scholars

The section below is a brief highlight of de Villiers's interaction with other proponents of ethics of responsibility.

5.4.1 Interactions with Max Weber

de Villiers has great respect for Max Weber's work, particularly his distinctive work in ethics of responsibility. It is difficult, de Villiers says, "not to be

---

58. Retrospective moral responsibility is when some or another negative outcome of the past is ascribed to a person. While with the new dimension, prospective moral responsibility, the responsibility of preventing humans and nature from being actively harmed or to realize desirable future conditions by taking necessary measures in the present, is ascribed to a particular person or persons, or more likely, to particular institutions. de Villiers, "Who Will Bear Moral," 16.

59. de Villiers, "Who Will Bear Moral," 17.

60. de Villiers, 18.

drawn into greater engagement with Weber's thought once you have become acquainted with it."⁶¹

His first encounter with Weber's work was in the new millennium when he began writing on proponents of Christian ethics of responsibility in the course of which he discovered Weber to have been the first to propose an ethic of responsibility. Ethics of responsibility was becoming widely spoken about from different contexts (Germany, America, and now in Africa), and within various disciplines (sociology, theology, philosophy, and economics/business).⁶² Since Weber's work has been studied in the previous chapter, here we will only be focusing on de Villiers's reception of Weber's ideas on ethics of responsibility.

In one of his addresses, de Villiers agrees that Weber's ethic of responsibility could serve to Christian ethicists as a model for doing social ethics in the twenty-first century.⁶³ Earlier, he had highlighted the devastating influence that late modernity poses on humanity and nature, hence, his acceptance of Weber's ethics of responsibility as an adequate tool to deal with those issues. Despite this recognition, de Villiers had some reservations that Weber's ethics of responsibility "needs some improvements because some of its aspects are "unacceptable to Christian social ethics."⁶⁴

5.4.1.2 Strengths of Weber's Ethics of Responsibility

The appeal for a contemporary ethics of responsibility, as expressed by de Villiers, took a turn from the observation of what was already obtainable. It is important to note that he regards the views of Weber, who was the first to use the expression "ethic of responsibility" and makes strong proclamations. One of those is that Weber was right in "asserting that modernization has had a significant negative impact on traditional Western ethics, and this impact has been as devastating as he asserted."⁶⁵ That assertion, amongst other things, makes Weber's thoughts significant, particularly in contemporary times that

---

61. de Villiers, *Revisiting Max Weber's*, vii.
62. de Villiers, vii.
63. de Villiers, "In Search," 4.
64. de Villiers, "In Search," 4, 1.
65. de Villiiers, *Revisiting Max Weber's*, 4.

have become "increasingly pluralistic that we have become more diverse and no longer share in a common religious and moral tradition."[66]

Firstly, de Villiers recognizes Weber's quest for the need to salvage the ethical dimension of life as vital.[67] Although he disagrees with Weber's claim on the demise of Christian ethics and religious ethics in general, owing to the influence of modernisation, he agrees that modernization presents challenges. These challenges, de Villiers avows, do not only affect adherents of religious moralities but also adherents of "thick" secular moralities related to views of life. This view suggests Weber's integrative consideration of the societal wellbeing that had to battle with the influence of modernization and to equally maintain its moral order. In such instances, Jersild's reminder that we live in a social environment which conditions and shapes our moral responses, and that we should not ignore changes taking place in our world, remains relevant.[68]

Since Weber had concluded on the demise of Christian ethics, he had little or no trust that it would provide any moral guidance. Weber feared that the ethical dimension of life would be eliminated from social orders, including the political order.[69] Interestingly, such arguments formed in Weber the conviction expressed in his lecture, *Politics as a Vocation,* that only the charismatic political leader is an effective representative of politics.[70]

In addition, de Villiers outlines the diminishing role of ethical considerations in contemporary societies as undermining the influence of morality in certain aspects of life, particularly in a consumerist global society.[71] As regards salvaging the ethical dimension of life in a global society that is thick with consumerist ideology, Douglas Meeks's observation can be taken as a point of departure. He observes, as his first problem, the perception that theology and church are not supposed to be responsible for questions of public life and have confined themselves to the issues concerning the meaning and purpose of eternal life. When theology and church become limited as such, Meeks reminds us that it has "omitted what was the primary concern of

---

66. Jersild, *Making Moral Decisions*, 10.
67. de Villiers, *Revisiting Max Weber's*, 187.
68. Jersild, *Making Moral Decisions*, 9.
69. de Villiers, *Revisiting Max Weber's*, 187.
70. Weber, *Politics as Vocation*.
71. de Villiers, *Revisiting Max Weber's*, 188.

traditional economy, namely livelihood."[72] The rise of consumerist ideology in this sense, one would say, has so much to do with the attitude of church and theology in engaging with the economics of the global era and its highlighted features. Here, the ethical dimension of human life is at stake in that millions of people have no sense of livelihood. Such situations suggest the official absence of God and human livelihood in the theory and practice of the market.[73] This notion, however, suggests a misconception of God, theology, and church in public life. It is instead the case that if Christian theology understands critically the trinitarian scope of the economy, namely creating, redeeming and new-creating work of God in the whole of creation, then it can answer the question if everyone in the household gets what it takes to live?[74] The whole view may explain why the global economic era could be considered, engaged, and has inputs from the theological perspective concerning the "household" concept of the earth and its resources. In view of all this, de Villiers applauds Weber's ethic of responsibility.[75]

Second, Weber's ethic of responsibility gets recognition by de Villiers because it calls for designing a new approach to ethics.[76] As previously discussed (see section 4.3.3), proponents of ethics of responsibility, other than de Villiers, have suggested new approaches to ethics relevant to the times we live in.[77] Here, de Villiers highlights Weber's three features for designing a new approach to ethics. These include first, that it is based on a process of consensus-seeking using selection, discussions and negotiation; second, it is based on the recognition of the validity of both applicable ethical values and non-ethical social order-specific, profession-specific, or organisation-specific values; and third, that it has both regulatory and aspirational intentions.

---

72. Meeks, "God's Oikonomia," 111.

73. Meeks, 112.

74. Meeks, 112.

75. See Ernst Conradie for further readings on the salvation of the earth and the concept of *Oikos*, "The Earth," 14.

76. de Villiers, *Revisiting Max Weber's*, 189.

77. Jonas, *The Imperative of Responsibility*, calls for a future ethics that ensures the survival of human beings in the future; (Huber suggests that traditional ethics is not sufficient to deal with issues of contemporary public morality facing the contemporary times: *Ethics: The Fundamental*; Schweiker suggests an integrated theory of responsibility comprizing of agential social, and dialogical perspectives, *Responsibility and Christian Ethics*.

Third, Weber's ethics of responsibility outlines the need for conceptualizing the new ethical approach as second-level normative ethics of responsibility.[78] The idea of suggesting a second-level normative ethical theory that focuses on politics, as Weber intends, holds if it involves all social orders and personal life with the hope to salvage the undermining effect of modernisation on ethical living.[79] Nevertheless, de Villiers draws our attention to contemporary philosophers but admits that as a conclusion, they would not concur. For him, Weber's criticism of religious ethical values would probably not agree with his dismissal for the social orders of the major secular normative ethical theories formulated by Western philosophers.[80] It seems these Western philosophical views were introduced to counter the growing ethical pluralism that could be applied by everyone in all spheres of life. Dismissing them would, therefore, result in partial disagreement of Weber's new ethical approach as second-level normative ethics of responsibility focusing on the charismatic political leader.[81] Yet, even if rejecting Weber's proposal for new ethical approach does gain acceptance by Western philosophers[82] and proponents of Enlightenment, de Villiers chooses to agree with Weber that those theories provide an effective antidote to the undermining effect of modernization on ethical living.[83]

Outlining reasons for his disagreement with the enlightenment philosophers, de Villiers holds to the first level normative approach to ethics as follows: First, they do not overcome the problem of increasing ethical pluralisation but contribute to it in a certain manner. Second, they cannot substantiate their claim that indubitable foundations for moral principles can be found. Third, they do not have unacceptable convincing ethical traits that render them inappropriate for proving ethical guidance in social orders. Fourth, they have little chance of eliciting the necessary essential commitment and motivation.[84]

---

78. de Villiers, *Revisiting Max Weber's*, 193.
79. de Villiers, 193.
80. de Villiers, 193.
81. de Villiers, 193.
82. Few of these philosophers include the deontological normative ethical theory of Kant, or the Utilitarianism of Bentham and Mill (de Villiers, *Revisiting Max Weber's*, 194).
83. de Villiers, 194.
84. de Villiers, 193–95.

The support by de Villier for Weber's new ethical approach holds. He argues that major secular normative ethical theories (that include the Enlightenment philosopher's proposals) are inadequate for providing ethical guidance in social orders for organisations and professions operating within them. He is, however, convinced that a new and more appropriate approach to ethics in these orders is needed,[85] which he supports in his proposal. Such an approach in de Villiers's view would, first, acknowledge that professional people and employees do not enter the workplace with minds that are *tabula rasa* with regards to ethics because they already have their ethical codes and convictions. Second, it would acknowledge that people in the workplace are primarily in need of ethical guidance on how they could relate their moral convictions to the ethical problems of the workplace, and to the ethical and non-ethical values already recognized in a meaningful way. In support of Weber, de Villiers notes that the new normative ethical theory would not be one that strives to identify and rationally justify universally valid first level moral principles as a substitute for personal moral principle. Rather, it would strive to provide second-level normative ethical guidance on how people ought to deal with their ethical convictions as well as with moral and non-moral guidelines recognized in the workplace.[86]

5.4.1.2 Weaknesses of Weber's Ethics of Responsibility

Although Weber made remarkable contributions to the field of ethics of responsibility, yet they are not without flaws for our time. A few of those flaws are outlined below.

First, de Villiers notes that Weber's designation of a charismatic political leader as the sole agent of responsibility is elitist, open to authoritarian abuse and one-sidedly political.[87] If de Villiers is understood well here, he observed what is central to Weber's over-upliftment of a political leader as one with the right moral standing to lead the cause for salvaging ethical living – in Weber's case, the political turmoil of his German context. Even in Weber's day, de Villiers notes, the reputation of the political leader had seriously tarnished and so could not be trusted for the claimed mandate. Taking examples

---

85. de Villiers, 195.
86. de Villiers, 195–96.
87. de Villiers, 197.

from the African political order, such a proposal for a charismatic political leader that Weber proposes would likely not find acceptance because of their attitude towards political participation. In that regard, de Villiers worries about our contemporary politicians and perhaps leaders, in today's Africa who, despite their professed solidarity with the poor, are more interested in enriching themselves by exploiting the available public resources, than in improving the plight of the poor. According to de Villiers, this happens because the focus of most of our democracies is placed on self-gratification than on the wellbeing of humanity and their societies. It also indicates why an alarmingly high number of politicians and government officials become rich as soon as they assume political offices, and are even willing to cross the line of immoral conduct and become involved in corruption.[88] If this is the charismatic political leader Weber referred to in his argument, in agreement with de Villiers, this author contends that such a leader is weak and would be unfit to address public morality, especially in the contemporary African, and specifically Nigerian context.

In another sense, de Villiers connects various contemporary ethical challenges facing us today to the ineffectiveness of leadership and narrow national interests. In the first instance, de Villiers equates poor attitude to addressing issues of climate change, migration, *insecurity, corruption, religious fundamentalism*, racial and national segregation, to a lack of strong leadership will. Interestingly, in Africa as elsewhere, politicians have got the power because of democratic forms of governance. On the second note, one could quite agree with de Villiers that these continue to happen because of narrow national interests.[89] As such, there are fewer concerns for national growth and development that could enhance the wellbeing of human lives which disregard the promotion of morality.[90]

The second problem in Weber's ethics of responsibility is his over-emphasis on the enclosed nature of differentiated social spheres and the contradictory

---

88. de Villiers, "The Recognition of," 7.
89. de Villiers, *Revisiting Max Weber's*, 199.
90. In the words of Jersild, morality is a controversial subject for every generation. Here it is taken as the enhancement of principles of conduct that differentiate right and wrong, but that work toward reviving ethical living, particularly in modern society. Jersild, *Making Moral Decisions*, 9.

nature of value-systems.[91] Here, de Villiers both argues for and against Weber in his connotation on moral value-systems. First, he agrees with Weber that "thick" moral values derived from either religious or secular life often clash with non-moral values of social orders. In his assessment, the clash occurs because of the contrary view of morality that exist between these orders. He thus warns that to implement policies using either of those moral orders could severely disrupt operations in these social orders on account of an inevitable conflict between the role players, and interference in the implementation of non-moral values. That, however, justifies Weber's thesis that thick moral values often clash. Second, de Villiers disagrees with Weber's conception that thin moral values are also incommensurable with the non-moral values of social orders. Clearing such doubts, de Villiers calls for sufficient agreement among role players on the applicable thin moral values that should be part of the ethical life of organisations, which when done would salvage any strife between moral values.[92] Considering the above views, Weber, in de Villier's view, made a mistake of equating all moral values with thick values that are derived from particular religious or secular views of life without considering the possibility that moral values might also be "thin." Weber also fails to recognize an important difference between moral and non-moral values,[93] namely that moral values play an orienting role in all spheres of life, although they are not applicable in the different spheres as identical.

The third problematic aspect of Weber's ethics of responsibility, as de Villiers and other scholars such as Breiner[94] opine, is that it does not depend or portray his nationalistic conviction.[95] So much so that the ethics of responsibility he proposes could only be accepted based on such convictions. It is surprising to note that Weber did not refer, even in *Politics as A Vocation*, to his nationalistic conviction while proposing the ethics of responsibility. Rather, as de Villiers points out, he argues based on first, a sociological analysis of the nature of modern politics and the role players, second, a demonstration of the inappropriateness of the ethic of conviction approach, and

---

91. de Villiers, *Revisiting Max Weber's*, 200.
92. de Villiers, 202.
93. de Villiers, 203.
94. Breiner, *Max Weber*, 43.
95. de Villiers, 203.

third, the identification of the features of an appropriate approach in modern politics. As a result, he succeeded in creating an avenue[96] for the political leader acting by this ethic to elevate an internationally strong German nation to an ultimate value.

In his argument to this issue, de Villiers's interest is in questioning the implication that in elevating a certain value, a charismatic political leader with good moral standing could bring other cultural values. A question can then be asked, "how does understanding morality help us in this regard?" Taylor opines that at the highest[97] theoretical level, much of contemporary moral theory assumes that morality can be defined in terms of a code of obligatory and forbidden actions, a code which can be generated from a single source or principle, while Wood states that "morality represents what is reflective, critical, and individualist in moral life."[98] Taylor's idea clarifies but also justifies de Villier's concern on the implication of Weber's assumption which rests on a single principle, namely the elevation of a charismatic political leader in a German context. Such an assumption, de Villiers warns, could result in elevating cultural values that could be harmful to particular individuals or groups of people.[99] However, de Villiers warns that elevation of ultimate values, including morality, should not be too formal or wide, as Weber argues; or a definition of morality be based on the efforts of modern liberal society in defining and applying codes of conduct, as Taylor says. Rather, our understanding of morality should borrow both from the Western world and the common use of language today.[100] If morality referred to "wellbeing or flourishing" in the history of the Western world philosophers and Christian ethicists, then it also agrees with the contemporary connotation.[101]

If we go by de Villiers's disagreement with Weber in situating morality not based on his nationalist but the charismatic political leader, his sociological side of ethics of responsibility depends on a person's surface. In either case, Weber's reference to morality is classified as, according to Taylor, a demonstration of the assumption that morality in terms of obligatory imposition

---

96. de Villiers, 203.
97. Taylor, *Dilemmas and Connection*, 314.
98. Wood, *Hegel's Ethical Thought*, 127.
99. de Villiers, *Revisiting Max Weber's*, 203.
100. de Villiers, 204.
101. Volf, *Flourishing: Why We Need*, ix.

from and to a single source. With such an assumption, one wonders if Weber's ethics of responsibility and his idea of morality would receive much attention in contemporary society, particularly in contexts other than his German. Perhaps, such considerations might have ignited the critical mind of de Villiers to propose a contemporary Christian ethic of responsibility that could effectively help to address the issues of ethical living in the context of technological advancement and globalisation, as well as their detrimental effects on human dignity.

5.4.2 Interactions with Hans Jonas

Another proponent of the ethics of responsibility that de Villiers engages with is Hans Jonas, whose concern rests on technological advancement and its effect on the future of humanity and nature. The concern here relates to how de Villiers wrestles with Jonas's view from his own (African) perspective with its peculiar challenges that certainly differ from Jonas.

He demonstrates three concerns regarding Jonas's ideas, which we shall focus our discussion on. These are the growing concern to bear moral responsibility in our time, the responsibility gap created by technology, and the form of responsibility Jonas takes and its implication for the future but perhaps also for the present.[102]

The expansion of moral responsibility outgrowing the ability to bear such responsibility is one of the most disturbing paradoxes of modern times.[103] It has been in connection with the influence of technological advancement, contributing to what de Villiers calls, "responsibility gap."[104] By this responsibility gap, a sort of confusion on who is responsible for the occurrence of certain actions becomes prominent. The question begging for answer in such regard, however, has to do with the call on who would bear moral responsibility; either human beings who manufacture the machines, the machines themselves, or those who operate the machines.

From the first issue mentioned on the growing concern to bear moral responsibility in our time, de Villiers consents that technology shares the blame because of the gap it causes. It would be recalled in the previous chapter,

---

102. Jonas, "Technology and Responsibility."
103. de Villiers, "Who Will Bear Moral," 16.
104. de Villiers, 16.

under the section on Hans Jonas (see section 4.3.3), that we studied his engagement with ethics of responsibility focusing on the future survival and sustenance of mankind while considering the effect that technology brings. Commenting on this, de Villiers consents that the effects of technological advancement have resulted in the responsibility gap thus: first, technology has created new modes of conduct and social institutions, new prohibitions, new virtues, new ways of helping and new ways of abusing people. Second, the application of technology has not only extended humankind's control over nature and helped limit the impact of the dangers in nature but has led to an increase in the number and the gravity of the risks facing humans. Third, technological advancement has made it difficult to link negative outcomes in industry and business to specific actions of human agents.[105] This, according to Jonas, has made technology assume ethical significance because of the central place it now occupies in human purpose, which was different from when it was a measured tribute to necessity and not the road to mankind's chosen goal that it has become. Additionally, Jonas explains technological perversion in human affairs further using the boundary between "city" and "nature" that has been obliterated so that:

> the city of men, once enclave in the nonhuman world, spreads over the whole of terrestrial nature and usurps its place. The difference between the artificial and the natural has vanished, the natural is swallowed up in the sphere of the artificial, and at the same time the total artefact (the works of man that have become "the world" and as such envelop their makers) generates a "nature" of its own, that is, a necessity with which human freedom has to cope in an entirely new sense.[106]

This is the extent to which human beings have come because of technology such that chances are that human extinction in the future could occur, following the lament of Jonas. He bases his argument on the future of humanity in the context of such a technological twist that is on the verge of substituting the roles of humans. Following this, de Villiers attests that Jonas's view of ethics

---

105. de Villiers, "Who Will Bear Moral," 17–18.
106. Jonas, *The Imperative of Responsibility*, 10.

of responsibility discourse relies more on a prospective[107] (positive, the new model) than on retrospective (negative, classical or old model) held by other philosophers. While in the classical sense responsibility looks back into the past and ascribes the responsibility for one or other negative outcomes in the past to a person, Jonas understands it differently. In his view, responsibility should look forward[108] to the future such that it actively ascribes to a particular person or institution, the responsibility in order to prevent future harm to humans and nature by taking the necessary measures in the present. According to the classical model, someone is only held responsible for the outcome of their actions in the past, a view which de Villiers objects to, while suggesting it would lead to a responsibility gap. Another shortcoming of the classical view, particularly concerning the African continent, is that the perils of public morality to human dignity would not be addressed since they are not effects of the past but of here and now. As Jonas states, therefore, we have a moral responsibility to safeguard and checkmark our actions and inactions here and now regarding either the promotion or protection of public morality while imagining future existence.

From the point of technological advancement and its effect on the possible extinction of human life in the future, and the focus on prospective responsibility put together, we can resonate with Jonas's position. This position raises concern on technology replacing humanity while creating a gap, hence, he argues for a prospective (positive) responsibility. With this model of responsibility, the blame is not placed on persons because of the consequences of their past actions, but what role they can play to prevent possible damages in the future here and now.[109]

Despite Jonas's appraisals on prospective ethics of responsibility for safeguarding the future of humankind, de Villiers disagrees with it as a substantive Christian ethics of responsibility model for our contemporary time. In this regard, three observations are outlined against Jonas's ethics of responsibility.[110] First, de Villiers declares that "any attempt to develop Christian ethics of responsibility that closely reflects Jonas' conception does not hold much

---

107. de Villiers, "Who Will Bear Moral," 17.
108. de Villiers, 17.
109. Jonas, "Technology and Responsibility," 33.
110. de Villiers, "Prospects of (part 2)," 89.

promise."[111] This is because, for him, Jonas's attempt to elevate responsibility to the substantive normative principle of the new ethics he proposes is problematic. Second, despite his convincing argument that the prospective responsibility for the survival of humankind should receive far more emphasis on contemporary ethics, his plea for the complete transformation of ethics into future ethics is one-sided. Third, Jonas's assumption that "only ethics based on a universally recognized foundation can warrant prospective responsibility for the future survival of humankind is inconclusive."[112]

5.4.3 Interactions with the German Christian Version of Ethics of Responsibility

Although the concept of ethics of responsibility was first developed in Germany by a sociologist, it has grown over the years to other disciplines, one of which is theology. Ever since theologians began the inquiry into this topic, it has expanded with a focus on the Christian ethics of responsibility among others. Here, the reader is therefore reminded that Christian ethics of responsibility is not new because famous theologians both from Germany and America dealt with it in their writings.[113] The focus of this section, however, is to engage with theologians who have developed ideas on Christian ethics of responsibility after the publication of Hans Jonas's book in the 1980s. These theologians took it upon themselves to develop Christian versions of ethics of responsibility while deviating slightly from Jonas's view that all contemporary ethics should focus on the future survival of humankind. This section, therefore, introduces the reader to de Villiers's engagement with the German theological version of the Christian ethics of responsibility and argues whether responsibility can, and should be, a qualifier for contemporary Christian ethics. In doing this, de Villiers wrote an article that engages these views which will be our guide in this exploration. Three theologians whose

---

111. de Villiers, 89.

112. de Villiers, 89.

113. "Renowned theologians like Dietrich Bonhoeffer and Richard Niebuhr wrote extensively on Christian responsibility in the middle decades of the twentieth century and presented their own versions of Christian ethics of responsibility. Their views have exercized enormous influence and have also received ample attention in theological dissertations and publications" (de Villiers, "Prospects of (part 2)," 88). As a result of the influence, the idea of ethics of responsibility has and still grows and is being developed in different contexts and further versions emerging.

views of Christian ethics of responsibility de Villiers engages are Wolfgang Huber, Johannes Fischer and Ulric Körtner.

In exploring the three German versions of Christian ethics of responsibility, de Villiers considers their place of commonality. In Huber's case, he pays much attention to Jonas and his future ethics but had also oriented himself to Max Weber's original conceptualisation of ethics of responsibility.[114] The result of that expanded and diversified his commitment and engagement with ethics of responsibility and how he presents his view. Of significance here is the fact that the result of Huber's engagement with early proponents "does not focus only on technological development and its ethical implication," but his attention is also taken "to other aspects of modernization and related ethical implications."[115] This probably informs his definition of ethics of responsibility (see section 5.5). Perhaps Huber could be right to focus not solely on Jonas's future ethics, but remain concerned and cautious about the here and now. When it comes to admitting responsibility as a qualifier for contemporary Christian ethics of responsibility, he agrees that it has contemporary connotations.[116]

Johannes Fischer's (Switzerland) view of responsibility seems to have had greater reception by de Villiers than both the views of Huber and Körtner. In one of his claims, de Villiers endorses Fischer's view of an ethics of responsibility as the most[117] qualified. The reason for that acceptance is his critical shift away from getting too close to Jonas's view of ethics for the future. Fischer finds that any "attempts to identify ethics of responsibility with ethics as a whole and to reduce it to future ethics with the survival of humankind as its sole aim, are relinquished, a legitimate, but limited role can, in his opinion, be assigned to such ethics."[118]

Although Fischer agrees to the late arrival of responsibility, he attests that its definitive roots are in the Judeo-Christian tradition. This led Fisher to ask three important questions he thinks every ethics should ask. First, "what is the good that we must strive for in this life? Secondly, what is the good we owe

---

114. Because his view of ethics of responsibility has been discussed in the previous chapter, little is said about him here.
115. de Villiers, "Prospects of a Christian Ethics of Responsibility," 91.
116. de Villiers, 96.
117. de Villiers, 93.
118. de Villiers, 93.

others that is our responsibility? Thirdly, what is the trans-subjective good that determines our lives, the Spirit?"[119] In Fischer's view, these questions portray the nature of what ethics, including Christian ethics, must strive towards giving answers to. Also, central to this Judeo-Christian tradition is the belief that human[120] beings are responsible to God in everything they do. Therefore, de Villiers concludes that ethics portrayed from this tradition is, in an eminent sense, ethics of responsibility.[121] It does not mean for Fischer, however, that Christian ethics can one-sidedly be seen in terms of ethics of responsibility. Instead, what he holds strong as central to ethics issues is not "what we are responsible for" but "what do we want or make each other responsible for."[122] For him, it is beyond our scope to discover moral responsibility rather than creating or constituting it mutually.

The third German theologian with the Christian version of ethics of responsibility is Ulric Körtner (Austria). He does differ from the two previous colleagues in his assessment of ethics of responsibility, but agreed that Christian ethics should be construed as an ethics of responsibility.[123] Körtner, like Huber, is sensitive to the challenges of our time that he resolves "responsibility should be the leading concept of Christian ethics attuned to the time we are living,"[124] where there is a growing need for responsibility. For him, adopting that all Christian ethics be based on responsibility is not his view, but the integration of concepts like good/values, duties and virtues with responsibility, prompts his thinking in that direction.[125] These concepts relate closely to Fischer's questions regarding how our responsibility to others should be. Considering global dynamics and their effects on humanity in our time that Schweiker talks about, Miroslav Volf[126] also has a description of our time

---

119. de Villiers, 93
120. de Villiers, 93.
121. de Villiers, 94.
122. de Villiers, 95.
123. de Villiers, "Prospects of (part 1)," 95.
124. de Villiers, 95.
125. Körtner, "Dem Risiko Trotzen," 581.
126. He sees that climate change's devastating impacts on the environment; global pandemics; great and growing discrepancies in power, wealth, and skills; emerging artificial intelligence menacing humans with redundancy; the global reach of barbaric terror burning and beheading enemies and destroying artifacts of our great civilizstion – these and other threats, he says, place an ashen mantle of melancholy on many (Volf, *Flourishing: Why We Need*, x).

resulting in the feeling that humanity is doomed to languishing.[127] These descriptions are timely and call for a re-think on our ethical engagements and how effectively they influence and enhance the sustenance of life both here and now, and for the hereafter.

A critical but constructive ethical consideration of our time suggests the desiring need for a good life. There are in existence views of what comprises a good life. As such, Volf finds that in our time (late-modernity), many define a good life as the "life that feels good, where pleasure overshadows the pain (happiness as pleasure)"; second, others think of the good life "as the life that goes well (happiness as wellbeing or satisfaction)"; and the third group views a good life "as the life that is lived well (happiness as excellent life)."[128] These three together are inextricably intertwined, which evokes an image of a living thing thriving in its proper environment.[129] It could be suggested, however, that what Christian ethics, including ethics of responsibility, should promote in the context of global dynamics is the condensed quest for a good life for the common good of society.

In comparing the three German theologians and their versions of Christian ethics of responsibility, de Villiers makes a careful study of their similarity and dissimilarity. In the first instance, he declares that the theologians both endorsed Christian ethics of responsibility and denied portraying ethics of responsibility as a substantive normative principle to be conceived as exclusively future ethics that needs a universally recognized foundation. Second, both have completely different views on the definitive features of Christian ethics of responsibility.[130] Understood properly, the German version that was surveyed, lay claim to formulate a Christian version of ethics of responsibility. Following their arguments, de Villiers proposes that:

> if Christian ethics does not follow Hans Jonas' view too closely, holding to the substantive principle and reducing itself to future ethics, but takes its cue from how responsibility should

---

127. Volf, *Flourishing: Why We Need*, ix.
128. Volf, "The Crown," 133; Marais, "Imagining Human Flourishing."
129. Volf, *Flourishing, Why We Need*, ix.
130. de Villiers, "Prospects of (part 2)," 97.

fundamentally stamp contemporary ethics, then the prospects of Christian ethics of responsibility are indeed quite promising.[131]

In support of the above hopeful proposal for the promising nature of responsibility stamping contemporary Christian ethics, de Villiers highlights how responsibility should qualify contemporary Christian ethics in his proposal.

5.4.4 Interactions with the American Version of Ethics of Responsibility

The perception of ethics of responsibility did not end in the German context, but has been prominent also in the English-speaking world, particularly America. In this case, two American traditions who emerged from two generations, have written on ethics of responsibility. Firstly, the Niebuhrian tradition (Richard Henry Niebuhr and Reinhold), and William Schweiker, a contemporary theologian. In this section, however, the reader is introduced to de Villiers's engagement with the view of the American version of ethics of responsibility, particularly those of Willian Schweiker. Since these contemporary versions of ethics of responsibility took their base after the publication of Hans Jonas's remarkable book, *The Imperative of Responsibility* which was published in 1979, and steers the discussion into the 1980s, it is wise to, therefore, situate each of their views against Jonas, first by looking at how Schweiker agrees or differs with Jonas, and how de Villiers engages him (Schweiker).

Following the challenges of his time and the German context, Jonas observed the absurdity of modern ethics and considered it irrelevant to combat contemporary ethical challenges. This is similar to what the philosopher, Alasdair MacIntyre, says in his book *After Virtue: A Study in Moral Theory* published in 1981, few years after Jonas,'s, concerning the irrelevance of modern ethics and went on to propose an alternative version, virtue ethics, that became dominant long after Aristotle.[132] Jonas, on the contrary, considered responsibility as an alternative model that, in his opinion, should be adopted by ethicists, suitable for contemporary times. His focus, however, centred on the survival of humanity in the future whilst they live in the

---

131. de Villiers, 106.
132. Macintyre, *After Virtue: A Study*, 12.

context of technological advancement and the detrimental effect on humanity. Unlike MacIntyre's virtue ethics that received prominence and acceptance among theologians such as Stanley Hauerwas, Jonas's future ethics of responsibility has not had an agreeable reception by those who began the inquiry after the publication of his book. It rather steered up conversations from various contexts while his view of ethics for the future became an interesting area of research. The various views on ethics of responsibility, whether it should be accepted as a theoretical framework for contemporary Christian ethics, has since been debatable among the proponents with various perceptions. One of the reasons for this, de Villiers observes is that:

> their views are quite disparate, mainly because they do not seem to share a common definition of "ethics of responsibility." To put it another way: the views put forward by proponents as Christian ethics of responsibility do not exhibit enough of a family resemblance to justify talk of a responsibility ethics school in Christian ethics.[133]

One of these proponents, who though has close views with Jonas but also differs, is William Schweiker, an American theologian whom we shall engage further in this section.

Although Schweiker has diverse views from Jonas on ethics of responsibility, he criticizes some and makes some adaptations, but he still sticks closely to Jonas's structure of ethics.[134] On one end, Schweiker, like Jonas, proposes an imperative of responsibility as the centrepiece of ethics of responsibility that "in all actions and relations respects and enhances the integrity of life before God . . . these actions he calls responsible actions and relations."[135] Differing in his view of ethics of responsibility from other proponents is Schweiker's qualification of the imperative of responsibility that he proposes, namely "before God" as seen above. That, for de Villiers, shows that Schweiker wants to make it clear that he is proposing "thoroughly theological ethics of responsibility . . . an attempt to demonstrate that a theological account of responsible

---

133. de Villiers, "Prospects of (part 1)," 470.
134. de Villiers, 470.
135. Schweiker, *Responsibility and Christian Ethics*, 2.

moral existence makes better sense of our intuitions about responsibility than important philosophical positions have done."[136]

Schweiker suggests that a universal realistic foundation for an ethics of responsibility is needed.[137] For him, it depicts a theological foundation for remembrance that all human beings are, above all, solely responsible to God but also to fellow human beings in all they do. Perhaps a reflection of Fischer's previous questions above on "what good we ought to strive for" and "what good we owe others" (see section 5.4.2). Going by Fischer's questions and Schweiker's theological ethics of responsibility position, two issues could be observed. First, by being responsible to God in all things suggests a conscious sense of what Christian ethics should pursue and exhibit. On the contrary, what we owe others depicts our interaction with others and how we treat the "other" who does not belong, or who shares a view different than ours. It is a reminder that human beings are defined by active relation to others, their world, and God.[138] A suggestive way to revisit ethics of virtue such as care and hospitality. Despite these depictions, de Villiers sees lop-sidedness in Schweiker's ethics of responsibility.

Additionally, there is a close similarity with Hans Jonas in Schweiker's ethics of responsibility which de Villiers cautions above (see section 5.4.2) that could minimise the possibility that responsibility would stamp contemporary Christian ethics. One of these is Schweiker's alliance with Jonas and the German theologians regarding taking responsibility for the survival of the future of life on earth. He agrees that "responsibility should take centre stage in contemporary ethics as a result of the risks involved with the radical extension of human power through rapid technological development."[139] Although such a view sounds one-sided from the German version above (see section 5.4.3), it is not completely accepted by Schweiker either. Accordingly, Schweiker shies away from this one-sided conceptualization of ethics as future ethics, even though he does not completely reject that it is concerned with only the future survival of life on earth.[140] From a more intentional sense,

---

136. de Villiers, "Prospects of (part 1)," 474.
137. de Villiers, 470.
138. Schweiker, *Responsibility and Christian Ethics*, 94.
139. de Villiers, 475.
140. de Villiers, 475; Schweiker, *Theological Ethics*, 94.

Schweiker's imperative of responsibility to enhance[141] the integrity of life before God is not futuristic in a sense, but connotes care, respect, protection, and promotion of humanity in every ramification.

With Schweiker's view of theological ethics of responsibility that alludes to Jonas's future ethics, de Villiers still asks if those are essential to ensure ethics of responsibility is suitable to be qualifier for the contemporary Christian ethics of responsibility. Considering the attempts that the above versions trying to postulate Christian ethics of responsibility, de Villiers is still uncertain whether those are enough to make responsibility a qualifier for contemporary Christian ethics of responsibility. To align the above versions, de Villiers proposes some features of a contemporary Christian ethic of responsibility.

5.5 Etienne de Villiers and the Contemporary Christian Ethic of Responsibility

In his engagement with other proponents of ethics of responsibility above, de Villiers has proven his quest for the reconceptualisation of contemporary Christian ethics of responsibility. Although he shows great respect for the views of other scholars, de Villiers dictates some gaps that require further strengthening. His conclusion that a contemporary Christian ethic of responsibility relevant to our time, with modifications from the earlier proposals is, therefore, required to address the challenges of public morality. The current section presents us with de Villiers's proposal for a contemporary Christian ethic of responsibility that has features other than those already mentioned by the foremost proponents. The reason for such an inquiry is to substantiate whether de Villiers's proposal helps us to address the menace of corruption responsible for undermining the dignity of human persons, particularly in the Nigerian context.

---

141. Schweiker, *Responsibility and Christian Ethics*, 2.

5.5.1 Features of de Villiers's Contemporary Ethics of Responsibility

5.5.1.1 Clarification of Terms

Before his argument in defence of contemporary ethics of responsibility, de Villiers devotes time clarifying some terms to showcase their usage and how he uses them. To have the flow of his opinions, we shall outline the terms here below.

Ethics of responsibility: de Villiers declares his intention in using ethics of responsibility that makes it more elaborate than the views already in existence. He, however, defines ethics of responsibility as an ethic comprehensively qualified by responsibility, or an ethic facilitating comprehensive responsibility.[142] This specific definition differs from others who have referred to responsibility either as dealing with the discourse of responsibility,[143] or as Levinas, who initially considered the relationship of one human being to another human being.[144] Hence his idea of infinite responsibility for the other, or those giving attention to retrospective moral responsibility for negative outcomes of past actions. These, de Villiers declares, should be referred to as "theory of responsibility" rather than "ethics of responsibility," to avoid confusing the terms. Meanwhile, the constituent parts of his definition above as facilitating responsibility by providing guidance on taking responsibility for the salvaging and promotion of ethical living responsibly or appropriately is worthwhile. In his view, this implies that what he considers as responsibility is to be understood as prospective responsibility, focusing on salvaging the present as for the future.

Contemporary: de Villiers constructs an ethic of responsibility as contemporary because it responds to the problem of the undermining of ethical living in contemporary societies, and the factors contributing to it.[145] This sort of response to contemporary challenges emanating from globalisation via technological advancement creates an irreplaceable responsibility gap. The idea of his ethic of responsibility being contemporary, in his opinion, is to

---

142. de Villiers, *Revisiting Max Weber's*, 208.
143. Schweiker, *Responsibility and Christian Ethics*.
144. Buddeberg, "Ernst Wolff, Political Responsibility," 709.
145. de Villiers, *Revisiting Max Weber's*, 209.

contribute to the salvaging and promotion of ethical living such that human dignity could be recognized and enhanced.

Normative ethical approach: de Villiers calls the contemporary Christian ethic of responsibility a normative ethical approach for various reasons: first, it provides guidelines on the most effective and contextually appropriate manner of promoting ethical living in the different spheres of life. Secondly, it reflects on the goals that need to be set and achieved, the virtues that need to be cultivated and instilled, and the norms that need to be followed in order to contribute to the promotion of ethical living. Thirdly, he calls this the normative ethical *approach* not a *theory* because it "expresses how to effectively and appropriately deal with the undermining of ethical living in contemporary societies."[146]

Second-level normative ethical approach: Earlier in this chapter (see section 5.4.1.2), de Villiers applauded Weber and other proponents of ethics of responsibility as a second-level normative approach. In his view, a second level normative ethical approach does not intend to identify and rationally justify the first-level moral goals to ideals to aspire to, moral virtues to exhibit, or moral principles to guide one's actions. Instead, it takes for granted that most people already have their moral ideals, virtues, principles and norms. The ethics of responsibility as a second-level normative ethical approach strives to find second-level guidelines to effectively enhance ethical living in all spheres of life.[147]

These terms serve as roadmaps to conceptualizing de Villiers's contemporary ethic of responsibility. The features he proposes to qualify this ethic are discussed in the section that follows.

5.5.1.2 Features of de Villiers's Ethic of Responsibility

For a distinctive argument against other views of ethics of responsibility, de Villiers specifies features accompanying his version. These features, in his opinion, could qualify or strive to make a case for responsibility qualifying the contemporary Christian ethic of responsibility that enhances salvaging and promotion of ethical living from factors contributing to its deterioration.

---

146. de Villiers, 209.
147. de Villiers, 210.

First, de Villiers argues that a contemporary Christian ethic of responsibility is an "in-between-ethic."[148] Recalling from de Villiers's awareness of the existing first-level normative ethical approach, he insists on a second-level normative ethical approach that Weber also subscribes to. As such, his agreement with Weber on adopting the second-level normative ethical approach does not seek to exclude the existing first-level normative ethical theories but seeks a balance and thus, brings the idea of an in-between-ethic. According to de Villiers, the "in-between-ethic," first "provides a rationale for being moral and acting morally and the enterprise of dealing with, and implementing first-level normative ethical principles."[149] Second, it provides guidelines on how out-dated and unacceptable ways of salvaging ethical living could be avoided, and how ethical living could be enhanced appropriately. He sees such an ethic as not to be equated with applied ethics since it does not seek to offer solutions to bio-ethical, economic ethical, political ethical or technological ethical issues. Rather, it does have relevance for how applied ethics is executed.[150] In this sense, a contemporary Christian ethic of responsibility, for de Villiers, would enhance the operations of normative and applied ethics by providing guidelines on how out-dated and unacceptable ways of salvaging ethical living could be avoided, and how ethical living could be enhanced appropriately. This perception is equated to both a camera and a GPS by de Villiers, but the emphasis on ethical life, which enhances ethical living attracts the attention of scholars such as Wood and Volf.

A better understanding of ethical living could better come through an ethical life.[151] He describes an ethical life as more concrete than an abstract right and morality not because it emphasises the collective over the individual but because of the ethical image of the individual self, and situates the self in living social order. Such a view of ethical self and life creates an awareness that highlights salvaging ways to ethical living. This, therefore, prevents an ethical self from the influence of modernisation problematizing them by transforming, pushing, energizing them against orderliness and strategizing

---

148. de Villiers, *Revisiting Max Weber's*, 214.
149. de Villiers, 214
150. de Villiers, 215.
151. Wood, *Hegel's Ethical Thought*, 26.

ethical codes and standards.[152] Such is an appeal to re-strategize ethical conduct amidst a global whirlwind, causing disorderliness to ethical life. Only in the world, Levinas appeals, where things are not in place such as politics and technology resulting in the negation of the projects, they guide and teach the inconsistency of humans that ethical living is problematized.[153] For de Villiers with his "in-between-ethic," the intention for it to fit in providing a rationale for being moral and acting morally could hold. This would include identifying the place of ethical life, as Wood says; and being cautious of the sharpening of moral codes, as Volf highlights. An in-between-ethic could, in a globalized world, provide better moral guidance for ethical living.

The second feature of a contemporary Christian ethic of responsibility for de Villiers is "the focus area."[154] By focus area, de Villiers refers to new issues undermining ethical living that the contemporary Christian ethic of responsibility could address. He specifically identifies the "difficulty experienced in contemporary societies with retrospectively holding specific agents morally and legally responsible for the war crimes (Holocaust and Apartheid), serious accidents as a result of the failure of technological systems (explosion of nuclear reactors),"[155] and could include the growing concern for corruption in Nigeria threatening the dignity of human persons. To address these concerns, de Villiers agrees to adapting two of Weber's proposals, namely dealing responsibly with values, and dealing responsibly with ethical decision-making as the focus areas of the contemporary Christian ethic of responsibility, in order to enhance his proposal.[156] These two focus areas would systematically deconstruct a retrospective model of responsibility Jonas had suggested, while proposing a prospective model which has received accolade among ethics of responsibility proponents (such as himself and Schweiker). Next, we discuss these proposals de Villiers adopted from the work of Weber.

The first relates to "responsibly dealing with values."[157] We must offer some clarification because the perception of values differs from culture and

---

152. Volf, *Flourishing: Why We Need*, 1.
153. Levinas, *Humanism of the Other* 45.
154. de Villiers, *Revisiting Max Weber's*, 215.
155. de Villiers, 215
156. de Villiers, 215
157. de Villiers, 215.

context, and so are variably conceptualized. As Kirkham asks, how[158] does one make moral judgments across cultural boundaries? Are such judgments truly moral or are they merely reflections of unenlightened tendencies towards cultural imperialism? Explaining how to deal with values responsibly, de Villiers follows thoughts projected by Walzer in his book, *Thick and Thin: Moral Argument at Home And Abroad*.[159] Thick moral values, on the one hand, refer to local, complex moral codes found in every society, intertwined with values, traditions and beliefs. On the other hand, thin moral value is the abstract[160] level at which one can understand fundamental moral issues across cultural borders. In clear terms, thick moral values are those propounded, promoted and exerzized by individuals within specific communities, religious institutions and/or secular enterprises. Thin moral values are found in social orders, organisations, professions and public life in general. According to de Villiers, Weber could not make a distinctive explanation regarding these moral codes in any case of making ethical decisions and, therefore, proposes that a contemporary Christian ethic of responsibility must pay careful attention to address focus areas.[161]

The tendency to absolutise moral values, de Villiers discloses, has no place in the contemporary ethic of responsibility because moral values only have a relative priority. The belief that thick moral values propounded by and for specific religious organizations or individuals, in de Villiers's view, changes with time either through transforming or adjusting them. Such adjustments consist in reinterpretation of particular moral values, the rearrangement for the hierarchal ordering of fundamental moral values, the elimination of certain traditional moral values, or the addition of new moral values to deal with new ethical problems.[162] Within such contexts, a contemporary Christian ethic of responsibility should provide guidance on, and encourage adherents of thick moral values to de-absolutize their thick moral convictions in public life; achieve optimal consensus on thick moral values in their communities and organizations; positively relate thick moral values to sets of thin moral

---

158. Kirkham, "Thick and Thin," 667.
159. Walzer, *Thick and Thin*, 34.
160. Kirkham, "Thick and Thin," 667.
161. de Villiers, *Revisiting Max Weber's*, 216.
162. de Villiers, 216.

values in public life; and positively contribute to the formation of sets of thin moral values.[163] Although de Villiers recognizes the impact of thick moral values from a religious point of view, he opines that we should distinguish between convictional certainty and epistemological certainty, which claims the correctness of these convictions beyond doubt.[164] Doing so, a contemporary Christian ethic of responsibility, in de Villiers's view, would become cautious to not absolutise either thick or thin moral values, nor proposing the prominence of one over the other. Rather, it seeks to give guidelines to help distinguish between acceptable and unacceptable compromises while emphasizing that the two views of moral codes are relevant for a contemporary Christian ethic of responsibility.[165]

The second focus area in a contemporary Christian ethic of responsibility for de Villiers is responsibly dealing with ethical decision-making.[166] Ethics must be grounded in a knowledge of human beings that enables us to say some modes of life are suited to our nature, whereas others are not, that is when ethical theories become those of human self-actualisation.[167] It is to such a context of self-actualization, and the place of human connection with each other that Levinas argues, it is not only possible but of the highest importance to understand one's humanity through the humanity of others.

---

163. This idea takes caution of secularisation and pluralisation as a "self-same process that can occur anywhere – and according to some people, is occurring everywhere." (Taylor, *Dilemmas and Connection*, 303). Reinterpretation referred here carries similar idea with what Jonas, *The Imperative of Responsibility*,) suggested for "an ethics for future sustenance of humanity"; and why Kant held that "all previous attempts to spell out the principles of ethics had been mistaken," Wood, "What is Kantian Ethics," 84; or as Schweiker suggests for "an integrated theory of responsibility," *Responsibility and Christian Ethics*, 94; and why Huber calls for an ethics that would appropriately address what "traditional ethics had insufficiently done"; or even why de Villiers raises an alarm that contemporary challenges seem to outweigh our capacity to address them; and his proposal for contemporary ethics of responsibility, capable to enhance and salvage ethical living in all spheres of life in contemporary society posed by the influence of modernisation (de Villiers, *Revisiting Max Weber's*,). These various views on ethics of responsibility only try to modernise and strengthen each other, and were accurate and effective at a specific time, but are almost obsolete in addressing public morality at present. It is what de Villiers says concerning rearrangement, reinterpretation of moral values. He argues that with inevitable change we are encountering through the influence of modernisation, certain moral values, particularly thick moral values, would be strange in social orders when they seek to replace thin moral values.

164. de Villiers, "A Christian Ethics."

165. de Villiers, *Revisiting Max Weber's*, 118.

166. de Villiers, 222.

167. Wood, *Hegel's Ethical Thought*, 17.

To responsibly deal with ethical decision-making, however, one must become cognisant of the context and content of such ethics, and the role driving goals of the stakeholders concerning such ethical decisions. In the case of context, the ethical issues in which decision is required, either from thick or thin moral values, would enhance a good decision, hence suggesting a sense of responsibility on the agent.

It is pertinent that all decisions, including ethical decision-making, are the responsibility of the one deciding. As a reminder, responsibility involving[168] recognizing that decisions on moral matters are one's own, who is obligated to provide a rational defence of them when challenged. As human agents, however, factors abound that influence decision on issues to give reasons why an action was not done adequately, hence denying responsibility for the actions. Indeed, as Tanner insists, those institutions influencing our decisions are "not substitute for one's own decisions on moral matters . . . because for her, taking responsibility for one's decisions also implies taking responsibility for one's life."[169] This would lead to a responsible life in keeping with responsible decision-making, which means recognizing that one has become the sort of person one is by making one's decision. It is to recognize one's life as a process of self-development through continuing critical deliberation about the proper ways to lead it.[170]

The responsible ethical decision-making de Villiers foresees in a contemporary Christian ethic of responsibility, calls for action in the following ways:

> perceiving the moral problem, accepting it as a moral problem that concerns oneself, clearly defining the moral problem, being self-critical of selfish and ideological motives in identifying and prioritising moral problems, and making sure that all the role players agree on the urgency of the moral problem at hand and understand it in the same way; analysing the concrete situation; designing and evaluating options for action; testing of norms, goods, and perspectives; testing the morally communicative

---

168. Tanner, "A Theological Case," 592.
169. Tanner, 593.
170. Tanner, 593.

obligatorycharacter of the selected option for action; and making the judgment decision.[171]

These factors suggest the appropriate way to responsibly deal with ethical decision-making. Here, one outstanding factor is the idea of co-responsibility, where more than one individual is required to participate. The reason for this is that many of the decisions that must be made today on effective morally direct actions or policies which could solve the complex ethical issues we are faced with, involve international agencies, governments, and the management of companies and other organisations. As stated earlier concerning the prospective nature of this ethic, (see section 5.4.2), the expected outcome is not to blame others for the effect of their past decision (right or wrong) – as a retrospective model of responsibility holds. Instead, it is to salvage ethical living for the common good of humanity and the society that ensures continual existence and possible flourishing of human persons.

The third feature of de Villiers's contemporary Christian ethic of responsibility is its two "levels of operation."[172] First is a primarily theoretical level at which academics and other professionals are involved, and second, a primarily practical level on which managers, educators, parents and individuals are involved. Often, theoretical frameworks or assumptions not transposed to practical realities end up with little or no relevance in the enhancement of human wellbeing. For instance, political debates to ending the scourge of corruption without proactive practical measures make no difference. In the same vein, de Villiers sees reasons to involve both professionals and mere individuals (referring to the unskilled) as actors if the contemporary Christian ethic of responsibility would serve the purpose of salvaging ethical living. He outlines some areas to demonstrate the place of theoretical level consisting of professionals.

First, he emphasises on empirical analysis by social sciences.[173] In this phase, analysis could be utilized to gain insight into the impact that factors at work in these contexts have on the ethical dimension. The analysis could also assist in the selection and formulation of values by revealing in which areas of social life shared moral values are lacking, and where moral gaps are

---

171. de Villiers, *Revisiting Max Weber's*, 224.
172. de Villiers, 225.
173. de Villiers, 225.

created as a result of technological innovation. It could also be utilized by companies, government agencies and NGOs to ensure the reliability of situational analysis when they have to decide on ethically directed actions and policies. Second, critical philosophical reflection could be implemented for different purposes. Being at its initial phase, the contemporary Christian ethic of responsibility would need further reflection on its shape and its relation to other forms of normative ethical approaches, and the challenges it faces.[174] Third, social and industrial psychological research could help to determine how boards, managers, and employees in organisations and communities, and individuals in their personal lives, could effectively be motivated to take responsibility for the enhancement of ethical living in their spheres of influence. This means that educational research has an important role to play in identifying effective ways to instil the virtue of willingness and readiness to take responsibility for enhancing ethical living in children, students, political leaders, company managers, and employees.

The second level of operation is a primarily practical level where theory is expected to convert to action steps. This level of operation consists of the responsibility for enhancing ethical living by personally setting examples (a responsibility everyone bears). It also consists of responsibility for enhancing[175] ethical living by teaching, inspiring and motivating other people or introducing effective measures that would encourage other people to contribute to ethical living (a responsibility not borne by everyone). The influence of thick moral values in some circles, however, restricts the effective display of ethical living or the enhancement of it. Regarding this, de Villiers observes that the more difficult it becomes for contemporary individuals in certain spheres of life to act morally while displaying some duties (due to institutional culture, or other reasons), the more urgent the need becomes to give special attention to strengthen the second sub-level of responsibility in our societies. Therefore, de Villiers warns against ethical absolutism when dealing with moral issues in that one should never absolutise the correctness of one's own moral convictions.[176]

---

174. de Villiers, 225.
175. de Villiers, 225.
176. de Villiers, "Christian Ethics and Secularisation."

The fourth feature of a contemporary Christian ethic of responsibility de Villiers envisages are the "Agents."[177] One of the differences between Weber and de Villiers is the agent of the ethic of responsibility. Whereas Weber strictly upholds a charismatic political leader as the sole agent, de Villiers suggests multiple agents for the contemporary Christian ethic of responsibility. He insists that "leadership, including political leadership, remains important when it comes to the implementation of the ethic of responsibility."[178] Arguing in support for multiple agents, de Villiers admits that enough people would have to behave in similar ways to have a significant collective impact in solving problems befalling our societies (such as global warming, environmental pollution and corruption).[179] In de Villiers's view, therefore, having multiple agents would contribute to strengthening the societal moral fibre. These agents, including parents (instilling moral virtues on children to be morally responsible human beings by setting a personal example), and leaders in all spheres of life to personally set an example by their incorruptibility and moral integrity, would exert enormous influence for the good of society. This is because it is indispensable in our time for both individual and co-responsibility (including collective and organisational responsibility to join forces in enhancing moral integrity in society.

Lastly, de Villiers suggests "modes" as another feature of a contemporary Christian ethic of responsibility.[180] For the fact that a

> contemporary Christian ethic of responsibility has been described as an 'in-between' ethic does not insinuate an accommodative mode for the sake of tolerance and agreement . . . rather, in the case of addressing the proclamation of extreme views, or the instigation of extreme practices in society, it might become necessary that the contemporary Christian ethic of responsibility adopt an activist, confrontational stance.[181]

This, de Villiers observes, could occur in either of two instances; first,

---

177. de Villiers, *Revisiting Max Weber's*, 226.
178. de Villiers, 226
179. de Villiers, 227
180. de Villiers, 227.
181. de Villers, 227.

in a situation where the functionalist denial of any recognition of moral consideration in a particular social order or organisation is proclaimed or practised and, secondly, where the functionalist absolutizing of one particular set of thick moral values is proclaimed or enforced in society.[182]

Seeing such a scenario as a tensed one, de Villiers thus declares that when the adherents of either extreme functionalist or fundamentalism refuse to become involved in constructive discussion and negotiation, the most responsible thing to do to enhance ethical living could be to strongly denounce and resist such attitude, and the views on which they are based. Such articulations, however, suggest a confrontational and activist dimension to address, particularly, extremely thick moral values that are detrimental to ethical living.

Despite these important depictions, clarity is needed to ascertain the reception and relevance of de Villiers's proposal in addressing issues of public morality in the African context. Prominently in this study is the concern that corruption undermines the dignity of human persons, particularly in the Nigerian context. From that backdrop, the goal of the entire study rests on modalities to enhance the promotion, protection and respect for the dignity of the Nigerian person in the context of corruption. The section that follows looks critically at de Villiers's proposal and how his features for a contemporary Christian ethic of responsibility are applicable in addressing the scourge of corruption to safeguard the dignity of human persons. By so doing, the ongoing study will, in the next chapter, propose features for a contemporary ethic of responsibility for the Nigerian context.

5.6 de Villiers on Moral Issues

Considering the problem being investigated in this study, corruption, and its effects of undermining the human dignity of a Nigerian person, this section explores what de Villiers's contemporary Christian ethic of responsibility proposal offers in salvaging such a situation. Here, the reader is introduced to the implication of de Villiers's ethic of responsibility in addressing the scourge of corruption in order to ascertain whether it provides a theoretical

---

182. de Villiers, 227.

framework to promote the enhancement of human dignity that ensures the common good of the Nigerian human person and society.

5.6.1 Corruption

As stated at the beginning of this chapter, de Villiers has devoted most of his academic writing to promote public morality and the good of society. This devotion has proven his pastoral integrity in contributing to the enhancement and upholding the truth of what he professes.[183] This section, therefore, discusses de Villiers's ethic of responsibility, and how it could help to address the scourge of corruption in Nigeria.

In one of his articles *A Christian Ethics of Responsibility: Does It Provide An Adequate Theoretical Framework for Dealing with Issues of Public Morality*, de Villiers makes useful remarks for the ongoing study. Focusing on his South African context, he identified three prevalent theological approaches to issues of public morality in the previous political dispensation, namely:

> apartheid theology, liberation theology and . . . church theology. Typical of the apartheid theology and the liberation theology approaches were that no sharp distinction was made between theological convictions on the one hand and political, economic and social convictions on the other hand. . . . The church theology approach accused both the apartheid theology and the liberation theology approaches of ideologically legitimising political policies and strategies favouring particular groups in society.[184]

This group of church theology wanted the church to find its "voice on issues of public morality and give public witness to its views."[185] Since the inception of the new South African political dispensation, apartheid theology has lost its grip, while liberation and church theology are still surviving, but have "little influence in the government and its policies"[186] because of a constitution that insists on the separation of religion and state. Also, the new political dispensation with challenges of modernization, politics, economics, and social

---

183. This is particular to his sharp criticism of apartheid and its justification by the Dutch Reformed Church in South Africa.
184. de Villiers, "A Christian Ethics," 24.
185. de Villiers, 24.
186. de Villiers, 24.

dimensions both problematizes and complicates the church's witness on the influence of these public moral issues. One reason for this is the separation of religion and state. The second reason has to do with the effectiveness of "thick" moral views of the church, which are inappropriate to those with different religious convictions. However, de Villiers makes suggestions on how ethics, including the contemporary Christian ethic of responsibility, could provide a theoretical framework in addressing public moral issues as follows: first, in salvaging and enhancing ethical living, and second, in ensuring fully and truly human living conditions.

Nigeria, like South Africa, is obsessed with public morality issues. In the case of South Africa, de Villiers basically projects views from Christian theological ethics of responsibility, possibly because of the majority Christian community and their influence on public issues in South Africa. The Nigerian case differs given its highly contested religious sentiments with frequent strife between the Christians and Muslim groups. Nevertheless, de Villiers's views for his South African context could serve Nigeria, albeit with some modifications.

First, his argument for dealing with public morality centres on "Christians to confront moral issues, and to develop a Christian ethical view based on thick religious and moral beliefs as a way to deal with public morality."[187] In Agang's argument, we could deduce that de Villiers's idea was driven by capitalist ideology, philosophy of market, and is rooted in a political agenda advocating for a one world order as the fuel for globalization.[188] He also adds that humans have discovered how to use their minds to transfer intellectual skills to material reality through technology, leading to globalizing public morality such as corruption and terrorism. The above idea problematizes de Villiers's suggestion of using thick Christian religious moral values to address public morality as those would be obsolete to proponents of other religions, particularly in Nigeria. On the contrary, Kunhiyop's view on the challenge of Christian morality in Africa could be useful in dealing with public morality in Africa. Kunhiyop agrees slightly with de Villiers in applying thick Christian moral values but differs from his methodology of applying them. Here, he warns against being too "satisfied with the gravitational

---

187. de Villiers, 33–34.
188. Agang, "Globalization," 1.

shift of Christianity to Africa" to close our eyes from many moral challenges facing the continent.[189] Rather, we must do some "serious soul searching for African Christianity."[190] Deducing from de Villiers, Agang, and Kunhiyop arguments, we could see that Africa is indeed faced with various challenges of public morality, either by the influence of modernity (Agang), or the nature of theologies that were transported from Europe (Kunhiyop). Applying thick religious moral values, as de Villiers suggests, could be effective in some spheres but ineffective in others such as Nigeria where the Christian faith is under severe strife with Islam. Instead, as Kunhiyop suggests, a "holistic approach to life"[191] where some African traditional norms such as communal life are integrated and revived. Doing so would reflects Kinoti's view on what the call to be a Christian today entails. The call to be a Christian, for Kinoti, is a call to "embody the values of creative fidelity to God, their creator and to other creatures in order to build up communities whose cultural, social, political and economic structures reflect responsibility, respect, care and love."[192] Kinoti goes further, alluding to the sameness of societal moral issues[193] African Christians face today, although some have taken a different dimension, hence, becoming very difficult and complex where forms and structures are rapidly changing.

Applying a contemporary Christian ethic of responsibility to deal with the issue of corruption from the above views would require a multi-dimensional approach, the use of agents that de Villiers suggests. Regarding the thick Christian moral values, de Villiers's proposal for the focus area for a contemporary Christian ethic of responsibility is helpful. Here, it is important to note that the application of thick moral values does not have as a goal to strip Christians from actively applying thick moral values in addressing moral issues. Rather, it is an invitation to both Christians and people of other

---

189. Kunihyop, "The Challenge of African," 70.
190. Kunhiyop, 79–80.
191. Kunhiyop, 70.
192. Kinoti, "African Morality," 74.
193. It seems, Kinoti asserts, African society is in the state of near chaos in the realm of morality because of people are disillusioned after suffering major cultural upheavals. But he insists there is hope when the African church stops shying away from the responsibility to call people to repentance, to set an example in moral integrity and to teach people the message of God who understands human frailty and is willing to heal wholly (Kinoti, "African Morality," 80–81).

faith traditions to see together, learn together, and dialogue on their different views on moral values and the detrimental effect on societal integrity. Doing so would allow, in the case of Nigeria, people with different religious views to submit proposals on what their belief systems consider moral and amoral. That perhaps could be the starting point to agree on issues of public morality, particularly corruption.

5.6.2 Human Dignity

Another key issue in this study is the notion of human dignity, and de Villiers too, has critically engaged it through the lens of an ethic of responsibility. Since a detailed discourse on human dignity is given in chapter 3, here we focus only on de Villiers's perception of human dignity from the perspective of a contemporary Christian ethic of responsibility.

The discussion on human dignity by de Villiers began by him raising an important concern regarding the role players who he thinks should champion the course of enhancing the human dignity of the African people. One reason for such a line of thought is not far from the idea of the communal nature of the Africans. So, he foresees that the task is so enormous that it would require more hands to actualise. Considering the complex nature of Africa, those role players should comprise the political, economic, and leaders of NGOs across Africa, but also include the leaders of ethnic and cultural groups, as well as those of religious denominations. According to de Villiers, "the leaders do not appear to be making a constructive contribution nor striving to protect elements undermining human dignity. Rather, they only appear to be sitting back and waiting on others to do so."[194] As a result, de Villiers foresees a "growing concern among African people, particularly those from thick ethnic and religious minorities and opposition parties, seeing themselves as victims"[195] completely at the mercy of others and with lack of control over their lives. These are two challenges that ethics of responsibility has got to deal with to safeguard or salvage the continuous undermining of the human dignity of the African person.

---

194. As a result of which, de Villiers adds, they have indulged in a blame game with their Western counterparts, while at the same time the Western leaders blame the African leaders for their inability to take measures toward protecting the continual undermining of human dignity in the continent, "Propheic Witness," 1.

195. de Villiers, "The Recognition of," 264.

From the contemporary Christian ethic of responsibility perspective, de Villiers outlines what recognition and enhancement of human dignity entails. First, "it should not only emphasize the recognition and enhancement of the human dignity of human beings living today. Secondly, we should also emphasize the need to recognize the human dignity of the future generation."[196] This should not be done, in his opinion, to the detriment of the rest of God's creatures. He draws our attention back to theories of ethics of responsibility we have studied which, in this case, make his proposal of a contemporary Christian ethic of responsibility influential.

Similarly, de Villiers alludes to the responsibility to enhance and recognize the human dignity of Christian individuals and churches. At one point, he suggests that Christians must collectively help affected people or protest against discrimination, exploitation and oppression which showcases undermining human dignity, a point that coincides with his view of "activist" and "confrontational" dimension of a contemporary Christian ethic of responsibility.[197] With any human person in such a life instance, it means their

> "sense of worth as human persons is curtailed, their participation in the life of society is limited, their need to create and recreate is frustrated, and the expression of their cultural feelings is subdued . . . in that case, there results in a more or less general breakdown of human respect and integrity."[198]

One of the points raised by Magesa here relates to the denial of freedom to be an individual one aspires to be, that correlates with God's intention. Since human dignity is described as an unquantifiable value of an individual, as already studied in chapter 3 (see section 3.3), it means refusing an individual their worth simply demeans their dignity. To avoid such extremes, our collective responsibility to safeguard the dignity of others in de Villiers's view, could be confrontational or in activism.

The violation of human dignity is more pronounced on the African continent than in most other places in the world because of the numerous challenges confronting the region.[199] Some of these causes include economic and

---

196. de Villiers, 268.
197. de Villiers, 270.
198. Magesa, *Christian Ethics*, 67.
199. Koopman, "Human Dignity in Africa."

social equity, racial discrimination, and lack of freedom. To this list, Koopman adds issues of injustice, sexism, xenophobia, crime, natural disasters, and abusive cultural practices, as challenges facing Africa from where often a violation of human dignity ensues.[200] These issues call for the co-responsibility of different stakeholders for the common goal to recognize and safeguard human dignity. This call by de Villiers with emphasis on only Christians in his contemporary ethics of responsibility, to take responsibility without adequately addressing other stakeholders, would be ineffective in a multicultural, multi-ethnic and multi-religious context like Nigeria. His view on engaging various agents, however, makes his proposal more promising than Weber's view of only a charismatic political leader as an agent of responsibility ethic. One reason for this could be contextual since communality is more understood in the African context than perhaps Weber's European context. That issues are better discussed and addressed by different stakeholders in the African context brings de Villiers's view of engaging various agents more promising than Weber's individualistic charismatic political leader.

Going by Magesa's suggestion that promotion of justice, freedom, and human dignity as of spiritual value, is broad. For him, the task involves, not merely the idea of promoting the greatest good for the greatest number, but the greatest good for all. This involves the active promotion of society based on equality and the interaction of individual freedom and social cohesiveness.[201] When concepts such as freedom, justice and equality are discussed alongside human dignity, it requires collective representative action to fight all forces responsible for regarding some human beings above others. This is why de Villiers calls Christians to establish the necessary institutions in order to address direct aspects of the problem.[202]

5.7 A Critical Reflection on de Villiers's Ethics of Responsibility

Writing from an African context, de Villiers's work on ethics of responsibility is commendable. Just as de Villiers attests to Weber being the first to use

---

200. Koopman, 242.
201. Magesa, *Christian Ethics*, 72.
202. de Villiers, "The Recognition," 270.

the expression ethic of responsibility, it can be argued here, that he too has been the outstanding theologian, who explicitly and deeply develops ethics of responsibility from the African continent.[203] Giving such credit to de Villiers, the above claim is validated by recent studies on ethics of responsibility in the African context suggesting that "nothing much has been done on the ethics of responsibility" compared to Europe and America.[204] Nevertheless, the discussion has started with de Villiers's depth enthusiasm in championing the course. In this regard, when we compare his works on the subject matter with what has been done in the African continent, one would not hesitate to classify him as the pioneer of the African Christian ethic of responsibility. To advance discussions on the ethics of responsibility in the African continent, however, de Villiers's work could be critiqued. The motive behind the critique is to develop the subject matter further, particularly by expanding its applicability in addressing public morality. The critique is, therefore, presented in three points. First, his failure to interact with African scholars, second, his critique of Weber's background, and third, his two-levels of operation.

Firstly, we have noted de Villiers's reluctance to converse with African scholars. Although being the first prominent African theologian to have written substantially on ethics of responsibility, this should not deny him interaction with African theological ethicists who might have suggested similar views from different dimensions and/or contexts. For instance, in de Villiers's interaction with Jonas on responsibility for the future of human beings and creation, there are links of similar ideas among African theologians. One of those is the Congolese priest and theologian, Bujo, who devotes a section in his works to discuss "the human being and ecological responsibility."[205] In one of his remarks, Bujo avows that "the proper treatment of creation ought to open an important perspective for the future . . . while he still recognizes the effect of technological civilization and its effect on creation, including human beings."[206] In de Villiers's non-recognition and lack of engagement with the few African counterparts makes his views somewhat strange or difficult to address a few common African issues.

---

203. de Villiers, *Revisiting Max Weber's*, 4.
204. Neequaye, "Towards an African Christian," 176.
205. Bujo, *The Ethical Dimension*.
206. Bujo, 215.

African theologians might have not explicitly delved into the discussion on ethics of responsibility, yet their theological interactions portray elements of responsibility. For instance, "whence has everything originated? why is everything in the universe the way it is now? and whither is everything proceeding?"[207] His submission that those questions can be regarded as constituting the problem of the meaning of destiny and concerns with ultimate origins, ultimate purpose, and ultimate goals suggest a sense of responsibility ethic. Collectively, Mugambi's concern in the above submission suggests a call of responsibility to provide answers that he thinks "challenge the mind of every thinking person."[208] Another example is drawn from de Villiers's South African counterpart, Charles Villa-Vicencio,[209] who makes three short remarks of ethics of responsibility asking us to act responsibly and requires us to be human beings, who are ready to risk ourselves in the service of others.[210] Even in his interaction with philosophers, de Villiers left the likes of Gyeke of Ghana, with his idea of "African social theory of responsibility."[211] Important as that idea is, African ethics of responsibility is said to "find expression in the social theory of responsibility."[212] Incorporating such existing thoughts of African scholarship in his proposal of contemporary ethics of responsibility, de Villiers would have probably used concepts[213] that are more familiar

---

207. Mugambi, *African Christian Theology*, 125.

208. Mugambi, 125.

209. Villa-Vicencio, "Ethics of Responsibility."

210. First, that the Christian tradition requires a christological understanding of God's redemptive purpose for creation – while he referred to Bonhoeffer's ethics. Second, an ethic of responsibility involves a hierarchy of values and norms; and third, it must take full recognition of human realisations and the inclination to self-justification. Villa-Vicencio, 86).

211. Read Gyekye, *An Essay on African*. It suggests what Brown states in *African Philosophy*, that both African theologians and philosophers have ventured into critical discourse portrayed by their Western counterparts by subsuming their thoughts on African to the larger discussions. This is done to avoid previous stereotypes, particularly of the cultures of sub-Saharan Africa that were viewed by the Western colonisers and missionaries as "primitive, backward, and in need of radical reconstruction. So also in terms of religion, Traditional Africa religions were viewed as grounded upon superstition, and metaphysical fantasy" (Brown, *African Philosophy*, 4). This said, should current studies irrespective of the discipline fail to present thoughts by African scholars, there is a tendency for continued negligence, and unsubstantiated assumptions about Africa and its people.

212. Neequaye, "Towards an African Christian," 217.

213. Rather de Villiers follows closely Edward Tödt's approach to tackling moral problems seriously in the formation of moral judgment as such approach entails the responsibility to do everything reasonable that is needed to solve the serious moral problem at hand (de Villiers, "An Ethics of Responsibility," 6), (de Villiers, *Revisiting Max Weber's*, 222). Although de Villiers

and African, those that better explain the experiences and perception of the African people.²¹⁴ In addition, had his thoughts been situated within the language frame that depicts the African mind, they would have had greater reception to African scholarship and persons. Perhaps doing so would earmark the nature and direction of the discourse on ethics of responsibility.

The second critique rests on de Villiers's critique that Weber was sociological in his approach, of which a similar case could be raised against his proposal of a contemporary Christian ethic of responsibility. A reference to Schweiker, who observes that "every work in ethics provides some account of what is going on"²¹⁵ is crucial here. Going by Schweiker's view, Weber was right on situating his ethics of responsibility from a "sociological analysis of the nature of modern politics and the role-players involved"²¹⁶ for that suggests the trend of events of his day and portrays his specialty, as a sociologist. Similarly, following his background as a theologian and pastor, de Villiers's views make a greater influence on the ecclesial context that suggests the perspective he speaks from. Although he makes several references showcasing his nationalistic identity in his involvement of public issues in South Africa, his arguments show greater concern on how the church should live and act in society.²¹⁷ As a public theologian, de Villiers's description of the public sphere being "global, torn and divided"²¹⁸ is an invitation to a theological and an ecclesial engagement with public issues confronting the wellbeing of society, particularly the South African.

---

affirms that Tödt's often referred to early thinkers who contributed to the development of an ethic of responsibility that made his thoughts appealing, yet he disagrees with Tödt by questioning and almost refused to present Tödt's theory of the moral formation of moral judgments as the definitive ethic of responsibility model for responsibly dealing with moral decision-making today (de Villiers, *Revisiting Max Weber's*, 224).

214. For example the notion of "Ubuntu" which referred by Neequaye as the "mutual caring and sharing within African community" (Neequaye, "Towards an African Christian," 277). Caring in this sense includes the wellbeing of human beings, as the proponents of human dignity mentioned (Koopman, "Human Dignity," 247), (Magesa, *Christian Ethics*, 22), (de Villiers,"Prophetic Witness," 2). Or caring for nature/ecology (Bujo, *The Ethical Dimension*, 14), (Conradie, "The Earth," 13). These require the concept of responsibility. As for Africans, communality is key to dealing with issues when they are spoken to be understood with images they easily associate with.

215. Schweiker, *Theological Ethics*, xi.
216. de Villiers, *Revisiting Max Weber's*, 203.
217. de Villiers, "How My Mind," 17; "The Vocation," 521.
218. de Villiers, "Responsible South African," 1.

Finally, his proposal from contemporary Christian ethics of responsibility in addressing public morality (including dealing with corruption and recognition of human dignity) centres more on what individual and corporate Christian ought to do.[219] With this evidence, we could also argue that de Villiers's ethics is too "Christian" in approach. Going by Schweiker's submission above, however, both Weber's and de Villiers's ethics, should be read and responded to based on the background from which it springs.

The contemporary ethics of responsibility proposal for two levels of operation by de Villiers is commendable. As a reminder, the crisis of humanism in our times undoubtedly originates from an experience of human inefficacy accentuated by the very abundance of our means of action and the scope of our ambitions.[220] We have human and material resources, we present speeches, symposiums and lectures on issues, but are equally unresponsive in implementation. That is what characterises most African nations, particularly Nigeria that is blessed with all it takes to thrive but misappropriation and mismanagement would not give way to the anticipated flourishing.[221] Therefore, de Villiers's call for both theoretical and practical levels is integrative with prospects for all stakeholders to participate, unlike Weber's charismatic political leader. In response to de Villiers, one of his theoretical points, namely the enhancement of educational research as an important role player, could be strengthened. It could begin by enforcing the teaching of ethics at different levels of learning. If de Villiers's teaching of Christian ethics and engineering ethics at the University of Pretoria yielded fruits, it is surprising why he did not include that recommendation to his proposal for the contemporary Christian ethic of responsibility, perhaps to suggest developing curriculums for teaching professional ethics both in higher places of learning and in organisations.

5.8 Chapter Summary

This chapter presented de Villiers's proposal for a contemporary Christian ethic of responsibility. Although de Villiers states the aim of his study as to "outline a cogent proposal to stimulate further discussion, he agrees to no

---

219. de Villiers, "A Christian Ethics," 23; "Prophetic Witness," 2.
220. Levinas, 45.
221. Jev, "Politics, Conflicts, and Nigeria's Unending Crisis."

claim for its complete newness as some adoptions are made from what is already in existence."[222] Nevertheless, his ideas have proven beyond doubt that he champions this field of theological engagement from the African continent.

His engagement with proponents of ethics of responsibility from an African context, showing his commendations and disagreement was demonstrated. It suggests his commitment to, first, align with global scholarship on a crucial and relevant theme as responsibility, which results in laying solid a foundation from African scholarship that similar conversation could continue. The reception of such scholarship would have greater significance on the African soil from the perspectives of suggesting ways to address moral issues confronting us, particularly, with special reference to corruption and its undermining effects on human dignity.

As core to this study, the devastating effects of corruption resulting in non-recognition of human dignity of the human persons are central with special reference to Nigeria. Also considered was de Villiers's proposal for contemporary ethics of responsibility with few modifications from Weber's earlier ethics. The response by de Villiers to corruption through the lens of an ethic of responsibility approach as a theoretical framework to the recognition and enhancement of human dignity has been explored. Considering his South African context and background are influential to what he writes and proposes on the two concepts, his ideas would likely require furthering to make them applicable to the Nigerian context. An invitation is made to interrogate how this study would further de Villiers's views in order to situate and make them relevant to the Nigerian context, while making an academic contribution to the theological ethical scholarship.

Following what has been presented in the foregoing chapters, the next chapter brings the findings together. The task to imagine ethics of responsibility's contribution to safeguarding the human dignity of the Nigerian person in a context obsessed with corruption will be considered. This is done with the aim of providing a theoretical framework that could appropriately deal with corruption, a scourge responsible for undermining human dignity, on the one hand and on the other hand, a bane to underdevelopment, misappropriation and mismanagement of abundant human and material resources, which can no longer be ignored.

---

222. de Villiers, *Revisiting Max Weber's*, 228.

CHAPTER 6

Toward an Ethics of Responsibility for Safeguarding Human Dignity in the Context of Corruption in Nigeria

6.1. Introduction

In this chapter, we shall present the findings from previous chapters concerning the secondary research questions. Such an inquiry will help us answer the primary research question that drives the secondary research questions. The first secondary research question sought to find out how corruption could be understood in Nigeria. Various approaches were used in perceiving corruption while factors responsible for fuelling its continued spread in Nigeria were outlined. From a theological perspective, it was presented that corruption occurs due to the inappropriate use of free will for the right action. Freewill enables choice-making either to do right or wrong without necessarily shifting blame to other persons. Here, when the choice to do wrong (indulging in corrupt acts) surpasses the choice to do right (frowning at things such as corruption), leads to an abuse of conscience.[1] That is similar when the moral strength is left unchecked.

Another form of corruption we surveyed in chapter 2 was political corruption, which involves mismanagement and misappropriation of public resources particularly by the political class. They make decisions informing

---

1. Further on corruption as abuse of conscience, see Umaru, "An Ethos," 199.

the governance of a state through policymaking, to ensure the smooth running of affairs that aims at enhancing the wellbeing of persons and society. The findings in chapter 2, however, did not arrive at this supposed ideal state. Rather, it found the prevailing abuse of these opportunities by the policymakers themselves. The issues of indecisiveness and complacency were found to be the major setbacks to curbing corruption.

Corruption was also discussed from the religious perspective regarding the church. As an institution with dictums as the "salt and light" of the world, the church has soiled its hands with corruption. We presented in the second chapter that two major reasons have caused this. First, the shifting nature of teachings, and second, the nature of lifestyle the church celebrates and applauds. As to the nature of teachings, the church seems to have shifted its focus and instead refrains followers from indulging in acts like corruption. The findings, therefore, indicated that the church shies away from declaring corrupt acts. On lifestyle, we found that the church emphasises ways of pleasure than teachings about the cross. The focus is more on success, wealth acquisition, and material gain with little or no emphasis on hard work, diligence, perseverance and honesty. As it were, the end justifies the means and not the other way round.

With the above findings, we saw how corruption is perceived in Nigeria and the actions towards curbing it. We found that despite the efforts, the menace still spreads, which calls for new dimensions of fighting it. The ethics of responsibility discussed in chapters 4 and 5 is the theological resource we have adopted. With specific reference to Etienne de Villiers, we shall incorporate ideas from ethics of responsibility and how they could contribute towards curbing the continuous spread of corruption in Nigeria that the dignity of human persons could attain recognition and enhancement. That forms the bedrock of this chapter. To do that, however, we will propose how ethics of responsibility could address the scourge of corruption in the Nigerian context in order to pave way for the recognition and enhancement of human dignity. We shall engage Etienne de Villiers's proposal for the contemporary Christian ethics of responsibility and how it could be applied to deal with issues of public morality such as corruption, on the one hand, while on the other hand, we shall come up with a proposal for the ethics of responsibility that befits the Nigerian context.

The second research question sought to find out the extent and consequences of corruption in Nigerian society with specific reference to human dignity. To answer this question, chapter 3 did an overview of the concept of human dignity through different periods and perspectives. It was gathered that the notion of human dignity is variably understood, which is perhaps the reason it is misrepresented and often misunderstood, hence, disregarded.

First, from an ontological perspective, we found that human dignity is embedded within human beings by their creatureliness. Such a view indicates the inviolability of human dignity by whatsoever means. It is humans' greatest gift received from creation that simply cannot be detached from them. The view holds similar perspectives with the Christian perception of human dignity. Since, from a Christian viewpoint, human dignity involves respect for the other, which does not occur because of one's contribution, but simply for being a human person made in God's image. Second, we looked at the social and psychological perspectives of human dignity. In this case, we found that dignity could both be given, reduced, increased or restricted, depending on one's social, psychological and physical output. It simply holds that one has dignity only when their performance or contribution justifies and qualifies them. Third, human dignity was considered from a humanist opinion, who view it in terms of self-esteem and belonging. Human dignity understood as such suggests re-imagination of inner fulfilment that indwells human persons. These findings on human dignity, however, will in this chapter be used to engage the perspectives of ethics of responsibility and the contribution it makes in understanding the human dignity of a Nigerian person within the context of corruption.

The third research question sought to engage with a theological resource, ethics of responsibility, and its contribution to addressing the scourge of corruption and its effect on the dignity of human persons in the Nigerian context. To answer this question, perspectives of ethics of responsibility were discussed in chapters 4 and 5 to showcase a developmental overview of the ethics of responsibility from the German, American and African contexts. The chapter engages multidisciplinary perspectives of ethics of responsibility, namely sociological, theological and philosophical dimensions. Chapter 5 specifically focused on the theological dimension from the African perspectives, particularly, the person of Etienne de Villiers, a South African Systematic Theologian. The choice of de Villiers was for a few reasons. First, as far as this project could find, Etienne de Villiers, like Max Weber in the German context, is the only African theologian that has written substantially on the ethics of responsibility.[2] Second, although Etienne de Villiers is not a Nigerian, he writes from an African context but does not specifically address the African audience – except for his South African context. Yet, he shares the concerns faced on the African continent. So, the choice to engage his ideas brings the study close to the Nigerian context. The goal of this question is to imagine the contribution which the ethics of responsibility could make for the common good that the Nigerian human persons could live truly and fully human lives.

The fourth research question sought to identify how the ethical resources contribute towards safeguarding human dignity in Nigeria. To answer this question, we shall identify some features of ethics of responsibility that serve the Nigerian context. Most importantly, we shall see how these characteristics would further academic engagement seeking contributions to safeguarding human dignity in Nigeria. Having arrived at some characteristics, it would provide us with a language to answer our research question four. At that stage, this study hopes to have proposed some useful theological-ethical resources that contribute to minimizing the scourge of corruption that is detrimental to the dignity of human persons.

6.1.1 First Research Question: Corruption in Nigeria

How could corruption be understood in the Nigerian context?

To answer this question, it was necessary to situate corruption in different phases. First, a theological-anthropological perspective. Here, a theological foundation of corruption was established. The idea of human fall and depravity began the moment humanity chose evil rather than good. Such a choice brought depravity of the human mind and enables the breeding of evils like corruption. This first research question, however, engages ethics of responsibility, particularly as demonstrated by Etienne de Villiers in chapter 5.

---

2. The reason for specifying the discipline is because there are African scholars, including theologians and philosophers, that have made critical references to ethics of responsibility. Those views were summarized in the last part of chapter 4.

6.1.1.1 Corruption and Governance

This section discusses, in relation to chapter 2, corruption and governance while engaging Etienne de Villiers's ethics of responsibility. The reason for that conversation is to ascertain the contribution of ethics of responsibility to curbing corruption, on the one hand, while on the other hand, using conversation extracts from de Villiers's contribution to demonstrate whether and how it helps in addressing the scourge of corruption. Also discussed in this section is de Villiers's engagement with issues that concern the public space, and the state.

The perception that good governance influences societal and human wellbeing cannot be overemphasized. As argued, the high demand for appropriate governance in most of the world, including Africa, is responsible for why those zones still battle to address concerns bewildering them. As stated in a previous study, one reason responsible for this is leadership's inability to coherently distribute power and resources.[3] Following this problem is a pervasive increase in a kleptocracy that keeps leaders, especially those of African descent, hostage to doing all but misusing and mismanaging public resources. This is why de Villiers succinctly refers to African political leaders as "more interested in enriching themselves once they are elected by exploiting the available public resources than in improving the plight of the poor."[4] Such body language keeps them off their responsibility to care for, and protect societal wellbeing. Instead, they focus on self-gratification, an attitude which leaves a good number of politicians and government officials as soon as possible – willing to cross the line of immoral behaviour and become involved in corruption.[5] The above hypothesis demonstrates how leadership plays a significant role in providing societal and human wellbeing. The leadership, therefore, has a responsibility to salvage a given society from the waves of public morality.

Although a democratic republic since 1994, many South Africans, including de Villiers, still wonder about the existence of certain leadership structures, notably racism. In particular, de Villiers sternly recognizes the rising tension between different racial groups years after the official end

---

3. Jev, "Politics, Conflicts, and Nigeria's Unending Crisis," 147.
4. de Villiers, "Prophetic Witness," 7.
5. de Villiers, 7.

of apartheid.⁶ While he was actively involved in prophetic proclamations during the heat of apartheid, de Villiers never relents in his struggle for justice and fairness. As seen in his work on social-ethical issues in South Africa, de Villiers's commitment largely demonstrates distinctive Christian answers to issues of peace and justice in society.⁷ Such is a demonstration by a Christian visionary leader, who seeks the wholeness of society. According to him, desiring such commitment should be a goal for societal transformation that envisions humanizing society.⁸ Such reflection was sensitive to human treatment during apartheid but also in post-apartheid South Africa. Yet the call for responsible reflection of organizational leaders remains active to ensure stoppage of blatant racist remarks by white people and equally blatant expressions of hate speech from black people.⁹ Here, two actions are required of responsible leaders, namely to address the problem confronting human and societal wellbeing and to speak out the implication of the problem, as seen with racism in the South African context. The failure to address these issues continues to widen[10] the inequality gap.

Corruption, like racism, requires similar responsible action. For governance to be qualified as good, certain attitudes towards leadership must be acquired and exercised. First, as in the case of racism above, leadership, in the case of Nigeria, would have to name the existence of the menace. Through the military dispensation, several efforts by the Nigerian leadership were made towards curbing[11] corruption. The return of democracy in 1999, however, intensified the fight against corruption when the leadership of the then-president, Olusegun Obasanjo, vowed to confront the monster head-on.[12] For Obasanjo, society only survives and flourishes in an orderly, reasonable, and predictable way where corruption is silenced.[13] Significantly so, such action was supported through the establishment of agencies to foresee anti-corruption campaigns, among them the EFCC and ICPC, which were

---

6. de Villiers, "Public Theology," 5.
7. de Villiers, "How My Mind," 19.
8. de Villiers, "The Vocation," 526.
9. de Villiers, "Public Theology," 6.
10. Koopman, "Human Dignity in Africa," 242.
11. Moyosore, "Corruption in Nigeria," 26.
12. Nwoba and Monday, "Appraisal of EFCC."
13. Salawu, "Towards Solving the Problem," 395.

discussed in chapter 2. From the action of Obasanjo's leadership, we could see his zeal to ensure the end of corruption. Such an action, in the context of this study, demonstrates readiness and responsiveness towards societal and human wellbeing. As stated above, the commitment that led to the institutionalization of anti-corruption agencies was to safeguard the survival of human existence and enhance societal development.

The foregoing comments invite us to integrate de Villiers's ethics of responsibility while interrogating how it could contribute to curbing the spread of corruption in Nigeria. In his response to how Christian ethics could be applied in addressing public morality in South Africa, de Villiers's views could serve well to address leadership and corruption in Nigeria. For his South African context, de Villiers suggests the formulation of more applicable and, sometimes, completely new norms based on the traditional Christian morality in addressing public issues.[14] Formulating new norms for approaching moral issues in the context of establishing anti-corruption agencies showcases what the Nigerian government did. As already noted, it is an act of responsible leadership from the government, which does not exclude the looming growth of challenges, particularly in the Northern part of Nigeria. In the previous chapters, particularly chapter 2, we gathered that a persistent culture of institutionalized corruption, greed, political thuggery and violence have contributed to a high level of unemployment. In summing the study, poor government policy and implementation, indiscipline caused by injustice, economic inequality, and poor leadership are factors believed to have caused the setback. The study suggests that leaders are at the centre of the matter because they know what is going on, which echoes Niebuhr. In the case of leadership in the context of corruption in Nigeria, what is going on is already known. The impending effects of institutional corruption are alarmingly visible to the leaders. The ability to envision society and human wellbeing, therefore, rests on them. Leadership power could usefully influence new ways to address a continual spread of corruption. One of the ways to do this is through public exposure of the culprits, naming the charges against them and decisively directing them through appropriate channels for proper action. When that happens, it would showcase reasonable action towards the enhancement and the recognition of human flourishing.

---

14. de Villiers, "A Christian Ethics," 33.

6.1.1.2 Corruption and Religious Institutions: The Church in Question

This section revisits the discussions on corruption in chapter 2 with specific reference to the church. This is done in order to bring de Villiers into the conversation. As a theologian and pastor, his engagement with church and issues of public morality is fundamental to this part of the study. Here, the ideas he develops through ethics of responsibility are brought into the conversation too. First, we shall outline how the church is marred with corruption. Second, we shall identify in conversation with de Villiers, how the church could redeem itself from the mess of corruption. Importantly, how the church could, in turn, fight the scourge of corruption. Considering de Villiers's proactive and steadfastness during the apartheid era in South Africa, we could learn and helpfully apply them in today's Nigerian church to intensify its anti-corruption crusades.

In chapter 2 of this study, we identified the imperial involvement of religious institutions, particularly the church, in corrupt activities. Despite the undeniable fact of these realities, this same institution has been actively involved in the fight against corruption. It is pertinent, however, that we integrate the anti-corruption enthusiasm of the Nigerian church within the perspectives of ethics of responsibility. This we do in order to ascertain how, and if, some helpful contributions would evolve to enhance the Nigerian church to adequately fight the scourge of corruption.

While addressing public morality in South Africa, Etienne de Villiers suggests the development[15] of Christian ethical views. The development of these views aims at confronting ethical values that are anti-ethical to Christian ethical standards. Here, Christian leadership and institutional responsibility should include developing moral codes. These codes include "character formation,"[16] "allowing Christian ethics to guide moral conduct,"[17] and the inculcation of "moral and ethical re-armament and spiritual resuscitation as the responsibility of the church."[18] These moral codes are suggested as proactive ways the church, particularly in Nigeria, could adopt to ensure

---

15. de Villiers, "A Christian Ethics," 33.
16. Coetzer and Snell, "A Practical-Theological Perspective," 29–30.
17. Ogbuehi, "Christian Ethics," 335.
18. Ige, "John the Baptist Approach," 584.

regaining its role of being the salt and light of the world, especially in its effort to contribute to the struggle against corruption.

From an ethics of responsibility perspective, the church becomes corrupt when it silently condones immoral conduct. That form of corruption makes both church leaders and the perpetrators of corruption complacent. On the one hand, the proceeds of corruption are used for church projects and aid in other religious functions. Such practices involving taking monies without alluding to the sources of the funds has become a doorway in which corruption is encouraged. On the other hand, the culprits of corruption freely move, and sometimes occupy important seats during religious functions. The question begging an answer in the above case is "what happens with the supposed character formation?" Instead of focusing on character formation, the above mentioned behaviour has been substituted. Accepting bribes or funds from suspicious sources is an act against the moral formation, hence, blocking the chances for moral, ethical, and spiritual re-armament. That is likely the reason why the church is losing the power to speak against the evils of corruption appropriately, because it lacks moral standing and perhaps, the reason why complacency is gaining way in the church. With this spiralling downward, the demand for prospective responsibility of the church that frowns at the abovementioned charges becomes imperative. That would mean having the church redressing its commitment both for the present and future challenges befalling it here and now, but also the effects on humanity and society.

6.1.1.3 Corruption and Society

This section will consider the society's two-fold contribution to corruption, namely how society contributes to the continuous spread of corruption in Nigeria as elsewhere on the one hand, and on the other hand, the role of society in curbing corruption. This is done with the aim of bringing into conversation Etienne de Villiers and his views of ethics of responsibility. This reflection is necessary in order to ascertain how the ethics of responsibility contributes towards not only to better our understanding of corruption but also to how it could be curbed.

In chapter 2, we outlined that the involvement of society in corruption is two-fold. First, positively through the proactiveness of society in the fight against corruption. This was seen through the involvement of civic society organizations and their determination in fighting the menace. Here, society was also seen as a perpetrating agent fuelling the spread of corruption. In the first instance, the raising failure of societal moral conduct was suggested to result in immoral activities, including corruption. On the second stance, a collaborative celebration of persons indicted with corruption charges results in further spread of corruption. Yet, another contributory role of society is in selective arrest and investigation of the corrupt. This, as we sketched in chapter 2, happens as a result of identity politics. It comes in the form of political parties, religious affiliation, ethnic diversity, and so on. When members of a particular group are indicted for corruption charges, those within the same fold and similar philosophy remain mute. They choose to become co-collaborators to protect the accused from public shame and disgrace. This study found the greater role, which society could play in fighting corruption, has to do with its proactiveness with a common goal towards the scourge. The argument here is that if the focus deviates from identity politicking, necessary steps would likely emerge. We shall also engage Etienne de Villiers in order to interrogate how his view of ethics of responsibility could help the Nigerian society in curbing corruption.

To this end, we first apply the Bonhoefferian view of vicarious representation. In his description, Bonhoeffer argues from Jesus's self-representation[19] for the selves of all human beings. Such ethical behaviour illustrates Jesus accepting[20] the responsibility with all the pain upon himself, an act that qualifies the real vicarious representative action, making Jesus the responsible person par excellence. Understanding such actions from the ethics of responsibility perspective suggests that ethical behaviour sometimes requires us to do what is, in the eyes of others, regarded abnormal. Gathered from a vicarious representative perspective, two facts stand out. First, in the case of Jesus, the ethical implication of the action was for the sake of underserved sinners for whose sake Jesus chose to die. Second, ethical benefit seeks to promote love and justice in the world. In all, vicarious responsibility refers to actions that result in both societal and human wellbeing.

Love for others and the promotion of justice are two elements for a vicarious representative action. In the context of corruption in Nigeria, perversion of the justice system has resulted in a disillusioned love for the other. This is

---

19. Bonhoeffer, "Ethics," 321.
20. Bonhoeffer, 232.

what displays the need to recognize and respond adequately to the aspirations of the citizens.[21] Some of these aspirations in the Nigerian context include a cry for an ethos of hospitality;[22] a quest for a fully and truly humanity that is nested in the humanity of others' compassion.[23] Clint Le Bruyns speaks of the notion of the societal common good differently concerning the need for the collective effort of persons. He suggests that the quality of democratic life has the potential to be enhanced and transformed as together, when ordinary[24] people take responsibility for their political life through the renewal of theological resources. The above views are indicative of the intensity and aspirations of human beings in society. While Akper and Forster view ethos of hospitality and compassion as needed in society, Le Bruyns stresses the yearning for the freedom to take responsible action, which guarantees the enhancement of the quality of human life that occurs in a society with freedom. It is then that a human person recognizes that they have a responsibility to care for themselves and others as well. Perhaps the time when humanity understands the connection of our own lives to the lives of those whose circumstances are altogether foreign to our own; not to say "this is not my affair"[25] or this is none of my own doing when another person lives on the margin. Living contrary to that affirmation, Sacks reminds us, is a conception of human life without responsibility which fails[26] to do justice to human dignity, and is no way to ensure our survival as a species. These thoughts remind us of the diverse needs befalling humanity and our ethical response in overcoming them.

The above submissions, in the context of Nigeria, suggest the need to intensify the ethics of recognition and care. In Nigeria, as for South Africa, such ideas engage the perils of corruption on the citizenry. First, as vicarious representatives, society is endowed with the responsibility to care for and protect the interest of the populace. As such, the essence civil organizations exist is beyond self-gratification but includes enhancing human development. Second, as civil society organizations, their roles significantly involve

---

21. Mercy, "The Effects of Corruption," 297.
22. Akper, "An Ethos of Hospitality."
23. Forster, "Affect, Empathy," 3.
24. Le Bruyns, "The Church, Democracy," 59.
25. Perpich, *The Ethics of Emmanuel*, 89.
26. Sacks, *To Heal*, 7.

societal wellbeing. The recognition of the social needs of hospitality and compassion seen above suggests that civil society organizations prioritize ways and opportunities that seek re-humanization from various forms of dehumanizing structures. Some of these include rejection of the other, racial discrimination, and other elements that limit the humane in other human beings. Re-humanization is described by de Villiers as being key to societal transformation. He finds that the optimal protection and enhancement of all life on earth or the flourishing of all God's creatures are formulations of a more inclusive goal that is worthwhile to explore.[27] From de Villiers's suggestion, a description of the goal for human flourishing arises.

The optimal protection and enhancement of all life on earth remain the responsibility of humans. The responsibility to recognize the wellbeing and sustainability of humanity and society in which they live rests on a conscious evaluation of, and engagement with public discourses. One of the ways of achieving this is to engage the field of public theology through thoughts from William Storrar, who recognizes the complexities of the public space and describes it as "torn and divided."[28] Such an idea echoes Stanley Hauerwas's description that "we live in a morally bankrupt age."[29] This is the world or the public space that Willian Schweiker describes as "the time of many worlds."[30] Accordingly, it is within such a context of the public space that public theology should speak about what is at stake, and which calls for collective involvement to address the issues of societal concern.[31] In a situation where different approaches would result in the enhancement of public sanity and the flourishing of lives, Storrar suggests a truly public theology as an alternative. In his assessment, a truly public theology should help to create a more inclusive public sphere in which public anger of the silenced and excluded voices of the oppressed and marginalized can be heard and addressed by the policymakers and practitioners. Here, he contends that public theologies have the task of bringing that public anger to effective policy resolution while resisting the privatization of areas of national life that were once scrutinized

---

27. de Villiers, "The Vocation," 526.
28. Storrar, "The Naming of Parts," 23.
29. Hauerwas, *The Peaceable Kingdom*, 2.
30. Schweiker, *Theological Ethics and Global*, xi.
31. Smit, "Does it Matter," 89.

in the public domain.³² Storrar concludes that public theologians have to identify issues of public concern that have already been removed from public scrutiny, then develop civic and political strategies to bring them back into an expanded public sphere.³³

The above outline on the public space relates the relevance for public theology on some specific notions. First, the task of a true public theology (its content); second, the nature of the situations it addresses (human condition), and third, the nature of the public space those situations are found (torn, chaotic and divided world). To integrate the three notions, Dirk Smit has further opinions. While he is concerned about the nature of the public space, Smit worries that something is at stake that matters, which in his view, public theology should seek to address. In that regard, he prefers public theology to be about what counts in public life, about what makes the difference, about what affects human beings and the created world, and what matters to real people in real life.³⁴ Although what matters to real people in real life may differ from one context to the other, yet Forster insists there is a great deal to be learned from the variety of the contexts. For him, this means that public theology ceases to address only a particular context, but calls for inter-contextual engagement, as one of its characteristics shows.³⁵

If public theology functions in diversifying contexts and concerns as seen above, it means applying it to the fight against corruption cannot be overemphasized. Public theology, therefore, becomes not only a way of academic discourses on what happens but also specifically those that matter. Since the detrimental effects of corruption on society are explored in chapter 2 (see section 2.5.3) of this study, the call for what matters, as Smit suggests, arises. First, something is already wrong (the nature of the public space), and second, the human persons' subjection to dehumanizing conditions through the pervasiveness of corruption. With that background information, public theology, as Storrar finds, would seek to create inclusive environments without boundaries. Perhaps building lost confidence in instances of estrangement,

---

32. See Forster for further discussions on why it should be theology(ies) in plural and not singular since their approaches to public engagement differs from various contexts, "Some Charateristics," 15.

33. Storrar, "The Naming of Parts," 23.

34. Smit, "Does it Matter," 89.

35. Forster, "Some Characteristics," 8.

lack of basic human needs results in public anger, dejection, loss of hope, oppression, and so on. These are common conditions in parts of Nigeria, particularly the North-Eastern zone, where the Islamic insurgency has gained momentum to the extent that Akper appeals for a new ethos of hospitality.[36]

From the ongoing conversation, we can see there is plurality in public morality. The role of public theology is made profound, as it could contribute to addressing the scourge of corruption. This is because public theology is suggested as a seeker of public interest in addressing public morality, which includes interrogating policy and decision-makers, who in the case of a democratic system of governance in Nigeria, are the politicians. As such, politicians are accused heavily for advancing the cause of corruption in different ways, particularly in what we described as political corruption in chapter 2. As policy and decision-makers, public theology functions not only in identifying the issues of public morality that are removed from public scrutiny but also seeks ways to bring them back into the public sphere. From an ethics of responsibility perspective, such an action reflects Bonhoeffer's vicarious representation discussed earlier (see section 4.3.1) as "stepping into an act" for the sake of others. According to Bonhoeffer, the failure of an individual to respond to, or address issues when necessary becomes an act of irresponsibility.[37] In the case of corruption, the public theologian does not only respond to issues that concern humans and their society. But as de Villiers points out, from a Christian perspective, humans are all responsible to God.[38] If being responsible in order to enhance the wellbeing of humans and other creatures equally implies being responsible to God, then the broader sphere of responsibility is opened. Being responsible for what God has created in order to ensure its advancement and sustenance culminates in David Kelsey's affirmation that human flourishing is inseparable from God's activities relating to human creatures, such that their flourishing is always depended upon God.[39]

These perspectives from the ethics of responsibility have problematized the complexities of societal public morality, particularly in relation to corruption, whose understanding demands a broader perspective. In the same

---

36. For the insurgency gaining momentum, see Adesoji," The Boko Haram Uprising," 95; Agang, "Globalization and Terrorism," 2; (Obamwonyi and Aibieyi, "Boko Haram Menace," 12.

37. Bonhoeffer, *Ethics*, 54.

38. de Villiers, "Prospects of (part 2)."

39. Kelsey, *The Eccentric Existene*.

way, the prospective solution would require combining efforts from different stakeholders. One of these perspectives is public theology. A true public theology, we found, concerns itself with human and societal wellbeing. It ensures some form of reconstruction of the remnant from which the chaotic world has left on humans. The next section looks at how the ethics of responsibility, particularly perspectives from de Villiers, could be applied in controlling the continuous spread of corruption in Nigeria.

6.1.1.4 Corruption and Control

This section seeks to outline the ways in which the ethics of responsibility is applicable in addressing the scourge of corruption. In chapter 2, we sketched a few modalities actively involved in fighting corruption in Nigeria. In this section, perspectives from the ethics of responsibility and how they would help intensify the existing anti-corruption crusaders in Nigeria will be employed. This is done with the aim of presenting the argument that ethics of responsibility could be a paradigm to reduce the menace of corruption, that human persons could rise above its effects. In other words, we argue that ethics of responsibility could contribute ways to strengthen the anti-corruption agencies for effective operation. For clarity and reminder, three agencies fighting corruption in Nigeria were highlighted in chapter 2, namely the government instituted agencies (ICPC, EFCC), civil society organizations and the religious institutions (the church in particular).

The Nigerian government has been obsessed with the plight of corruption. Having grown to become a blight in Nigeria, corruption is considered, among other factors, the bane distorting development in the country. Within such a frame of concern, the return of democracy in 1999 influenced the establishment of two among many other anti-corruption agencies. Since we have discussed their roles in chapter 2 (see section 2.6.1), we will not dwell on that here. Rather, we shall engage de Villiers's perspectives of the ethics of responsibility and how they could helpfully strengthen the operations of the existing anti-corruption agencies in Nigeria. This engagement is necessary given the assumed ineffectiveness of the anti-corruption agencies to set Nigeria free from the blight of corruption ever since their establishment To do this, it is essential to identify a few challenges the agencies strive to combat.

First, the two government-established anti-corruption agencies we refer to in chapter 2 face the challenge of non-compliance from the judiciary. One of the determinants of justice in a state is the judiciary, which is one of the three arms of government, with the other two being the Executive and the Legislature. In the aspect of interpretation of laws and execution of punishment, the judicial arm of government plays the central role. When applied to corruption cases, this arm of government in Nigeria has been faulted, particularly when reports are brought to them from the anti-corruption agencies. One of these is that the courts grant bail to corrupt-convicted individuals.[40] A judiciary in such a state of complacency creates bottlenecks that inhibit prompt, timely, and sincere prosecution of culprits. Such dramatic events give rise to suspicion in governance and are suggestive of a state that lacks a strong and well-developed institution.[41] Carefully considered, this is one of the reasons why corruption has gained prominence in Nigeria. If good governance were to survive, therefore, there must be an interplay of such factors as justice, fairness and equity.[42] When the opposite happens, it not only limits and frustrates the activities of the anti-corruption agencies, but also exposes the fallen state of the government institutions that should boost their actions on the perpetrators of corruption. In the language of responsibility, we could say the Nigerian judiciary has become complacent with regard corruption cases.

Since the treatment of corruption-related issues deters the activities of the anti-corruption crusades in Nigeria, de Villiers's ethics of responsibility has some suggestions. Although these suggestions are not solutions to Nigeria's problem, they could be applied to enhance the responsible handling of corruption cases. From the onset, de Villiers warns that the Christian ethics of responsibility should avoid some extremes; an emphasis that moral responsibility is over and above role responsibility, and not to separate moral and role responsibilities nor to reduce role responsibility to functionality. In his view, that should both be avoided and criticized.[43] This warning aligns with his conviction that thick moral values be made available to accommodate thin moral values in ethics of responsibility discourse.[44] For instance, de

---

40. Nwankwo, "The Official Corruption," 309.
41. Asaju, "Sustaining Democratic Rule," 6.
42. Yagboyaju, "Political Corruption," 174.
43. de Villiers, "A Christian Ethics," 34–35.
44. de Villiers, *Revisiting Max Weber's*.

Villiers maintains that if the sole responsibility of a public office holder or institution, say the judiciary, constitutes maintenance of law and order or presiding over corruption allegations, it should be recognizedas important in its own right.[45] In this sense, ethics of responsibility has to emphasize that politicians, business owners and other public or private stakeholders, also have moral responsibility. Equally, ethics of responsibility would seek to demonstrate that the widespread assumption that acting in a morally right way is not conducive[46] to efficient politics and business is wrong.

It is common to hear public office holders dismissing their endowment with moral responsibilities. Often, they see moral obligations as belonging to a few persons and professions which influence their treatment of public issues. In the case of handling corruption cases, opposite actions are played or not treated properly for prosecution or delaying judgments. Sometimes, delay in the action results in moral failure, while in some occasions, moral responsibility is dismissed from the conversation where de Villiers suggests that ethics of responsibility is not limited to religious people. Rather, all rational beings have the moral obligation of treating God's good creation with dignity. Humanity is mandated to be stewards of God's good creation, including the state. The responsibility to ensure a more humane society rests on the shoulders of those that have discovered this task. As Sacks reminds us, we are to "create, not destroy, for it is my world you are destroying, my creatures you are killing."[47] Going by that view, one could add that we should cultivate concepts such as justice, hospitality, compassion and recognition, because God desires them in abundance amid creatures. This understanding calls attention to the consequences of moral actions with their implications for here and now and the future generation. Similarly, with non-compliance from the judicial system, which threatens the effectiveness of the anti-corruption bodies, it widens the gap that supports the spread of corruption. The ethics of responsibility must, therefore, endeavour to work out the prospective implications for persons whose lives are at present under the siege of their dignity being undermined. As it were, corruption neither glorifies God nor enhance the course of God's creation. Rather, it dishonours God's intention for the

---

45. de Villiers, "A Christian Ethics," 35.
46. de Villiers, 35.
47. Sacks, *To Heal*, 9.

flourishing of creation via the distortion of human dignity. A responsible defence for God's good creation, therefore, defines the moral responsibility every human person possesses.

6.1.2 The Second Research Question: Human Dignity in Nigeria

In what ways is the dignity of human persons challenged by corruption in Nigeria?

To answer this question, it was necessary to outline various views toward the conceptualisation of human dignity. While the view of this study on human dignity is from a theological perspective which links having dignity to being truly human, it was concluded that human dignity is a right that every human being deserves to not only have but it should be protected, promoted and be respected by all. To substantiate the aforementioned hypothesis, the second research question engages Etiene de Villiers's views on ethics of responsibility as discussed in chapter 5, and how they would help us with ways recongise and safeguard human dignity from the scourge of corruption.

6.1.2.1 Human Dignity and Ethics of Responsibility

This section explores the contribution of ethics of responsibility towards recognition, enhancement and protection of human dignity. It seeks to understand the nature of resources that ethics of responsibility brings to the discourses on human dignity inquiry, with regard to safeguarding it from humiliation and torture. This is done to deepen the understanding that humans could fully and truly live, on the one hand, while, on the other hand, exploring how ethics of responsibility would contribute towards the actualisation of the common good of human beings and their environment.

The notion of human dignity and ethics of responsibility have been integrated by de Villiers. Here, he focuses on Christian leaders and individual churches taking responsibility for recognizing the dehumanizing activities bedevilling society, while calling for the establishment of principles that could foster the enhancement of human dignity that reduces the chances of non-recognition. This would, in turn, bring about awareness on the protection of human dignity. While aware of this, de Villiers's suggestion is for thick Christian moral values to lead in the conversation on human dignity recognition and enhancement. Although this is appropriate in a sense, one would cautiously remember that human dignity talk is not limited to one religious group.

Going by de Villiers's opinion, a thick moral value of human dignity relies on the theory that humanity is God's image-bearer. This theory holds a universal idea that every human being has an unquantifiable dignity that should be respected, protected and promoted. It comes in contrast to what was considered human dignity before the Enlightenment Era. The universal idea promoted by Immanuel Kant calls for acting such that humanity, either in oneself or in another, be always considered as an end and never be taken as a means to an end. To engage with these notions of human dignity and responsibility, we shall explore three dimensions, namely human dignity and personal liberty, human dignity and societal responsibility, and human dignity and personal responsibility.

6.1.2.2 Human Dignity and Personal Liberty

This section seeks to establish the relationship between human dignity and personal liberty in conversation with Abraham Kuyper[48] and Michael Novak.[49] This is done in order to arrive at some contested realities of modern societies and human liberty, particularly about the economy. It will be argued that modern economics reduces human beings to mere commodities, an idea already objected to by Immanuel Kant in chapter 3 (see section 3.3.3).

The idea of human liberty is associated with human dignity. Human dignity, like other concepts, requires both societal and individual efforts for its recognition and enhancement, but within the context where freedom flourishes to enable them to live fully and truly human lives. One of Abraham Kuyper's important contributions was to elaborate a theology that recognizes and glorifies man's work on earth.[50] Such a contribution clarifies, amongst many things, the responsibility of a human person to others and society. While the responsibility to others involves, in the context of this study, the quest for recognizing and enhancing the dignity of humans, the responsibility to society includes seeking the welfare of society by promoting public

---

48. Lived between 1837–1920, was Prime minister of the Netherlands between 1901–1920. He was an influential neo-Calvinist theologian, and a journalist.

49. Lived between 1933–2017, was an American Catholic philosopher, journalist, novelist, and diplomat.

50. Novak, "Human Dignity, Persnal Liberty," 76.

righteousness.[51] As to the latter, Kuyper used a biblical cultural mandate as an enduring command for humanity to develop the potential endowed in creation as service to God. He made cultural engagement a strategic priority for his followers in the context of their times.[52] Such a broad perspective of human involvement in societal development agrees with the presupposition of his lectures on Calvinism. The emphasis is made that Calvinism did not stop at a church-order, but expanded in a life-system while influencing worldviews.[53]

This provides us with Kuyper's theological depiction that recognizes and glorifies man's work on earth. It works in promoting societal good which does not only signify societal wellbeing but human dignity also. In the case of human dignity, there is a call for caution. Novak imagines that since humans are made in the image of God who endowed each of us with a certain innate worth when we enter into our creative endeavours, anything counter[54] to dignity must be avoided. Hence, Kuyper suggests that we[55] have to care about the welfare of our fellow human beings, and we must act honourably in their midst. Novak, perhaps following Kuyper above, concludes that "good Christians should band together and take initiative to promote and to protect the dignity of ourselves, and the dignity of our brothers and sisters."[56] To actively indulge in such practice, however, requires some form of liberty within which modern economics delves into quantifying the worth of humans by variables. Yet, Kuyper and Novak's approaches to reclaiming the worth of a human person from the modern economic milieu are paramount.

Contemporary realities possess uneasy questions concerning societal morality. Christians, being part of society are sometimes left perplexed with two decisions, where instead of asking the question "what should be our outlook, or what should be our role, some rather conclude, let us look the other way and forget about it."[57] The second group threatens to withdraw either by underestimating their innate worth with abilities to live, or they intentionally

---

51. Mouw, *Abraham Kuyper*.
52. Bratt, *Abraham Kuyper*.
53. Kuyper, *Lectures on Calvinism*, 53.
54. Novak, "Human Dignity, Persnal Liberty," 76.
55. Mouw, *Abraham Kuyper*, 107.
56. Novak, 76.
57. Colson, "How Now Shall We Live," 289.

choose to stay aloof. The other group, however, recognizes Kuyper's view of human worth. In his theological argument that recognizes and glorifies man's work on earth, Kuyper made remarkable reflections. He saw the glorification of man's work through the role it plays in satisfying a deep human need, in allowing each of us to provide for our family and others in need, and in our effort to build up the kingdom of God.[58] This is only possible when the willingness to provide the needs of others is complemented by liberty to doing the same. At some point, doing good for the sake of humanity that one considers a divine mandate is either frustrated or suppressed by those who oppose the good. An example can be drawn of most African democracies where basic human needs are in the shortest supply. Most efforts to satisfy these needs of particularly the marginalized majority, experience difficult opposition by those who prefer a continuous usage of people as a means of meeting their ends. Within such a context, the recognition and enhancement of human dignity becomes problematic because of the lack of freedom to act responsibly for the sake of the "other." To think reasonably on how to combat such a challenge, however, some thoughts by Thomas Aquinas on human dignity and liberty are worth reflecting on.

In his theological contribution to human dignity and liberty, Thomas Aquinas viewed liberty in two ways. First, recalling that both Jews and Christians explain human dignity by pointing to human liberty, human liberty is, thus, considered a fundamental datum of God's revelation to humanity.[59] For Aquinas, his first concept of human liberty focuses on human understanding on one thing rather than another. This he called liberty of specification. In the context of this study, one could attempt to say liberty to seek the protection and promotion of human dignity without interference or to speak for those who lack the power to defend themselves while dehumanizing the context of, for instance, corruption.

Second, the liberty to involve in reaching a determination that enough evidence is at hand for reaching judgment, and the decision not to evade the evidence, but to be faithful to it – to go ahead and make the judgment. Aquinas called this "liberty of exercise."[60] Again, one could attempt to equate

---

58. Novak, "Human Dignity, Persnal Liberty," 76.
59. Novak, "The Judeo-Christian Foundation," 111.
60. Novak, 113.

Aquinas's reference to faithful exercise to fighting for the cause of justice without resistance. It means to exercise the right of human beings for the cause of human beings, to defend and protect their rights to be human. This is liberty that seeks the interest of making life better for others to ensure they thrive. This is the freedom to choose the kind of life an individual has reason to value freedom, which is considered a basic ingredient of a flourishing human life.[61] That sort of exercise promotes synergy to fight and defend a good cause. Consequently, the moral harm of corruption, in this case, could be the limitation of freedom to fighting it. These two forms of human liberty – specification and exercise – are significant yet applicable within the context of liberty. They specifically outlined the necessity of knowing the cause of action (specification) and its relevance thereof (exercise). In the context of this study, specifying the problem – corruption undermining the dignity of human persons – reignites the passion towards resisting it, which is the attitude involving the exercise to recognize and enhance the dignity of human beings.

6.1.2.3 Human Dignity and Societal Responsibility

In this section, the concern is to emphasize the need for co-responsibility of society in safeguarding human dignity. In doing so, some notions in African theology, such as concepts of communality, will be explored. This is done in order to establish that safeguarding human dignity requires communal collaboration. We shall journey with thoughts from de Villiers and how they are helpful in this regard. In addressing public issues in the South African context, de Villiers makes contributions through ethics of responsibility where he outlines the responsibility of the society in safeguarding moral issues. When such an understanding is established, the reader will be directed to comments that although we are responsible for each other, we all are, above all things, responsible to God. By being responsible to God, we first are responsible for other human beings and to God's good creation. That way, humans reclaim their creatureliness in the image of God to fulfilling the task of taking care (being stewards) of creation.

Although the recognition and enhancement of human dignity have become a concern, society could make significant influence to reverse the

---

61. Graf, and Schweiger, "Poverty and Freedom," 261.

social order. From the way society looks and places value on human persons, the stereotypes on individual persons would take a new tone when the enhancement of human dignity takes centre stage. Perhaps, that commences when the inhabitants of society recognize the reason for their existence. Speaking with specific reference to Christians as part of society, Hunter suggests that,

> the passion to engage the world, to shape it, and finally change it for the better, would seem to be an enduring mark of Christians on the world in which we live. To be Christian is to be obliged to engage the world, pursuing God's restorative purposes over all of life, individual and corporate, public, and private. For this is the mandate of creation.[62]

The above address indicates the attitudinal expectation of Christians in the world. Obsessed with conflicting views and ideas about absolutes, particularly with regards to the dignity of human persons, the mandate of Christians is to influence change – change in a culture that seemingly presents different ideals. Such ideals retain society, including Christians, in a fix that keeps people in despair as if Christians "do not care."[63] Amid such complexities in society, however, Abraham Kuyper reminds us that "there is not a square inch in the whole domain of our human existence over which Christ, who is sovereign over all, does not cry: Mine."[64] If every domain of creation subscribes to Christ's love and care, humans would have no exemption but to do the same.

As Christians, such a culture of despair should not threaten our existence and influence in the world. Realities should instead abound on how to substantiate the complexities of the time we live.[65] One of these complexities is the secularization theories summarized by some studies.[66] Of the theories of secularization, the authors presented one strand of an argument that

---

62. Hunter, "To Change the World," 4.
63. Colson, "How Now Shall We Live," 288.
64. Bratt, *Abraham Kuyper*, 195.
65. Some descriptions of the time we live have already been mentioned in the previous sections of this study. Refer to Stanley Hauerwas "chaotic world" (Hauerwas, *A Community of Character*, 14) and William Schweiker "the time of many worlds" (Schweiker, *Theological Ethics*, xi).
66. Pollack, "Varieties of Secularization theories," 60–62; Swatos and Christiano, "Secularization Theory," 209; Beyers, "Self-Secularisation as Challenge," 2.

stands out; one that suggests a decline in devotion to divine imperatives that Christians are left in the dilemma of choices. Within that atmosphere, however, Bratt's suggestion is helpful. He agrees that secularization is the stamp of the age, yet even so, "the Lord must have also provided the means for believers to sound the claims of faith in that context."[67] In the context of this study, one of the ills of the age relates to the non-recognition, hence, the violation of human dignity. One of the reasons for this is variation in its meaning and application, as already presented in chapter 3 (see section 3.3). The controversy has reached such a climax that human dignity does not matter anymore to many people. Amid these controversies, what role should society play to safeguard the dignity of human persons, holding that effective recognition and enhancement of it requires collective effort? We shall briefly suggest an answer to this question below.

First, stereotyping and stratifying human beings is key to the non-recognition of human dignity. Previously in chapter 3 (see section 3.3), we highlighted dimensions at which human dignity is perceived. Some of those dimensions from the social and psychological perspectives promote the stratification of human beings. Also, the anthropological perspective of human dignity portrays some stereotypes in that not only do they suggest the non-recognition of human dignity, but also both are caused by human society. This is a form of evil that Huber describes as the worst, when humans do evil to fellow human beings.[68] Here, what matters is an invitation to societal responsibility towards recognition and enhancement of human dignity. Certainly, there are no easy answers nor solutions, but hard and difficult questions, says Jonathan Sacks, a Jewish Rabbi. He asks, "what is our responsibility to humanity as a whole? what bonds of obligation link us to those with whom we do not share a country, a political structure, a language or culture? what proportion of our wealth, if any, are we duty-bound to share?"[69] We shall attempt to provide answers to these questions here below.

To understand Sacks's question of our responsibility to humanity would require that we establish the dilemma humans are in. One of the concerns

---

67. Bratt, *Abraham Kuyper*, 196.
68. Huber, *Violence: The Unrelenting Assault*.
69. Sacks, *The Dignity of*, 111.

Sacks raises is the endemic[70] increase in inequality both within and between countries. Such is a similar concern the anthropological perspectives from Koopman and Bedford-Strohm suggest. With such a growing concern, human beings are reduced to mere objects of ridicule and pity. They are left with no dignity. This has remained so within human society owing to a lack of compassion for other human beings, a feeling of non-human equality that others assume a more human position than others. What matters, in some spheres, is the placement of priority on things rather than on people. For instance, "Americans spend more on cosmetics, and Europeans on ice cream, than it would cost to provide schooling and sanitation for the two billion people who currently go without both."[71] Worst still, such engrained inequality is visible such that we can no longer claim that we did not know as we claimed centuries ago.[72]

Such a world where only a few prosper and many starve, offends our deepest sense of fairness and human solidarity.[73] This is a call to the rediscovery of what fully and truly humanity means for others. Fairness in the treatment of others not for what we could do, but because they are humans and are deserving. In this case, freedom towards human solidarity is reignited, so that they begin to clamour for a better life. This is similar to what Marcel Sarot calls "self-actualization which is a moment of re-humanization and regaining of self-respect."[74] Seemingly, the absence of freedom and fairness results in dependency on livelihood. But referring to the ancient Israelite society, "they were charged with creating a society where everyone has a basic right to a dignified life and to be equal citizens."[75] Such a society was to be a reverse of what the Israelites had "experienced in Egypt: poverty, persecution, and enslavement . . . to freedom."[76] Sacks, with his focus on the Jewish context's suggestion, illustrates that poverty humiliates and that no good society will

---

70. Sacks, 105.
71. Sacks, 106.
72. Sacks, 108.
73. Sacks, 111.
74. Sarot, "Models of," 181.
75. Sacks, *The Dignity of*, 114.
76. Sacks, 115.

allow humiliation.⁷⁷ If no society prefers the humiliation of its citizens, then no society will desire the existence of humiliating structures.

Such a suggestion calls for a responsibility involving human beings in society. In living together with others, we discover our true sense of humanity. We share our human limitations with others, we experience the unification of our needs, we learn tolerance, we become reminded of our vulnerabilities. In fact, "we learn patience."⁷⁸ In all these, we discover our worth because, in so doing, we realize the dignity of others, we become sensitive to discover dehumanizing structures that we cause for ourselves in most cases. We tend to forget that "society is ordained by God as a necessary remedy for corrupt nature."⁷⁹ Only when we discover the role of society in the recognition of humiliating structures, and seek for ways to combat those, can we say "society must ensure equal dignity."⁸⁰ Individuals have a positive duty to join others to change institutions of society to uphold the dignity of man.⁸¹ Here, not only does the responsibility of recognizing and enhancing human dignity bestowed on society, individual persons equally have a role to ensure the recognition but also respect for their dignity.

6.1.2.4 Human Dignity and Personal Responsibility

This section presents the argument that safeguarding human dignity has a personal dimension. That human dignity is the focus here suggests that humans have a responsibility to protect and promote their self-worth. Such an inquiry invites us to problematize the notion of altruism, a strict focus on living for others with less attention on oneself. Altruism in human dignity discourse, for instance, argues that individuals have a responsibility toward the recognition and enhancement of their dignity. It is not all an outward concern towards others but has an inward reaction. Such perception invites a person to reflect inwardly o their self-worth, to recognize and reignite self-respect beyond both the psychological and social dimensions of human dignity that bases on self-esteem rather than the inviolable worth. It means

---

77. Sacks, 119.
78. Hauerwas and Pinches, "Practicing Patience," 202.
79. Thielicke, *Theological Ethics*, 143.
80. Sacks, *The Dignity of*, 120.
81. Novak, "Human dignity," 68.

recognizing and enhancing one's dignity becomes a gateway through which the dignity of others is recognized, respected and promoted. Put differently, the human dignity of others would better be respected when we recognize the value of our own dignity. That idea we shall discuss as personal dignity. To do this, we shall focus on a perspective emphasizing that personal dignity could be developed through the discovery of self-respect.

Immanuel Kant's idea on the obligations of an individual to oneself would be a good starting point in our conversation on personal responsibility to human dignity. Kant insists that "the first duty of a human being as an animal being is to preserve himself in his animal nature."[82] Such an idea perhaps comes from the fact that, inwardly, self-recognition propels outward action, particularly to others, which becomes an obligation to oneself. Such obligations, in Kant's view, are accompanied by two resolutions that a human being views himself as the subject of duty. First, as a sensible being who is a member of one of the animal species, and second, as an intelligible being whose perception goes beyond mere reasoning, since reason as a theoretical faculty could well be an attribute of a living corporeal being.[83] Here, Kant submits "I can recognize that I am under obligation to others only insofar as I at the same time put myself under obligation."[84] Such obligation put across by Kant suggests that acknowledging it as an obligation, to recognize and enhance our human dignity, provides us with a perspective towards others.

Additionally, an inward reflection of oneself influences their existence. It provides a sensation that one has untapped hidden abilities. The non-recognition of such value has resulted in why humans accept designations of "who they are" from society and others around them. Such ideological beliefs result in false acceptance of the worth of human beings. On the contrary, the discovery of true worth generates inner self-worth and a reclaiming of the defaced notion of humans. That is a scenario, Nico Koopman assures while referring to the urgency that necessitates the end of apartheid in South Africa. Apartheid dehumanized White South Africans by teaching them that they were superior human beings and dehumanized the Black people by

---

82. Kant, "Frontmatters," 189.
83. Kant, 186.
84. Kant, 185.

teaching them to accept they were inferior to the Whites.[85] So, part of the re-humanization process entails that Whites be freed from the superiority, and Blacks from inferiority complexes. That is what happens when there is no inner discovery of self-worth. The question begging for an answer here is, how could the inner worth of a people be discovered that they may know? To answer that question, we engage Frits de Lange's thoughts on self-respect.

Frits de Lange uses the notion of self-respect as a pointer to the inner discovery of self-worth. The inner worth begins from inward actualization that one is endowed with an inward unquantifiable variable called dignity. Since "being human suffices for having dignity,"[86] there are no exemptions and limitations on who has dignity. In that case, the nullification of psychological and social dimensions of human dignity emphasizing it could be increased, reduced, or taken away holds. Understood this way, human dignity ceases to be measured based on an individual's input in society other than as an unquantifiable, indwelling variable. This idea is theologically supported in that people's dignity does not rest in their rationality or on their social merits, but in the fact that they are called[87] by God to live as his creatures. In his concluding remarks on the alien dignity of human beings, Koopman adds that creatures are not only called by God to live, but that they live in freedom and are treated with justice.[88]

Living fully as human beings entails living with freedom. This gives humans a sense of belonging and participation in society. Within such a context comes self-awareness, which as de Lange puts it, brings to the knowledge that you are a human being equal to other people. It also brings the understanding that you be held responsible for your actions and have plans and projects to be respected. Here, self-awareness implies being conscious of your human worth, which is only achievable within the context of freedom and justice.[89] With freedom and fairness, people exhibit self-confidence leading to self-respect. As de Lange points out, only those able to imagine

---

85. Koopman, "Some Theologial and Anthropological Perspectives."
86. de Lange, "Having Faith in Yourself," 215.
87. de Lange, 213.
88. Koopman, "Some Theologial and Anthropological Perspectives," 185.
89. de Lange, 214.

a self-esteemed future for themselves acquire it. Indeed, faith in oneself is a prerequisite of self-respect.[90]

The above finding follows Sarot's conclusion that each human being has some innate capacities that are worth actualizing. Those capacities are obtainable where human beings live in fellowship with God and with other human beings.[91] This is found in what John Rawls describes as a just society, where the liberties of equal citizenship are taken as settled,[92] and the rights secured by justice are not subject to political bargaining or the calculus of social interests. Rather, they are measured on the scale of freedom and justice made available. This is societal responsibility that should seek the recognition and enhancement of the dignity of human persons, a notion consisting of a collaborative effort to recognizing and enhancing the dignity of others. Such attempts, however, result in some emotional exhaustion that denies an individual self-discovery of their inner worth. It could also lead one to accepting that enhancing humanity is altruistic, living exhaustively seeking the recognition and enhancement of other people's dignity while failing to discover one's inner worth. As it were, self-respect is actualized by re-conceptualizing self-love, a view contrary to altruism.[93]

The ongoing discussion invites us to re-evaluate and re-consider our commitment towards ensuring ethical and responsible living in society. We highlighted that for the recognition and enhancement of human dignity, the responsibility rests on both society and individual persons. Yet, personal responsibility towards promoting human dignity occurs where freedom and justice flourish.

---

90. de Lange, 218.

91. Sarot, "Models of," 192.

92. Rawls, *A Theory of Justice*, 3.

93. The concept was first coined by the French philosopher, Auguste Comte, to support his moral doctrine that one's moral obligation solely depends on the impact made on other people (Campbell, "Altruism in August Comte," 357). It is an important idea that closely relates with the concept of good life in ethics, making life better for others. The difference, however, is that altruistic motive has tendencies of leaving the altruist in a state of nagging guilt, emotional exhaustion, physical burn-out, and going to any extent to avoiding being called selfish. We are not interested in theorizing the entire idea of altruism here, but to make a case using altruism in relation to the recognition and enhancement of human dignity. The argument in relation to human dignity is formulated as follows, "recognition and enhancement of human dignity does not start and end at aiming others, but has an inward dimension, too where one does not all seek to enhance the dignity of others at the detriment of their own." Cambell, 359.

6.2 Proposing Some Features of an Ethics of Responsibility for the Nigerian Context

The task of this section is to put forward a proposal for the features of ethics of responsibility that would be suitable to address the scourge of corruption undermining the dignity of human persons in Nigeria. The previous section engaged de Villiers's contemporary Christian ethic of responsibility and how it addresses public morality. Consequently, a few limitations were observed and were outlined in the form of critical engagement in chapter 5 (see section 5.7). The idea behind the critical engagement was to seek ways to further the discussion on the subject matter. The critique, however, serves as a springboard to what we shall argue in this part of the study.

With Nigeria being the focus area for this study, this section desires to suggest the characteristics of the ethics of responsibility that is relevant to enhancing the recognition and protection of human dignity from the scourge of corruption. Due to Nigeria being multi-ethnic, multi-cultural, and contested religious, any features for such ethics would have to take cognisance of the possible divisiveness. This is important in order to start conversations concerning public morality. As de Villiers has suggested, there is a need to recognize and respect the various ethos of people in communities, both the thick and thin ethical norms. Following that suggestion, formulating ethics of responsibility to address the scourge of corruption ought to make considerations on both the people and their context. That would mean having likeminded stakeholders willing to engage with the issues of concern, or we simply talk of public theology.[94] Veldsman refers to the function of public theology in such a context as

> a call that all seekers and strangers[– concerned persons –] should stand up as public theologians, acknowledging religion and religious experience as products of rationality, and be held accountable as we are moving from one context to another and make statements that hold our values.[95]

Formulating a new model entails that the old is unlearned or modified. In most cases, modification ensures an existing idea still makes contributions

---

94. For more on public theology, see Smit, "Does it Matter;" Forster, "Some Charateristics;" Agang, "The Need for."

95. Veldsman, "Discussing Publicness," 546.

to ongoing conversations. Other times, an existing idea could be ignored or perhaps modified to ensure a continuity of ideas, or be unlearned to create space for new ones. Although this does not seldom apply in critical scholarship, chances are that such ideas are left with fewer references, which gradually become obsolete. In this study, however, we do not intend to unlearn the ideas developed by de Villiers on the contemporary Christian ethic of responsibility, but seek to continue the conversation from a different context. Particularly, his proposal for contemporary ethics of responsibility where he insists on a second-level normative ethical approach, the idea cannot be overruled considering the relevance it has to the current study.

Here, we shall highlight features of a contemporary ethic of responsibility concerning the Nigerian context. So far, this study has outlined the impending problem of corruption on human dignity, and, at this stage, continues the conversation that de Villiers started on what the features of this ethics should look like. All this while being conscious of the Nigerian context, and how the features would befit discussing public morality which characterises our time.

In his description of the times in which we live, Sacks has made some helpful remarks. His description of our world as "fractured" ignites the intention for its healing.[96] The argument in his book presents an outcry for the return of religion to its true purpose, namely to enhance ethical and moral living. According to Sacks, these have been compromized, perhaps due to the influence of modernity. In his remarks on the twenty-first century, Sacks notes the following as contributing challenges of our time. First, environmental problems including global warming, erosion of the biosphere, the destruction of rain forests, and the greatest extinction of species since civilization began. Second, the growing inequality between the rich and the poor. Third, political problems including ethnic conflict, civil wars, successive waves of asylum seekers, the proliferation of violence and international disorder, and the danger posed by failed, failing and rogue states.[97] In consideration of Sacks's concern, there comes to mind concern for what Emmanuel Levinas calls the "other." This other, for Levinas, is the one for whose wellbeing we have the responsibility to look after, which is our obligation.[98] Understanding our

---

96. Sacks, *To Heal*, 264.
97. Sacks, 264.
98. Levinas, *Humanism of the Other*.

obligation in responsibility talk, however, invites us to an ultimate perception about life. Sacks describes this life as "God's call to responsibility."[99]

This, is a call for critical engagement on issues of concern for humanity and society. From a Christian perspective, Smit's opinion is appropriate here. He states that "we are one on a much deeper level than anything that makes us different from one another, that distinguishes, divides, and separates us, and that we should find ways of embodying this unity also in our common life together in the polis."[100] If by embodying the unity within human society, Smit relates to what Sacks sees as our responsibility, and what Levinas calls the exhibition of our "moral conscience," it means, Christians and perhaps every human person, has a moral obligation both within his/her circles and to the wider society. These obligations whose focus is to heal the fractured world full of violence and divisiveness requires an ethos of commonality, not of indifference but concern for the wellbeing of the other. By healing the other, we equally heal ourselves; a conducive environment for one is, in turn, conducive also for ourselves.

The above description of our time becomes an invitation to what is of concern to this study. The fragmentation this study has investigated includes the devastating effect of corruption on the dignity of human persons in Nigeria. Calls are made towards curbing the menace, but these calls are insufficient to halt its continuous spread. This then becomes the drive for a theological resource to add to the conversation on the anti-corruption campaign in Nigeria. An ethic of responsibility being this theological rhetoric, we shall outline some features which could be relevant to initiate discussion on the subject matter. It is pertinent to note that corruption, if it remains uncontrolled, would further the fracturing of our world. In this case, it would mean leaving humanity and its environment, as in the case of Nigeria, in hopeless situations. That would mean not doing justice to God's good creation. As Sacks reminds us, "a conception of human life without responsibility fails to do justice to human dignity and is no way to ensure our survival as a species."[101] This is an invitation to engage the impending issues of corruption to safeguard human dignity, on the one hand, while, on the other hand, seeking the

---

99. Sacks, *To Heal*, 3.
100. Smit, "Does it Matter," 296.
101. Sacks, 8.

enhancement of ethical-living and acting to ensure personal, corporate and social responsibility. With such highlights, we shall advance to propose some features of the contemporary ethic of responsibility for the Nigerian context.

The features proposed in this study are built from de Villiers's line of agreement with Weber, who suggests that a contemporary ethic of responsibility should be considered a second-level normative approach.

6.2.1 A Matter of Urgency

Mitigating the spread of corruption is necessary to reduce the continual undermining of human dignity in Nigeria. Perhaps, it is the more reason why corruption is one of the defining issues of our time. As such, speaking to the African continent regarding issues of concern, Agang worries that "we see abundant evidence that all is not well in Africa."[102] Considering the issues facing us on the African continent, including the scourge of corruption that is devastatingly affecting the very fabric of humanity – its dignity – "we hear and read the urgent cry that we in Africa need action now."[103] This cry is not only to safeguard the present human condition from what Schweiker calls "the time of many worlds" affecting us here and now, but also for the coming generation.[104] The contemporary Christian ethic of responsibility that seeks to address the scourge of corruption must, therefore, do so with a sense of urgency.

Corruption affects us all but not to the same extent. The people who suffer first and worst as a result of corruption, just like climate change, are those who did close to nothing in causing it: the poor and the vulnerable members of society. They are affected when corruption squanders the basic needs meant for their wellbeing and dignity. These poor and helpless members of society become useful tools and a means for a selfish end – another way human dignity is undermined, which this study argues for. They are left in traumatic circumstances that life sometimes loses its value in their thoughts. As Sacks reminds us, however, "a conception of human life without responsibility fails to do justice to human dignity and is no way to ensure our

---

102. Agang, "The Need for," 3.
103. Veldsman, "Science," 175.
104. Read this further in Schweiker, *Theological Ethics*, xi.

survival as a species."¹⁰⁵ This, therefore, makes our response to the plight of humanity in trouble from corruption and irresponsive measurement toward sending a matter of urgency. Such action confirms our creaturely identity that warrants that "we have a contribution to make to the human heritage."¹⁰⁶ Our expectation in this context entails formulating modalities from which to speak about what is going on.

From some thoughts of Dirk Smit speaking for a pluralistic South African context, we could glean to build our own. The nature of what we see happening in Nigeria has discouraged individual and societal values. One of these is what Godwin Akper elaborated while advocating for an ethos of hospitality as a desirable need in Nigerian society at present. Adding to Akper's quest for an ethos of hospitality, there is also the need for an ethos of forgiveness, tolerance, confession, truth-telling and unity owing to the injustices done against humanity by itself. Here, Smit suggests that "unity, reconciliation, forgiveness and an embrace will remain superficial and under continuous threat, if the continuing legacies of inequality and oppression are not addressed."¹⁰⁷ Additionally, in the case in Nigeria, we have not only inherited structures of injustice, violence and inequality, but also have successfully created some for ourselves, using religion, ethnicity and regionality.¹⁰⁸ It would simply be unjust to continue as if these present dehumanizing structures and systems created by us do not impact us now and the future generation.

This leaves us with the question "shall we continue this way folding up our arms to allow these dehumanizing structures to keep growing in our society?" This study would not hesitate to answer in the negative. We can not continue living with these structures. We have a mandate to ensure the healing of any existing wound. As Sacks suggests, it is not a task expected to be done by a single person, but one that requires many hands. While lamenting on how to heal this fractured world, Sacks insists that

> each of us must be conscious that we can't complete the task: we need someone else to make the shekel whole. But neither is our contribution insignificant. We can contribute our half,

---

105. Sacks, *To Heal*, 8.
106. Sacks, 10.
107. Smit, "Contributions of Religions," 296.
108. Kure, "Leadership , Corruption ," 2–3.

confident that others will join us, perhaps inspired by what we do. We can change the world, but we need partners, and the best way of finding them is to lead by personal example.[109]

From Sacks's perception towards the healing of our fractured world, this study finds that an ethic of responsibility is needed in Nigeria, with a sense of urgency, now more than ever before.

To heal the fractures inflicted on the Nigerian persons, the ethic of responsibility must urgently seek to know what is going on. In our case, however, we already know what is going on – it is corruption undermining the dignity of human persons within a weak-willed leadership atmosphere. Our collective response then entails speaking the possibilities in order to salvage the human person from dehumanizing structures. Naming the problem gives room for its possible solutions. Our problem here consists of the degradation of human dignity through the scourge of corruption. The quest, however, is for the recognition and enhancement of human dignity to enable the flourishing of God's good creation. Only when we discover that as our duty, could we stop being silent in the face of wrongdoing or injustice parading the Nigerian human person.[110] That would further motivate us to use whatever influence we can justly use to salvage ethical living and enhance moral formation. Foreseeing some complex and difficult situations, the contemporary Christian ethic of responsibility could adopt an activist and a confrontational approach to addressing ethical issues (see section 5.5.1.2). Given that such an approach could result in some sort of struggle emphasises that "if we succeed, we have made a difference, and if we fail, we have honoured our obligation by doing what we could."[111]

The intention of an ethic of responsibility in such regard is not only to have a state but a society. In society, Sacks explains,

> we feel that common sense of belonging that comes from a sense that we are neighbours as well as strangers; that we have duties to one another, to the heritage of the past and the hopes of

---

109. Sacks, *To Heal*, 267.

110. Knowing fully that silence in the midst of injustice, violence, and all forms of dehumanisation suggest a sense of affirmation. Bonhoeffer, calls it irresponsibility (Bonhoeffer, *Ethics*).

111. Sacks, *To Heal*, 123.

the generation yet unborn; that society is not a hotel where we receive services in exchange for money, but a home to which we feel attached and whose history is our own.[112]

That must concretely be a commitment towards bettering a place. The Nigerian persons and society must endeavour to work for such a humane society that respects, regards and upholds humanity in its whole.

The point here is that a contemporary Christian ethic of responsibility in the context of corruption in Nigeria would have to urgently act in order to salvage the ongoing dehumanizing structures.

6.2.2 Dialogical Dimension

The contestable diversity of Nigeria requires a multi-dimensional approach to issues, particularly those affecting public morality. These public moralities, including corruption, are subsumed into every sector of the Nigerian society, causing a downturn in the enhancement of human dignity. In a view to re-ignite sensitivity to denial of human dignity, there arises a need to dialogue within these divisions. For the sake of this study and section, three units are selected, namely religion, region and ethnicity. This choice resonates from the continuous conflict between Christians and Muslims (religion); the idea of the Southern and Northern Nigeria (region); and the idea of multiple tribes (ethnicity). These factors must be brought together under the platform called "a dialogical dimension," which we shall consider as a feature of a contemporary ethic of responsibility. This idea of dialogue disagrees with Weberian attribution of a charismatic political leader as a sole agent of responsibility, but agrees with de Villiers on recruiting different stakeholders. The idea is further supported by Veldsman who points out that "we need to work together to formulate clearer and broader guidelines for our own contexts."[113] The ethic of responsibility we propose here, like de Villiers's, therefore, desires collective responsibility in order to actualise its purpose.

Take an instance from a photographer who carries their camera when they are shooting quickly and informally, but when they want to be stable for accurate, well-aimed, and focused shots, they use a multi-dimensional mechanism in the form of a tripod. The secret to using this mechanism does

---

112. Sacks, 125.
113. Veldsman, "Science," 187.

not depict which segment is the most important, but what matters most is the contribution that each makes. Perhaps, it is not about the authenticity of each dimension but its presence and the contribution towards stabilizing the entire tripod. In the case of Nigeria and the three factors mentioned, the unity required in the fight against public morality does not favour the popularity or strength of one people group or religion over the other. Neither is it an indication of prominence or dominance. Rather, it is a call to form united forces to fight a common enemy, which signifies the essence of unity of purpose to ensure significant results. We want to use this scenario in applying ethics of responsibility that seeks to address public morality in Nigeria.

The divisions that interest us here have been blissful in some ways but also detrimental at some point. Religion, for instance, as argued in chapter 2 of this study (see section 2.5.4), has fuelled most of the crisis that claimed numerous lives and led to the destruction of property. Yet the same religion acts as a reconciling agent and speaks for the promotion of morality (see section 2.6.3). It is not correct, however, to assume that ideals of any of these divisions (religion, region, ethnic) are solely responsible for actions than the behaviour of individuals serving as their leaders. Left to some, nothing guarantees that, on their own, those individuals will act to positively advance the ideal mission of the society rather than their self-interest. Perhaps within the confluence of three variables, namely responsibility, authority and privilege.

Responsibility, authority and privilege could play a significant role in dialogical dimension theory. In instances where responsibility is given that exceeds one's authority, the outcome is likely that one leaves a job undone. Consequently, if the authority is too much for a responsibility, they become dictators, barking orders regardless of whether they make sense or accomplish anything. At the last stage, if they have privilege without responsibility, and without adequate explanations, it results in suspicion of how the privilege is earned. These three cases could be used to reiterate a dialogical dimension model for an ethic of responsibility. As it is, the recognition that we both have a personal and corporate responsibility to safeguard human dignity dismisses the notion of waiting on an external authority before acting. Any ethic of responsibility that seeks to address public morality such as corruption in Nigeria must not neglect these divisions, otherwise, it encounters opposition due to non-inclusion and involvement. This is one of the reasons Nigeria still considers issues of federal character daring. It is useful because the three divisions highlighted play a central role in job provision and other political appointments. So, an ethic of responsibility that would fit such a context must take cognizance of those divisions to ensure concrete conversation on public issues. Such an ethic must endeavour to address differences without prejudices. It must bring to dialogue the various divisions on the implication of corruption on the dignity of human persons and seek a common language to addressing it. It must be an ethic above religion, ethnicity or region, but one that seeks the wellbeing of humanity in the face of dehumanisation.

6.2.3 Strong Ethical Value-oriented

The culture of an ethical person or nation is defined starting from the very top of the national or societal chart. From an individual stance, being ethical calls for standing for, and doing the right thing, irrespective of the consequences. For de Villiers, he presumes that an in-between-ethic (see section 5.5.1.2), as an ethical approach to a contemporary Christian ethic of responsibility, provides better moral guidance for ethical living.

The agent does what is right because, to them, that is the right thing to do; which suggests being responsible for those whose sake the right thing is done. He/she, therefore, understands that "life is God's call to responsibility."[114] In doing this, Levinas maintains, "I find myself responsible not owing to such and such a guilt which is mine or to offenses that I would have committed, but because I am responsible for a total responsibility which answers for all the others and all in the others, even for their responsibility."[115] Such perception of responsibility objects individual claims to responsibility as only when they have done an action (good or bad). It, however, agrees with Sacks's view of general responsibility as an intention of God that we have been gifted with all credentials by God for acts of good.[116] We could deduce from above, the character of an ethical individual from their determination to living and acting right without being mindful of consequences that make ethical behaviour possible. God, who responsibly loves good creation, invites us to replicate similar attitudes towards other creatures, particularly human beings. Being responsible, in this case, becomes responsiveness towards both

---

114. Sacks, *To Heal*, 3.
115. Perpich, "The Ethics of Emmanuel," 84.
116. Sacks, 3.

God and other creatures, which includes "upholding human dignity, seek justice in all human affairs of life and obey the laws of God."[117] Such is a reminder of Levinas's idea for an ultimate obligation that annihilates agent-centred options. To be infinitely responsible is to be "ever on call, always at one's post, impaled upon one's obligation, never quits with it, never with an option to take a day or an hour or even a minute for one's cares."[118]

From a societal or national case, being ethical entails some expectations of consistency and regularity in moral behaviour. For instance, in the case where law enforces moral standards, the preservation of these standards by every member in society becomes hard, especially with the challenge of the plurality of norms that some have lost their monopoly in all spheres of life. The provision of ethical codes could, therefore, grant members of such society the expectation of what is required of them in keeping societal moral codes. For this to happen in society or a nation, its leaders must demonstrate ethical practices in any situation. From what they say to what they do, the outright display of readiness to ethical living and acting must be displayed. The true test of such leadership is in the decision-making process when there is a choice between what is ethically responsible and its outcome.

In the search for features of the ethics of responsibility in Nigeria within the context of corruption and its impending effect on human dignity, it must have a strong ethical value orientation. Of this ethical value orientation, an individual or an idea is given adherence when it promises practical steps towards its implementation. For a contemporary Christian ethic of responsibility to foresee the inculcation of practical ethical values for the societal common good in Nigeria, particularly in the fight against corruption, it would mean actions complementing speeches.[119] In other words, a strong determination to actively live and act morally right in order to ensure an ethical society.

6.2.4 Guided by Integrity, Fairness and Equity

Integrity is an all-encompassing characteristic of an ethical person and society. It is a feature that goes along with fairness, equity, compassion, justice,

---

117. Aben, "The Trinity and Public Theology," 46.
118. Perpich, "The Ethics of Emmanuel," 84.
119. Kure, "Corruption and the Dignity."

and seeks to create a humane environment. In summary, integrity shows regard for the "other." It searches for what is going on, and seeks to treat dehumanizing structures such that human persons could live and thrive. The attitude of persons or a society of integrity is seen from the manner in which the concerns of humanity within its power are handled. How the poor are treated, the less-privileged cared for, if basic human needs are provided, how they are fairly distributed and so on. That would determine a society where integrity flourishes.

As a nation, Nigeria is in search of people with integrity. It is a search that includes leaders, but also followers who would live and act with integrity in both public and private affairs. People whose private lives publicly display their true essence in terms of duty performance or job description where no supervision is provided. In terms of effective duty performance, integrity is antithetical to non-performance, ineffectiveness, unproductivity and, in fact, to corruption. Unfortunately, the only limited attention has been placed on how to evaluate policy systems and institutions to bolster integrity to enhance the discharge of official duties, the performance of institutions, and the exercise of public or other entrusted power in tackling the issue.[120] Until that is achieved, the quest for wellbeing, flourishing and the recognition of human dignity would receive little to no consideration. In connection with the ongoing focus of this section of the study, integrity could be regarded as a feature of a contemporary ethic of responsibility in Nigeria in that it timely sees and acts for the wellbeing of human persons. If the ethic of responsibility does so, it escapes from being an irresponsible ethic.

As a feature of a contemporary ethic of responsibility, integrity search covers more than an individual actor, but their interactions and relationships with likeminded different actors for common goals. Such a relationship put together, enables the actors' collective effort, and evolves unity of purpose to act, respond and plan for either public or private organizations. In so doing, they collectively work to limit and counteract public issues distorting the wellbeing of human persons, such as corruption.[121] From a public theology perspective with the concern of common good, this approach is helpfully applied. In their consideration of the common good and contemporary

---

120. Brown and Heinrich, "National Integrity Systems."
121. Brown and Heinrich, 290.

politics, Bradstock and Russel put it that common good refers to seeking the welfare of the city, and the wellbeing of all members of a community. For them, if that is the goal for pursuing the common good, the idea of sectional-based models of political action – where the concerns and interests of one faction prevail over those of others – will be inappropriate.[122] Regarding integrity, the contemporary Christian ethic of responsibility quest for the common good could drive for rapid response to the scourge of corruption. Following the argument on collective effort towards the common good of human persons, it is fundamental to note that there are no special qualifications for persons of integrity in the context of fighting the common enemy, namely corruption in Nigeria. Rather, "it is the responsibility of all members of society to promote and work for the common good."[123] Such common good refers to, among other things, "responsible justification and substantiation of our values and beliefs."[124] A emphasis of this nature was made in chapter 2 of this study (see section 2.4.2), when we discussed the collective role in enhancing morals.[125] Additionally, positive collaboration between different measures provided, is perhaps the first[126] real empirical indication that integrity works to enhance accountability and control of corruption, and is a good reason for continuing approaches to anti-corruption policy. Such an idea affirms what Sacks says regarding our role in making God's world that is fractured, a better place. He succinctly puts it that

> we are here to make a difference, to mend the fractures of the world, a day at a time, an act at a time, for as long as it takes to make it a place of justice and compassion where the lonely are not alone, the poor not without help; where the cry of the vulnerable is heeded and those who are wronged are heard.[127]

---

122. Bradstock and Russel, "Politics, Church," 171.
123. Bradstock and Russel, 175.
124. Veldsman, "Discussing Publicness," 557.
125. In chapter 2 we discussed the need for developing morals that would ensure a habitable society. Three places namely, family, church, and schools were mentioned as important places where morals could be taught, specifically on how to detest corrupt practices. Bringing this idea here would mean that living with integrity as a prerequisite for ethics of responsibility could have meaningful impact while discussing the scourge of corruption on human dignity.
126. Brown and Heinrich, "National Integrity Systems," 290.
127. Sacks, *To Heal*, 5.

Adding to Sacks's concern, to imagine having a world – like in Nigeria – without dignity being undermined, would mean intensifying our efforts to ensure the recognition and the enhancement of human dignity. Only people of integrity can offer hospitality to a stranger that Sacks finds to be "an act greater than receiving the divine presence because that is religion at its most humanizing and humane."[128] This echoes what Williams said about a Christian's faith in corporate life. He avows that it is life that takes on the task of ensuring habitation for God who is visible only when a human life gives place and offers hospitality to God.[129] For a contemporary Christian ethic of responsibility eligible to address issues of corruption in Nigeria, therefore, integrity in the discussions and of the people must be held in high regard. Integrity in seeing and responding to issues of public morality must be given high priority.

6.2.5 The Need for Confession

Following the previous point on integrity, the ethic of responsibility in Nigeria should also have a confessional paradigm. Confession, as refers here, goes beyond the usual acknowledgment of wrongs committed against the other. Rather, it involves voicing and accepting blame for things not done appropriately, whether not speaking or standing for the course of justice for the other. In that case, whether done deliberately or not, provided they have contributed to fuelling demeaning activities against human persons, the need arises for professing. It is an idea that dissociates from retrospective perspective of responsibility that seeks legal actions on past actions without an onward-looking attitude. Instead, confession here takes as a point of departure from the past actions, both those the agent was actively involved in or not; whether s/he acted ignorantly or consciously. The focus is to speak out the involvement or knowledge regarding the past. This falls in line with de Villiers's mention of "focus area" as a feature of a contemporary Christian ethic of responsibility (see section 5.5.1.2). By so doing, there would be better prospects for the future that are learned from past errors. We shall, therefore, look at confession as a feature for the proposed ethic of responsibility in Nigeria and how it could address the notion of corruption with its daunting effects on human dignity.

---

128. Sacks, 5.
129. Williams, *Faith in the Public*.

Toward an Ethics of Responsibility for Safeguarding Human Dignity 319

With the Nigerian context being multi-diversified, for the sake of relevance, the ethic of responsibility must first name its calling, given the present realities befalling the nation. As it is no longer news that the Nigerian nation faces debilitating challenges confronting the flourishing and wellbeing of its citizens through the scourge of corruption, ethics of responsibility must be responsible to identify these challenges.[130] On the one hand, it should explain its objectives which include, but are not limited to, the need for religious, ethnic and regional tolerance, and the quest to combine efforts to combat the common enemy (corruption). On the other hand, it must declare an intention for collective responsibility to safeguard and enhance the human dignity of the Nigerian persons. Such a declaration must be accompanied by a commitment to the unity of purpose such as coming to agree on the task of co-responsibility for the common good of society.

Confession, as Smit observes, is an important contribution to public life. In it, following the experiences of apartheid in South Africa, he emphasises that confession is important for three reasons: first, saying yes, affirming what we are committed to, what we believe in and what we find important; second, it is saying no, denying what we regard as false and exposing and rejecting what we want to resist (in the light of our eyes); and third, it is saying we feel implicated in what went wrong, we are sorry, we do not fully see, we do not understand, we have not listened properly, we did not care enough, we are also part of the problem, not the solution.[131] Smit's analysis of confession was for what had already happened. In the case of Nigeria, this study speaks of confession in present continuous terms of what is currently happening. In that case, as a people, Nigerians would have to ask and provide answers to the following question: how does persistent undermining of human dignity affect our religious beliefs, political affiliation, and what gains or losses (if any) exist? There must be a conscious commitment to examine our participation in public affairs to see what contribution it makes in building societal wellbeing and human flourishing. We perhaps would need to see differently, think differently and act differently. Only then shall we realize our misappropriation, misunderstanding, and mistreatment of human persons, which

---

130. For more on human flourishing, see Volf, *Flourishing: Why We Need*, and Marais, "Imagining Human Flourishing."

131. Smit, "Contributions of Religions," 298.

we either have directly or indirectly contributed, by being part of making the actualisation of basic human needs difficult, what this study in chapter 2 calls denial of human dignity. Or we have been silent when our voices, faces and commitment to safeguarding human dignity was needed – what Bonhoeffer calls irresponsibility[132] and, Kretzschmar calls immoral leadership.[133]

Following the above argument, we gathered the need for confession. It is confessing our lack or failure of involvement in making a positive impact on public life, as Smit suggests. It is confessing that we have acted below the expectation to protect, respect, and promote the inherent dignity of human persons. It is confessing that we share the guilt committed against humanity at the time we live – this, is accepting co-responsibility. It is confessing the tinted legacy we prepare for the future generation, a legacy which they would have no clear lines to direct and live in a nation they proudly call their own. Perhaps it is confessing our failure to protest the evil befalling humanity. In all these, the ethic of responsibility in Nigeria ought to call for confession for a meaningful anticipated public life thereof. Such ethic seeks to not only understand the plight of the people but provide responsible ways to act and live. It is such an ethic that would thoroughly address the sins committed against humans both in the past and present, not by probing for a retrospective, but prospective responsibility. An ethic whose interest is the wellbeing of human persons, in this context, promoting human dignity.

6.2.6 An Orientation towards the Future

Theories are formulated to provide frameworks for understanding human behaviour, thought, and development. In some cases, they exist to explain, predict and seek to understand concepts while challenging the existing knowledge with critical assumptions. In the context of this study, the formulation of a theory entails providing a framework that informs the human attitude towards combating corruption, and seeks to challenge the effectiveness of the existing anti-corruption campaigns. This is done with the aim of exposing the blight of corruption on the dignity of human persons. The contemporary Christian ethic of responsibility for the Nigerian context must, therefore, orientate towards the future. This refers to how people ponder about assessing,

---

132. Bonhoeffer, *Ethics*, 54.
133. Kretzschmar, "The Formation of Moral," 86.

viewing and creating the future for themselves and others. It describes how humans express dissatisfaction with what is going on while seeking, thinking, and planning for better ways for themselves. It informs people's readiness for bettering not only their wellbeing but also of the "others." By this model of orientation, what concerns the "other" at present, and the future generation, is treated with much enthusiasm. Also, this model clearly captures the drive of prospective model of responsibility.

From what we learn from Levinas and his concept of the "other," a true Levinasian would always submit to a previously adopted strategy for scrutiny under the inspiration for the ethical appeals of the others.[134] Levinas recognizes that the consequences of ethical conduct have ethical meaning, namely that consideration regarding the consequences belongs to the essence of the moment of decision making in the face of the plurality of others.[135] The ethical meaning conceived from ethical conduct, however, determines the consequences. Wolff finds that if the consequences of ethical conduct have ethical meaning, then it is impossible to avoid thinking about ethics not exclusively in terms of the meaning of the face of the other, but to think strategically.[136]

Here, to think strategically means having to prioritise and to ultimately make a sacrifice in the name of the maximisation of justice. It means having to live beyond the norm that threatens freedom and flourishing of the other, but seek to defend the course of livelihood for others. It means choosing to be a good person, who Larocco equates to being civic. To be uncivil by questioning or criticizing the justice of instituted suffering in its various forms becomes paradoxically unjust, and an unfair way to treat those who are defending the order of what is.[137] This is thinking not only for here and now, but also for future. First, to sacrifice for the course of justice to whom the same is denied, and second, a choice not to obey anything that supports infringing on the "other" of freedom to live and thrive. That means, what becomes the ethical appeal for the "other" goes further than a desire for human fulfilment. Human realisation considered from the context of human struggles, some would suggest, is found beyond the shores of the world we live in. Purcell,

---

134. Wolff, *Political Responsibility*, 209.
135. Wolff, 215.
136. Wolff, 215.
137. Larocco, "The Other," 3.

however, views human fulfilment differently as not a withdrawal[138] from the world, but rather as a commitment to the world . . . being in the world for him is to be incarnate and enfleshed. Perceiving human fulfilment as such requires that a human person becomes real to the concerns of others with a readiness to create a future that promises protection, respect and promotion of human dignity. This would mean the provision of ways to live dignifying lives in the world that is chaotic and fractured with corruption, as in the case of Nigeria. This gives rise to the need to responsibly think for here and now, but importantly, for the future while thinking and planning to actualise the aspirations for a more humane society.

A futuristic orientation as a feature of the contemporary Christian ethic of responsibility in addressing the scourge of corruption in Nigeria would need to understand the significance of the other in order to uncover the existing barriers keeping us from seeing humanity through and in others. This is done not only for the "other" here and now, but also for the future generations and how they go on living. This was Bonhoeffer's concern as well. The fragmentation of the humanity of the "other" in Nigeria does not only call for an ethos of hospitality but also of acceptance and tolerance. Accepting the "other" with the acknowledgment that we, too, are considered the "others" in God's world. The contemporary Christian ethic of responsibility then invites for an intentional dialogue to investigate the divisive factors hindering the humanity of the "other" from recognition. The contours of corruption becoming harmful to human dignity should ignite sensitivity for the wellbeing of those on the margins. Those in Nigeria include victims of insecurity, sexual harassment, marginalization, and who are living without basic human needs. Their rights for being human are exchanged for selfish ambitions by the policy-makers, who care litle regarding the wellbeing of those on the margins.[139] These persons are hopeless with both the present predicaments as well as the future. They ask questions on what would be of their children's generation in the future with no concrete answers. Within such a situation, the need for responsible action, which in this case, involves how we think, plan and respond to those issues of concern befalling us here and now as well as those that concern the future which would be lived without us.

---

138. Purcell, *Levinas and Theology*, 73.
139. Umaru, "Corruption as a Threat."

6.2.7 Relational Anthropology

The discipline of anthropology covers studies related to humanity. In theological anthropology, for instance, the relationality between God and creatures, particularly human beings, is made clear. This, therefore, suggests that anthropology deals with studies that inform human existence with other humans and nature. In our search for features of the ethic of responsibility in Nigeria, however, we shall argue that it be relationally anthropological, to seek and identify ways of dealing with the human creatures who are both relational and social beings. Those are human creatures whose lives are endangered constantly through the violation of their dignity. To ensure commitment to salvaging the dilemma, the ethic of responsibility would aim to humanize the Nigerian society, making it suitable for human existence and flourishing, and thereby develop a model that addresses ethical living and action.

The politics of being human has engulfed different fields of study. The argument holding on what should characterize a human person has neither spared[140] the theology discipline nor others such as sociology, psychology, biology, neuroscience, or cultural anthropology. Such conversations have influenced the way human dignity is perceived (see section 3.3). Within such differentiation in meaning, human history reveals why ill-treatment of others became and still is the norm by other human beings. In one of these theories, Richard Kearney aligns this to the time we live when he says that "in an age crippled by a crisis of identity and legitimation, it would seem particularly urgent to challenge the polarization between Us and Them."[141] The continuous imagination of, and perhaps involvement, is Kearney's concern on the crisis of identity[142] blindfolds humanity from recognizing the essence of the other. Terry Eagleton, thus, outlines some of the primary elements of the imaginary and says that:

> a projection or imaginative transposition into the interior of another's body; the physical mimesis of 'by the very mien and gesture (of the other) we arise and fall in their condition;' the 'contagiousness' by which two human subjects share the same inner condition; the visual immediacy with which the other's

---

140. Horan, "Beyond Essentialism," 94, 96.
141. Kearney, *Strangers, Gods, and Monsters*, 5.
142. Further on identity politics, see Fukuyama, *Identity: Contemporary Identity Politics*.

inner state is communicated, so that the inside seems inscribed on the outside; and the exchange of positions or identities ('one man's eyes are spectacles to another').[143]

The above quotation reminds us of the connectivity and relationality that exist amongst human beings. It is one that indicates we are much closer and better together than apart; we have more elements that unite than separate us; as humans, we belong to each other. Eagleton summarises his comment by pointing out that "the necessary corollary of treating others as oneself is to treat oneself as another."[144] That reminds us of the notion of compassion which Forster thinks "could move diverse groups of persons toward a shared goal, namely the intention of achieving the fullness and flourishing of humanity."[145] From the concerns presented above, Kearney's sense of urgency to address the separating elements between "us and them," and Eagleton's view of the interconnectedness of human beings, when taken critically, inform us of the essence of our relationality that should generate a sense of compassion, as Forster puts it.

The human person here is the agent and centre of emphasis. As an agent, the human person can create an atmosphere suitable that both fellow humans and non-humans would co-exist, for if there be no agent there can be no action. To characterise an ethic of responsibility for the Nigerian context, the focus must be on the agent. The agent in question is one whose dignity is violated, but also is the perpetrator. Taking Kearney's concept of a stranger, for instance, the human person becomes the perpetrator of the human dignity of others when "others are not acknowledged as themselves . . . then we turn the Other into a monster and a god."[146] Such happenings occur when a human person loses the sense of humanness from the "other," who treats them in a violently inhumane manner. Since the stereotypical alluding of the "other" either as an alien or stranger blindfolds the sense of humour, the individual receives treatment not befitting its creatureliness. For the ethic of responsibility to address the debilitating effects of corruption on human dignity, it must take the recognition and placement of the human person,

---

143. Eagleton, *Trouble with Strangers*, 13.
144. Eagleton, 14.
145. Forster, "Affect, Empathy," 9.
146. Kearney, 5.

the agent, at the focal point. In this sense, the human person, as the victim of inhumanity, realizes and re-conceptualizes the essence of their being. On the contrary, the human agent, as the perpetrator, is called to confession over their involvement in the maltreatment of the "other." In that sense, the ethic of responsibility speaks responsibly.

Arguably, in recognizing relational anthropology, the ethic of responsibility understands a human person as a rational being. From a theological perspective, Huber explains this notion as it links to interpretation. He declares that relational[147] interpretation sees the creation of the human person in the image of God as a relatedness between God and his creature. Since relational anthropology seem to originate from creatureliness, as Huber puts it, the relatedness of human beings receives a boost which ethics of responsibility could explore to expand upon. When taking ethics of responsibility as relational anthropology, human persons are understood as communicative beings, as people who do not only listen to the call but answer the call, as Sacks understands it "life is God's call to responsibility."[148] According to Sacks, the call to responsibility urges our reactionary mode towards continuing what God calls us into. Again, he puts it well that "God, the ultimate Other, asks us to reach out to the human other. More than God is a strategic intervener, he is a teacher. More than God does our will, God teaches us how to do his."[149] To sum it all, we could agree with Sacks that "the ethic of responsibility is the best answer to the meaning and meaningfulness of a life."[150]

Similarly, relational anthropology helps us to better our understanding of a human person. Perhaps just as human dignity is understood by others as nothing anymore, there arises the need for the proper perception of a human person as a responsible being.[151] Here, Huber helps us to see four dimensions to understanding a responsible being, which showcases human relatedness.[152] First, a human person is related to God, second, related to the world, third, related to other humans, and lastly, related to oneself. Seen that way, a human person either as a perpetrator or victim is charged for the consequences of

---

147. Huber, "Ethics of Responsibility," 9.
148. Sacks, *To Heal*, 5.
149. Sacks, 3.
150. Sacks, 6.
151. Bedford-Strohm, "Human Dignity," 210.
152. Huber, 9.

their action or inaction to God, to the world, to others, and to oneself. This understanding helps us to see the value of life as a whole, which would make us realize that "most time we spent pursuing things turn out to be curiously irrelevant."[153] We fail to discover the social reality in human beings that guard our perception of the "other." Jesus, for example, presented in the gospels analogically as *Immanuel*, "God with us," invites us to be "with" the others. Being with the others, particularly when the "other" who, in the Nigerian context, does not belong to our company, is broad. In the one sense, it could be a call for tolerance of the difference we see in the "other" that makes them less than "us," or in another sense, agreeing on common grounds to fight a common human enemy. In the latter case, the collaboration suggests our relational human identity that seeks the interest of other human beings. In the former case, the idea of tolerating the differences in others reminds us that we also are different from their side, hence, they think differently about us. That way, relational anthropology reminds us of our shared humanity.

6.3 Chapter Summary

In this chapter we revisited the discussions in the previous chapters with the aim of bringing to the reader the effectiveness of the contemporary Christian ethic of responsibility proposed by de Villiers in chapter 5. In doing so, we integrated his thoughts on how to deal with public morality, particularly in the Nigerian society. The discussions led us to emphasise the place of compatibility in the recognition and enhancement of human dignity. Helpfully so, we discovered the need to further the discussion on ethics of responsibility to the Nigerian context in which we highlighted some of its features.

Regarding the promotion and enhancement of human dignity, we outlined three modalities through which human dignity could be recognized, enhanced, and be protected. First, we argued that the enhancement and promotion of human dignity require societal responsibility. Arguing from the perspective of togetherness and unity of purpose towards achieving a goal, there comes a strand of responsibility that society must exhibit. This involves acknowledging the differences there are in roles of society, and those of individual persons regarding their worth. It involves the realisation that

---

153. Sacks, *To Heal*, 6.

humiliating structures are threatening human flourishing, hence, we must seek ways to combat them to create a more humane society. Also, societal responsibility involves the discovery that individuals must join others to change institutions threatening human wellbeing. Collective responsibility of society emerges when society seeks the interest of the "other," who could be anyone. This "other" is one whose hope for life might be failing. In all, recognizing that everyone in society matters for simply being human, would create a sense of compassion for all. As such, the society's unity of purpose for specific goals would result in an unimaginable outcome.

Second we considered human dignity and personal responsibility. We argued here that an individual has a responsibility towards enhancing their human dignity. It was argued using a theoretical framework of self-respect while rejecting a thorough assumption portrayed by altruism. Human persons are entitled to safeguard their dignity and inculcate their self-respect. Such a realisation, however, comes through the discovery of the worth they have without having to rely on what is accorded. These phenomena are indicators that by discovering one's self-image and respect, the same applies to identifying humanity in others. It enables one to re-imagine the humanity in others as well as their own. Although personal responsibility towards the enhancement of individual worth is possible, one of the conditions that necessitate this possibility is the notion of freedom or liberty.

Third, we considered that the recognition and enhancement of human dignity requires personal liberty. In discussing that notion, we engaged some thoughts from Thomas Aquinas on specification and exercise. These two concepts emphasized on the need to specify a problem and the attitude towards proffering a solution to it. The problem in this context is the undermining condition of corruption on the dignity of human persons. Identification and specification of the problem, however, determines the attitude in fighting its cause. We, therefore, concluded that knowing a specific problem (corruption) as the blight to human dignity requires a certain amount of freedom to combat it. The freedom referred to here is to choose the kind of life an individual has reasoned to value which, in this case, involves the freedom to protect and enhance the dignity of oneself and other human beings. It is a positive sort of liberty that seeks the interest and flourishing of others.

In all, the threats that corruption poses on human dignity could be engaged through different dimensions. First, it must become a personal responsibility for everyone; second, it must become a responsibility for communities to combat against vices such as corruption that are a threat to public morality; third, freedom must be used for a just course in that personal liberty must be guided by ethical-moral standards.

Going by the above discussion, we can gather that recognition and enhancement of human dignity is multidimensional. Corruption being the common enemy grants that we both have the responsibility of intensify our engagement with it, both as individuals and through societal collaboration that requires liberty. To ensure this understanding gets through to the Nigerian human persons, the ethics of responsibility must be taken seriously. It must seek certain qualifications to become an effective model to enhance the fight against corruption and to enhance the promotion and protection of human dignity. In that regard, the last section of this chapter proposed some features of ethics of responsibility that would sufficiently befit the context of Nigeria. These features seek to bring together stakeholders from different circles of influence for dialogue on what such ethics entail.

In conclusion, we say the ethics of responsibility is an effective tool to enhance the fight against corruption. First, it provides the existing anti-corruption agencies in Nigeria a boost for effective operation. Second, it addresses the significance of human and societal wellbeing through exploring what being responsible for human and society entails. Third, it teaches on the attitude of a responsible agent who seeks not only self-interest, but also the interest of the "other."

CHAPTER 7

Summary and Conclusions

7.1 Introduction

This study sought to outline the extent to which corruption undermines human dignity in Nigeria. The study began by sketching some root causes of corruption in Nigeria (see section 2.4). It was gathered that a continuous spread of corruption in a country full of numerous religious claims suggests a loss of conscience towards the recognition and enhancement of human dignity. This study, therefore, proposes the need for a new ethos of approach to addressing moral issues that are hampering human and societal wellbeing.[1]

Considering the above, the aim of this study was to present a more contextual and theological understanding of human dignity as it is often misinterpreted, which in turn, leads to the assumption that some people are to be treated with more dignity than others. Or simply put, some people are considered to have more dignity or are more human than others. With that in mind, the study unveils the extent to which human dignity is violated through acts of corruption in Nigeria. In summary, this study sought to achieve the following research objectives:

1. To gain an understanding of how corruption is perceived in Nigeria, the ways in which it is being curbed, and the extent to which it violates human dignity

---

1. Kure, "Leadership, Corruption," 1–7; Umaru, "An Ethos of Responsibility," 199–213.

2. To unpack the concept of human dignity with the variation in meaning, and how the lack of a coordinated perception of it results in violation through various human actions such as corruption
3. To interrogate the theological contribution that an ethic of responsibility could offer in the struggle against corruption in Nigeria
4. To examine the ways in which ethical resources could contribute to human dignity in Nigeria.

These objectives triggered the formulation of the following secondary questions that the study sought to answer:

1. How could corruption be understood in the Nigerian context?
2. In what ways is the dignity of human persons challenged by corruption in Nigeria?
3. What theological resources could an ethic of responsibility offer to address corruption in the Nigerian context?
4. How might these identified ethical resources contribute to combating the scourge of corruption towards the safeguarding of human dignity in Nigeria?

Moreover, the above secondary questions contributed toward answering the primary research question of: How could an ethic of responsibility contribute toward the safeguarding of human dignity within the context of corruption in Nigeria?

These questions were answered through the different chapters of the study as summarized in the section below.

7.2 A Discussion of the Major Findings

This section presents the major summary from individual chapters and proposes answers to the research questions highlighted above. This study is divided into seven chapters with the following pivot and some of their conclusions presented below.

Chapter 1 presented the general introduction and background to the study and highlighted the methodology employed in the study. In this chapter, the background to the key themes was given, which served well to present the reader with general ideas of the research therein. The chapter also provided a statement of the problem, the research aim and objectives, as well as the methodology employed in the study.

Chapter 2 traced, outlined and evaluated the general perception of corruption in Nigeria. Key components of the chapter were perceptions of corruption from theological/anthropological viewpoints, political form of corruption, and religious form of corruption; the causes of corruption in Nigeria; the effects of corruption in Nigeria, and the existing efforts toward curbing the spread of corruption in Nigeria. The chapter is summarized as follows:

1. The chapter provided some perspectives from which corruption was considered. These include theological/anthropological, moral, and religious, and political forms of corruption. These perspectives suggested that corruption is a human problem that began since the fall.[2] To understand corruption properly would mean understanding the extent of human intention toward self and material things. It further gathered that the result of such human choice is why we leave scars. These scars require what Igboin calls "moral transformation" such that humanity can be redeemed from itself and the excessive yearning for material things.[3]

2. Equally, the chapter outlined some reasons for a continuous spread of corruption in Nigeria. These include, failure of leadership, greed, failure in moral upbringing, loss of a sense of humanity, and holistic poverty (see section 2.4). It is no longer news that leadership crisis and corruption are among the greatest obstructions to democratic stability and economic development in Nigeria today.[4] If the relationship between leadership and corruption becomes mutually inclusive – as we see happening in Nigeria today – it grants access to the rise in corruption and other human vices. At such an emergence, it is a demonstration that leaders have failed and lack the wheel to lead. Such leaders are described as "immoral"[5] and are "irresponsible

---

2. Aben, "The Trinity and Public Theology," 39–47.
3. Igboin, *Corruption: A New Thinking*, 1.
4. Ebegbulem, "Corruption and Leadership," 221.
5. Kretzschmar, "The Formation of Moral," 27.

to lead."[6] Only leaders who are responsible can: speak against any evil committed against humanity, speak for the marginalized and seek to enhance their wellbeing, objectively seek the flourishing of society and its inhabitants. Such leaders do not rejoice when their subjects are subjected to dehumanisation.

3. The chapter went further to outline the effects of corruption in Nigeria. The following areas were considered: the effects on the people, the effects on the Nigerian economy, and the escalation of terrorism (see section 2.5). On the people, corruption has resulted in basic human needs not being provided for Nigerians. This happens because of mismanagement of human and material resources that are meant to serve the needs of the populace. As a result, human dignity is violated because what is needed to make life worth living for an average Nigerian is not provided. This is not because of shortages in supply, but selfishness, insensitive conscience toward the cruelty against humanity.[7] More importantly is the unimaginative rise in insecurity where countless human lives are taken either through kidnappings, killed by bandits, Boko Haram insurgency, or Fulani herdsmen. The continuous exposure of human lives to danger as such, in the opinion of this study, suggests a total failure of leadership to its primary responsibility – to protect human lives. Otherwise, recent opinions from some quarters suggest that citizens should arise and defend themselves else they are killed one after the other.[8]

4. The last section of the chapter looked at the current effort toward anti-corruption in Nigeria by analysing three agencies, namely, the government instituted agencies (EFCC and ICPC), civil society organisations, and religious institution (see section 2.6). It was outlined that these agencies have made some giant strides and have recorded some successes. However, they are accused of not doing enough. One way to get rid of such criticisms would be that the agencies, especially the government instituted ones, reconsider their goals and objectives, and focus on doing their job. One of the goals for

---

6. Kure, "Leadership, Corruption," 6.
7. Kure, 4–5.
8. Umaru, "Corruption as a Threat."

their establishment was to ensure there are "no sacred cows" with corruption cases when it comes to prosecution (see section 2.6.1). That way, the fight against corruption would be intensified beyond speeches and into responsible actions.

The chapter gathered that corruption is still an impending moral, social, theological and political problem in Nigeria, whose marketers and distributors remain human beings. The need to go beyond the traditional "speeches without action," "public life parallel to private life," "religious beliefs void of seeking human wellbeing and societal development" is urgent and necessary (see 6.2.1). The study, therefore, suggests that corruption be painted as it is: a blight to human dignity. This study also proposes that for corruption to be under control in Nigeria, an "ethic of living must be accompanied by an ethic of doing." This means that what is said, whether in public or private, a religious or moral belief that abhors immoral acts such as corruption must have full public expression and be rendered immoral by all. Any attempt to justify an immoral act, irrespective of the motivation, renders the effort against corruption futile.

Chapter 3 presented an overview of the concept of human dignity. The focus of the chapter was to present a more textured, theological understanding of human dignity and its relation to violation by incessant corruption in Nigeria. The chapter was divided into four major sections:

1. An overview of why human dignity discourse has become relevant in recent times. It was gathered that cruel human activities towards themselves and nature are among the pointers towards the current human dignity discourse (see section 3.3). This remains so because humans are meaning-seekers who desire recognition and lives worth living. While recognizing that we are "in the time of many worlds"[9] where what was unthinkable in the time past – such as human cruelty towards each other – has now become our reality.[10] Such forms of violence committed by humans against other human beings has been described as the worst kind of violence.[11] Considering corruption,

---

9. Schweiker, *Theological Ethics*, xi.
10. Hauerwas, *The Peaceable Kingdom*, 4.
11. Huber, *Violence: the Unrelenting*, 6.

an evil perpetrated by human beings, which results in the violation of human dignity, we could resonate with why discourses regarding the recognition and enhancement of human dignity are timely and urgent (see section 6.2.1).

2. The second segment of the chapter was a historical overview of the notion of human dignity. This idea was covered through the early church, the middle ages and the wake of the enlightenment. Prominently in this section was Immanuel Kant's categorical imperatives of "doing to humanity either in your person or in the person of others, always as an end and never as a means only" (see section 3.3.3).[12] This statement affirms the inalienability of human dignity (see section 3.4.2).

3. The chapter equally highlighted some perspectives on human dignity. The idea was to uncover how best to understand the concept in relation to what informed the study. In this regard, human dignity was understood from an ontological, inherent and inviolable, social, humanist and from a Christian anthropological perspective (se section 3.3). The emphasis was made in relation to Kant's categorical imperative regarding human dignity.[13]

4. Since the context of the study is Nigeria, a section of the chapter reviewed how human dignity is perceived using a few cultures as microcosm for the whole (see section 3.4). The point of departure from that section is the need to live in harmony[14], and accord human dignity to one another, which is a sure way to be truly humans.

5. It was equally gathered that human dignity discourses would be objectively verified without a mention of human rights (see section 3.5). A section of the chapter presented a sort of relationship between these two important concepts. One thing worthy of mention is the fact that Human Rights were instituted to safeguard human dignity.

This chapter gathered that lack of a unified understanding of human dignity is key to its non-recognition and undermining. Being almost a universal concept enshrined in the constitutions of many countries and the United

---

12. Novak, "The Judeo-Christian Foundation," 108.
13. Kant, *Groundwork for the Metaphysics*.
14. Aben, "The Trinity and Public Theology," 46.

Nations, human dignity still varies in meaning. As result of these various conceptions, the violation takes different forms which does not, in some contexts, seem as violation because of variation therein the meaning of it. Two ways human dignity is violated, particularly in Nigeria are lack of provision of basic human needs to enhance livelihood and societal wellbeing, and the second is the use of human beings as means to achieving ends. This is something that must be addressed if human dignity matters to all, and if the discourse about it is to be taken to a more intentional level. From these findings, this study observes some reasons for a continual nonhuman dignity undermining of human dignity. First, there is no universal and common perception of human dignity which might have resulted in why different concepts are used to define something that should be a universal component. In this view lies the awareness of different belief systems but holds from the fact that every belief system deals with human beings whose dignity, in all cases, is violated. For this to be addressed, human dignity as enshrined in many national constitutions, must be revisited with clearer explanations of its worth. One of these reminders would be that "without dignity the human person loses their sense of humanity" (see section 3.4.5). To recognize and enhance human dignity is to uphold and celebrate humans, the carrier of dignity. The second reason for a continuous violation of human dignity which this study gathers is depravity of the human mind. Despite the proper universalisation of human dignity, human beings must learn to live and treat each other with dignity for simply being humans. This is an instinct that must develop from an individual, communal, and to the global space (see section 6.1.2). Agitation claiming certain privileges for a few individuals while depriving a majority of their sense of livelihood, for whatsoever reason, must be rejected and taken as a point of concern for every human being anywhere. No one is more human than another just as no human has more dignity than another. As a human family, any violation of this communal responsibility results in undermining human dignity.

Chapter 4 introduced the theological resource, ethics of responsibility from different dimensions and contexts as follows:

1. The chapter set the historical setting of ethics of responsibility by surveying the works of Max Weber, who was the first to coin the idea (see section 4.2). His quest for a representative and responsible

democracy, whose interests should be on enhancing humans and their communities, led him to choose an ethic of responsibility over the ethic of conviction.

2. The chapter took to present the reception of ethics of responsibility in the German theological context. In doing this, two notable German theologians, Deitrich Bonhoeffer and Wolfgang Huber had their works surveyed as a representation for the context (see sections 4.3.1 and 4.3.2).

3. Also from the German context was the works of the philosopher, Hans Jonas, whose work had made tremendous contribution in the field of ethics of responsibility, with specific focus on the impact of technological advancement on future generation (see section 4.3.3).

4. Following the German context, the chapter extended the search for ethics of responsibility to the American context. In doing this, the views of H. R. Niebuhr and his brother, Reinhold Niebuhr, were consulted. Following this were the views of William Schweiker, a contemporary theologian that has taken the discourse on ethics of responsibility further in the American context after the Niebuhrian brothers (see section 4.3.4).

5. The last part of the chapter traced ethics of responsibility in the African context (see section 4.4). This section revealed some concepts regarding ethics of responsibility from the African context. It was, however, clearly stated that nothing substantial has been made until the work of Etienne de Villiers, which is discussed in chapter 5.

From the above summary, the study found it interesting to observe the ongoing conversations in the area of ethics of responsibility, and how promising they could be towards salvaging ethical living in contemporary society. There were, however, challenges that are worth mentioning here for the purpose of further study. One of these is the incompatible views of the proponents of ethics of responsibility regarding its definition, and perhaps its meaning and applicability. This is something that makes engaging the idea in its whole difficult, despite most of the proponents drawing their sources from Max Weber. The context in which every inquiry that is informed by ethics of responsibility is based determines its applicability, and the school of thought informing one's thinking; either social, theological, ethical or philosophical.

Chapter 5 was more specific to the African context, but particularly studied the works of Etienne de Villiers, who is the foremost contemporary proponent of Christian ethics of responsibility in Africa. One specific interest of this chapter was that it provided the road map to the crux of this study in chapter 6. In chapter 5, de Villiers's proposal for a contemporary Christian ethic of responsibility presents some helpful approaches to deal with issues of public morality. Among others, these issues range from corruption, social injustice, undermining of human dignity, economic inequality, racism, tribalism, xenophobia and all other forms of marginalisation. As a result of the guidelines from chapter 5, the study was able to propose some features of a contemporary Christian ethic of responsibility for the Nigerian context (see section 6.2).

Chapter 6 summed up the discussion of the study. The first part of the chapter (see sections 6.1.1 and 6.1.2) attempted to respond to the research questions that were highlighted in chapter one (see section 1.3.1). The second part of the chapter, however, focused on making a proposal for a contemporary Christian ethic of responsibility to make a theological contribution to the struggle against corruption in Nigeria (see section 6.2). In doing this, the chapter made a proposal with features that would inform such an ethic, and how it would fit into the struggle against corruption to salvage human dignity from violation. The idea of combating corruption which informed this study is the fact that human dignity is under siege because of corruption. Due to the diversity in Nigeria, including diverse religious views, the proposal took notice of those factors to present an ethic that would be all encompassing and all accommodative, whose aim is to salvage ethical living, recognize and enhance the integrity of human life in the context of corruption.

In the summary of the chapter, this study reports a few things. First, just as the fight against corruption has a personal responsibility, the protection, respect, and promotion of human dignity also has a personal dimension. Second, combating corruption has a communal dimension where immoral behaviour gets communal objection or praise, as it is with human dignity. The responsibility, however, rests on individual persons to make ethical decisions for moral living by rejecting and frowning at immoral lifestyles. This is possible because of personal liberty in the form of freedom, which has constitutional backing in some spheres. Although this be true, the individual or society is responsible for moral decisions and actions they take and must be ready to give an answer to either their actions or inactions, particularly regarding moral decision and living.

Chapter 7 sums up the highpoints of the study. The chapter recapped the major findings from the preceding chapters. In doing this, the chapter brings the whole study to a close with some concluding remarks

7.3 Contribution of This Research

7.3.1 Theological Ethics

At the core of a theoretical contribution of this study rests the principles that calls for a contextual interaction with concepts and ideas and how they impact and are impacted by communities. In this study, the challenge of corruption and its impact on human dignity of Nigerians was considered to have possibilities for a new view to public morality and ways to salvage ethical living through an ethic of responsibility.

- Ethics of responsibility opens possibilities that transpose blame games to being proactive for the good of oneself and the good of the "other."
- There are possibilities that threats to public morality could be addressed through an ethic of responsibility.

7.3.2 The Nigerian Context

At the heart of a practical contribution rests the principles that call for active participation and responsibility by every Nigerian in the face of dehumanizing consequences of corruption.

- Intentionality as a base for the struggle against corruption: To ensure some level of success in this struggle against corruption in Nigeria, there ought to be an intentional commitment which aims at salvaging the country from devaluation and ridicule by the global community. This is because corruption has been a contributory factor as to why many Nigerians are regarded often as fraudsters for simply being Nigerians.
- Doing the right thing even when no one else does: In the case of avoiding immoral acts such as corruption, which is celebrated in some corners, there is always a room for developing a personal

ethic. Such an ethic builds and modifies one's perspective towards what is right and wrong regarding ethical moral values, but also develops in one a perspective to life and moral values.
- A rediscovery of societal/communal moral values: The synergy that was used in the struggle against colonialism and many other social injustices was a demonstrated commitment against the evil done to humanity. Similarly, corruption being a moral evil, requires such collaboration which aims at salvaging humanity against the evils done in the form of dehumanisation of human dignity.
- It could be anyone's fault: Both those that have been indicted, those that are currently engaging irresponsibly, and those who watch without saying or taking positive actions against the evils of corruption on human dignity could be grouped as perpetrators of corruption. It takes people of courage and commitment, which everyone could choose to be, to seek the interest of others with the aim of enhancing the integrity of their lives. It is, therefore, a responsibility for all, and not just for some people, to ensure that corruption in all circles be described "a national disaster" in Nigeria.

7.4 Possibilities for Future Research

Unity in understanding and application of ethics of responsibility: If ethics of responsibility could be developed to have some unifying idea this would make it promising to address public morality than when its proponents have a parallel view of it.

Ethic of responsibility as a virtue in theological ethical discourse: If an ethic of responsibility could be developed as a contemporary moral virtue among existing ethical virtues.

The integration of ethics of responsibility with corruption proved that other societal vices such racism, poverty, inequality, and unemployment could be studied under the influence of an ethic of responsibility.

7.5 Final Conclusion

Corruption has enormous effects and metamorphoses daily in human affairs which, in turn, results in untold dehumanizing consequences. It is, however, not possible to bring an end to this menace until human beings who are its promoters, intentionally resolve to do so. Even when corruption is known as a blight eating up the human conscience, the combating effort against it remains a daunting task because it still enjoys patronisers who are blinded to its deception. This is one of the reasons why the yearning for recognition, promotion and protection of human dignity grows exponentially so that the existing efforts in curbing the spread of corruption in Nigeria have been unsuccessful. To this end, the struggle against corruption must be triggered by the increasing violation to human dignity. Where the worth of a human being is considered above and over human greediness is where responsible actions and decisions are taken.

Some failures of the existing anti-corruption agencies in Nigeria were mentioned in this study, perhaps their efforts have been evidently unsuccessful. One of the reasons for failure is that the majority population have always assumed corruption as solely a political, social and economic issue, and almost ignored the moral fabric of it. Following the complexity in understanding corruption, it is suggested that concerted efforts are needed to stop it. Shifting blames and accusing a few persons for corruption has not really helped in this regard which is why a theory of responsibility is needed. Collective efforts must, however, be employed to consider the struggle against corruption as "our struggle" and desist from calling it "their struggle." This calls for responsible decisions and actions which are contained in the theory that is proposed in this study.

Nigeria is embattled with uncontrollable phases of corruption. Two reasons are suggested in this study to have caused this: First, the country is full of inept leadership, which has become insensitive towards recognition and enhancement of human dignity, and second, a myopic view of corruption. In response to this reality, there is an urgent need for responsible decision, living, and action – the need to develop, and consciously cling onto having a "personal, communal and national ethic of responsibility" - in addressing societal moral issues such as corruption that has become a blight depriving human dignity of protection, promotion, and respect. Also needed, is having leaders that are intentional and are consciously sensitive towards the plight of humanity. To do this appropriately is to engage concrete deliberation suggested from ethics of responsibility. This theory of ethics of responsibility, as Etienne de Villiers foresees, would be adequate in addressing public moral issues in contemporary (Christian) society – but also in a diverse religious context like in Nigeria – a society that is plagued by corruption, whose effects undermines human dignity.

Bibliography

Action Aid Nigeria. *Corruption and Poverty in Nigeria*. Abuja, Nigeria, 2015.

Aben, T. "The Trinity and Public Theology." In *African Public Theology*, eds. S. B. Agang, H. J. Hendriks, and D.A. Forster, 39–47. Carlisle: HippoBooks, 2020.

Ackerman, D. "Becoming Fully Human: An Ethic of Relationship in Difference and Otherness." *Journal of Theology for Southern Africa* 102 (1998): 13–27.

Ackerman, R. S. *Corruption and Governance: Causes, Consequences, and Reform*. Cambridge: University Press, 1999.

AUABC. "Combating Corruption, Improving Governance in Africa: Regional Anti- Corruption Programme for Africa." Vol. 1. 2011.

Ademowo, A. J. "Boko Haram Insurgency and the Imperative of Promoting the Culture of Peace in Nigeria." *The International Journal of Business and Management* 3(2015): 224–229.

Adenike, E. T. "An Econometric Analysis of the Impact of Corruption on Economic Growth in Nigeria." *Journal of Business Management and Economics* 4 (2013): 54–65.

Adenuga, A. A., and S. A. Omolawal. "Religious Values and Corruption in Nigeria: A Dislocated Relationship." *Journal of Educational and Social Research*, 4 (2014): 522–528.

Adesoji, A. "The Boko Haram Uprising and Islamic Revivalism in Nigeria." *Africa Spectrum* 2 (2010): 95–108.

Adkins, W. H. "Honour and Punishment in the Homeric Poems." *Bulletin of the Institute of Classical Studies* 7 (1960): 23–32.

Afolabi, O. O. "The Role of Religion in Nigerian Politics and its Sustainability for Political Development." *Net Journal of Social Sciences* 3 (2015): 42–49.

Agang, S. B. "Globalization and Terrorism: Corruption as a Case to Ponder." *Pyrex Journal of Law and Conflict Resolution* 2 (2016): 1–8.

———. "The Need for Public Theology in Africa." In *African Public Theology*, eds. S. B. Agang, J. H. Hendriks, and D. A. Forster, 3–14. Carlisle: HippoBooks, 2020.

Aguas, J. J. S. "The Notions of the Human Person and Human Dignity in Aquinas and Wojtyla." *Kritike,* 3 (2009): 40-60.

Ajibefun, M. B. "Social and Economic Effects of the Menace of Fulani Herdsmen Crisis in Nigeria." *Journal of Educational and Social Research* 8 (2018): 133-139.

Ajie, H.A and Gbenga, O. "Corruption and Economic Growth in Nigeria : An Empirical Analysis 1996 – 2013." *European Journal of Business and Management* 7 (2015): 224-243.

Akanbi, S. O. and J. Beyers. "The Church as a Catalyst for Transformation in the Society" *Theological Studies* 74 (2017): 1-8.

Akinbi, J. O. "Examining the Boko Haram Insurgency in Northern Nigeria and the Quest for a Permanent Resolution of Crisis." *Global Journal of Arts, Humanities and Social Sciences,* 3 (2015): 32-45.

Akindola, R.B., and Ehinomen, C.O. "Military Incursion, Tribalism, and Poor Governance: The Consequences for Development in Nigeria." *Mediterranean Journal of Social Sciences,* 8 (2017): 151-157.

Akinyemi, L. S. "Civil Society and the Anti-Corruption Struggle in Nigeria." *International Journal of Business and Social Science* 7 (2016): 115-127.

Akper, G. "An Ethos of Hospitality as Public Morality in the Face of the Disorderly Process in Nigeria Today?" *Stellenbosch Theological Journal* 1 (2015): 283-298.

———. "Is God in Nigeria ? Land Dislocation and the Challenge of Confessing Belhar in Nigeria Today." *Stellenbosch Theological Journal* 4 (2018): 61-72.

Aleyomi, M. B. "Corruption and Democratization Process in Nigeria's Fourth Republic."*International Journal of Politics and Good Governance* 4 (2013): 1-25.

Allen, P. L. "Sin and Natural Theology: An Augustinian Framework Beyond Barth." *NZSTh,* 57 (2015): 14-31.

Anazodo, R. O., C. J. Igbokwe-Ibeto, and B. C. Nkah. "Leadership, Corruption and Governance in Nigeria:Issues and Categorical Imperatives." *African Research Review* 9 (2015): 41-58.

Andorno, R. and A. Pele. "Human Dignity." In *Encyclopedia of Global Bioethics,* ed. H. Henk, 1-12. Switzerland: Springer, 2015.

Andorno, R. "Human Dignity and Human Rights as a Common Ground for a Global Bioethics."*Journal of Medicine and Philosophy* 34 (2009): 223-240.

Anthony, I. "'New Nigeria': 'A Socioreligious Dimension of Prophetics Envisioning." *Theological Studies* 74 (2018): 1-7.

Aquinas, T. *Nature and Grace.* Ed. A. M. Fairweather. Philadelphia: The Westminster Press, 1954.

———. *Virtues of Justice in the Human Community. Volume 41"* . Blackfriars, Oxford: Eyre & Spottiswoode, London, 1971.

———. *St Thomas Aquinas Summa Theologiae: The Gospel of Grace. Volume 30*. Blackfriars, Oxford: Eyre & Spottiswoode, London, and Mcgraw-Hill Book Company, New York, 1972.

Arendt, H. "Organized Guilt and Responsibility." *Jewish Frontier* 12 (1945): 146–212.

Aristotle. *Aristotle Nicomachean Ethics*. Indianapolis: Bobbs-Merrill Educational Publishing, 1981.

———. *Politics*. Kitchener: Batoche Books, 1999.

———. *Nicomachean Ethics*. London: Aeterna Press, 2015.

Asaju, K. "Sustaining Democratic Rule in Nigeria: The Corruption Tide." *Advanced in Social Sciences Research Journal* 1 (2014): 1–12.

Augustine. *The City of God. VIII–XVI*. Washington, DC: Catholic University of America Press, 2008.

Awojobi, O.N. "Political Corruption and Underdevelopment in Nigerian Fourth Republic." *International Journal of Innovation and Scientific Research* 11 (2014): 151–157.

Bagaric, Mirko and James Allan. "The Vacuous Concept of Dignity." *Journal of Human Rights* 5 (2006): 257–270.

Bagu, K. J. "Human Rights." In *African Public Theology* eds. S. B. Agang, J. H. Hendricks, and D. A. Forster, 205–219. Carlisle: HippoBooks, 2020.

Balot, R. K. *Greed and Injustice in Classical Athens*. Princeton: Princeton University Press, 2001.

Baloyi, G. T. "When Culture Clashes with Individual Human Rights: A Practical Theological Reflection on the Dignity of Widows." *Verbum et Ecclesia* 38 (2017): 1–11.

Bamidele, O. "Combating Terrorism: Socio Economic Issues, Boko Haram, and Insecurity in the North-Eastern Region of Nigeria." *Military and Strategic Affairs* 8 (2016): 109–131.

Banda, C. "Poverty." In *African Public Theology* eds. S. B. Agang, J. H. Hendricks, D. A. Forster, 113–126. Carlisle: HippoBooks 2020.

Bappah, H. Y. "Nigeria's Military Failure Against the Boko Haram Insurgency." *African Security Review* 25 (2016): 146–158.

Barbour, I. G. *Ethics in An Age of Technology: The Gifford Lectures Volume 2*. New York: HarperSanFrancisco, 1993.

Barth, K. *Church Dogamtics: The Doctrine of God Vol II*. Edinburgh, New York: T. & T. Clark, 1957.

———. *The Christian Life: Church Dogmatics IV, Lecture Fragments*. Grand Rapids: William B. Eerdmans Publishing Company, 1981.

———. "Respect for Life." In *On Moral Medicine: Theological Perspectives in Medical Ethics* eds. M.T. Lysaught, J. J. Kotva, S. F. Lammers, and A. Verhey, 724–733. Grand Rapids: Eerdmans, 2012.

Bayefsky, R. "Dignity, Honor, and Human Rights: Kant's Perspective." *Political Theory* 41 (2013): 809–837.

Bazin, D. "A Reading of the Conception of Man in Hans Jonas' Works: Between Nature and Responsibilty. An Environmental Ethics Approach." *Ethics and Economics* 2 (2004): 1–17.

Bedford-Strohm, H. "Human Dignity: A Global Ethical Perspective." *Scriptura* 104 (2010): 211–220.

Berry, R. J. *God's Book of Works: The Nature and Theology of Nature*. London/ New York: T. & T. Clark, 2003.

Beyers, J. "Self-Secularisation as Challenge to the Church." *Theological Studies* 71 (2015): 1–10.

Boesak, Allen. "A Hope Unprepared to Accept Things as They Are: Engaging John de Gruchy's Challenges for the 'Theology at the edge.'" *NGTT DEEl*, 1 (2014), 1055–1074.

Bonhoeffer, D. *Dietrich Bonhoeffer Ethics second ed*. The Fontana Library: Theology and Philosophy, 1968.

———. *Ethics: Dietrich Bonhoeffer's Works vol 6*. Minneapolis: Fortress Press, 2005.

Bradstock, Andrew and Hilary Russel. "Politics, Church and the Common Good." In *A Companion to Public Theology*, eds. S. Kim, and S. Day, 150–183. Leiden/ Boston: Brill, 2017.

Brand, G. *Speaking of a Fabulous Ghost: In Search of a Theological Criteria with Special Reference to the Debate on Salvation in African Theology*. Frankfurt: Peter Lang, 2002.

Bratt, J. D. *Abraham Kuyper: Modern Calvinist, Christian Democrat*. Grand Rapids: Eerdmans, 2013.

Breiner, P. *Max Weber and Democratic Politics*. Ithaca and London: Cornell University Press, 1996.

Brown, A. J. and F. Heinrich. "National Integrity Systems: An Evolving Approach to Anti-Corruption Policy Evaluation." *Crime Law Social Change* 68 (2017): 283-292.

Brown, L. M. *African Philosophy: New and Traditional Perspectives*. Oxford: Oxford University Press, 2004.

Le Bruyns, C. "Human Dignity and Moral Renewal." *Scriptura* 95 (2007): 202–212.

———. "The Church, Democracy, and Responsible Citizenship." In *Between Capital and Cathedral: Essays in Church-state Relationships*, eds. W. Bentley, and D.A. Forster, 59–72. Pretoria: Research Institute for Theology and Religion University of South Africa, 2012.

Buddeberg, E. "Ernst Wolff, Political Responsibility for a Globalized World: After Levinas' Humanism." *Ethic Theory Moral Practice* 15 (2012): 709–710.

Bujo, B. *The Ethical Dimension of Community: The African Model and the Dialogue Between North and South*. Nairobi: Paulines Publications in Africa, 1998.

Caiden, G. E. "Corruption and Governance." In *Where Corruption Lives*, G. E. Caiden, O. P. Dwivedi, and J. Jabbra, Bloomfield: Kumarian Press, 2001.

Campbell, R. L. "Altruism in August Comte and Ayn Rand." *The Journal of Ayn Rand Studies* 7 (2006): 357–369.

Campos, A. S. "Responsibility and Justice in Aristotle's Non-Voluntary and Mixed Actions." *Journal of Ancient Philosophy* 7(2013): 100–121.

Carlsson, A. B. "Blameworthiness as Deserved Guilt." *Journal of Ethics* 21 (2017): 89–115.

Chayes, S. *Thieves of State: Why Corruption Threatens Global Security*. New York: W.W. Norton & Company, 2015.

Chetwynd, E., F. Chetwynd, and B. Spector. *Corruption and Poverty: A Review of Recent Literature*. Washington, DC: 2003.

Cliteur, P., R. V. Wissen, and D. Haag. "Human Dignity as the Foundation for Human Rights." *Rechtstheorie* 35 (2004): 157–173.

Coetzer, W., and L. E. Snell. "A Practical-theological Perspective on Corruption: Towards a Solution-based Approach in Practice." *Acta Theologica* 33 (2013): 29–53.

Colson, C. W. "How Now Shall we Live?" *Journal of Markets & Morality*, 5(2002): 287–304.

Conradie, E. M. "Human Distinctiveness as a Journey of Discovery of (Human) Finitude." *Journal of Theology for Southern Africa* 128 (2007): 4–17.

———. "The Earth in God's Economy: Reflections on the Narrative of God's work." *Scriptura* 97 (2008): 13–36.

———. *The Earth in God's Economy: Creation, Salvation, and Consummation in Ecological Perspectives*. Zurich: Lit Verlag, 2015.

Coughlin, J. J. "Pope John Paul II and the Dignity of the Human Being." *Harvard Journal of Law & Public Policy* 27 (2003): 65–80.

D'Souza, J. "Greed: Crises, Causes, and Solutions." *International Journal of Humanitiesand Social Sciences* 5(2015): 1–6.

Dada, J. A. "Human Rights under the Nigerian Constitution: Issues and Problems." *International Journal of Humanities and Social Sciences* 2 (2012): 34–43.

Dales, R.C. "A Medieval View of Human Dignity" *Journal of History of Ideas*, 38 (1977): 557–572.

Daniel, A. and D. Nuebert. "Civil Society and Social Movements: Conceptual Insights and Challenges in African Contexts." *Critical African Studies* 11 (2019): 176–192.

Davis, W. "Max Weber on Religion and Poltical Responsibility." *Religion* 29 (1999): 29–60.

Doig, A. "Good Government and Sustainanble Anti-Corruption Strategies: A Role for Independent Anti-Corruption Agencies?" *Public Administration and Development* 15 (1995): 151–165.

Dolamo, R. T. "The Legacy of Black Consciousness: Its Continued Relevance for Democratic South Africa and its Significance for Theological Education." *Theological Studies* 73 (2017): 1–7.

Donnelly, J. "Human Rights and Human Dignity: An Analytical Critique of Non-Western Conceptions of Human Rights." *The American Political Science Review* 76 (1982): 303–316.

Duschinsky, R. "Tabula Rasa and Human Nature." *Philosophy* 87 (2013): 509–529.

Eagleton, T. *Trouble with Strangers: A Study of Ethics*. Chichester: Willey-Blackwell, 2009.

Ebegbulem, J. C. "Corruption and Leadership Crisis in Africa: Nigeria in Focus." *International Journal of Business and Social Science* 3 (2012): 221–227.

Eberl, J. T. "Aquinas in the Nature of Human Beings." *The Review of Metaphysics*, 58(2004): 333–365.

———. "The Ontological and Moral Significance of Persons." *Scientia et Fides*, 5 (2017): 217–236.

Ejidike, O. M. "Human Rights in the Cultural Traditions and Social Practice of the Igbo of South-Eastern Nigeria." *Journal of African Law* 43 (1999): 71–98.

Eliaeson, S. "Max Weber and Plebiscitary Democracy." In *Max Weber, Democracy, and Modernization*, eds. R Schroeder, 47–60. London: Palgrave Macmillan, 1998.

Emeghara, N. "The Dignity of the Person in African Belief." Theology Annual (1992): 14–137.

Enderle, G. "The Ethics of Conviction Versus the Ethics of Responsibility: A False Antithesis for Business Ethics." *Journal of Human Values* 13 (2)007: 83–94.

Ene, I., J. Williams, and Y. Dunnamah. "Corruption Control and Political Stability in Nigeria: Implication for Value Re-Orientation in Politics." *Global Journal of Human Social Sciences Interdisciplinary* 13 (2013): 6–12.

Enslin, J. V. "Kant on Human Dignity: A Conversation Among Scholars." Boston College, 2014.

Eseoghene, V. E. and H. O. Efanodor. "Boko Haram Insurgency and Its Impact on Nigeria's External Image." *Research and Development* 9 (2016): 308–345.

Esidene, C. "Effects of Corruption on Nigeria's Political and Democratic Objectives: The Way Forward," *Afro Asian Journal of Scial Sciences* V, no. 3 (2014): 1–9.

Eshleman, A. "Moral Responsibility." *Philosophy Faculty Publications and Presentations* 1 (2014): 1–13.

Faleye, O. A. "Religious Corruption: A Dilemma of the Nigerian State." *Journal of Sustainable Development in Africa* 15 (2013): 170–185.

Farris, S. R. Max Weber's Theory of Personality: Individuation, Politics, and Orientation in the Sociology of Religion. Leiden/Boston: Brill, 2013.

Fatile, J. O. "Corruption and the Challenges of Good Governance in the Nigerian Public Sector." *Africa's Public Service Delivery and Performance Review* 1 (2014): 46–65.

Feinberg, J. S. *The Many Faces of Evil: Theological Systems and the Problem of Evil*. Grand Rapids: Zondervan Publishing House, 1994.

Feldman, R. L. "The Root Causes of Terrorism: Why Parts of Africa Might Never be at Peace."*Defense & Security Analysis* 25 (2009): 355–372.

Ferrera, M. "Objectivity, Political Order, and Responsibility in Weber's Thought." *Critical Review: A Journal of Politics and Society* 30 (2018): 256–293.

Fisman, R. and M. A. Golden. *Corruption: What Everyone Needs to Know*. Oxford: Oxford University Press, 2017.

Fletcher, Joseph F. *Situation Ethics: The New Morality*. Philadephia: Westminster Press, 1966.

Ford, D., and R. Muers. eds. *The Modern Theologians: An Introduction to Christian Theology Since 1918*. Malden: Blackwell Publishing, 2005.

Forster, D. A. "God's Kingdom and the Transformation of Society." In *Between Capital and Cathedral: Essays in Church-State Relationships*, eds. W. Bentley, and D.A. Forster, 73–88. Pretoria: Research Institute for Theology and Religion University of South Africa, 2012.

———. "Affect, Empathy, and Human Dignity? Considering Compassion at the Intersection of Theology and Science." In *Consider Compassion: Global Ethics, Human Dignity, and the Compassionate God*, eds. J. L. Claassans, and F de Lange, 3–16. Eugene: Pickwick Publications, 2018.

———. "Some Charateristics of Public Theolog.y" In *African Public Theology*, eds. S. B. Agang, H. J. Hendriks, and D. A. Forster, 1–12. Carlisle: HippoBooks, 2020.

French, P. A. "The Corporation as a Moral Person." *American Philosophical Quarterly*, 6 (1979): 207–215.

———. *Responsibility Matters*. Lawrence: University of Kansas, 1992.

Fukuyama, F. Identity: Contemporary Identity Politics and the Struggle for Recognition. London: Profile Books, 2018.

Galvin, K. and L. Todres. "Dignity as Honour-Wound: An Experiential and Relational View." *Journal of Evaluation in Clinical Practice* 21 (2015): 410–418.

Gane, N. "Max Weber on the Ethical Irrationality of Political Leadership." *Sociology* 30 (1997): 549–564.

Gberevbie, D. E. "Ethical Issues and Nigeria's Quest for Development." *Rwanda Journal*, 1 (2013): 21–35.

Graf, G., and G. Schweiger. "Poverty and Freedom." *Human Affairs* 24 (2014): 258–268.

Granville, L. "Christianity and the Responsibility to Protect." *Studies in Christian Ethics* 25 (2012): 312–326.

Griswold, W. "Formal Capacities and Relational Understandings: Greed in Literature, arts and Sociology." *Sociologias* 20 (2018): 86–104.

Guyette, F. "Thomas Aquinas and Recent Questions about Human Dignity." *Diametros*, 38 (2013): 113–127.

Gyekye, K. *An Essay on African Philosophical Thought: The Akan Conceptual Scheme*. Cambridge: Cambridge University Press, 1987.

Habermas, J. "The Concept of Human Dignity and the Realistic Utopia of Human Rights." *Metaphilosophy* 41 (2010): 464–480.

Hanf, M., A. Van-melle, F. Fraisse, A. Roger, B. Carme, and M. Nacher. "Corruption Kills: Estimating the Global Impact of Corruption on Children Deaths." *PLoS ONE* 11, no. 6.

Hauerwas, S. *A Community of Character: Toward a Constructive Christian Social Ethics*. Notre Dame: University of Notre Dame Press, 1981.

———. *The Peaceable Kingdom: A Primer in Christian Ethics*. London: University of Notre Dame Press, 1983.

———. "Virtue." in *Readings in Christian Ethics: Theory and Method (vol 1)*, eds. D. K. Clark, and R. Rakestraw, 251–256. Grand Rapids: Baker Books, 1994.

Hauerwas, S. and C. Pinches, "Practicing Patience: How Christians Should be Sick" *Christian Bioethics* 2 (1996): 202–221.

Hicks, D. *Dignity: The Essential Role it Plays in Resolving Conflict*. New Haven: Yale University Press, 2011.

Horan, D. P. "Beyond Essentialism and Complementarity: Toward a Theological Anthropology Rooted in Haecceitas." *Theological Studies* 75 (2014): 94–117.

Huber, W. "Toward an Ethics of Responsibility." *The Journal of Religion* 74 (1993): 573–591.

———. *Violence: The Unrelenting Assault on Human Dignity*. Minneapolis: Fortress Press, 1996.

———. "The Dignity of the Different: Towards a Christian Ethics for Pluralistic Societies." In *Living Theology: Essays Presented to Dirk J. Smit on His Sixtieth Birthday*, eds. L. Hansen, N. Koopman, R. Vosloo, 427–440. Wellington: Bible Media, 2011.

———. *Ethics: The Fundamental Questions of our Lives*. Washington, DC: Georgetown University Press, 2015.

———. "Why ethics?" *Stellenbosch Theological Journal* 1(2015): 151–166.

———. "Ethics of Responsibility in a Theological Perspective" Unpublished paper, South Africa: Stellenbosch Univeristy, January 2020.

Hunter, J.D. *To Change the World: The Irony, Tragedy, & Possibility of Christianity in the Late Modern World*. Oxford,: Oxford University Press, 2010.

van Huyssteen, J.W. *Alone in the World? Human Uniqueness in Science and Theology.* Grand Rapids: Eerdmans, 2006.

I-Morphé, R. O. Africa's Social and Religious Quest: A Comprehensive Survey and Analysis of the African Situation. Jos, Nigeria: Logos Quest Publishing, 2011.

Idang, G. E. "African Cultural Values." *Phronimon* 16 (2015): 97–111.

Igboin, B. O. "Corruption in Nigeria: The Transformative-Mosaic Model as a Panacea." *African Ecclesial Review* 58 (2016): 43–65.

———. *Corruption: A New Thinking in the Reverse Order.* Oyo: Ajayi Crowther University Press, 2018.

Ige, A. S. "John the Baptist Approach to Corruption: A Recipe for the Church in Nigeria." *Law and Politics* 14 (2016): 577–582.

Ighaekeme, G. O, M. T. Abbah, and M. M. Gaidem. "The Effect of Corruption on Socio- Economic Development of Nigeria." *Canadian Social Science* 10 (2014): 149–157.

Ijewereme, O.B. "Anatomy of Corruption in the Nigerian Public Sector: Theoretical Perspectives and Some Empirical Explanations." *SAGE Open* 5 (2015). http://www.uk.sagepub.com/aboutus/openaccess.htm

Ikezue, E. C., and P. C. Ezeah. "Boko Haram Insurgency in Nigeria: A Public Perception Approach." *Journal of African Studies* 5 (2015): 1–16.

Irwin, T. *Classical Philosophy.* New York: Oxford University Press, 1999.

Isyaku, A. "Terrorism: A New Challenge to Nigeria's Stability in the 21st Century." *International Affairs and Global Strategy* 12 (2013): 16–24.

Jalocho-Palicka, M. "Thomas Aquinas' Philosophy of Being as the Basis for Wojtyla's Concept and Cognition of Human Person." *Studia Gilsoniana* 3 (2014): 127–153.

Jersild, P. *Making Moral Decisions: A Christian Approach to Personal and Social Ethics.* Minneapolis: Fortress Press, 1990.

Jev, A. A. "Politics, Conflicts, and Nigeria's Unending Crisis." *Journal of Global Peace and Conflict* 2 (2014): 147–158.

John, P. H. "Narratives of Identity and Sociocultural Worldview in Song Texts of the Ham of Nigeria: A Discourse Analysis Investigation." PhD Dissertation, Stellenbosch University, South Africa, 2017.

Johnson, M. "Syndromes of Corruption: Wealth, Power, and Democracy" Cambridge: Cambridge University Press, 2005.

Jonas, H. "Technology and Responsibility: Reflections on the New Tasks of Ethics." *Social Research* 40 (1973): 31–54.

———. *The Imperative of Responsibility: In Search of an Ethics for the Technological Age.* Chicago: The University of Chicago Press, 1984.

Jones, H. E. *Kant's Principle of Personality.* Madison: The University of Wisconsin Press, 1971.

Kant, I. *Groundwork for the Metaphysics of Morals*. New Haven and London: Yale University Press, 2002.

———. "Frontmatters." In *Kant: The Metaphysics of Morals* eds. L. Denis, Cambridge: Cambridge University Press, 2017.

Karp, D. J. "The Responsibility to Protect Human Rights and the R to P: Prospective and Retrospective Responsibility." *Global Responsibility to Protect* 7 (2015): 1–20.

Kass, L. *Being Human: Core Readings in the Humanities*. New York: W.W. Norton & Company, 2004.

Kato, B.H. *Theological Pitfalls in Africa*. Kisumu: Evangel Publishing House, 1975.

Kearney, R. *Strangers, Gods, and Monsters*. London: Routledge, 2003.

Kelsey, D. H. *Eccentric Existence: A Theological Anthropology. Volume 1*. Louisville: WestMinster John Knox Press, 2009.

Kim, B. H. "Dietrich Bonhoeffer's Ethics of Obedience and Responsibility in the Context of Pacifism and Just-War." Boston University, 2015.

Kinoti, H. W. "African Morality: Past and Present." In *Moral and Ethical Issues in African Christianity: A Challenge for African Christianity*. eds. J. N. K. Mugambi, and A. N. Wasike, 73–82. Nairobi, Kenya: Acton Publishers, 1999.

Kirchhoffer, D. G. "Becoming What You Are: On the Value of Human Dignity as an Ethical Criterion in Light of Contemporary Critiques." *International Journal of Philosophy and Theology* 70 (2009): 45–66.

———. *Human Dignity in Contemporary Ethics*. Amherst: Teneo Press, 2013.

———. "Human Dignity and Human Enhancement." *A Multidimensional Approach Bioethics* 31 (2017): 375–385.

Kirkham, C.W. "Thick and Thin: Moral Argument at Home and Abroad." *Journal of International Affairs* 48 (1995): 667–671.

Koopman, N. "Some Theological and Anthropological Perspectives on Human Dignity." *Scriptura* 95 (2007): 177–185.

———. "Human Dignity in Africa: A Christological Approach." *Scriptura*, 204 (2010): 240–249.

———. "Belhar: A Transforming and Dignifying Tradition." *Journal of Theology for Southern Africa* 139 (2011): 32–41.

Körtner, U. H. J. "Dem Risiko trotzen: Grundzüge einer zeitgemässen Verantwortungsethik." *Evangelisch Kommentare* 29 (1996): 581–586.

Kreikebaum, H. "Corruption as a Moral Issue." *Social Responsibility Journal* 4 (2008): 82–88.

Kretzschmar, L. "The Formation of Moral Leaders in South Africa." *Journal of Theology for Southern Africa* 128 (2007): 18–36.

Kunhiyop, S. W. *African Christian Ethics*. Carlisle: HippoBooks, 2008.

———. "The Challenge of African Christian Morality." *The Journal of South African Theological Seminary* 7 (2009): 60–80.

Kure, K. U. "Leadership, Corruption and the Dignity of Humans : Some Reflections from the Nigerian Context." *Theological Studies* 76 (2020): 1–7.

Kuyper, A. *Lectures on Calvinism*. New York: CosimoClassics, 2007.

de Lange, F. "Having Faith in Yourself": Self-Respect and Human Dignity." *Scriptura* 95 (2007): 213–223.

Larocco, S. "The Other, Shame, and Politics: Levinas Justice, and Feeling Responsible." *Religions* 381 (2018): 1–17.

Lebacqz, K. "Alien Dignity." In *On Moral Medicine: Theological Perspectives in Medical Ethics*, eds. M.T. Lysaught, A. Verhey, S.E. Lammers, and J. J. Kotva, 724–733. Grand Rapids: Eerdmans, 2012.

Levinas, E. *Humanism of the Other*. Urbana: University of Illinois, 2006.

Linden, T. "The German Christians' Influence on Barth's Harmatiology of Pride." PhD Disertation, The University of Western Ontario, 2016

Lovin, R. W. "Becoming Responsible in Christian Ethics." *Studies in Christian Ethics* 22 (2009): 389–398.

Lucas, J. R. *Responsibility*. Oxford: Clarendon Press, 1993.

Luków, P. "A Difficult Legacy: Human Dignity as the Founding Value of Human Rights." *Human Rights Review* 19 (2018): 313–329.

Macintyre, A. *After Virtue: A Study in Moral Theory*. London: Duckworth, 1981.

———. *Dependent Rational Animals: Why Human Beings Need the Virtues*. Chicago: Open Court, 1999.

Magesa, L. *Christian Ethics in Africa*. Nairobi: Acton Publishers, 2002.

Makinde, T. "Global Corruption and Governance in Nigeria." *Journal of Sustainble Development* 6 (2013): 108–117.

Maluleke, T. S. "African Theology." In *The Modern Theologians: An Introduction to Christian Theology Since 1918*, eds. D. Ford, and R. Muers, 485–501. Malden: Blackwell Publishing, 2005.

Malvestiti, B. "Human Dignity as a Status vs Human Dignity as a Value: A Double Nature." *Phenomenology and Mind* 2 (2016): 152–159.

Maslow, A. "A Theory of Human Motivation." *Psychological Review* 50 (1943): 370–396.

Marais, N. "Happy? A Critical Analysis of Salvation in Ellen Charry that Portrays Human Flourishing as Healing, Beauty and Pleasure." *Verbum et Ecclesia* 36 (2015): 1–10.

———. "Imagining Human Flourishing? A Critical Analysis of Contemporary Soteriological Discourse." PhD Dissertation, Stellenbosch University, South Africa, 2015.

Mauro, P. "Corruption: Causes, Consequences, and Agenda for Further Research." *Finance and Development* (1998): 11–14.

McCrudden, C. "Human Dignity and Judicial Interpretation of Human Rights." *The European Journal of International Law* 19 (2008): 655–724.

McKenna, S. C. S. *The Fathers of the Church: A New Translation*. Vol. 45. Washington, DC: The Catholic University of America Press, 1970.

Meeks, M.D. "God's Oikonomia and the New World Economy." In *Christian Social Ethics in a Global Era*, M. L. Stackhouse, P. L. Berger, D. P. McCann, and M. D. Meeks, 111–126. Nashville: Abingdon Press, 1995.

Meilaender, G. *Neither Beast nor God: The Dignity of the Human Person*. New York: Encounter Books, 2009.

Meith, D. "Human Dignity in Late-Medieval Spiritual and Political Conflicts." In *The Cambridge Handbook of Human Dignity: Interdisciplinary Perspectives*, M. Düwell, J. Braarvig, R. Brownsword, and D. Meith, 74–84. Cambridge: Cambridge University Press, 2014.

Mercy, O. A. "The Effects of Corruption on Good Governance in Nigeria." *International Journal of Development and Sustainanbility* 4 (2015): 292–307.

Mike, U. *Corruption in Nigeria: Review, Causes, Effects, and Solutions*. Lagos, 2018.

Moltmann, J. *On Human Dignity: Political Theology and Ethics*. London: SCM Press, 1984.

———. *Faith and the Future: Essays on Theology, Solidarity, and Modernity*. Maryknoll: Orbis Books, 1995.

———. *God in Creation: A New Theology of Creation and the Spirit of God*. Minneapolis: Fortress Press, 1993.

———. *God for a Secular Society: The Public Relevance of Theology*. Minneapolis: Fortress Press, 1999.

———. *Ethics of Hope*. Minneapolis: Fortress Press, 2012.

Mommsen, W. J. "Max Weber in America." *The American Scholar* 69 (2000): 103–109.

Morris, T. *Hans Jonas' Ethics of Responsibility: From Ontology to Ecology*. Albany, New York: State University of New York Press, 2013.

Mouw, R. J. *Abraham Kuyper: A Short and Personal Introduction*. Grand Rapids: Eerdmans, 2011.

Moyosore, S. O. "Corruption in Nigeria : Causes , Effects and Probable Solutions." *Journal of Political Science and Leadership Research* 1 (2015): 22–36.

Mozaffari, M. H. "Human Dignity: An Islamic Perspetive." *An International Journal of Academic Research* 54 (2011): 2–15.

Muers, R. "Pushing the Limit: Theology and Responsibility to Future Generation." *Studies in Christian Ethics* 16 (2003): 36–51.

Muftugil, O. "Human Dignity in Muslim Perspective: Building Bridges." *Journal of Global Ethics* 13 (2017): 157–167.

Mugambi, J. N. K., and A. N. Wasike. *Moral and Ethical Issues in African Christianity:A Challenge for African Christianity*. Nairobi: Acton Publishers, 1999.

Mugambi, J. N. K. *African Christian Theology: An Introduction*. Nairobi: Heinemmann Kenya, 1989.

———. *From Liberation to Reconstruction: African Christian Theology after the Cold War*. Nairobi: East African Educational Publishers, 1995.

Muis, J. "Human Rights and Divine Justice." *Theological Studies* 70 (2014): 1–8.

Naudé, P. "Virtue and Responsibility: Economic-Ethical Perspectives in the Work of Etienne de Villiers." *Verbum et Ecclesia* 33 (2012): 1–6.

———. "Economics." In *African Public Theology*, eds. S. B. Agang, J. H. Hendricks, and D. A. Forster, 97–111. Carlisle: HippoBooks, 2020.

Neequaye, G. K. "Towards an African Christian Ethics for the Technological Age: William Schweiker's Christian Ethics of Responsibility in Dialogue with African Ethics." PhD Dissertation, University of Pretoria, South Africa, 2013.

Niebuhr, H. *The Responsible Self: An Essay in Christian Moral Philosophy*. New York: Harper & Row, 1963.

Niebuhr, R. "Must we do Nothing?" In *From Christ to the World: Introductory Readings in Christian Ethic*, eds. W. G. Boulton, T. D. Kennedy, and A. Verhey, 422–425. Grand Rapids: William B. Eerdmans Publishing Company, 1994.

Van Niekerk, A. C. J. "Personal-Ethical Perspectives in the Work of Etienne de Villiers." *Verbum et Ecclesia* 33 (2012): 1–6.

Nikelly, A. "The Pathogenesis of Greed: Causes and Consequences." *International Journal of Applied Psychoanalytic studies* 32006(1): 65–78.

Nilsson, M. "Civil Society Actors in Peace Negotiations in Central America." *Journal of Civil Society* 14 (2018): 135–152.

Nordenfelt, L. "Varieties of Dignity." *Health Care Analysis* 12 (2004): 69–81.

Novak, M. "The Judeo-Christian Foundation of Human Dignity, Personal Liberty, and the Concept of the Person." *Journal of Markets & Morality* 1 (1998): 107–121.

———. "Human Dignity, Personal Liberty: Themes from Abraham Kuyper and Leo XIII." *Journal of Markets & Morality* 5 (2002): 59–85.

Nwankwo, R. N. "Official Corruption and Povery Reduction in Nigeria: A Critical Assessment (2003–2010)." *International Journal of Arts & Sciences* 6 (2013): 305–329.

Nwaodu, N., D. Adam, and O. Okereke. "A Review of Anti-Corruption wars in Nigeria." *Africa's Public Service Delivery and Performance Review* 2 (2014): 153–174.

Nwoba, M. O. E., and N. P. Monday. "Appraisal of Economic and Financial Crimes Commission in the Fight Against Corruption in Nigeria." *The Social Sciences* 13 (2018): 94–104.

Obamwonyi, Samson E and Stanley Aibieyi. "Boko Haram Menace: Need for Collective Security for National Development." *International Affairs and Global Strategy* 44 (2016): 11–17.

Ober, J. "Three Kinds of Dignity." Working paper (Standford University), 2009
Oberdorfer, B. "Human Dignity and the Image of God." *Scriptura* 204 (2010): 231–239.
Obuah, E. "Combating Corruption in A "Failed" State: The Nigerian Economic and Financial Crimes Commission." *Journal of Sustainable Development in Africa* 12 (2010): 27–53.
Odi, N. "Impact of Corruption on Economic Growth in Nigeria." *Mediterranean Journal of Social Sciences* 5(2014): 41–46.
Odo, L. U. "The Impact and Consequences of Corruption on the Nigerian Society and Economy." *International Journal of Arts and Humanities* 4 (2015): 177–190.
Oduyoye, M. A. "Alive to What God is Doing." *The Ecumenical Review* 41 (1989): 194–200.
———. "Reducing Welfare and Sacrificing Women and Children." *Journal of Theology for Southern Africa* 104 (1999): 74–77.
Ogbeide, O. A. "Fulani Herdsmen and Communal Clashes in Nigeria: Issues and Solutions." *Mayfair Journal of Agricbusiness Management* 1(2017): 50–61.
Ogbonnaya, A. K. "Effects of Corruption in Nigeria's Economy: A Critical View." *International Journal of Academic Research in Business and Social Sciences,* 8 (2018): 120–128.
Ogbuehi, F. I. "Christian Ethics in a Corrupt Society: A Challenge to Christians in Nigeria." *UJAH,* 18(2017): 320–340.
Ogini, O.S., and A. D. Omojow. "Sustainable Development and Corporate Social Responsibility in Sub-Saharan Africa: Evidence from Industries in Cameroon." *Economies* 4 (2016): 1–15.
Ojo, O. and P. F. Adebayo. "Food Security in Nigeria: An Overview." *European Journal of Sustainable Development* 1 (2012): 199–222.
Okon, E. O. "The Root Causes of Domestic Terrorism in Nigeria: An Empirical Investigation." *Asian Review of Social Sciences* 5 (2016): 6–24.
Ola, A. S, A. Mohammed, and M. S. Audi. "Effects of Corruption on Economic Development in Nigeria." *Global Journal of Interdisciplinary Social Sciences* 3 (2014): 209–215.
Oladipo, S. E. "Moral Education of the Child :Whose Responsibility?" *Journal of Social Science* 20 (2009): 149–156.
Olalekan, A. B. "Human Rights, Governance, and the Nigerian Constitution: A Historical Survey." *Journal of Humanities and Social Science* 17 (2013): 59–64.
Oleinik, A. "Volunteers in Ukraine: From Provision of Services to State and Nation Building" *Journal of Civil Society* 14 (2018): 364–385.
Omenka, I. J. "The Effect of Corruption on Development in Nigeria." *Journal of Humanities and Social Science* 15 (2013): 39–44.

Omonijo, D. O., O. O. C. Uche, O. A. U. Nnedum, and B. C. Chine. "Religion as the Opium of the Masses: A Study of the Contemporary Relevance of Karl Max." *Asian Research Journal of Arts and Social Sciences* 1 (2016): 1–7.

Omonijo, D. O., M. J. T. Nwodo, O. C. Uche, and E. N. Ezechukwu. "The Proliferation of Churches and Moral Decadence in Nigeria: The Socio-Economic and Religious Implications." *Scholars Bulletin* 2 (2016): 637–648.

Omotola, J. "The Intellectual Dimensions of Corruption in Nigeria." *The Social Sciences* 11(2007): 29–41.

Onongha, K. "Corruption, Culture, and Conversion: The Role of the Church in Correcting a Global Concern." *Journal of Applied Christian Leadership* 8 (2014): 67–82.

Osunwokeh, C. I. "Human Dignity Stance of Umunna Solidarity in Igbo Traditional Society: A Challenge to African Christianity." *Journal of Scientific Research and Report* 8 (2015): 1–11.

Ottati, D. F. "The Niebuhrian Legacy and the Idea of Responsibility." *Studies in Christian Ethics* 22 (2009): 399–422.

Page, M. T. *A New Taxonomy for Corruption in Nigeria*. Massachusetts Avenue, NW Washigton, DC: Carnegie Endowment for International Peace, 2018.

Pellizzoni, L. "Responsibility and Ultimate Ends in the Age of the Unforeseable: On the Current Relevance of Max Weber's Political Ethics." *Journal of Classical Sociology*, (2008).1–18.

Perpich, D. *The Ethics of Emmanuel Levinas*. Stanford: Stanford University Press, 2008.

Piechowiak, M. "Thomas Aquinas: Human Dignity and Conscience as a Basis for Restricting Legal Obligations." *Diametros* 47 (2016): 64–83.

Pink, A. W. *The Doctrine of Human Depravity*. Lafayette: Sovereign Grace Publishers, 2001.

Pollack, D. "Varieties of Secularization Theories and their Indispensable Core." *The Germanic Review: Literature, Culture, Theory* 90 (2015): 60–79.

Porter, J. *Morality and Christian Ethics*. New Studies in Christian Ethics. Cambridge: Cambridge University Press, 1995.

Pring, C., and J. Vrushi. "Global Corruption Barometer Africa 2019: citizen's views and experiences of corruption." Transparency International.

Purcell, M. *Levinas and Theology*. Cambridge: Cambridge University Press, 2006.

Raimi, L., I. B. Suara, and A. O. Fadipe. "Role of Economic Financial Crimes Commission and Independent Corrupt Practices and other Related Offenses Commission at Ensuring Accountability and Corporate Governance in Nigeria." *Journal of Business Administration and Education* 3 (2013): 105–122.

Rawls, J. *A Theory of Justice*. Cambridge: The Belknap Press of Harvard University, 1999.

Reinders, H. S. "Understanding Humanity and Disability: Probing an Ecological Perspective." *Studies in Christian Ethics* 26 (2013): 37–49.

Ringer, F. *Max Weber: An Intellectual Biography*. Chicago: The University of Chicago Press, 2004.

Robinson, M. *Corruption and Development*. London: Frank Cass, 1998.

Rondet, H. *Original Sin: The Patristic and Theological Background*. Staten Island: Alba House, 1972.

Root, M. "Aquinas, Merit, and Reformation Theology After the Joint Declaration on the Doctrine of Justification." *Modern Theology* 20 (2004): 5–22.

Sacks, J. *The Dignity of the Difference: How to Avoid the Clash of Civilization*. London/New York: Continuum, 2002.

———. *To Heal a Fractured World: The Ethics of Responsibility*. New York: Schocken Books, 2005.

Salawu, B. "Towards Solving the Problem of Corruption in Nigeria: The ICPC Under Searchlight." *Pakistan Journal of Social Sciences* 5 (2008): 391–398.

Sarot, M. "Models of the Good Life." In *Religion and the Good Life*, eds. M. Sarot, and W. Stoker, 175–194. Assen: Royal Van Gorcum, 2004.

Scanlon, T. M. *What We Owe to Each Other*. Cambridge: The Belnap Press of Harvard University Press, 1998.

Schelling, F. W. J. *First Outline of a System of the Philosophy of Nature*. Albany: State University of New York Press, 2004.

Schuster, J. "Human Dignity in the Light of Anthropology and the History of Ideas." In *Human Dignity: Discourses on Universality and Inelienability*, eds. K. Krämer, and K. Vellguth, 3–16. Quezon City: Clareton Communication Foundation, 2017.

Schweiker, W. "Radical Interpretation and Moral Responsibility: A Proposal for Theological Ethics." *The Journal of Religion* 73 (1993): 613–637.

———. *Responsibility and Christian Ethics*. Cambridge: Cambridge University Press, 1995.

———. *Theological Ethics and Global Dynamics: In the Time of Many Worlds*. Malden: Blackwell Publishing, 2004.

———. "The Ethics of Responsibility and the Question of Humanism." *Literature & Theology* 18 (2004): 251–270.

Sebahene, A. U. "Corruption Mocking at Justice: A Theological-Ethical Perspective on Public life in Tanzania and its Implication for the Anglican Church of Tanzania." PhD Dissertation, Stellenbosch University, South Africa.

Sensen, O. "Kant's Conception of Human Dignity." *Kant-studien* 100 (2009): 309–331.

———. "Human Dignity in Historical Perspective: The Contemporary and Traditional Paradigms." *European Journal of Political Theory* 10 (2011): 71–91.

Shuaibu, S. S, M. A. Salleh, and A. Y. Shehu. "The Impact of Boko Haram Insurgency on Nigerian National Security." *International Journal of Academic Research in Business and Social Sciences*, 5(2015): 254–266.

Shubane, K. "Civil Society in Apartheid and Post-Apartheid South Africa." *Theoria: A Journal of Social and Political Theory* 79 (1992): 33–41.

Smiley, M. *Moral Responsibility and the Boundaries of Community: Power and Accountability from a Pragmatic Point of View*. Chicago: University of Chicago Press, 1992.

Smit, D. J. "Does it Matter? On Whether there is Method in the Madness." In *A Companion to Public Theology* eds. S. Kim, and K. Day, 67–92. Leiden: Brill, 2017.

———. "Contributions of Religions to the Common Good in Pluralistic Societies from a Christian Perspective? Some Critical Remarks." *International Journal of Public Theology* 11 (2017): 290–300.

Soulen, R. K. and L. Woodhead. *God and Human Dignity*. Grand Rapids, Michigan: Eerdmans, 2006.

Soyinka, W. *The Climate of Fear*. London: Profile Books, 2004.

Starr, B. "The Structure of Max Weber's Ethics of Responsibility." *Journal of Religious Studies* 27 (1999): 407–434.

Steinmann, A. C. "The Legal Significance of Human Dignity." Thesis submitted in fulfillment of the Requirements for the degree Doctor of Laws at the North-West University: South Africa, 2016.

Stoecker, R. "Three Crucial Turns on the Road to an Adequate Understanding of Human Dignity." In *Humiliation, Degradation, Dehumanization: Human Dignity Violated*, eds. P. Kaufmann, H. Kuch, C. Neuhauster, and E. Webster, 7–17. Dordrecht: Springer, 2010.

Storrar, W. "The Naming of Parts : Doing Public Theology in a Global Era." *International Journal of Public* 5 (2011): 23–43.

Suleiman, A. O. "Political Corruption is the Despicable Spectrum Responsible for the Economic Downturn in Nigeria: Religious Perspective." *Journal of Global Economics* 5 (2017): 1–5.

Suntai, D. I., and T. S. Targema. "Media and Civil Society in the Fight Against Corruption: The Case of Nigeria." *IJORAS* 1 (2018): 49–67.

Swatos, W. H. and K. J. Christiano. "Secularization Theory: The Course of a Concept." *Sociology of Religion* 60 (1999): 209–228.

Swinburne, R. *Responsibility and Atonement*. Oxford: Clarendon Press, 1989.

Talbert, Matthew. "Moral Responsibility." *The Stanford Encyclopedia of Philosophy*, Winter 2019 Edition, ed. Edward N. Zalta. https://plato.stanford.edu/archives/win2019/entries/moral-responsibility.

Tanner, K. "A Theological Case for Human Responsibility in Moral Choice." *The Journal of Religion* 73 (1993): 592–613.

Taylor, C. "Dilemmas and Connection: Selected Essays." Cambridge: Harvard University Press, 2014.

Taylor, M. K. Paul Tillich: *Theologian of the Boundaries*. London: Collins, 1987.

Tella, C. M., S. M. Liberty, and P. Y. Mbaya. "Poor Leadership, Indiscipline & Corruption Undermines Peace in Nothern Nigeria." *American International Journal of Social Science* 3 (2014): 207–214.

Theobald, R. *Corruption, Development, and Underdevelopment*. Houndmills: Macmillan Press, 1990.

Thielicke, H. *Theological Ethics Volume 2*. Grand Rapids: William B. Eerdmans Publishing Company, 1979.

Tillich, P. *Systematic Theology*. Digswell Place: James Nisbet & Co LTD, 1968.

Tom, E. J., and P. O. Bamgboye. "The Role of Religioin in Combating Corruption: The Nigerian Experience." *International Journal of Social Sciences* 11 (2017): 128–142.

Tonwe, D. A., and O. Oarhe. "Corruption Management in Nigeria: Interrogating Civil Society as an Anti-Corruption Actor." *Dynamics of Public Administration* 32 (2015): 16–30.

Tormusa, D. O., and A. M. Idom. "The Impediments of Corruption on the Efficiency of Healthcare Service Delivery in Nigeria." *Online Journal of Health Ethics* 12 (2016). http://dx.doi.org/10.18785/ojhe.1201.03.

Towner, W. S. *Genesis*. Louisville, London: Westminster John Knox Press, 2001.

Transparency International. *Corruption Perceptions Index 2018*. https://www.transparency.org/files/content/pages/2018_CPI_Executive_Summary.pdf

Udo, E., E. Samuel, and I. Prince. "The Effects of Corruption on Economic Sustainanbility and Growth in Nigeria." *International Journal of Economics, Commerce and Management* VI (2018): 657–669.

Ukase, P., and B. Audu. "The Role of Civil Society in the Fight Against Corruption in Nigeria's Fourth Republic: Problems, Prospects and the Way Forward." *European Scientific Journal*, 11 (2015): 171–195.

Ukiwo, U. "Politics, Ethno-Religious Conflicts, and Democratic Consolidation in Nigeria." *Journal of Modern African Studies* 41 (2003): 115–138.

Umaru, K. K. "Corruption as a Threat to Human Dignity: Some Reflections in the Nigerian Situation." In *A Multi-Dimensional Perspective on Corruption in Africa: Wealth, Religion, and Democracy*, S. B. Agang, P. Pillay, and C. Jones, 224–231. Newcastle upon Tyne: Cambridge Scholars Publishing, 2019.

———. "An Ethos of Responsibility as a Theological Paradigm for Anti-Corruption in Nigeria." In *Fighting Corruption in African Contexts: Our Collective Responsibility*, eds. C. Jones, P. Pillay, I. Hassan, 199–213. Newcastle upon Tyne:Cambridge Scholars Publishing, 2020.

United Nations. "Global programme Against corruption: UN anti-corruption policy." Vienna, 2001.

United Nations Economic Commission for Africa. *Measuring Corruption in Africa: The International Dimension Matters, 2006.* https://repository.uneca.org/handle/10855/23012.

Veldsman, D. "Discussing Publicness on the Public Square?" *Stellenbosch Theological Journal* 3 (2017): 547–559.

———. "Science." In *African Public Theology*, eds. S.B Agang, H. J. Hendriks, and D. A. Forster, 175–187. Carlisle: HippoBooks, 2020.

Veldsman, D. P. and C. J. Wethmar. "For and About Etienne de Villiers as Ethicist of Responsibility." *Verbum et Ecclesia* 33 (2012): 1–2.

Villa-Vicencio, C. "Ethics of Responsibility." In *Doing Ethics in Context: South African Perspectives*, eds. C. Villa-Vicencio, and J. De Gruchy, 75–88. Maryknoll: Orbis Books, 1994.

Villa, D. R. "Max Weber: Integrity, Disenchantment, and the Illusions of Politics." *Constellations: An International Journal of Critical and Democratic Theory* 6 (1999): 540–560.

de Villiers, E. "How My Mind has Changed." *Journal of Theology for Southern Africa*, 111 (2001): 17–21.

———. "Who Will Bear Moral Responsibility?" *Communicatio* 28 (2002): 16–21.

———. "A Christian Ethics of Responsibility: Does it Provide an Adequate Theoretical Framework for Dealing with Issues of Public Morality?" *Scriptura*, 82 (2003): 23–38.

———. "Religion, Theology, and the Social Sciences in a Socieity in Transition." *Theological Studies* 60 (2004): 103–124.

———. "The Vocation of Reformed Ethicist in the Present South African Society." *Scriptura*, 89 (2005): 521–535.

———. "Prospects of a Christian Ethics of Reponsibility (part 1): An Assessment of an American Version." *Verbum et Ecclesia* 27 (2006): 468–487.

———. "Prospects of a Christian Ethics of Responsibility (part 2): An Assessment of three German Versions." *Verbum et Ecclesia* 28 (2007): 88–109.

———. "The Recognition of Human Dignity in Africa: A Christian Ethics of Responsibility Perspective." *Scriptura* 104 (2010): 263–278.

———. "Prophetic Witness: An Appropriate mode of Public Discourse in Democratic South Africa?" *Theological Studies*, 66 (2010): 1–8.

———. "Responsible South African Public Theology in a Global Era." *International Journal of Public Theology* 5 (2011): 1–4.

———. "The Distinctiveness of Christian Morality: Reflections After 30 Years." *Verbum et Ecclesia*. 33 (2012): 1–7.

———. "An Ethics of Responsibility Reading of Eduard Tödt's Theory of the Formation of Moral Judgment." *NGTT* 54 (2013): 1–9.

———. "In Search of an Appropriate Contemporary Approach in Christian Ethics: Max Weber's Ethic of Reponsibility as Resource." *Theological Studies* 71 (2015): 1–8.

———. *Revisiting Max Weber's Ethic of Reponsibility*. Tübingen: Mohr Siebeck, 2018.

———. "Christian Ethics and Secularisation :Business as Usual?" *Verbum et Ecclesia*. 39 (2018): 1–9.

———. "Public Theology and the Present Debate on Whiteness in the Democratic South Africa." *International Journal of Public Theology* 12 (2018): 5–23.

———. "Does the Christian Church have any Guidance to offer in Solving the Global Problems we are Faced with Today?" *Theological Studies* 76 (2020): 1–9.

Volck, B, and J. Shuman. "Dignity of the Body: Reclaiming what Autonomy Ignores."*Journal of Moral Theology* 4 (2015): 121–140.

Volf, M. *Flourishing: Why We Need Religion in a Globalized World*. New Haven: Yale University Press, 2015.

———. "The Crown of the Good Life: A Hypothesis." In *Joy and Human Flourishing: Essays on Theology, Culture, and the Good Life*, eds. M. Volf, and J. E. Crisp, 127–146. Minneapolis: Fortress Press, 2015.

Vorster, N. "A Theological Perspective on Human Dignity, Equality, and Freedom." *Verbum et Ecclesia*. 33(1): 1–6.

Vosloo, R. "Public Morality and the Need for an Ethos of Hospitality." *Scriptura* 82 (2003): 63–71.

Waldron, J. "Dignity, Rank, and Rights." *Public Law & Legal Research Paper Series* (2009): 1–69.

Walzer, M. *Thick and Thin: Moral Argument at Home and Abroad*. Notre Dame: University of Notre Dame Press, 1994.

Wannenwesch, B. "Responsible Living or Responsible Self? Bonhoefferian Reflections on a Vexed Moral Notion." *Studies in Christian Ethics* 18 (2005): 125–140.

Weber, M. *Politics as Vocation*. New York: Oxford University Press, 1946.

———. "Max Weber: An Intellectual Biography." In *From Weber*, ed. H. H. Gerth, and M. Wright. London: Routledge, 1970.

———. *From Max Weber: Essays in Sociology*. Abingdon, Oxon: Routledge, 1991.

———. "Domination and Legitimacy." *German Sociology* (1998), 24–37.

Williams, R. *Faith in the Public Square*. London: Bloomsbury Publishing, 2012.

Wiredu, K. *Cultural Universals and Particulars: An African Perspective*. Bloomington: Indiana University Press, 1996.

Wolbert, W. "Human Dignity, Human Rights and Torture." *Scriptura* 95 (2007): 166–176.

Wolff, E. *Political Responsibility for a Globalized World: After Levinas' Humanism Volume II*. Bielefeld: Verlag, 2011.
Wolterstorff, N. P. *Justice, Rights and Wrongs*. Princeton: Princeton University Press, 2008.
———. *Justice in Love*. Grand Rapids: William B. Eerdmans Publishing Company, 2011.
———. *Journey Toward Justice: Personal Encounters in the Global South*. Grand Rapids: Baker Academic, 2013.
Wood, A. W. *Hegel's Ethical Thought*. Cambridge: Cambridge University Press, 1990.
———. "What is Kantian Ethics?" In *Groundwork for the Metaphysics of Morals*, ed. A. W. Wood, 158–181. New Haven: Yale University Press, 2002.
———. *Kantian Ethics*. Cambridge: Cambridge University Press, 2008.
Yagboyaju, D. A. "Political Corruption, Democratization, and the Squandering of Hope in Nigeria." *Journal of African Elections* 10 (2011): 171–186.
———. "Religion, Culture, and Political Corruption in Nigeria." *Africa's Public Service Delivery and Performance Review* 5 (2017): 1–10.

Langham Literature, with its publishing work, is a ministry of Langham Partnership.

Langham Partnership is a global fellowship working in pursuit of the vision God entrusted to its founder John Stott –

> *to facilitate the growth of the church in maturity and Christ-likeness through raising the standards of biblical preaching and teaching.*

Our vision is to see churches in the Majority World equipped for mission and growing to maturity in Christ through the ministry of pastors and leaders who believe, teach and live by the word of God.

Our mission is to strengthen the ministry of the word of God through:
- nurturing national movements for biblical preaching
- fostering the creation and distribution of evangelical literature
- enhancing evangelical theological education

especially in countries where churches are under-resourced.

Our ministry

Langham Preaching partners with national leaders to nurture indigenous biblical preaching movements for pastors and lay preachers all around the world. With the support of a team of trainers from many countries, a multi-level programme of seminars provides practical training, and is followed by a programme for training local facilitators. Local preachers' groups and national and regional networks ensure continuity and ongoing development, seeking to build vigorous movements committed to Bible exposition.

Langham Literature provides Majority World preachers, scholars and seminary libraries with evangelical books and electronic resources through publishing and distribution, grants and discounts. The programme also fosters the creation of indigenous evangelical books in many languages, through writer's grants, strengthening local evangelical publishing houses, and investment in major regional literature projects, such as one volume Bible commentaries like the *Africa Bible Commentary* and the *South Asia Bible Commentary*.

Langham Scholars provides financial support for evangelical doctoral students from the Majority World so that, when they return home, they may train pastors and other Christian leaders with sound, biblical and theological teaching. This programme equips those who equip others. Langham Scholars also works in partnership with Majority World seminaries in strengthening evangelical theological education. A growing number of Langham Scholars study in high quality doctoral programmes in the Majority World itself. As well as teaching the next generation of pastors, graduated Langham Scholars exercise significant influence through their writing and leadership.

To learn more about Langham Partnership and the work we do visit **langham.org**